SAT®

DRILLS

STUDENT EDITION

280 +
READING QUESTIONS

600 +
GRAMMAR QUESTIONS

540 +
MATH QUESTIONS

NOT FOR SELF-STUDY: DOES NOT CONTAIN ANSWER KEYS. REQUIRES TEACHER GUIDANCE.

- **Repeated, Isolated Practice Per SAT Section**
- Time-Saving **Advice**, Proven **Techniques**
- **Teacher Edition Available**

Authors
Arianna Astuni, Co-Founder IES Test Prep
Khalid Khashoggi, Co-Founder IES Test Prep

Editorial
Christopher Carbonell, Editorial Director
Johnna Landau, Editor
Marc Wallace, Editor
Cassidy Yong, Editor

Design
Christopher Carbonell

Contributors
Hannah Thorpe
Rajvi Patel

Published by IES Publications
www.IESpublications.co

ON BEHALF OF
Integrated Educational Services, Inc.
304 Amboy Avenue
Metuchen, NJ 08840
www.iestestprep.com

We would like to thank the IES Publications team as well as the teachers and students at IES Test Prep who have contributed to the creation of this book.

ISBN-13: 9798811580682
QUESTIONS OR COMMENTS? Visit us at iestestprep.com

TABLE OF CONTENTS

DISCLAIMER

- The *SAT Drills: Student Edition* book is **NOT for self-study**.
- **This book does NOT have answer keys and requires teacher guidance.**
- More information can be found in the *SAT Drills: Teacher Edition* book.

Dear Student,

Honing your accuracy on the SAT can be challenging—especially when you have not built the stamina to manage the stress and anxiety that comes from poor time management. Your test-taking skills are strong at the beginning of each section, but your precision tends to waiver as the test continues and your energy dips. This is a common pitfall for many students, but it can be overcome!

After 20 years of teaching, I've discovered that the best way to master your time management on a full, three-hour SAT is to focus on smaller, individualized passages and sections first. Always keep in mind the following:

"Do a small job well done."

This mentality will be your test prep foundation. If you can master your timing on smaller sections, you will gradually build the stamina needed to approach a full SAT. By focusing on incremental improvements, you will learn to pace yourself on each question or passage without sacrificing strategy.

The *SAT Drills* book is the culmination of "doing a small job well done." Each chapter focuses on a specific SAT section —reading, grammar, or math—and is filled with repeated, individual drills that cover the common question-types on the SAT. Build your stamina by timing yourself on one or two drills at a time. Eventually, these stepping stones will lead to the comfort and confidence needed to tackle a full test!

If you are working with a tutor, this educator can time you per drill to comprehensively assess how to improve your timing and ultimately, increase your score.

The above philosophy has been the backbone that my past students have used to find their own successes on the SAT and even further into their college careers. I am confident that by applying this mindset onto every section of the SAT, you, too, can achieve your dream score!

Wishing you the best of luck,

Arianna Astuni

Welcome to IES Test Prep!

Overview of Chapters

This book is divided into three main chapters:

Chapter 1: Reading Drills
Chapter 2: Grammar Drills
Chapter 3: Math Drills

How to Use This Book (for IES Test Prep Workshops)

Per workshop, you will practice applying IES techniques and strategies on the assigned drills with your teacher in a timed setting.

Do **not** complete the drills before your assigned workshop. You will complete the drills **during** the workshop to practice under a time limit. Your teacher will guide you on the time limits per drill or may assign multiple drills at a time.

See below pacing information as a reference.

PACING INFORMATION FOR DRILLS

This clock symbol provides directions on **timing limits** or **pacing guides** per chapter. Read this information first before practicing on the assigned drills.

13 MINUTES per **Reading** Passage/ Drill

8-9 MINUTES per **Grammar** Passage/ Drill

25 MINUTES per **Math-No Calculator** Drill

28 MINUTES per **Math-Calculator** Drill

CONTINUE

Chapter 1
Reading Drills

Directions: For each drill, use about 13 minutes to read the passage and answer its questions. It is normal to finish either a minute before or after this time limit.

IES Workshops: You will **complete 2 reading drills per workshop**. Please follow the time limits provided by your workshop teacher. Remember, you will complete these drills **during** workshop.

Good luck!

Questions 1-10 are based on the following passage.

Adapted from Thomas Hardy, *Jude the Obscure*, originally published in 1895. At this point in the narrative, the young Jude is living in a rural community and aspires to attend Christminster, a fictional British university that Hardy modeled on Oxford.

During the three or four succeeding years a quaint and singular vehicle might have been discerned moving along the lanes and by-roads near Marygreen, driven in a quaint and singular way.

In the course of a month or two after the receipt of the books Jude had grown callous to the shabby trick played him by the dead languages. In fact, his disappointment at the nature of those tongues had, after a while, been the means of still further glorifying the erudition of Christminster. To acquire languages, departed or living in spite of such obstinacies as he now knew them inherently to possess, was a herculean performance which gradually led him on to a greater interest in it than in the presupposed patent process. The mountain-weight of material under which the ideas lay in those dusty volumes called the classics piqued him into a dogged, mouse-like subtlety of attempt to move it piecemeal.

He had endeavored to make his presence tolerable to his crusty maiden aunt by assisting her to the best of his ability, and the business of the little cottage bakery had grown in consequence. An aged horse with a hanging head had been purchased for eight pounds at a sale, a creaking cart with a whity-brown tilt obtained for a few pounds more, and in this turn-out it became Jude's business thrice a week to carry loaves of bread to the villagers and solitary cotters immediately round Marygreen.

The singularity aforesaid lay, after all, less in the conveyance itself than in Jude's manner of conducting it along its route. Its interior was the scene of most of Jude's education by "private study." As soon as the horse had learned the road and the houses at which he was to pause awhile, the boy, seated in front, would slip the reins over his arm, ingeniously fix open, by means of a strap attached to the tilt, the volume he was reading, spread the dictionary on his knees, and plunge into the simpler passages from Caesar, Virgil, or Horace, as the case might be, in his purblind stumbling way, and with an expenditure of labor that would have made a tender-hearted pedagogue shed tears; yet somehow getting at the meaning of what he read, and divining rather than beholding the spirit of the original, which often to his mind was something else than that which he was taught to look for.

The only copies he had been able to lay hands on were old Delphin editions, because they were superseded, and therefore cheap. But, bad for idle schoolboys, it did so happen that they were passably good for him. The hampered and lonely itinerant conscientiously covered up the marginal readings, and used them merely on points of construction, as he would have used a comrade or tutor who should have happened to be passing by. And though Jude may have had little chance of becoming a scholar by these rough and ready means, he was in the way of getting into the groove he wished to follow.

While he was busied with these ancient pages, which had already been thumbed by hands possibly in the grave, digging out the thoughts of these minds so remote yet so near, the bony old horse pursued his rounds, and Jude would be aroused from the woes of Dido by the stoppage of his cart and the voice of some old woman crying, "Two today, baker, and I return this stale one."

He was frequently met in the lanes by pedestrians and others without his seeing them, and by degrees the people of the neighborhood began to talk about his method of combining work and play (such they considered his reading to be), which, though probably convenient enough to himself, was not altogether a safe proceeding for other travelers along the same roads. There were murmurs. Then a private resident of an adjoining place informed the local policeman that the baker's boy should not be allowed to read while driving, and insisted that it was the constable's duty to catch him in the act, and take him to the police court at Alfredston, and get him fined for dangerous practices on the highway. The policeman thereupon lay in wait for Jude, and one day accosted him and cautioned him.

CONTINUE

1

The passage is best described as

A) a humorous description of the downfall of a reckless young man.

B) an instructive tale about the dangers of excessive knowledge.

C) a light-hearted account of one individual's devotion to study.

D) a condemnation of the impracticality of dead languages.

2

It can be reasonably inferred that Jude is

A) a melancholy young man forced to deliver bread as punishment for an unnamed misdeed.

B) a poor young man with ambitions to dramatically alter his lifestyle.

C) an orphan with no aptitude for study or work.

D) a good-natured boy with little knowledge or conception of the world beyond his community.

3

As used in line 17, "piqued" most nearly means

A) confused.

B) irritated.

C) urged.

D) forced.

4

The first paragraph serves to anticipate the author's later discussion of

A) the intrinsic oddities of Marygreen.

B) Jude's unusual driving habits.

C) the dangers of traveling along country roads in late nineteenth-century England.

D) the delays and mishaps involved in the delivery of Jude's books.

5

Which choice provides the best evidence for the answer to the previous question?

A) Lines 10-14 ("To acquire . . . patent process")

B) Lines 19-22 ("He had . . . in consequence")

C) Lines 29-32 ("The singularity . . . private study")

D) Lines 48-50 ("But, bad . . . good for him")

6

As used in line 35, "ingeniously" most nearly means

A) resourcefully.

B) brilliantly.

C) imaginatively.

D) cunningly.

7

The passage most strongly suggests that Jude's studies "would have made a tender-hearted pedagogue shed tears" (lines 40-41) because

A) Jude applied a great deal of effort to understanding the texts.

B) Jude habitually misinterpreted even the simplest passages to a point of nonrecognition.

C) Jude approached his studies in a lazy and haphazard way.

D) Jude excelled in the interpretation of Latin texts to an extent that would impress established teachers.

8

It is reasonable to conclude that Jude's studies were

A) sufficient to establish his academic credentials.

B) worthless except for the diversion they provided the townspeople.

C) valuable insofar as they set him along the path that he desired.

D) of immense importance in helping him to understand human nature.

CONTINUE

9

Which choice provides the best evidence for the answer to the previous question?

A) Lines 7-10 ("In fact . . . Christminster")
B) Lines 32-41 ("As soon . . . tears")
C) Lines 54-57 ("And though . . . follow")
D) Lines 73-79 ("Then a . . . highway")

10

It can be reasonably inferred that "Dido" (line 63) is

A) an educated woman from Jude's earlier years.
B) a nickname given to Jude's aunt.
C) a character from one of Jude's books.
D) an idealized figure from Jude's own imagination.

CONTINUE

Questions 1-10 are based on the following passage.

Written by a specialist in higher education, this passage considers the career prospects of college and university students who have majored in the humanities.

Fields of study that have often been characterized as completely impractical—literature, art history, philosophy—have been getting a lot of positive press lately. The standard line that such press takes goes something like this: over the past two decades, advanced economies focused overwhelmingly on skills in quantitative analysis and produced an over-abundance of engineers, data analysts, and investment bankers. What weren't produced were enough students and professionals with exceptional written, spoken, and interpersonal aptitudes. Yet these aptitudes, which are actually fostered by those "impractical" disciplines, are what employers need in an increasingly large and complex world economy. There are more than enough college graduates who can crunch numbers; there aren't enough who can sit a client down and effectively explain why those numbers matter.

Perhaps the best exemplification of this standard line is a 2013 article entitled "Why English Majors Are the Hot New Hires," written by entrepreneurship and leadership specialist Bruna Martinuzzi. Long satirized as the most otherworldly of all otherworldly fields, college-level English, in Martinuzzi's view, is instead a passport to a set of skills that employers crave: most obviously, good writing and coherent critical thinking; somewhat less obviously, exceptional sympathy and empathy. According to Martinuzzi, one basic online search of monthly job postings returned "over 1,000 listings for highly paid jobs where employers list empathy as a necessary qualification. And these were not just jobs in traditionally compassionate sectors, such as health care and nonprofits; they included companies in technology, finance, consulting and aerospace, to name a few."

You can't argue with hard numbers, but you can argue with the wisdom of some of the conclusions they have yielded. Most obvious is something of an inconsistency in sheer cause and effect: the average English major studies English to become a scholar, teacher, or professor of English, not an aerospace consultant. And for those in English and other characteristically impractical disciplines who do leave academia and enter the commanding heights of the world economy, the journey involves far more than responding to a few employer listings.

A somewhat more accurate explanation of what really happens has recently been furnished by cultural anthropologist and Memling Institute Fellow Amanda Flock. "Students in the humanities," notes Flock, "do not programmatically absorb the skills that make them into successful businessmen or entrepreneurs." What they absorb, instead, are what Flock calls "side-effect skills." The average English major, for instance, will sit down to read Jane Austen's *Emma* with the aim of understanding Austen's narrative devices, approach to characterization, and perspective on society. As the side effect of such analysis—not its original intention—that English major will probably learn a thing or two about human nature and good decision making, or about other business fundamentals. Such skills manifest themselves especially well under duress: an English major, for instance, may leave college, find no jobs within the field of literature, fall on his or her resources of personality, and improvise a way to employment.

These side-effect skills can be enormously potent, if that English major is ever nudged out of academia. More likely, that English major has signed up for a lifetime of reading and re-reading Jane Austen. Desirable though they may be, humanities students find themselves secured within small circles of humanists, partially as the result of hard economics. On average, students in engineering and business come from lower-income households than students in the humanities do. On average as well, mid-career engineers, architects, and statisticians make $30,000 more per year than do their counterparts in English, philosophy, history, and theater. Those who study the humanities aren't setting out to take control of the job market or even to out-earn their parents. It is more likely, in a large number of cases, that they just need enough money to remain comfortably impractical.

CONTINUE

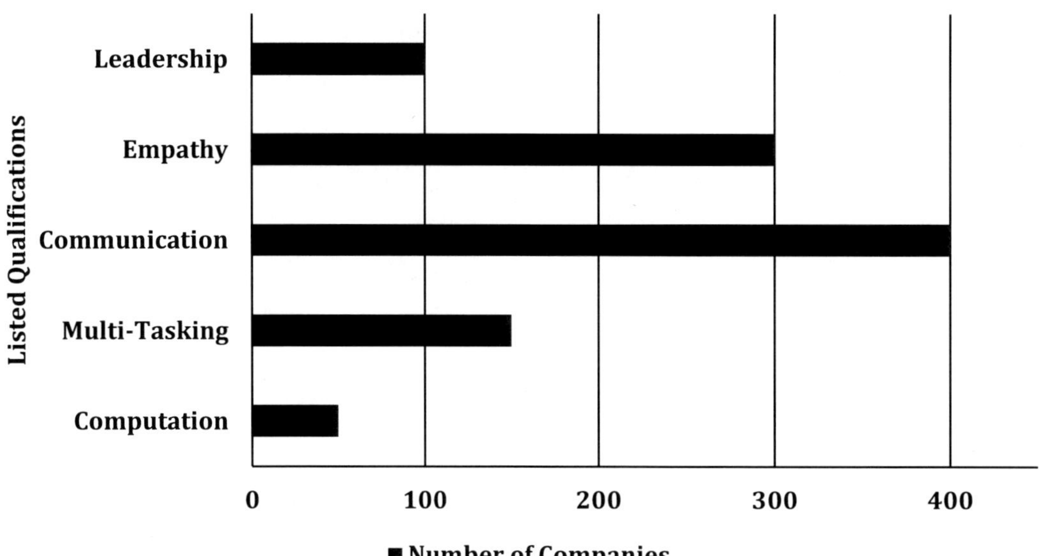

1

Which choice best describes the structure of this passage?

A) A description of a trend followed by an argument as to the danger of that trend
B) A generalization about a group that is refuted by a deeper analysis of that group
C) A description of a changing attitude that leads into a critical analysis of that change
D) A defense of a phenomenon that is substantiated by a rigorous analysis of the national economy

2

The author of the passage introduces the "standard line" in line 4 in order to

A) disprove a dangerous myth about the composition of the workforce.
B) support a later claim regarding the economic desirability of humanities majors.
C) introduce a popular claim that will be openly critiqued later in the passage.
D) focus on the unreliability of those who advise students on choosing courses of study.

3

Which choice provides the best evidence for the answer to the previous question?

A) Lines 21-27 ("Long satirized . . . empathy")
B) Lines 37-41 ("Most obvious . . . consultant")
C) Lines 53-56 ("The average . . . on society")
D) Lines 78-80 ("Those who . . . parents")

4

As used in line 50, "programmatically" most nearly means

A) methodically.
B) confidently.
C) punctually.
D) exhaustively.

CONTINUE

5

The author of this passage suggests that humanities majors are most likely to leave academia when

A) they are provided financial incentives above and beyond those provided by academic positions.
B) they are recruited by employment agencies for large corporations.
C) they fail to find positions with academic sectors.
D) they realize the high value of their interpersonal skills.

6

Which choice provides the best evidence for the answer to the previous question?

A) Lines 14-17 ("There are . . . matter")
B) Lines 30-34 ("And these . . . few")
C) Lines 60-65 ("Such skills . . . . employment")
D) Lines 72-78 ("On average . . . theater")

7

It can be inferred that the employers surveyed in the graph would generally respond to the ideas put forward by Bruna Martinuzzi with

A) agreement, because humanities curricula include direct study of interpersonal skills such as empathy and sympathy.
B) agreement, because the skills Martinuzzi cites directly are in higher demand than qualities such as computation and multi-tasking.
C) disagreement, because strong leadership aptitude is a necessary prerequisite for attaining the empathy and communication skills that Martinuzzi values.
D) disagreement, because all business sectors, not just traditionally compassionate ones, can use the skills of English majors.

8

The author mentions *Emma* as an example of a book that

A) communicates valuable lessons about human behavior.
B) epitomizes the frivolous studies of English students.
C) remains one of the best guides to successful business practices in the literary canon.
D) disproves Flock's characterization of humanities studies.

9

The author refers to the comparative incomes of the families of humanities and science majors in order to

A) argue that science majors face more significant obstacles to success.
B) explain that humanities students tend to be less financially ambitious than those who study science.
C) observe that humanities majors are ultimately unlikely to exceed their parents in income.
D) refute the misconception that students of the humanities come from relatively disadvantaged backgrounds.

10

Which of the following can be reasonably concluded from the passage and from the data in the graph?

A) College students with strong interpersonal skills are generally uninterested in developing similarly strong computation skills.
B) Most college graduates fail to develop the leadership skills that are necessary in high-paying jobs.
C) Computation skills are currently a lower priority for employers than these skills were in the past.
D) Employers are likely to place a renewed emphasis on multi-tasking and a lowered emphasis on communication over the next few years.

STOP

Questions 1-10 are based on the following passage.

Recently, increased study of epidemic diseases has been prompted by crises in public health. The authors of the two passages below consider issues in the history of medicine; the first passage is from an article on intellectual history published in 1998, while the second article is from an editorial that appeared in an American newspaper in 2014.

Passage 1

The word "plague" has always created fear in the human soul; it makes us aware not only of our own mortality, but also of that of our race. Indeed, there have been periods in history when human extinction has seemed quite possible. In the Middle Ages, "the Black Death"—which we now know as Bubonic plague—was carried by black rats and spread throughout Europe, claiming the lives of between 30% and 50% of the population. In 1918, the "Spanish" Flu pandemic claimed more lives than had been taken by the violence of the First World War. At the time, these contagions, silently arriving and claiming their victims, appeared to be unstoppable and, so it seemed, beyond the control of mere mortals. It was as if all of civilization felt powerless in the face of the inevitable.

Yet in 1796, Dr. Edward Jenner first created the hope that there might be a means of controlling, and even of eradicating, such devastating diseases. Jenner's engineering of the first effective vaccine against smallpox led to the belief, now commonly held, that all plagues could eventually be defeated. This eighteenth-century success emboldened scientists to explore the origins of what were previously assumed to be intractable afflictions. For example, by examining the water supplies in areas where cholera was rampant, scientists gained the knowledge necessary to treat this disease. Studying the disease at its source was of paramount importance, yet such study would not have been attempted without the heartening success of Jenner's discoveries. Thanks to the pioneering efforts of Dr. Jenner, the dogged courage of scientific exploration has continued unabated, showing us that it is possible to control and eradicate what earlier civilizations regarded as incurable contagions. As a result, vaccination is now commonplace. The world is a safer place for it.

Passage 2

Just because one has the right tool for the job does not necessarily mean that one will use it. If my air conditioner is broken, for example, and I have the right pair of pliers to tackle the task at hand, you can rest assured that I will get to work; my comfort and my well-being are directly at stake. However, if another man on the other side of town has a broken air conditioner, and has no pliers to fix it, I might not be immediately inclined to help. After all, I don't live in that man's house. Depending on the news coverage, I might not even be aware of that man's plight. What difference does it make to me?

As self-interested and complacent as this might sound, it is a common public attitude towards the ever-growing threat of the devastating Ebola virus, which made headlines after a recent, high-drama outbreak. To be fair, our indifference is understandable. Due to the astounding successes of such medical advances as the development of smallpox and polio vaccines, which all but eradicated those diseases from the face of the earth, we tend to feel secure in our knowledge that there is no disease that cannot be cured by science. And while this certainly may be the case, the indisputable fact remains that no disease will ever be cured without real research and serious effort.

We must remind ourselves that the vaccines for smallpox and polio did not come out of thin air, and did not appear simply because scientists willed them to; these measures were developed through hard work and toil. We cannot presume that, thanks to the scientific breakthroughs of the past, we will forever be healthy and safe. As we all know, the world grows smaller by the day; with daily trans-Atlantic flights from West Africa to New York City, we cannot afford to act as though Ebola exists elsewhere, in an alternate universe that cannot affect us. After all, this is not just a case of a broken air conditioner, but a very real and dangerous disease that could potentially land on our very doorstep. As a developed nation at the forefront of medical science, it is necessary for us to devote our considerable energy and resources to confronting Ebola at its source—in the West African nations where it grows more threatening by the day. Only then will we stand a chance of eradicating this disease, just as our forebears eradicated smallpox and polio.

CONTINUE

1

The author of Passage 1 is best described as

A) a proponent of scientific research.
B) a scholar criticizing a particular use of terminology.
C) a historian revealing modern misconceptions.
D) a writer reflecting on a personal experience.

2

Which choice provides the best evidence for the answer to the previous question?

A) Lines 1-3 ("The word . . . race")
B) Lines 16-18 ("Yet in . . . diseases")
C) Lines 19-21 ("Jenner's . . . defeated")
D) Lines 30-34 ("Thanks to . . . contagions")

3

As used in line 35, "commonplace" most nearly means

A) approachable.
B) uninteresting.
C) overused.
D) widespread.

4

Both passages are primarily concerned with the issue of

A) public health.
B) incurable diseases.
C) scientific controversy.
D) global economics.

5

The author of Passage 1 does which of the following to suggest that vaccination was revolutionary?

A) Details the political upheaval that followed a medical breakthrough
B) Describes the power of disease prior to the discovery of vaccination
C) Compares modern medical techniques to those from the Middle Ages
D) Implies that humans are no longer required to worry about their own mortality

6

The author of Passage 2 most likely mentions an air conditioner in order to

A) add humor to an otherwise somber debate.
B) elaborate on an earlier statement.
C) differentiate two likely threats.
D) explain why certain technologies are unnecessary.

7

The author of Passage 2 refers to trans-Atlantic flights (line 68) primarily to

A) imply that anyone in the world could easily contract Ebola.
B) suggest that people who lived centuries ago were safer than people today.
C) substantiate the claim that diseases can spread rapidly.
D) provide an unexpected example of a positive effect of modernization.

8

As used in line 77, "grows" most nearly means

A) becomes.
B) sprouts.
C) flourishes.
D) augments.

CONTINUE

9

Like the author of Passage 1, the author of Passage 2 would agree with which of the following statements?

A) The increasing mobility of the public poses a challenge to those trying to contain disease.

B) Triumphing over Ebola will require years of serious medical research.

C) The advent of vaccination has made people less fearful of disease.

D) The public has become too relaxed about the prospect of a modern epidemic.

10

Which choice provides the best evidence for the answer to the previous question?

A) Lines 36-37 ("Just because . . . use it")

B) Lines 52-57 ("Due to the . . . by science")

C) Lines 61-65 ("We must . . . and toil")

D) Lines 74-78 ("As a . . . day")

CONTINUE

Questions 1-11 are based on the following passage.

This passage is adapted from a speech delivered by William Lloyd Garrison on February 14, 1854, to the Broadway Tabernacle in New York. In the passage, Garrison discusses slavery in the United States and the abolitionist movement.

Notwithstanding the lessons taught us by Pilgrim Fathers and Revolutionary Sires, at Plymouth Rock, on Bunker Hill, at Lexington, Concord and Yorktown; notwithstanding our Fourth of July celebrations, and ostentatious displays of patriotism; in what European nation is personal liberty held in such contempt as in our own? Where are there such unbelievers in the natural equality and freedom of mankind?

Our slaves outnumber the entire population of the country at the time of our revolutionary struggle. In vain do they clank their chains, and fill the air with their shrieks, and make their supplications for mercy. In vain are their sufferings portrayed, their wrongs rehearsed, their rights defended. As Nero fiddled while Rome was burning, so the slaveholding spirit of this nation rejoices, as one barrier of liberty after another is destroyed, and fresh victims are multiplied for the cotton-field and the auction-block.

For one impeachment of the slave system, a thousand defences are made. For one rebuke of the man-stealer, a thousand denunciations of the Abolitionists are heard. For one press that bears a faithful testimony against Slavery, a score are ready to be prostituted to its service. For one pulpit that is not "recreant to its trust," there are ten that openly defend slaveholding as compatible with Christianity, and scores that are dumb. For one church that excludes the human enslaver from its communion table, multitudes extend to him the right hand of religious fellowship.

The wealth, the enterprise, the literature, the politics, the religion of the land, are all combined to give extension and perpetuity to the Slave Power. Everywhere to do homage to it, to avoid collision with it, to propitiate its favour, is deemed essential—nay, is essential to political preferment and ecclesiastical advancement. Nothing is so unpopular as impartial liberty. The two great parties which absorb nearly the whole voting strength of the Republic are pledged to be deaf, dumb and blind to whatever outrages the Slave Power may attempt to perpetrate. Cotton is in their ears—blinds are over their eyes—padlocks are upon their lips. They are as clay in the hands of the potter, and already moulded into vessels of dishonour, to be used for the vilest purposes.

The tremendous power of the Government is actively wielded to "crush out" the little Anti-Slavery life that remains in individual hearts, and to open new and boundless domains for the expansion of the Slave system. No man known or suspected to be hostile to "the Compromise Measures, including the Fugitive Slave Law," is allowed to hope for any office under the present Administration. The ship of State is labouring in the trough of the sea—her engine powerless, her bulwarks swept away, her masts gone, her lifeboats destroyed, her pumps choked, and the leak gaining rapidly upon her; and as wave after wave dashes over her, all that might otherwise serve to keep her afloat is swallowed by the remorseless deep. God of heaven! if the ship is destined to go down "full many a fathom deep," is every soul on board to perish? Ho! a sail! a sail! The weather-beaten, but staunch ship Abolition, commanded by the Genius of Liberty, is bearing toward the wreck, with the cheering motto, inscribed in legible capitals, "WE WILL NOT FORSAKE YOU!" Let us hope, even against hope, that rescue is not wholly impossible.

To drop what is figurative for the actual, I have expressed the belief that, so lost to all self-respect and all ideas of justice have we become by the corrupting presence of Slavery, in no European nation is personal liberty held at such discount, as a matter of principle, as in our own.

CONTINUE

1

The stance Garrison takes in the passage is best described as that of

A) a critic of the status quo.
B) an advocate for nationalistic principles.
C) an opponent of political revolution.
D) a scholar of African-American history.

2

Based on the passage, which choice best describes how Garrison feels about slavery?

A) It will inevitably be abolished by the United States.
B) It is more accepted in Europe than in the United States.
C) It has only continued for economic reasons in the United States.
D) It has degraded the founding principles of the United States.

3

Which choice provides the best evidence for the answer to the previous question?

A) Lines 10-12 ("In vain . . . mercy")
B) Lines 27-29 ("For one . . . fellowship")
C) Lines 45-49 ("The tremendous . . . Slave system")
D) Lines 66-71 ("I have . . . own")

4

The main rhetorical effect of the third paragraph (lines 19-29) is to

A) suggest that abolitionists face insurmountable challenges.
B) convey the threat that the slave system poses to democracy.
C) show that abolitionists are outnumbered by those who support slavery.
D) indicate that slavery is a system that denies individuals their inalienable rights.

5

As used in line 22, "bears" most nearly means

A) approaches.
B) produces.
C) receives.
D) endures.

6

In his speech, Garrison does which of the following to argue against slavery?

A) Explains how abolition will restore the strength of the current government administration
B) Implies that Americans do not live by the ideals that they celebrate
C) Compares the accomplishments of freed slaves to those of other Americans
D) Details the daily tortures and injustices suffered by slaves

7

Which choice provides the best evidence for the answer to the previous question?

A) Lines 1-7 ("Notwithstanding the . . . our own?")
B) Lines 9-10 ("Our slaves . . . struggle")
C) Lines 30-32 ("The wealth . . . Power")
D) Lines 49-52 ("No man . . . Administration")

8

As used in line 37, "absorb" most nearly means

A) captivate.
B) acquire.
C) understand.
D) encompass.

9

Lines 52-58 ("The ship . . . deep") serve primarily to

A) explain the similarities between a country and a ship.
B) highlight the state's resilience.
C) dramatize the nation's peril.
D) vilify the current administration.

10

It can be reasonably inferred from the passage that politicians are generally

A) candid about their objectives.
B) independent and unbiased thinkers.
C) subject to abolitionist influence.
D) responsive to popular opinion.

11

In the passage, Garrison establishes a contrast between

A) the aggressive influence of Slave Power and the passive compliance of society.
B) the cautiousness of American historical figures and the assertiveness of the Abolitionists.
C) the good work done by the Government and the injustice of the Compromise Measures.
D) the duplicity of American political parties and the honesty of European politicians.

STOP

Questions 1-10 are based on the following passage.

The following passage is excerpted from an article about whale evolution.

In a space of only fifty million years, whales have evolved from four-legged land animals into the wonderful aquatic creatures they are today. Relative to the evolution of other life forms, the whale's is fast. The sharks we see swimming around us have remained the same for over 350 million years, though they are, as we all are, in a process of slow evolutionary change.

We may not know exactly why or how one species evolves faster than another, but we can certainly identify climate change and dwindling food supplies as primary causes. Fossils of the now-extinct Pakicetus, recently discovered in sedimentary rock formations, have elucidated some of the mysteries surrounding the whale's departure from land. This earliest-known ancestor of the whale walked around on four legs and sported a tail. It was approximately the size of a wolf. Evidence from the geologic record surrounding these fossils reveals that there was an abrupt increase in global temperature at the time Pakicetus was alive. This leads us to believe that its regular food supply may have been abruptly altered, forcing Pakicetus to forage for food in the water. Fifty million years later, after several transitional phases of evolution, Pakicetus became the blue whale, the humpback, the dolphin, and all other members of the cetacean order. Unlike many of the life forms that became extinct (think dinosaur) the whales are successful at responding to drastic environmental change.

And they are still evolving.

In the mid 1980s, an unusual sound was picked up by scientists. It bore the signature of a whale song and was detected along well-documented migration routes used by whales, but it was at a frequency of 52 Hertz, which is significantly outside the 15-20 Hertz range used by, and audible to, whales. This sound has been monitored and studied over three decades. No sighting of any animal responsible for this sound has ever been made, but marine biologists are certain of one fact: this is the sound of a whale that has no friends. No other whale activity has ever been recorded in the vicinity of or in response to this sound. Biologists have dubbed the creature emitting the sound "Whale 52." Different theories have emerged in the attempt to explain this phenomenon. Some have posited that Whale 52 is a hybrid, or a deformed, or a deaf whale. But what if this is a perfectly healthy animal, the newest specimen of whale evolution?

Indeed, the home of the whale was transformed overnight by Man. We arrived on the scene only two million years ago and became significant to whales only in the last one hundred years: our rapid and formidable technological evolution has given rise to underwater noise pollution through submarine sonar activity, nuclear bomb testing, and incessant pings from scientific devices that measure everything in the oceans. These disturbances are believed to be responsible for the disorientation of whales that rely on sound for their own survival. Whale songs are thought to function on multiple levels: courtship, navigation, food sourcing. By interfering with the natural processes of reproduction, migration, and feeding, our artificial underwater sounds may be spurring the latest phase of the whale's evolution. After all, we are altering their environment and they have proven able to respond rapidly.

Figure 1

COMPOSITION OF UNDERWATER NOISE

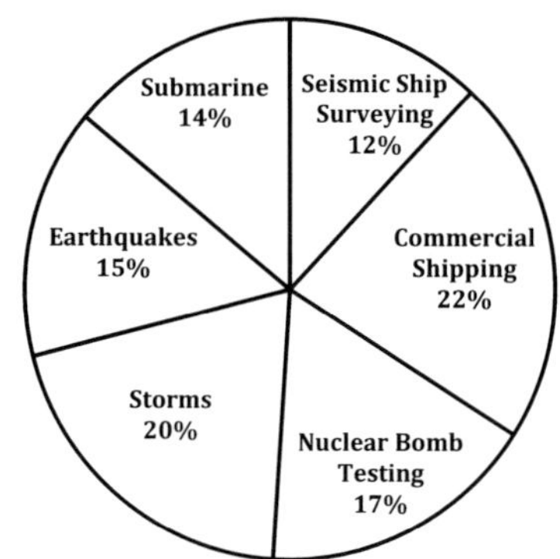

Figure 2

Country	Dead or Beached Whales with Brain or Inner Ear Injuries, 2013 (%)
Bahamas	47
Greece	72

Figure 1 and Figure 2 are adapted from the Oceanic Preservation Society website, www.opsociety.org. Figure 1 depicts underwater noise and Figure 2 provides data for autopsied whales that died from injuries associated with intense underwater sound.

CONTINUE

1

The author refers to “fifty million years” in the first paragraph primarily to

A) introduce a thesis about whale evolution.
B) note a particularly long evolutionary history.
C) outline an implausible scientific theory.
D) assess the relative physical strength of two species.

2

The passage most strongly suggests that evolution occurs as a direct result of

A) genetic variation and selective pressure.
B) migrations and anatomical transformations.
C) a changing environment and food scarcity.
D) the passage of time and foraging behavior.

3

Which choice provides the best evidence for the answer to the previous question?

A) Lines 4-6 (“The sharks . . . years”)
B) Lines 8-11 (“We may . . . causes”)
C) Lines 14-16 (“This earliest-known . . . a tail”)
D) Lines 22-25 (“Fifty million . . . order”)

4

As used in line 31, “bore” most nearly means

A) held up.
B) wore.
C) assumed.
D) exhibited.

5

The author’s attitude towards whales could best be described as

A) appreciative.
B) amused.
C) perplexed.
D) disappointed.

6

Which choice provides the best evidence for the answer to the previous question?

A) Line 16 (“It was . . . wolf”)
B) Lines 26-28 (“the whales . . . change”)
C) Lines 44-45 (“Some have . . . whale”)
D) Lines 58-59 (“Whale songs . . . sourcing”)

7

As used in line 41, “dubbed” most nearly means

A) copied.
B) named.
C) mimicked.
D) soothed.

8

Based on the passage, which statement best describes the human impact on whale species?

A) Our relatively new technology has quickly altered the environment in which the whales operate.
B) Our disruption of whale communication will eventually eliminate the entire whale population.
C) The noise pollution that we have created is forcing whales to communicate more effectively.
D) The effects of our development are negligible when compared to the long history of the whale species.

9

Based on Figure 1 and the passage, which choice gives the correct percentages of underwater noise that does NOT contribute to the disorientation of whales?

A) 15% and 12%
B) 20% and 15%
C) 22% and 17%
D) 14% and 12%

10

Which choice is supported by the data in the second figure?

A) A large percentage of Greece's coastline is inhabited by whales.
B) The number of whales that suffered injury is highest near the Bahamas.
C) The percentage of whales with recorded injuries is highest near Greece.
D) The number of whales that suffered injury is roughly the same for Greece and the Bahamas.

11

Based on the two figures, the author would most likely conclude which of the following?

A) Whales near the Bahamas are less affected by human-sourced underwater noise pollution than those near Greece.
B) Whales near the Bahamas will be more likely to survive natural disasters than those near Greece.
C) Greece's thriving fishing industry accounts for its underwater noise pollution.
D) The volume of commercial shipping is lower in the Bahamas than in Greece.

Questions 1-10 are based on the following passage.

This passage is adapted from a 2013 short story about a Midwestern man named Jermaine Wright, who has left his small town in Wisconsin to move to Boston, Massachusetts.

This was a new coffee shop. It was actually an old coffee shop, one of the oldest in America, first opened in 1874. But to Jermaine, it was a new coffee shop. Everything was new to Jermaine. The Northeast ran at a different speed than Jermaine did, but he found himself able to catch up, to run past the lazy ambling of his native Wisconsin. This was a new coffee shop, and he was a new Jermaine.

He didn't even necessarily want to leave Wisconsin, but his therapist thought it would be a good exercise in independence and confronting his fears to move somewhere new, somewhere farther along. Frankly, Jermaine thought his therapist wanted a break from their sessions, and had even heard the therapist say something of the sort to his receptionist, but Jermaine told himself that his old paranoid fears of worthlessness were just dogging him. Regardless of the reason for his new shift in location, Jermaine still called his therapist weekly, sometimes biweekly, to which his therapist would reply, "Hello Jermaine, what's the crisis this time?"

Jermaine sat down with his coffee, a large-sugar-no-Splenda-soy-milk-no-dairy-hazelnut-and-as-little-froth-as-possible-brew, and thought about his new roommate. Jeff was an odd fellow, a little too happy and a little too friendly for Jermaine, but Jermaine supposed the situation could be worse. Jermaine Wright and Jeff Wozniak. "Double JW!" Jeff said. "JW squared!" Jeff laughed. Jeff seemed to construe himself as a comedian, but Jermaine couldn't manage to find him funny. He simply smiled and waited for it all to be over.

What's worse were Jeff's cleaning habits. Jeff would leave his clothing strewn all about the apartment. Jermaine was rather strict about tidiness, but only once had he found the courage to confront Jeff about it, a situation resulting in Jeff's comment, "Oh yeah, thank goodness we no longer live with our mothers!" Jermaine answered with a weak smile, and then a sigh, and he didn't bring up the topic again. He did begin to clean the apartment, a development to which Jeff adjusted immediately.

Jermaine sipped his coffee, and pulled his laptop from his bag. He'd done enough thinking about Jeff for the day, he told himself. He pulled up the document he was working on; he was a freelancer, often picking up government projects, but he'd been having problems lately. The websites and his friends had all said it was so easy to change your address, but Jermaine was having a hard time finding all the authorities he had to inform of the change. An immeasurable amount of work, yet it was supposedly no work at all. He would eventually get to it, but who could stomach a day in line at the motor vehicle agency?

When all was said and done, Jermaine missed his native Wisconsin. When he remembered his time there, he remembered his old life with a tender pain, as he might remember an old friend who had moved away long ago. He thought of his coworkers—here was the pain, with none of the tenderness—and he thought of his neighbors. He thought of his family—oh, his mother never quite let him be, maybe she was the one thing he was truly glad to be rid of. But he remembered fondly the way Ontario Drive swooped around in curves and buckled under bridges. He missed the flat plains, and the way you could see a hundred trees stretched out over what felt like a hundred miles, and the way a snow drift could create a monument in just one night.

He couldn't say he hated the Northeast, though he could say that Boston was not nearly as comfortable as Wisconsin was. He couldn't say Boston was less enjoyable, but he could say that it was more stressful. He didn't feel as lost as he thought he would, though. He didn't feel as helpless as he thought he would. He had come here to get a break from the everyday particulars, and he was certainly finding that, but with an important caveat: all days are the same in some sense.

CONTINUE

1

The main purpose of this passage is to

A) catalog the differences between New England and the Midwest.
B) describe one man's inability to adapt to his new home.
C) portray the personality of an eccentric individual as he adjusts to a new location.
D) record the problems often encountered by roommates struggling to adapt to each other's idiosyncrasies.

2

It can be inferred that Jermaine views his move to New England as

A) less disorienting than he imagined.
B) impossible to accept.
C) temporary because of changing job opportunities.
D) agonizing because Jermaine misses his family.

3

Which choice provides the best evidence for the answer to the previous question?

A) Lines 9-12 ("He didn't . . . along")
B) Lines 36-40 ("Jermaine answered . . . immediately")
C) Lines 53-59 ("When all . . . neighbors")
D) Line 71 ("He didn't . . . though")

4

Jermaine's therapist answers the phone in the manner he does in line 20 ("Hello Jermaine . . . time") most likely because

A) the therapist suspects that the move was a bad idea for someone as sensitive as Jermaine and fears the worst.
B) the therapist is an old friend of Jermaine's family and is accustomed to the ups and downs of his relationship with Jermaine.
C) Jermaine's frequent complaints have led the therapist to expect a set pattern of behavior.
D) the therapist hopes that he and Jermaine will grow even closer if Jermaine returns.

5

Which of the following appears to provide Jermaine with the most stress?

A) Mundane details
B) Existential anxieties
C) Separation from his mother
D) Financial insecurities

6

As used in line 28, "construe" most nearly means

A) analyze.
B) reinvent.
C) present.
D) argue for.

7

As described in the third paragraph (lines 21-30), Jermaine's relationship with his roommate Jeff can best be characterized as

A) awkward but endurable.
B) hostile and contemptuous.
C) manipulative and unstable.
D) competitive but rewarding.

8

As used in line 51, "stomach" most nearly means

A) relish.
B) digest.
C) consume.
D) tolerate.

9

One of the primary problems that Jermaine faces is

A) anger management.
B) emotional dependence.
C) absentmindedness.
D) low self-confidence.

10

Which choice provides the best evidence for the answer to the previous question?

A) Lines 4-8 ("The Northeast . . . Jermaine")
B) Lines 15-17 ("but Jermaine . . . him")
C) Lines 49-52 ("An immeasurable . . . agency?")
D) Lines 63-66 ("He missed . . . night")

STOP

Questions 1-11 are based on the following passage.

In the following passage, the author discusses the "slavery footprint" of every individual and how we can work to reduce global slavery.

Consumerism is on the rise: we want more, we want it fast, and we want it cheap. Our landfills are growing as we accumulate and quickly disregard more and more possessions. So it shouldn't come as a shock to know that our carbon footprint is getting larger. But most people are unaware that our slavery footprint is expanding as well. This happens whenever we buy products that in some way support modern slavery. If you own a computer, a decent number of shoes, or a bike of just about any sort, you probably have somewhere in the neighborhood of 100 slaves working for you.

A recently launched website called slaveryfootprint.org, which is backed by the U.S. State Department, defines a slave as "anyone who is forced to work without pay, is being economically exploited, and is unable to walk away." Through this site, we can calculate how connected to human trafficking and slave labor we are. Knowing that we might have a hand in perpetuating such evils, we should at least take a moment to think about the consequences of our role in consumer society.

The site offers a survey that, when completed, determines the exact slavery footprint of any given visitor. Participants in the survey feed in information about their lifestyles and purchasing trends, and a sophisticated algorithm calculates where geographically their possessions were made. After that, the site searches its database to estimate the prevalence of slavery in these areas and produces a number representing the slavery footprint. The results are staggering. The average person has about 27 slaves working for him or her, and half of those slaves are active at any given moment. This means that the majority of the products we use on a daily basis has at some point passed through the hands of a slave.

With roughly 30 million slaves in the world today, chances are that most of what we buy has at one time or another come into contact with a slave. Chocolate, though processed and packaged by fancy European boutiques, is made from cocoa beans which are gathered by the small hands of slave children across West Africa. Leather from India is often obtained through the forced labor of lower-caste workers. The Thai seafood industry relies on the labor of Cambodian, Burmese, and Malaysian slaves. Coltan, a superconductor used in electronics such as cell phones, is mined by slaves in the Democratic Republic of the Congo. Even in the cosmetics industry, tens of thousands of Indian children mine mica, the little sparkles in makeup, and China's migrant population often produces the silica in nail polish. And these are only a few of the products we come across daily that depend on slave labor.

This does not mean that all the companies we patronize endorse slave labor, or knowingly run sweatshops. Nor does it necessarily mean that we should vilify a company upon finding out that it is somehow connected to slave labor. What we need to do is understand the supply chains at the heart of the problem; most companies rely on other companies for processed and raw materials, unaware sometimes of where these materials originate. We as consumers have the obligation to do the research, and it is incumbent on us, as the end-users of these products, to bring modern slavery to the attention of influential companies. Only if we can rally together and do this in a large way can we have a shot at combating slavery.

On the Slavery Footprint website, users can download the "Free World" software and use it to research brands and stores. Users can also send letters to various companies, requesting inquiries into their supply chains. Companies that receive these letters, fearing negative press about their links to slavery, are more likely to check whether or not their suppliers are in fact utilizing slave labor. Nothing mobilizes business more than the threat of a public relations fiasco. But steps toward a solution can't start until consumers become more aware of the problem.

For most people, slavery is something that happens in distant places, or only happened long ago. But slaveryfootprint.org brings this affliction to our doorstep, and reminds us that by staying unaware and inactive, we are complicit in slavery today.

CONTINUE

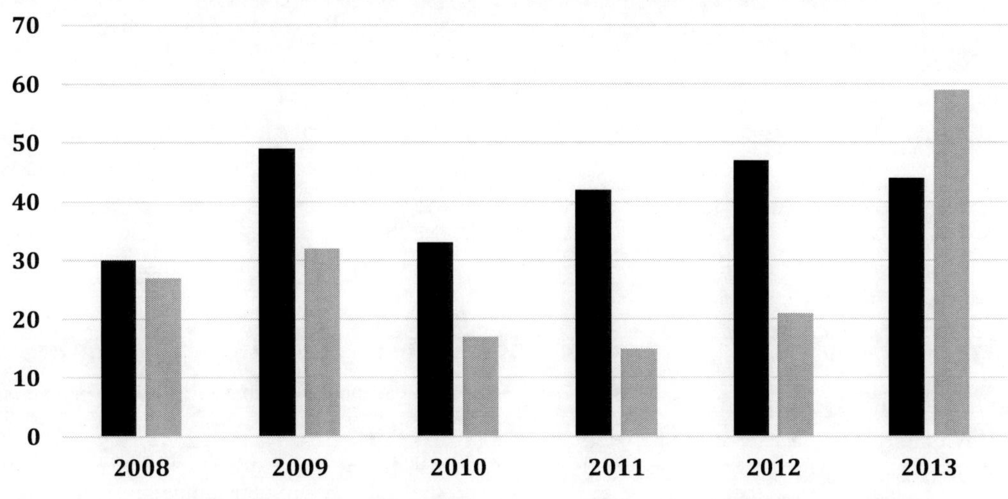

1

The primary purpose of the passage is to

A) remind readers that slavery still exists today in one continent.

B) introduce a website that can help to combat a problem.

C) argue that the electronics industry is solely responsible for slavery.

D) highlight certain industries that should be boycotted.

2

The main effect of the author's phrasing in lines 4-7 ("So it . . . as well") is to

A) illustrate the impact of human civilization on the natural landscape.

B) explain the connection between humanitarian struggles and the U.S. State Department.

C) use the language of a well-known problem to introduce a lesser-known one.

D) create an analogy between two seemingly disparate environmental concerns.

3

As used in line 18, "connected to" most nearly means

A) combined with.

B) tied to.

C) akin to.

D) aware of.

4

According to the author, what is responsible for increasing a slavery footprint?

A) Lowering trade restrictions

B) Creating overseas factories

C) Developing new technologies

D) Consuming products

5

Which choice provides the best evidence for the answer to the previous question?

A) Lines 7-8 ("This happens . . . slavery")

B) Lines 31-34 ("The average . . . moment")

C) Lines 54-56 ("This does . . . sweatshops")

D) Lines 58-62 ("What we . . . originate")

6

The author develops an argument in lines 37-53 by

A) demonstrating the widespread prevalence of slavery.

B) listing every national economy that depends on slavery.

C) suggesting a course of action that will combat slavery.

D) analyzing the productivity of slave-dependent nations.

7

Which of the following does the author suggest that the reader do?

A) Publicly criticize expensive brands
B) Investigate company suppliers
C) Avoid purchasing imported merchandise
D) Visit the U.S. State Department

8

Which choice provides the best evidence for the answer to the previous question?

A) Lines 17-19 ("Through . . . we are")
B) Lines 20-22 ("we should . . . society")
C) Lines 37-39 ("With roughly . . . a slave")
D) Lines 70-72 ("Users can . . . chains")

9

As used in line 72, "chains" most nearly means

A) cords.
B) confines.
C) bindings.
D) networks.

10

Do the data in the graph directly support the author's ideas about effective ways to combat slavery?

A) Yes, because the amount of legislation increased sharply between 2012 and 2014.
B) Yes, because the most victims were identified in 2009.
C) No, because the author never discusses slavery-related legislation.
D) No, because the number of identfied victims has not decreased significantly.

11

Which claim about human trafficking is supported by the graph?

A) The number of victims identified directly corresponds to the amount of new or amended legislation.
B) Both the highest number of victims identified and the highest amount of new or amended legislation were seen in 2013.
C) The lowest number of victims identified was recorded in 2011.
D) Both the number of victims identified and the amount of new or amended legislation were higher in 2013 than in 2008.

Reading Drill 8

Questions 1-10 are based on the following passage.

Over the past decade, environmentalists and engineers have attempted to find new ways to deal with the scarcity of natural resources in central Africa. The author of this passage considers one new invention and its possible impact on society and ecology in Ethiopia.

The *Ficus vasta* or, to give its everyday name, the Warka tree is immense in size. Its massive trunk grows to a height of twenty-five meters and its branches spread to form an inverted bowl that can reach fifty meters in width. As its Latin name indicates, this mammoth plant is a member of the fig (*Ficus*) family; indeed, it produces a fruit which can be eaten by sheep, goats, baboons, monkeys, and children.

Typically, the Warka tree grows along the banks of rivers, though it can also be found in the savannas of Uganda and Tanzania and in ecosystems well beyond these countries, particularly in the Horn of Africa. This plant has grown in the Sudan, in Somalia, and in Ethiopia. However, visitors to these nations would be hard-pressed to find any Warkas—or, in some regions, any trees of any kind. There was a time when this was not the case, yet one of the consequences of the extreme poverty in these parts of the world has been deforestation. When trees are chopped down to provide wood for cooking fires, but cannot be replaced by local communities, the result is barren land where life of all sorts begins to die out. These African countries expose, in a particularly stark manner, the consequences of the human struggle for basic survival.

Over seven million of the people who live in sub-Saharan Africa do not have regular access to water; these Africans rely on water holes that are often approximately fifty kilometers from their homes and that can only be accessed on foot. Even in the areas of Ethiopia where there is water at hand, this water lies one thousand and fifty feet below tough, rocky terrain. To break through without heavy machinery is impossible. Even if such excavation could be achieved, there is little chance that the water could be pumped to the surface without electrical power, which is also hard to come by in these regions. On account of such scarcities, solutions that are at once minimal and ingenious are necessary.

One promising proposal for these troubled regions of Africa has come from Arturo Vittori, an Italian artist, architect, and industrial designer. Vittori has designed subways, yachts, and the largest existing airliner, the A380. He has even created prototypes for an extreme environment tent and for a pressurized rover that humans could use to drive across Mars. Most recently, he traveled to Ethiopia and witnessed the devastating problems caused by the lack of available water. He also saw, for the first time in his life, a magnificent *Ficus vasta*. Then he went home and designed the WarkaWater.

In appearance, the WarkaWater mimics the tree that inspired its design: a "trunk" eight meters high narrows at its top (just like the neck of a bottle) before suddenly expanding to a width of almost eight meters. Nobody has yet weighed an actual Warka tree: this facsimile weighs, in total, sixty kilograms, and can be created by four people with the aid of a simple cutting machine. Bamboo strips are bound together in the shape of a Warka tree, forming a pattern of crossed stalks. These stalks are then linked by a mesh of nylon and polypropylene fibers. Thus, a scaffold for condensation has been built: overnight, dew forms on the fibers and rolls down the strands into a collecting basin at the base of the structure. In this way, over one hundred liters of drinkable water can be collected every day.

The whole construction is hand-crafted yet is based on the same precision modeling that is used to create the interior of an aircraft. The highly portable WarkaWater is both artistic and practical: it links the needs of Ethiopia's nomadic communities with the scientific ambitions of the twenty-first century. In a sense, Vittori has shown that elements of traditional societies, far from being hindrances to progress, can show us how to preserve the earth we inhabit.

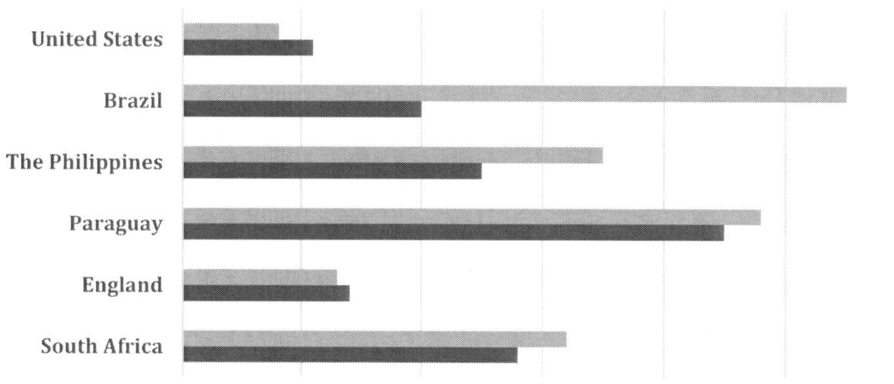

1

The passage suggests that deforestation is primarily a by-product of

A) a booming lumber industry.
B) changing weather conditions.
C) irresponsible farming methods.
D) widespread chronic poverty.

2

It can be inferred from the passage that Vittori designed the WarkaWater because

A) he saw the invention as a means of turning an enormous profit.
B) he wanted to re-create a natural marvel for aesthetic pleasure.
C) he wanted to alleviate suffering.
D) he needed a new architectural challenge.

3

Which choice provides the best evidence for the answer to the previous question?

A) Lines 40-42 ("Vittori . . . A380")
B) Lines 44-46 ("Most recently . . . water")
C) Lines 46-48 ("He also . . . *Ficus vasta*")
D) Lines 50-53 ("In appearance . . . meters")

4

The information in the third paragraph (lines 25-37) conveys the idea that the problem of water shortage in Africa is

A) trivial.
B) dramatic.
C) manageable.
D) localized.

5

As used in line 37, the word "minimal" most nearly means

A) low-profile.
B) negligible.
C) inexpensive.
D) insignificant.

CONTINUE

6

The author includes a list of Vittori's achievements primarily in order to

A) underscore Vittori's ingenuity in solving engineering problems.
B) reinforce Vittori's growing reputation for creativity.
C) indicate the background needed to solve a humanitarian problem.
D) contrast Vittori's humble origins with his present-day renown.

7

Which of the following statements is best supported by the passage?

A) The Warka tree grows abundantly throughout Africa.
B) Though native to many regions, the Warka tree is now rare.
C) The Warka tree is a significant source of nourishment.
D) The Warka tree resists cultivation.

8

Which choice provides the best evidence for the answer to the previous question?

A) Lines 5-8 ("As its . . . and children")
B) Lines 9-12 ("Typically . . . Africa")
C) Lines 13-16 ("This plant . . . kind")
D) Lines 19-22 ("When trees . . . die out")

9

As used in line 56, the word "created" most nearly means

A) conceived.
B) inspired.
C) designed.
D) produced.

10

Which of the following statements is most supported by the graph?

A) Average deforestation is always directly proportional to a country's average poverty level.
B) Average poverty level is determined directly by the average deforestation per month.
C) Average deforestation is inversely related to a country's poverty level.
D) The average poverty level of a country exists in independence of its monthly deforestation.

10

Based on information in the graphic and the passage, the relation between deforestation and poverty in Ethiopia is least similar to the situation in which country?

A) Brazil
B) The Philippines
C) Paraguay
D) South Africa

STOP

Questions 1-10 are based on the following passage.

Originally published under the title "Docility and Dependence," this passage is one of the short essays that appears in *A Treatise on Parents and Children* by George Bernard Shaw (1856-1950).

If anyone, impressed by my view that the rights of a child are precisely those of an adult, proceeds to treat a child as if it were an adult, he (or she) will find that though the plan will work much better at some points than the usual plan, at others, it will not work at all; as it happens, this discovery may provoke him to turn back from the whole conception of children's rights with a jest at the expense of bachelors' and old maids' children. In dealing with children what is needed is not logic but sense. There is no logical reason why young persons should be allowed greater control of their property the day after they are twenty-one than the day before it. There is no logical reason why I, who strongly object to an adult standing over a boy of ten with a Latin grammar, and saying, "you must learn this, whether you want to or not," should nevertheless be quite prepared to stand over a boy of five with the multiplication table or a copy book or a code of elementary good manners, and practice on his docility to make him learn them. And there is no logical reason why I should do for a child a great many little offices, some of them troublesome and disagreeable, which I should not do for a boy twice his age, or support a boy or girl when I would unhesitatingly throw an adult on his own resources. But there are practical reasons, and sensible reasons, and affectionate reasons for all these illogicalities.

Children do not want to be treated altogether as adults: such treatment terrifies them and over-burdens them with responsibility. In truth, very few adults care to be called on for independence and originality: they also are bewildered and terrified in the absence of precedents and precepts and commandments, but modern Democracy allows them a sanctioning and canceling power if they are capable of using it, which children are not. To treat a child wholly as an adult would be to mock and destroy it. Infantile docility and juvenile dependence are, like death, the products of Natural Selection; and though there is no viler crime than to abuse them, yet there is no greater cruelty than to ignore them. I have complained sufficiently of what I suffered through the process of assault, imprisonment, and compulsory lessons that taught me nothing, which are called my schooling. But I could say a good deal also about the things I was not taught and should have been taught, not to mention the things I was allowed to do which I should not have been allowed to do. I have no recollection of being taught to read or write, so I presume I was born with both faculties, but many people seem to have bitter recollections of being forced reluctantly to acquire them. And though I have the uttermost contempt for a teacher so ill mannered and incompetent as to be unable to make a child learn to read and write without also making it cry, still I am prepared to admit that I had rather have been compelled to learn to read and write with tears by an incompetent and ill mannered person than left in ignorance. Reading, writing, and enough arithmetic to use money honestly and accurately, together with the rudiments of law and order, become necessary conditions of a child's liberty before it can appreciate the importance of its liberty, or foresee that these accomplishments are worth acquiring. Nature has provided for this by evolving the instinct of docility. Children are very docile: they have a sound intuition that they must do what they are told or perish. And adults have an intuition, equally sound, that they must take advantage of this docility to teach children how to live properly or the children will not survive. The difficulty is to know where to stop.

CONTINUE

1

Bernard Shaw uses repetition in lines 10-25 ("There is . . . resources") in order to

A) suggest that the way adults treat children should be more logical.
B) indicate that he disagrees with traditional modes of education.
C) imply that he finds children disagreeable.
D) emphasize that sensible actions are not always logical.

2

It can most reasonably be inferred that Bernard Shaw believes that children

A) have the same rights as adults and should be treated as such.
B) will naturally acquire the ability to read and write.
C) cannot yet appreciate the importance of education.
D) enjoy learning with their peers more than learning with adults.

3

Bernard Shaw implies that his education was

A) neither fruitful nor comprehensive.
B) essential to his writing career.
C) similar to that granted to most children.
D) guided by illogical procedures.

4

According to the author, the "difficulty" (line 70) that adults face is knowing when to stop

A) exercising control over children.
B) teaching basic skills to children.
C) believing that children have rights.
D) treating children like adults.

5

According to the passage, adults are able to compel children to learn because

A) adults have more power in a democracy.
B) children are naturally obedient.
C) adults treat children as their equals.
D) children depend on adults for sustenance.

6

Which choice provides the best evidence for the answer to the previous question?

A) Lines 3-5 ("he . . . at all")
B) Lines 44-46 ("But I . . . taught")
C) Lines 55-58 ("still I . . . ignorance")
D) Lines 64-65 ("Nature . . . docile")

7

According to the passage, adults are similar to children because they

A) feel uncertain without guidance.
B) enjoy sanctioning and canceling powers.
C) can survive without relying on others.
D) dislike persons of higher authority.

8

Which choice provides the best evidence for the answer to the previous question?

A) Lines 6-9 ("as it . . . maids' children")
B) Lines 32-33 ("they also . . . commandments")
C) Lines 36-37 ("To treat . . . it")
D) Lines 50-52 ("but many . . . them")

9

As used in line 2, “proceeds” most nearly means

A) approaches.

B) undertakes.

C) advances.

D) evolves.

10

As used in line 66, “sound” most nearly means

A) universal.

B) valid.

C) tested.

D) tangible.

CONTINUE

Questions 1-10 are based on the following passage.

In these passages, two authors consider how food shortages relate to concepts from plant biology.

Passage 1

The cultivated peanuts of today have lost most of their former genetic resistance to disease; as a result, peanut plants have immense trouble reproducing, and peanut crops have nearly been decimated. Imagine a world without jars of peanuts on the shelves or peanut butter cups in vending machines—hard, right? The same goes for the banana: did you know that it is sterile? The yellow bunched fruit that can be found at the market is actually a genetically cloned mutant and cannot reproduce on its own. The wild type, which is capable of spreading seeds (and seeds the size of capers), is neither as delectable nor as marketable as its barren counterpart. Because of their diminished immunities and nonexistent reproductive capabilities, these foods are at risk of disappearing from global commerce as increasingly robust pathogen populations threaten the futures of peanut and banana crops.

The cases of the peanut and the banana are only two examples of how a lack of biological diversity can diminish a plant population necessary to a cash crop industry. Concern with plant inbreeding hearkens back to The Great Famine of 1845, when the Potato Blight eradicated a staple of Irish nutrition; in the course of this crisis, mass starvation took the lives of nearly one million people over six years.

Indeed, the Potato Blight's cost in human life was staggering, but the loss of expertise and labor should not be underestimated: almost 4.5 million Irish, the horrors of the potato blight ever in mind, left their home country between 1850 and 1921. Greater cross-breeding of potatoes would have facilitated genetic variation, would have fostered more robust strains, and might have prevented a nationwide catastrophe. Sadly for those remaining in Ireland, some of the agricultural talent needed for cross-breeding had been eradicated, or driven out of the country, by the Potato Blight itself.

Passage 2

For some, hardships pave the way for ingenuity. Even in nations that have been afflicted by food shortages, it is possible to push back against the worst economic and agricultural pressures. Nikolai Vavilov (1887-1943), who eventually became one of Russia's most prominent geneticists and botanists, grew up in an era when hunger was omnipresent and food was scarce. Determined to create a better existence for his family and for mankind as a whole, Vavilov dedicated his life to comprehending the root of starvation and to developing the means of preventing food crises. To consolidate his work on these problems, he collected agricultural seeds from five continents and established a seed bank.

Vavilov's seed bank was instrumental in promoting genetic classification and preservation as a truly modern system of scientific inquiry—and of humanitarian involvement. Because orthodox seeds (those that can survive drying or freezing, and that are suited to remote conservation) can remain in a dormant state for decades with properly controlled temperature and humidity conditions, their DNA will sustain little damage and the seed itself can remain viable, functioning almost as an organic time capsule. It is possible to compare this famous seed bank to the civilization-saving storehold of Noah's Ark; Vavilov, certainly, was interested in protecting civilization, not with paired-off animals but with the plant strains that would ensure a healthy future.

CONTINUE

1

In discussing the science of seeds, the author of Passage 1 and the author of Passage 2 both present

A) specific historical examples.
B) profiles of famous scientists.
C) cutting-edge technological solutions.
D) literary and religious references.

2

As used in line 1, "cultivated" most nearly means

A) modified.
B) proliferating.
C) refined.
D) cultured.

3

The examples of "Greater cross breeding" (Passage 1, line 30) and "orthodox seeds" (Passage 2, line 53) would best support the idea that

A) research must be undertaken to counteract starvation.
B) agricultural scientists can foster especially durable plants.
C) the Potato Blight involved genetically manipulated seeds.
D) agriculture based on inbred strains of seeds will ultimately fail.

4

The primary purpose of Passage 2 is to

A) illustrate the variety of seeds available to counteract hunger.
B) directly contradict the ideas put forward in Passage 1.
C) show how an early life filled with hardship can lead a scientist to success.
D) discuss the significance of work that addressed a specific humanitarian problem.

5

Which choice provides the best evidence for the answer to the previous question?

A) Lines 40-43 ("Nikolai . . . scarce")
B) Lines 47-49 ("To consolidate . . . seed bank")
C) Lines 53-59 ("Because . . . capsule")
D) Lines 59-61 ("It is possible . . . Noah's Ark")

6

If Nikolai Vavilov's development of "orthodox seeds" had taken place by 1845, the discovery would most likely have had what effect on the scenario described in Passage 1?

A) One million Irish deaths would have happened over ten years instead of over six years.
B) Genetic variation would have allowed fruit and nut crops to remedy Ireland's potato shortage.
C) Ireland might not have lost so many great minds and diligent workers to the Potato Blight.
D) Some of the world's greatest agricultural talent would never have been discovered.

7

The author of Passage 1 would most likely regard Vavilov's findings as discussed in Passage 2 as

A) enlightening, since the findings prove that genetic uniformity tends to weaken plant species over time.
B) questionable, since none of Vavilov's ideas have been experimentally validated.
C) limited, because Vavilov had little interest in the psychological effects of famine.
D) valuable, because disasters can result from poor knowledge of the best agricultural practices.

CONTINUE

8

Which choice provides the best evidence for the answer to the previous question?

A) Lines 1-4 ("The . . . decimated")

B) Lines 26-28 ("Indeed . . . underestimated")

C) Lines 30-33 ("Greater . . . catastrophe")

D) Lines 33-35 ("Sadly . . . eradicated")

9

As used in line 10, "wild" most nearly means

A) original.

B) unruly.

C) energized.

D) unregulated.

10

Passage 1 and Passage 2 examine the topic of seed biology in a manner best described as

A) hypothetical and experimental.

B) factual yet counterintuitive.

C) anecdotal and scientific.

D) informal and accessible.

STOP

Questions 1-10 are based on the following passage.

Adapted from *A Room with a View* by E.M. Forster (1908). In this scene, a young Englishwoman named Lucy Honeychurch is visiting Florence with an older relative, Miss Bartlett.

It was pleasant to wake up in Florence, to open the eyes upon a bright bare room, with a floor of red tiles which look clean though they are not, with a painted ceiling whereon pink griffins and blue amorini sport in a forest of yellow violins and bassoons. It was pleasant, too, to fling wide the windows, pinching the fingers in unfamiliar fastenings, to lean out into sunshine with beautiful hills and trees and marble churches opposite, and close below, the Arno, gurgling against the embankment of the road.

Over the river men were at work with spades and sieves on the sandy foreshore, and on the river was a boat, also diligently employed for some mysterious end. An electric tram came rushing underneath the window. No one was inside it, except one tourist, but its platforms were overflowing with Italians, who preferred to stand. Children tried to hang on behind, and the conductor, with no malice, spat in their faces to make them let go. Then soldiers appeared—good-looking, undersized men—wearing each a knapsack covered with mangy fur, and a great-coat which had been cut for some larger soldier. Beside them walked officers, looking foolish and fierce, and before them went little boys, turning somersaults in time with the band. The tramcar became entangled in their ranks, and moved on painfully, like a caterpillar in a swarm of ants. One of the little boys fell down, and some white bullocks came out of an archway. Indeed, if it had not been for the good advice of an old man who was selling button-hooks, the road might never have got clear.

Over such trivialities as these many a valuable hour may slip away, and the traveler who has gone to Italy to study the tactile values of Giotto, or the corruption of the Papacy, may return remembering nothing but the blue sky and the men and women who live under it. So it was as well that Miss Bartlett should tap and come in, and having commented on Lucy's leaving the door unlocked, and on her leaning out of the window before she was fully dressed, should urge her to hasten herself, or the best of the day would be gone. By the time Lucy was ready her cousin had done her breakfast, and was listening to a third one of the hotel's guests, a clever lady, among the crumbs.

A conversation then ensued, on not unfamiliar lines. Miss Bartlett was, after all, a wee bit tired, and thought they had better spend the morning settling; unless Lucy would at all like to go out? Lucy would rather like to go out, as it was her first day in Florence, but, of course, she could go alone. Miss Bartlett could not allow this. Of course she would accompany Lucy everywhere. Oh, certainly not; Lucy would stop with her cousin. Oh, no! that would never do. Oh, yes!

At this point the clever lady broke in.

"If it is Mrs. Grundy who is troubling you, I do assure you that you can neglect the good person. Being English, Miss Honeychurch will be perfectly safe. Italians understand. A dear friend of mine, Contessa Baroncelli, has two daughters, and when she cannot send a maid to school with them, she lets them go in sailor-hats instead. Every one takes them for English, you see, especially if their hair is strained tightly behind."

Miss Bartlett was unconvinced by the safety of Contessa Baroncelli's daughters. She was determined to take Lucy herself, her head not being so very bad. The clever lady then said that she was going to spend a long morning in Santa Croce, and if Lucy would come too, she would be delighted.

"I will take you by a dear dirty back way, Miss Honeychurch, and if you bring me luck, we shall have an adventure."

Lucy said that this was most kind, and at once opened the Baedeker, to see where Santa Croce was.

"Tut, tut! Miss Lucy!" Thus said her clever companion "I hope we shall soon emancipate you from Baedeker. He does but touch the surface of things. As to the true Italy—he does not even dream of it. The true Italy is only to be found by patient observation."

CONTINUE

1

It can be reasonably inferred from the passage that Lucy is

A) an expatriate who wishes to make Florence her home.
B) a tourist visiting Florence with her husband.
C) an academic studying politics in Italy.
D) a person who has limited familiarity with Florence.

2

Which choice provides the best evidence for the answer to the previous question?

A) Lines 32-37 ("Over such . . . under it")
B) Lines 48-50 ("Lucy would . . . go alone")
C) Lines 58-61 ("A dear friend . . . . instead")
D) Lines 77-79 ("He does . . . observation")

3

The author repeats the phrase "It was pleasant" in lines 1 and 5-6 primarily in order to

A) emphasize the hedonism of the central character.
B) contrast the charms of one city with the unpleasantness of another.
C) introduce a detailed description of a setting.
D) foreshadow a later criticism of Florentine society.

4

The metaphor "a caterpillar in a swarm of ants" (line 26-27) indicates that the observer is

A) critical of the slow pace of Florentine traffic.
B) appalled at the recklessness of those who are walking on the tracks.
C) detached from the scene as though watching another species.
D) wary of utilizing public transportation in Florence for fear of injury.

5

The observation in lines 32-37 ("Over such . . . under it") primarily serves to

A) indicate that the novelty and distraction found in Italy are unique.
B) transition from an impressionistic account to a social encounter.
C) enumerate the reasons why a person may travel to Italy.
D) allude to the effects of Giotto's artistic methods on foreign paintings.

6

Miss Bartlett's behavior in lines 51-53 ("Of course . . . yes!") is best characterized as

A) abrasive disregard.
B) delicate suggestion.
C) shy curiosity.
D) aggressive solicitude.

7

The clever lady mentions Contessa Baroncelli's children to make the point that

A) children are rarely bothered in Italian cities.
B) Italians are easily confused with the English.
C) it is inappropriate for a maid to accompany English children.
D) Lucy Honeychurch does not need an escort in Florence because she is English.

CONTINUE

8

Why does the “clever companion” (lines 75-76) wish to “emancipate” (line 76) Lucy from her guidebook?

A) To convince Lucy to ignore Miss Bartlett

B) Because Baedecker does an especially poor job of cataloging Italian art and culture

C) Because Baedecker does not relate an authentic version of Florence

D) To free Lucy of the negative opinion of Italians fostered by Baedecker’s guidebook

9

The author would likely agree that “patient observation” (line 79) is best represented by

A) an exhaustive tour of museums, chapels, and other sites of historical interest.

B) a detailed study of the artistic nuances epitomized by the works of Giotto.

C) a profound understanding of the Italians’ deep nobility of spirit.

D) a leisurely exploration of the daily scenes of Florentine life.

10

Which choice provides the best evidence for the answer to the previous question?

A) Lines 5-10 (“It was pleasant . . . of the road”)

B) Lines 15-17 (“No one . . . preferred to stand”)

C) Lines 45-48 (“A conversation . . . go out?”)

D) Lines 64-66 (“Miss Bartlett . . . so very bad”)

CONTINUE

Questions 1-10 are based on the following passage.

The passages below, adapted from works published in 2012, discuss in-school bullying and how this problem has recently been addressed.

Passage 1

It's no secret that getting bullied is hurtful. But when a student, or any individual, gets bullied in person, there's only so much damage a bully can do before the possibility of someone stepping in arises. Yet in cyberspace, bullying takes on a whole new meaning. Now, perpetrators can gain momentum as others chime in as well. And those others who do decide to join the bullying don't need to leave the ease and comfort of their chairs; they simply press a few buttons on their keyboards and they're done. But the impact for those who are bullied is lasting.

Bullying is just as much a public health problem as it is a victim's or individual's problem, as it causes major concerns for entire school environments. High schools with a high rate of bullying have scored much lower on standardized tests than those with lower rates of bullying. These lower test scores affect a given school's capacity to meet federal requirements and hinder the education of the many students who do not pass the exams. This is a problem for schools on account of the No Child Left Behind Act, under which students must receive passing scores on standardized tests to even graduate. Under this act, schools are now under pressure to do something urgent about bullying.

To stop bullying, we need to work together to educate everyone and get everyone involved: administrators, parents, and students. President Barack Obama recently started a campaign against bullying and Lady Gaga has her own foundation, called Born This Way, to help spread the message. But these are just a few outlets, and unless society as a whole does what is needed to combat this problem, the consequences of bullying will only grow worse. We do not permit harassment and the abuse of adults in the workplace, so why should similar protections not be afforded to children in school?

Passage 2

After school specials are not as popular now as they were in the 1980's, but those who watched them can recall at least one or two specials on bullying. But what some seem to forget is that bullying has been around long before the media put it in the hot seat. Bullying has not gotten worse over the years, according to studies in the field; rather, the media attention it has received, as a product of the devastating results of bullying, has highlighted this major problem.

According to StopBullying.gov, a popular website that tracks bullying, "Bullying is unwanted, aggressive behavior . . . that involves a real or perceived power imbalance. The behavior is repeated, or has the potential to be repeated, over time. Bullying includes actions such as making threats, spreading rumors, attacking someone physically or verbally, and excluding someone from a group on purpose." The argument that these instances are simply cases of "children being children" is no longer a viable excuse. In an age of interconnectedness, bullying delivers easy and immediate pain. The perpetrators don't have to pose a physical threat at all; they now have the Internet at their disposal and can do their damage without leaving the comfort of their own homes.

The act of bullying doesn't only have an effect on the victim. For the perpetrators, bullying can be the beginning of a trajectory of trouble, including disorderly conduct, skipping school, substance abuse, and, quite possibly, adult criminal behavior. For the victims, being bullied leads not simply to immediate physical and emotional pain; many times, the impact can extend into later life. The scars don't go away, but stay with the victims into adulthood. The ripple effect doesn't stop at the bully and the bullied, either, since those who are simply witnesses and are not directly involved in bullying are more likely to skip school or abuse alcohol. A climate of fear affects everyone.

Unfortunately, the old way of doing things (suspension and expulsion) doesn't stop bullying. Punishment-based strategies don't give students the tools they need to make lasting behavioral changes. Those who have a tendency to victimize others usually have weak social skills and little emotional regulation, which can definitely be contributors to bullying behaviors. Therefore, the best strategy for combating bullying is a comprehensive approach. This includes getting the bullies involved. It may sound counterintuitive, but the bullies need help too, maybe the most help. If we can get through to them, we can come close to eliminating the problem altogether.

CONTINUE

1

As used in line 36, “afforded” most nearly means

A) managed.
B) provided.
C) donated.
D) paid.

2

As used in line 57, “viable” most nearly means

A) developed.
B) successful.
C) vital.
D) adequate.

3

In Passage 1, the author implies that schools are working to address bullying partially because

A) schools are increasingly aware of the negative and long-lasting consequences of bullying.
B) federal legislation obligates schools to be more concerned about bullying.
C) parents are becoming more vocal about making schools into bully-free environments.
D) bullying in school is significantly more severe than bullying in cyberspace.

4

Which choice provides the best evidence for the answer to the previous question?

A) Lines 4-5 (“Yet in cyberspace . . . meaning”)
B) Lines 12-13 (“Bullying is . . . problem”)
C) Lines 23-25 (“Under . . . bullying”)
D) Lines 26-27 (“To stop . . . involved”)

5

How would the author of Passage 2 most likely respond to point made in the final paragraph of Passage 1?

A) Victims should be protected from bullying, but the perpetrators must be given constructive attention.
B) The problem of Internet-based bullying needs to be addressed as a public health concern.
C) It is unnecessary to focus primarily on protecting children from bullies at school.
D) Drawing parallels between the workplace and the school removes focus from issues unique to children.

6

Which choice provides the best evidence for the answer to the previous question?

A) Lines 40-42 (“But what . . . hot seat”)
B) Lines 58-62 (“The perpetrators . . . homes”)
C) Lines 78-79 (“Punishment-based . . . changes”)
D) Lines 85-87 (“It may . . . most help”)

7

Which best describes the overall relationship between Passage 1 and Passage 2?

A) Passage 2 addresses a different aspect of the issue presented in Passage 1.
B) Passage 2 calls into question the central points advanced in Passage 1.
C) Passage 2 argues against the effectiveness of the solution proposed in Passage 1.
D) Passage 2 analyzes a dilemma described in more general terms in Passage 1.

CONTINUE

8

The central claim of Passage 2 is that bullying

A) can be defined in multiple ways depending on the circumstances.

B) negatively affects perpetrators, victims, and bystanders.

C) must be directly addressed by the government.

D) is unrelated to the declining popularity of after school specials.

9

On which of the following points would the authors of both passages most likely agree?

A) Punishment is an effective way to make schools safer.

B) Bullying behavior suggests underlying psychological issues.

C) Receiving lower test scores correlates with being bullied.

D) The Internet plays a role in facilitating bullying.

10

What function does the quotation in lines 48-55 serve in Passage 2?

A) It examines the consequences of a problem discussed in the previous paragraph.

B) It offers evidence for a claim made in the previous paragraph.

C) It clarifies a term that appears in the previous paragraph.

D) It rejects a major assumption of the previous paragraph

STOP

Questions 1-11 are based on the following passage.

The following passage is taken from an article on new medicines that are being used to combat diseases that affect the human eye.

Imagine that you are wearing sunglasses. Everything you see is darkened because you are looking not only through your eyes' own lenses as usual, but also through the dark lenses of the sunglasses. Now imagine that you are looking through sunglasses coated in white paint. You would not able to see anything clearly, perhaps only vague shadows and light spots. Millions of people live with this reality in the form of cataracts, white cloudy formations in the eye.

Cataracts are formed when crystallins (which, in their normal state, help the eye to maintain its transparency and structure) clump together and obscure the lens of the eye. Although their formation is not fully understood, cataracts are very common and tend to affect older people. According to the National Eye Institute, most Americans who are at least 80 years old have, or have had, cataracts. The only current treatment for cataracts is eye surgery; unfortunately, many people, particularly those living in economically disadvantaged countries, do not have access to this procedure. Without surgery, cataracts can thicken and cause blindness. In fact, according to the Fred Hollows Foundation, cataracts are responsible for approximately half of all cases of blindness in the world.

Despite the increasing correlation of cataract frequency and old age, some forms of cataracts are genetic and appear in children. Ling Zhao, a molecular biologist from the University of California, decided to study children with inherited forms of cataracts in the hopes of discovering what causes cataract formation. Her research team discovered that these children have a genetic mutation that prevents their bodies from producing lanosterol, a steroid normally found in humans.

One of the researchers who has worked alongside Zhao is Dr. Kang Zhang, a professor of ophthalmology at the University of California. Zhang explained that, "by screening families across the world for mutations that affect vision, we found four kids in two families with genetic aberrations in an enzyme called lanosterol synthase." As its name suggests, lanosterol synthase synthesizes lanosterol. Dr. Zhao's team then hypothesized that perhaps a lack of lanosterol, caused by the absence of lanosterol synthase, was responsible for cataract formation.

To evaluate this hypothesis, the researchers tested lanosterol eye drops on lab models of human lens cells clouded by cataracts. The results, which showed clear diminution of cataract thickness, were dramatic. The scientists then tested the eye drops on rabbits with severe cataracts. After six days, 11 out of the 13 rabbits had very mild cataracts or exhibited completely clear eyes. The team then tested the eye drops on dogs, with very similar results.

Dr. Zhao and her team published their results in the scientific journal *Nature* in July 2015. The findings led molecular biologist and cataract researcher Jonathan King of the Massachusetts Institute of Technology (MIT) to exclaim, "This is a really comprehensive and compelling paper—the strongest I've seen of its kind in a decade."

In addition to its potential to treat animals, lanosterol holds a lot of promise as a human medicine. If the drops work as well for human patients as they did for the rabbits and dogs, the eye drops would not only save millions of people from the cost and inconvenience of surgery, but also save the eyesight of millions more who do not have access to cataract surgery. Clara Eaglen of the Royal National Institute of Blind People remarked, "Anything that removes the need for invasive surgery will be hugely beneficial to patients. If eye drops could be self-administered, this would remove the burden on eye clinics." It is possible, now, to imagine a world without cataracts.

CONTINUE

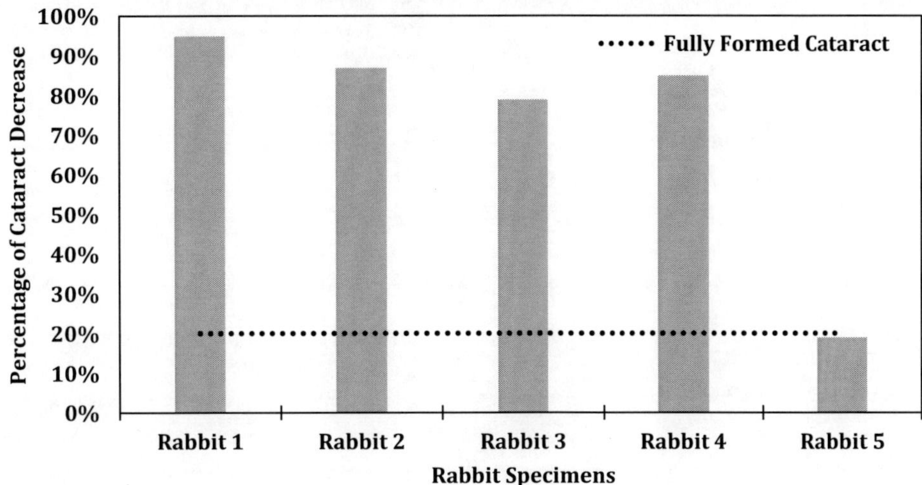

1

The primary purpose of the first paragraph is to

A) advocate for those living with blindness.
B) illustrate the process of cataract formation.
C) demonstrate the effect of cataracts on vision.
D) introduce a research project conducted at MIT.

2

According to the research discussed in the passage, it can most reasonably be inferred that cataracts form due to

A) complications in surgery.
B) over-activity of enzymes.
C) lower hygienic standards.
D) a steroid deficiency.

3

The primary purpose of the quotation in lines 61-63 is to

A) add legitimacy to Dr. Zhao's findings.
B) undermine a dissenting opinion.
C) give further insight into the cause of cataracts.
D) suggest that Jonathan King and Ling Zhao will eventually collaborate.

4

Childhood cataracts are different from adult cataracts because they

A) are explained largely by heredity.
B) do not lead to blindness.
C) are more common in males.
D) have been ignored by researchers

5

Which choice provides the best evidence for the answer to the previous question?

A) Lines 18-19 ("The only . . . surgery")
B) Lines 23-26 ("In fact . . . the world")
C) Lines 27-29 ("Despite . . . children")
D) Lines 48-50 ("To evaluate . . . cataracts")

6

According to the passage, the treatment of cataracts with lanosterol

A) has not yet been proven effective for humans.
B) cannot replace traditional methods.
C) could cause more complications than surgery.
D) causes thickening of the lens of the eye.

CONTINUE

7

Which choice provides the best evidence for the answer to the previous question?

A) Lines 51-53 ("The scientists . . . cataracts")
B) Lines 57-58 ("Dr. Zhao . . . July 2015")
C) Lines 66-69 ("If the drops . . . surgery")
D) Lines 75-76 ("It is . . . cataracts")

8

As used in line 42, "aberrations" most nearly means

A) misinterpretations.
B) anomalies.
C) refractions.
D) idiosyncrasies.

9

As used in line 51, "diminution" most nearly means

A) removal.
B) reduction.
C) depletion.
D) depreciation.

10

Based on the graph, which rabbit from the experiment would provide the weakest evidence for the author's claims?

A) Rabbit 1
B) Rabbit 2
C) Rabbit 4
D) Rabbit 5

11

How does the graph corroborate the findings of Dr. Zhao and her team?

A) It indicates that lanosterol treatment is most effective for large mammals.
B) It indicates that lanosterol treatment can be frequently though not absolutely effective.
C) It indicates that lanosterol treatment has no adverse side-effects for mammal species.
D) It indicates that lanosterol treatment will always improve a patient's vision.

Questions 1-11 are based on the following passage.

The following is an excerpt from the book *Anarchism and Other Essays* by Emma Goldman (1869-1940), a proponent of political anarchism who relocated from Europe to the U.S. (The term "anarchism" refers to a school of thought that radically opposes government intervention in day-to-day life—and that, at its most extreme, supports the abolition of formal government.)

It is generally conceded that unless the returns of any business venture exceed the cost, bankruptcy is inevitable. But those engaged in the business of producing wealth have not yet learned even this simple lesson. Every year the cost of production in human life is growing larger (50,000 killed, 100,000 wounded in America last year); the returns to the masses, who help to create wealth, are ever getting smaller. Yet America continues to be blind to the inevitable bankruptcy of our business of production. Nor is this the only crime of the latter. Still more fatal is the crime of turning the producer into a mere particle of a machine, with less will and decision than his master of steel and iron. Man is being robbed not merely of the products of his labor, but of the power of free initiative, of originality, and the interest in, or desire for, the things he is making.

Real wealth consists in things of utility and beauty, in things that help to create strong, beautiful bodies and surroundings inspiring to live in. But if man is doomed to wind cotton around a spool, or dig coal, or build roads for thirty years of his life, there can be no talk of wealth. What he gives to the world is only gray and hideous things, reflecting a dull and hideous existence—too weak to live, too cowardly to die. Strange to say, there are people who extol this deadening method of centralized production as the proudest achievement of our age. They fail utterly to realize that if we are to continue in machine subserviency, our slavery is more complete than was our bondage to the King. They do not want to know that centralization is not only the death-knell of liberty, but also of health and beauty, of art and science, all these being impossible in a clock-like, mechanical atmosphere.

Anarchism cannot but repudiate such a method of production: its goal is the freest possible expression of all the latent powers of the individual. Oscar Wilde defines a perfect personality as "one who develops under perfect conditions, who is not wounded, maimed, or in danger." A perfect personality, then, is only possible in a state of society where man is free to choose the mode of work, the conditions of work, and the freedom to work. One to whom the making of a table, the building of a house, or the tilling of the soil, is what the painting is to the artist and the discovery to the scientist—the result of inspiration, of intense longing, and deep interest in work as a creative force. That being the ideal of Anarchism, its economic arrangements must consist of voluntary productive and distributive associations, gradually developing into free communism, as the best means of producing with the least waste of human energy. Anarchism, however, also recognizes the right of the individual, or numbers of individuals, to arrange at all times for other forms of work, in harmony with their tastes and desires.

Such free display of human energy being possible only under complete individual and social freedom, Anarchism directs its forces against the third and greatest foe of all social equality: namely, the State, organized authority, or statutory law—the dominion of human conduct.

Just as religion has fettered the human mind, and as property, or the monopoly of things, has subdued and stifled man's needs, so has the State enslaved his spirit, dictating every phase of conduct. "All government in essence," says Emerson, "is tyranny." It matters not whether it is government by divine right or majority rule. In every instance its aim is the absolute subordination of the individual.

Referring to the American government, the greatest American Anarchist, David Thoreau, said: "Government, what is it but a tradition, though a recent one, endeavoring to transmit itself unimpaired to posterity, but each instance losing its integrity; it has not the vitality and force of a single living man. Law never made man a whit more just; and by means of their respect for it, even the well disposed are daily made agents of injustice."

1

As used in line 13, "will" most nearly means

A) character.
B) insistence.
C) volition.
D) desire.

2

The author most strongly implies which of the following about "the power of free initiative" (line 15)?

A) It is not valued in the current business of production.
B) It is thriving because of the mechanization of labor.
C) It never contributed significantly to productivity.
D) It is a serious threat to the centralized economy.

3

Goldman describes those who do not share her viewpoint as

A) selfish.
B) irresponsible.
C) oblivious.
D) uncreative.

4

Which choice provides the best evidence for the answer to the previous question?

A) Lines 1-3 ("It is generally . . . is inevitable")
B) Lines 22-24 ("What he gives . . . cowardly to die")
C) Lines 27-30 ("They fail utterly . . . to the King")
D) Lines 76-78 ("Law never made . . . injustice")

5

Goldman presents "the proudest achievement of our age" (line 27) as a characterization that

A) is used by those who do not agree with her.
B slightly overstates the country's progress.
C) is used by those who have acquired great wealth.
D) accurately depicts the current economic system.

6

As used in line 29, "complete" most nearly means

A) unmodified.
B) total.
C) exhaustive.
D) finished.

7

The discussion of work in lines 43-48 ("One to whom . . . creative force") primarily serves to

A) demonstrate that it is unlikely that most people enjoy their jobs.
B) describe the manner in which work should be approached.
C) call attention to particular vocations that have recently been neglected.
D) emphasize that working with machines would streamline certain processes.

8

According to the Goldman, what is an advantage of Anarchism?

A) It fosters the consolidation of wealth among few individuals.
B) It frees citizens from a violently oppressive central government.
C) It gives people freedom to make personal decisions about work.
D) It establishes regulations to organize production and trade organizations.

CONTINUE

9

Which choice provides the best evidence for the answer to the previous question?

A) Lines 17-19 ("Real wealth . . . to live in")
B) Lines 52-55 ("Anarchism . . . and desires")
C) Lines 56-61 ("Such free . . . human conduct")
D) Lines 70-75 ("Referring to . . . living man")

10

As they are presented in the passage, Emerson and Thoreau would most probably view the United States federal government as

A) detrimental.
B) legitimate.
C) prejudiced.
D) revolutionary.

11

Goldman contends in the passage that individuals are profoundly influenced by

A) the environment where they are normally employed.
B) the growing recognition that government is unjust.
C) the ideas of respected thinkers and philosophers.
D) the desire to make government smaller but more efficient.

STOP

Questions 1-10 are based on the following passage.

The following passage is from an article about the effects of industrial agriculture on the atmosphere.

Greenhouse gases like carbon dioxide (CO_2), methane (CH_4), and nitrous oxide (N_2O) absorb infrared light and warm the globe. They are also all components of biological cycles: CO_2 is consumed in photosynthesis and emitted in animal respiration; N_2O is one component of the nitrogen cycle; CH_4 is consumed and emitted by certain species of microorganisms. In balance with their natural cycles and at relatively constant atmospheric concentrations, these gases have kept the earth habitable. But industrialization has increased the concentration of each substance.

Current agricultural practices exacerbate the problem. For example, soil naturally holds carbon, which in turn helps the soil retain nutrients, filter water, and regulate temperature. In fact, soil holds three times more carbon than does the atmosphere. But today's commercial farmers use chemical fertilizers and pesticides that deplete the soil's carbon-capturing ability. About one third of the excess carbon in the atmosphere can be attributed to mismanaged and destroyed soils.

Our current food system also affects CH_4 concentration. Methanogens (CH_4-producing microorganisms) live in the guts of cows, termites, and even humans, helping us break down and absorb our food. Digestion creates CH_4 for release into the atmosphere, and U.S. cattle contribute 20 percent of emissions. This could be reduced: most commercially raised cattle subsist on grain, which forces the digestive system to work harder, leading to more CH_4. To see how diet affects CH_4, Stonyfield Farm conducted a study wherein 15 Vermont farms added more grasses to their cows' grainy diets. This study and a similar one in France found a significant drop in methane emissions: as much as 30 percent.

Industrial agriculture has an even greater effect on N_2O concentration. Commercial agriculture demands large amounts of ammonium-rich fertilizer. The natural nitrogen cycle produces ammonium, but not enough to support our large population. To accommodate mega-farms, scientists discovered how to create fixed nitrogen on a commercial scale. This industrial "Haber-Bosch" process is energy intensive and bad for the environment. In fact, synthetic nitrogen fertilizers account for 69 percent of N_2O emissions in the U.S.

When the elements of today's food system are added up—deforestation, land use change, food processing, transportation, refrigeration, packaging, retail, food waste, and agriculture itself—they comprise between 44 and 57 percent of global human-sourced greenhouse gas emissions. Some might shrug this off, suggesting that today's methods are more efficient than those of the past. Actually, the reverse is true. In 1940, 1 calorie of energy produced 2.3 calories of food. Today, 10 calories of energy produce less than half of that—just 1 calorie of food. Some will accept this inefficiency, touting the use of large farms, chemical products and uniform seeds to "feed the world." However, the relationship between food production and world hunger is unclear. We produce more food per capita today than at any time in history—about 4.3 pounds per person per day. Yet hunger persists.

The benefits of our current food system are unclear, but the environmental damage is starkly apparent. In the face of changing climate and potentially harsher farming conditions, it would be wise to start taking organic and local farms—those that prohibit chemicals, foster biodiversity, and heal the soil—more seriously.

CONTINUE

Atmospheric Concentration of Methane Gas Over Time

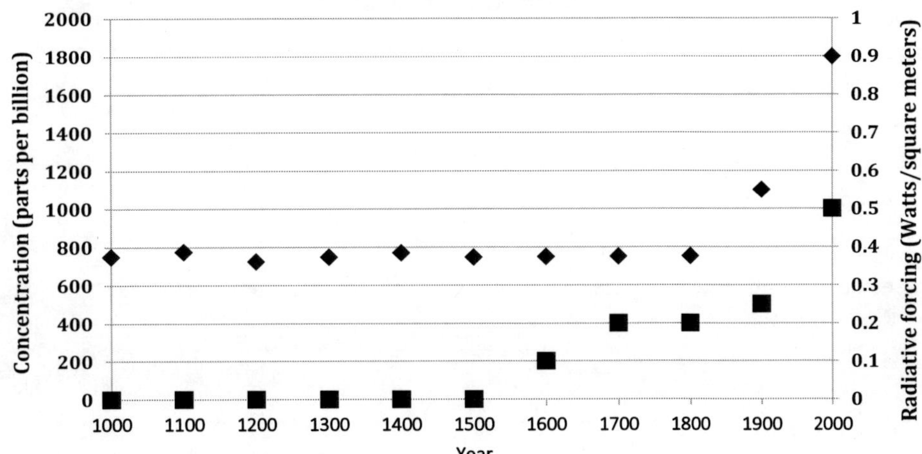

1

The primary purpose of the passage is to

A) summarize the effects of greenhouse gases on the environment.

B) introduce a new strategy for industrial-scale food production.

C) indicate that current agricultural practices have destructive side effects.

D) explain how human activity damages the natural carbon cycle.

2

Which choice provides the best evidence for the answer to the previous question?

A) Lines 16-18 ("But today's . . . ability")

B) Lines 39-41 ("To accommodate . . . scale")

C) Lines 45-50 ("When the . . . emissions")

D) Lines 55-57 ("Some will . . . the world")

3

As used in line 13, "holds" most nearly means

A) regards.

B) absorbs.

C) restrains.

D) dominates.

4

Based on the passage, which choice best describes the relationship between the research in Vermont and that in France?

A) The research in Vermont contradicts that in France.

B) The research in Vermont expands on that in France.

C) The research in France corrects that in Vermont.

D) The research in France corroborates that in Vermont.

5

As used in line 39, "support" most nearly means

A) condone.

B) finance.

C) comfort.

D) sustain.

6

In lines 50-52 ("Some might . . . the past"), what is the most likely reason the author mentions a potential opinion?

A) To anticipate a flawed counterargument

B) To concede an important point in a debate

C) To mock proponents of industrial efficiency

D) To validate a seeming misconception

CONTINUE

7

Which choice provides the best evidence for the answer to the previous question?

A) Lines 10-11 ("But industrialization . . . substance")
B) Line 52 ("Actually, the . . . true")
C) Lines 59-61 ("We produce . . . per day")
D) Lines 62-63 ("The benefits . . . apparent")

8

The passage and the accompanying graph most strongly suggest that the use of chemicals in agriculture has what effect?

A) Elimination of world hunger
B) Streamlined food production
C) Damage to the environment
D) Contaminated crop yields

9

Based on the graph, the ratio of methane gas concentration to radiative forcing was highest in what year?

A) 1600
B) 1700
C) 1900
D) 2000

10

It can reasonably be inferred from the passage and from the graph that

A) since 1800, the atmospheric concentration of methane has increased with a corresponding increase in radiative forcing.
B) since 1800, the atmospheric concentration of methane has increased while radiative forcing has remained constant.
C) since 1800, the atmospheric concentration of methane has decreased while radiative forcing has increased.
D) the atmospheric concentration and radiative forcing of methane have largely remained constant since 1000.

CONTINUE

Questions 1-10 are based on the following passage.

This passage is taken from a humorous short story written early in the twenty-first century.

It's another April day with intermittent heavy showers. "Good for the garden!" says my neighbor, and yes, I can see that the plants I had carefully installed in the front last week are making some effort to emerge. The clematis in the pot by the front door has survived the winter and is growing rampantly, although the clematis against the wooden fence merely displays a few timid green shoots. The apple tree is beginning to show buds here and there, but it still looks hesitant, and there is no sign that a single one of the bulbs I planted in autumn is making an effort to push through. I sigh. I am a terrible gardener, really: all enthusiasm and no patience. I wonder if whoever moves into this house after I leave will keep the garden going.

My reverie is interrupted by the arrival of a white van, which double-parks outside my gate. On the vehicle's side are painted the words: "Mr. Dutton, Removals and Storage." I look at my watch. Mr. Dutton has arrived only an hour late. Mr. Dutton gets out of his van and walks up the path. He is a rather stocky man. His hair is cropped close to his skull and he sports a small earring in his left ear. He wears heavy boots, a sagging pair of jeans, and a heavy belt, which is partially obscured by his overhanging belly. His T-shirt is emblazoned with a motorcycle logo and he also dons an open, ill-fitting jacket with leather shoulder pads. The fingers of his right hand vigorously work his mobile phone. He pauses at the gate, pockets his phone, grins broadly at me, and approaches the door with the air of a busy executive. I invite him in and show him the items that I need to send into storage; we then sit down in the front room while Mr. Dutton works out the estimated price for the job, all the while pursuing a monologue that requires few interventions on my behalf.

Mr. Dutton tells me that he understands that I am moving to Oregon, which is funny because he had an uncle who lived there. This uncle joined the Peace Corps over twenty years ago: Mr. Dutton hasn't heard from him since. Mr. Dutton then informs me that he is paying top taxes in this country and that by the end of 2012 there will be an economic black hole because everyone paying top taxes will have moved elsewhere—as they are already doing. I try to work this logic out, but by the time I have, Mr. Dutton has moved on to his interest in pre-Roman history. Do I realize that every thousand years, the earth suffers a cataclysmic disaster, as in 535 A.D. when Krakatoa exploded? (The actual date had escaped me.) It caused darkness for twenty years, and crop growth became minimal. And that affected societies all over the world: the Ming Dynasty in China collapsed, as did the Aztec Empire in Mexico. If that were to happen today, this country would be finished. (I nod in agreement.) We would turn to cannibalism, since we import all our food. We would not know what to do, although, of course, the answer resides in one word: N.A.S.A. According to Mr. Dutton, the U.N. should force everyone in the world to give up 5% of what they earn in order to finance spaceships, which would bring about the colonization of both Mars and the Moon. That, he says, is the future, and the quotation for storage for one year will be $1735.25. Will I be paying in advance?

With that, Mr. Dutton takes his leave, telling me just before he goes that MTV is a brilliant channel, since its costumes and music give young people the opportunity to learn about the world, and that it has been a pleasure to meet me, for I am clearly someone with a view to the future. More people like us, he apparently feels, are needed if we are to survive the present difficulties. I see him to the front door, and watch him take out his mobile phone, enter his car, and roar off. I look once more at the garden, shrug my shoulders, and go back indoors.

1

It can be inferred that the author of the passage is

A) deeply enraged by the digressions of Mr Dutton.
B) enthralled by the idiosyncratic yet prudent ideals of Mr. Dutton.
C) slightly disoriented by Mr. Dutton's loquacity.
D) vexed by Mr. Dutton's unsavory political opinions.

2

As used in line 33, "pursuing" most nearly means

A) chasing.
B) conducting.
C) seeking.
D) scrutinizing.

3

Mr. Dutton's view on current affairs can best be described as

A) alarmist in its conclusions and somewhat sketchy in its evidence.
B) sanguine in its short term projections but ultimately pessimistic.
C) cautious in logical method and conservative in outlook.
D) politically brash but informed by extensive education in economics.

4

Which choice provides the best evidence for the answer to the previous question?

A) Lines 28-30 ("He pauses . . . executive")
B) Lines 45-49 ("Do I . . . minimal")
C) Lines 51-54 ("If that . . . food")
D) Lines 62-65 ("With that . . . the world")

5

The narrator describes Mr. Dutton in lines 15-30 ("My reverie . . . executive") in order to

A) portray the singular nature of Mr. Dutton's appearance and mannerisms.
B) attempt to put out of mind the ill treatment the garden has suffered as the result of negligence.
C) emphasize the narrator's own lack of a cultivated and sophisticated countenance.
D) suggest that Mr. Dutton is too distracted by his mobile phone to perform his job adequately.

6

The question in line 61 ("Will I be paying in advance?") can best be characterized as

A) worried.
B) angered.
C) ironic.
D) thoughtful.

7

According to Mr. Dutton, the solution to the dire state of the world's future can best be found in

A) gardening.
B) hard work.
C) tax reform.
D) space exploration.

8

As used in line 63, "brilliant" most nearly means

A) blinding.
B) elite.
C) valuable.
D) knowledgeable.

CONTINUE

9

It can be inferred from the passage that Mr. Dutton thinks of the narrator as

A) an unconcerned individual who has little to say about the important matters facing society.
B) a dependable ally in desperate times.
C) a shrewd yet eloquent adversary.
D) a devoted friend who can adapt to changing social circumstances.

10

Which choice provides the best evidence for the answer to the previous question?

A) Lines 28-34 ("He pauses . . . behalf")
B) Lines 43-45 ("I try . . . history")
C) Lines 54-59 ("We would not . . . Moon")
D) Lines 65-69 ("it has been . . . difficulties")

STOP

Questions 1-10 are based on the following passage.

How do societies change as they become increasingly large and complex? In these readings, two authors consider this issue from different perspectives.

Passage 1

Complexity kills. You should know this well if you have ever tried to develop a long, intricate argument, only to find that everyone has stopped paying attention to you a tenth of the way through. But there are times in history when, quite literally, complexity has exerted a lethal influence. As a society grows larger, it necessarily develops new capacities to meet new challenges, yet in so doing expands and expands until its basic operations are no longer sustainable.

This is exactly the argument that was laid out in *The Collapse of Complex Societies* by Joseph Tainter, a book that first appeared in 1988 and that continues to be a house favorite among sociology and anthropology buffs. Among the societies that Tainter has considered are some of the most remarkable the world has seen, including the Romans and the Mayas. To demonstrate how these societies failed, Tainter marshals concepts from classic economic and political theory: an aggressively expanding society would inevitably decentralize, stretch, and weaken, since the costs of expanding would eventually outstrip the benefits to be gained from such expansion. Such an attenuated society would then be forced (often to its detriment) to rely on new allies, or would be forced (certainly to its detriment) to accumulate crippling debts. There is much that Tainter's theory explains, yet there is also much about sociology and anthropology that has changed since 1988. Tainter has little interest in genuinely small societies with primitive technologies. He also neglects the very forces—including ideological and religious bonds—that can hold even a dying society together for an astonishingly long period of time. These considerations make sociological ideas of complexity more unruly, more unpredictable, and indeed more complex. Do ideologically-centralized societies exhibit healthy growth, or are they little more than eventual victims of the complexity that kills?

Passage 2

What is it that makes a society grow larger and more complex? A recent study put forth by Joseph Watts, an anthropology student at the University of Auckland, presents an interesting hypothesis. Apparently, the development of small-scale communities into large chiefdoms and city-states hinges upon the nature of the religious beliefs of the general populace. After studying 96 different cultures spread across Australia and Indonesia, Watts found a correlation between the belief in deities that are capable of punishing selfish behavior and the development of relatively large and complex societies. The reason for this, argues Watts, is that in smaller communities, everyone knows everyone else, and people tend to behave and abide by the rules because friends and family are always watching; to transgress would be to lose one's reputation. As societies grow larger, however, crime becomes more of a problem: it is much easier to steal from someone you don't know than from someone you have to see each day.

According to Watts, this is where the belief in punishing deities becomes a kind of "glue" that keeps a society together. The punishing god functions as a kind of invisible cop in the sky, watching and making sure no one breaks the rules. Fewer rules are disobeyed and the society prospers.

This is certainly an interesting theory, and Watts' recent study seems to confirm it. Among the 96 tribes studied, thirty-seven held beliefs in supernatural deities capable of punishing selfish acts, such as shirking a sacrifice or flouting a taboo. The statistics also suggest that belief in such gods predates the development of societies with greater political complexity. If Watts' theory proves true, it may replace older modes of thought, which held that an all-powerful, moralizing deity was the impetus for a more complex society. The truth, however, may lie with the "small gods," not with the big ones.

CONTINUE

1

It can be inferred that the author of Passage 1 believes that complexity

A) is inevitably destructive to large civilizations.
B) can weaken but never completely destroy a prosperous civilization.
C) should be produced through decentralized governance and local reforms.
D) may not be explained by a single unified theory.

2

Which choice provides the best evidence for the answer to the previous question?

A) Lines 4-6 ("But there . . . influence")
B) Lines 14-16 ("Among the . . . Mayas")
C) Lines 28-29 ("Tainter has . . . technologies")
D) Lines 32-35 ("These considerations . . . complex")

3

According to Joseph Tainter, complex societies tend to collapse because

A) they are often easy targets for foreign invasion or internal rebellion.
B) too much is spent and not enough gained in the process of political expansion.
C) they are often spread out to such an extent that a single identity is no longer feasible.
D) they lack the trust and emotional bonds present within small societies.

4

The author of Passage 1 refers back to the publication date (line 28) of Tainter's book in order to

A) emphasize how outdated Tainter's archaeological information is.
B) observe that Tainter's breakthrough in anthropology was relatively recent.
C) transition from a description to a critique of Tainter's theory.
D) argue that new cases of collapsed societies since 1988 necessitate revisions to Tainter's argument.

5

As used in line 17, "marshals" most nearly means

A) commands.
B) arranges.
C) disciplines.
D) utilizes.

6

The references to "glue" (line 59) and the "cop in the sky" (line 61) serve to indicate how

A) the threat of divine retribution can keep a society functioning.
B) the belief in supernatural powers can inhibit scientific and technological advancement.
C) societies with strong religious convictions tend to revere and preserve their natural surroundings.
D) Western anthropologists still have incomplete ideas about the role of myth and belief in primitive societies.

7

The last paragraph of Passage 2 suggests that the development of a "moralizing deity" (lines 72-73) is important primarily because this development

A) can cripple certain tribes while assisting others.
B) is instrumental in the transformation of large rural societies into urban civilizations.
C) was believed to be a precondition for creating a complex society out of small tribes.
D) is impossible without the religious institutions provided by large and complex societies.

CONTINUE

8

Which describes the overall relationship between Passage 1 and Passage 2?

A) Passage 1 endorses a theory about a phenomenon, while Passage 2 expresses reservations about that theory.
B) Passage 1 critiques a theory about a phenomenon, while Passage 2 investigates the causes of that phenomenon.
C) Passage 1 presents and then disproves an argument, while Passage 2 defends some of the argument's assumptions.
D) Passage 1 takes issue with a methodology and Passage 2 uses a separate methodology to arrive at a similar conclusion.

9

How would the author of Passage 1 most likely respond to the theory set forward by Joseph Watts in Passage 2?

A) Complex societies would not need punishing deities if they were capable of maintaining functional civil institutions.
B) The development of punishing deities among small tribes will most likely lead to the destruction of those tribes.
C) Shared belief in punishing gods might keep even otherwise declining societies from collapse.
D) Unifying religious convictions enable a small tribal society to organize into a large empire.

10

Which choice provides the best evidence for the answer to the previous question?

A) Lines 6-9 ("As a society. . . sustainable")
B) Lines 19-22 ("an aggressively . . . expansion")
C) Lines 22-25 ("Such an . . . debts")
D) Lines 29-32 ("He also . . . of time")

Questions 1-10 are based on the following passage.

The passage below is taken from a 2014 essay that considers the possibility of sympathy between humanity and different animal species.

David Blunkett is a member of the British Parliament, one who is held in particular affection by the general public. The reason for this is two-fold. First, he has been blind since childhood, yet has not been prevented from holding high office. Second, he is always seen on television and in public accompanied by his guide dog. There have been six in his life so far, most of which have sat through noisy sessions in the House of Commons, apparently indifferent to the hubbub surrounding Blunkett, concerned only with the role of devoted guide and guard.

Blunkett is retiring from Parliament this year, and he has been writing about the relationship between his dogs and himself; it is his conviction that dogs have a remarkable ability to read and understand the emotions of humans. For him, dogs can interpret the body language of their owners and react with the same caring responses that humans often direct at one another: soothing, gently correcting, sometimes cautioning gestures. Inspiring though this conception is, it is a conception with a complex history.

It is believed that the dog has existed in its present forms for at least eleven thousand years, although some experts would suggest that the dog appeared even before that, perhaps as early as sixteen thousand years ago. Yet it is generally accepted that the dog we know today has its ancestral roots in a wolf species—not the common European grey wolf, but a now-extinct earlier wolf population. Charles Darwin, in his definitive work *The Origin of Species*, could only conclude that the domestic dog may be descended from more than one wild ancestor. The same, perhaps, is the case for kindred species such as the Arctic Wolf, the Red Fox, and the Coyote. It is generally assumed that, like these distant cousins of today's dogs, the original dog was a "hunter gatherer" species, one that formed packs to harass its prey. However, none of these natural "relations" really anticipates the bond of domesticity. Very rarely do "hunter gatherer" animals cooperate with alien species—and almost never to the extent that the dog has cooperated with human beings.

In his article "How Dog Became the Dog," American journalist Mark Derr suggests that the dog could only have developed its present relationship with humans as a result of "attentiveness, curiosity, necessity, and recognition of the advantage gained through collaboration." At first glance, Derr's conclusion might seem to be relatively logical, though the more deeply his logic is considered, the more disturbing it becomes. Perhaps a dog's sympathetic ability to recognize human emotion is not a special "ability" at all, just evolutionary common sense—an essential means of separating encouraging and threatening stimuli. However, what would be common sense in the dog's original, uncertain natural environment should not be misread when it is displayed elsewhere. One consequence of Derr's idea that the dog recognizes "the advantage gained though collaboration" is that dogs may be better manipulators than we think. They put on shows of devotion to secure survival, knowing that humans value these apparent reactions, but perhaps not feeling anything like the emotions we humans feel.

Whatever the cause of a dog's actions may be, we have to accept that many people are prone to attribute all kinds of intelligence and sensitivity to dogs. Why wonder? A dog is a cheerful companion, especially if one lives alone, and can ignite an innately human sense of responsibility. What is revealed by such a relationship tells us more about the fallibility and sentimentality of humans than about the ulterior motives of dogs. For example, many people are as convinced as David Blunkett is that dogs share our ideas of anger and sorrow. Others declare that a dog will defend the person with whom it lives. (Disgruntled postmen can certainly attest to this.) Yet perhaps the motivations can be disregarded, when dogs and humans are both the better for their bonds.

CONTINUE

Guide Dog Responses to Human Gestures (Training)

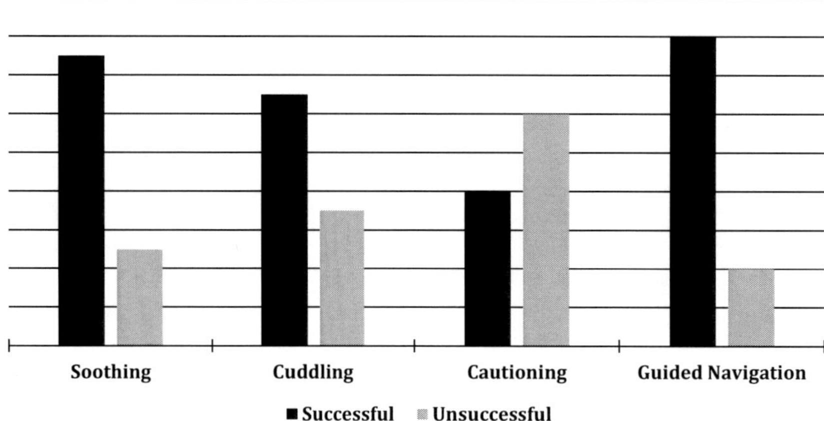

The graph indicates the average response for guide dogs in the Guide Dogs of America training sequence. These dogs responded either successfully or unsuccessfully with the associated trained response to the trainer's various human gestures.

1

What function does the third paragraph (lines 22-41) serve in the passage as a whole?

A) To shed doubt on David Blunkett's theory
B) To underscore the characterization of dogs as docile
C) To discuss the inconclusive ancestry of the dog
D) To introduce Mark Derr's ideas and theories

2

Which choice does the author explicitly cite as a possible advantage of the bond between dogs and humans?

A) Dogs can help humans to understand and communicate strong emotions.
B) Dogs are easily trained to perform simple tasks.
C) Dogs offer their owners practical assistance and protection.
D) Dogs readily sympathize with handicapped people.

3

Which choice provides the best evidence for the answer to the previous questions?

A) Lines 7-11 ("There have . . . guard")
B) Lines 38-40 ("Very rarely . . . alien species")
C) Lines 59-61 ("They put on . . . reactions")
D) Lines 75-77 ("Yet perhaps . . . bonds")

4

One of the central assumptions of the passage is that

A) dogs are motivated solely by the need for food.
B) dogs are motivated by emotion, not by logic.
C) the dog's original environment required cooperation with other animal species.
D) dogs may be more opportunistic than they are popularly believed to be.

5

Which choice provides the best evidence for the answer to the previous question?

A) Lines 50-53 ("Perhaps a . . . stimuli")
B) Lines 53-56 ("However . . . elsewhere")
C) Lines 56-59 ("One consequence . . . we think")
D) Lines 66-68 ("A dog . . . responsibility")

6

As used in line 38, "anticipates" most nearly means

A) explains.
B) expects.
C) predicts.
D) considers.

CONTINUE

7

In the final paragraph, the author refers to “many people” in order to

A) indicate the growing popularity of Mark Derr’s ideas.
B) underscore the prevalence of possible misconceptions about dogs.
C) highlight a development that weakens David Blunkett’s claims.
D) resolve a debate about the motives of dogs.

8

As used in line 54, “uncertain” most nearly means

A) unusual.
B) unknown.
C) dangerous.
D) intriguing.

9

Based on the passage and the graph, which of the following guide dog responses would the author cite as contradictory to Blunkett’s claims?

A) Soothing
B) Cuddling
C) Cautioning
D) Guided Navigation

10

Which choice is best supported by the information in the graph?

A) Trained dogs and humans share an inherent sympathetic bond.
B) Human trainers failed to provide appropriate gestures to elicit the cautioning response.
C) Guide dogs are most successful overall in guided navigation.
D) Disciplined dogs only react with sympathy to non-threatening human gestures.

STOP

Questions 1-11 are based on the following passage.

This consideration of American enterprise is an excerpt from *Random Reminiscences of Men and Events* (1909), the memoir of businessman John D. Rockefeller.

I confess I have no sympathy with the idea so often advanced that our basis of all judgments in this country is founded on money. If this were true, we should be a nation of money hoarders instead of spenders. Nor do I admit that we are so small-minded a people as to be jealous of the success of others. It is the other way about: we are the most extraordinarily ambitious, and the success of one man in any walk of life spurs the others on. It does not sour them, and it is a libel even to suggest so great a meanness of spirit.

In reading the newspapers, where so much is taken for granted in considering things on a money standard, I think we need some of the sense of humor possessed by an Irish neighbor of mine, who built what we regarded as an extremely ugly house, which stood out in bright colors as we looked from our windows. My taste in architecture differed so widely from that affected by my Irish friend, that we planted out the view of his house by moving some large trees to the end of our property. Another neighbor who watched this work going on asked Mr. Foley why Mr. Rockefeller moved all these big trees and cut off the view between the houses. Foley, with the quick wit of his country, responded instantly: "It's invy, they can't stand looking at the ividence of me prosperity."

In my early days men acted just as they do now, no doubt. When there was anything to be done for general trade betterment, almost every man had some good reason for believing that his case was a special one different from all the rest. For every foolish thing he did, or wanted to do, for every unbusiness-like plan he had, he always pleaded that it was necessary in his case. He was the one man who had to sell at less than cost, to disrupt all the business plans of others in his trade, because his individual position was so absolutely different from all the rest. It was often a heart-breaking undertaking to convince those men that the perfect occasion which would lead to the perfect opportunity would never come, even if they waited until the crack o' doom.

Then, again, we had the type of man who really never knew all the facts about his own affairs. Many of the brightest kept their books in such a way that they did not actually know when they were making money on a certain operation and when they were losing. This unintelligent competition was a hard matter to contend with. Good old-fashioned common sense has always been a mighty rare commodity. When a man's affairs are not going well, he hates to study the books and face the truth. From the first, the men who managed the Standard Oil Company kept their books intelligently as well as correctly. We knew how much we made and where we gained or lost. At least, we tried not to deceive ourselves.

My ideas of business are no doubt old-fashioned, but the fundamental principles do not change from generation to generation, and sometimes I think that our quick-witted American business men, whose spirit and energy are so splendid, do not always sufficiently study the real underlying foundations of business management. I have spoken of the necessity of being frank and honest with oneself about one's own affairs: many people assume that they can get away from the truth by avoiding thinking about it, but the natural law is inevitable, and the sooner it is recognized, the better.

One hears a great deal about wages and why they must be maintained at a high level, by the railroads, for example. A laborer is worthy of his hire, no less, but no more, and in the long run he must contribute an equivalent for what he is paid.

CONTINUE

1

According to Rockefeller, the "men" in line 50

A) were fully aware of their company's finances.
B) struggled to keep the Standard Oil Company open.
C) were initially skeptical of John D. Rockefeller's business practices.
D) were young and vivacious opportunity-seekers.

2

The primary purpose of the first paragraph is to establish that

A) John D. Rockefeller struggles to feel compassion for poor businessmen.
B) some people make defamatory claims about the United States.
C) the success of others generates ambition, not jealousy.
D) people should spend money rather than save it.

3

As used in line 2, "advanced" most nearly means

A) proposed.
B) learned.
C) improved.
D) evolved.

4

John D. Rockefeller describes himself as "old-fashioned" primarily because he

A) is older and more experienced than other businessmen.
B) realizes that he is not modernizing along with the rest of his industry.
C) does not value what younger men value.
D) believes that the basics of enterprise are immutable.

5

The third paragraph (lines 26-40) is concerned with establishing a contrast between

A) self-absorption and pragmatism.
B) malice and generosity.
C) privacy and publicity.
D) current problems and possible reforms.

6

The example in the last paragraph primarily serves to

A) advocate for fair wages across the transportation industry.
B) illustrate a basic tenet of sound business management.
C) introduce the concept of business ethics.
D) suggest that it is difficult to put a monetary value on labor.

7

It can most reasonably be inferred that Rockefeller differs from other American businessmen because he

A) unavoidably feels envious of others' success.
B) appreciates the need to accurately assess his business.
C) values acquiring land over maintaining neighborly relationships.
D) finds humor in difficult business situations.

8

Which choice provides the best evidence for the answer to the previous question?

A) Lines 1-3 ("I confess . . . money")
B) Lines 17-18 ("My taste . . . friend")
C) Lines 47-48 ("Good . . . commodity")
D) Lines 61-62 ("I have . . . affairs")

CONTINUE

9

According to the passage, John D. Rockefeller would most likely agree that

A) Mr. Foley often acts unreasonably during discussions about architecture.
B) American businessmen are sensible but neither clever nor witty.
C) some businessmen selfishly introduce disorder into other businesses.
D) the men of the past were more rational than Rockefeller's contemporaries in America.

10

Which choice provides the best evidence for the answer to the previous question?

A) Lines 9-10 ("It does . . . spirit")
B) Lines 33-36 ("He was . . . the rest")
C) Lines 41-42 ("Then . . . affairs")
D) Lines 53-54 ("At least . . . ourselves")

11

As used in line 22, "cut off" most nearly means

A) shortened.
B) bypassed.
C) obstructed.
D) silenced.

Questions 1-11 are based on the following passage.

The following passage was written by a specialist in inorganic chemistry

Down at the bottom of the periodic table lie the lesser-known elements: halfnium, seaborgium, meitnerium, and many other obscurities that are not discussed in any introductory chemistry course. There is a reason for this. Due to their extremely heavy nuclei, these elements are highly unstable, and they undergo spontaneous radioactive decay into smaller, more stable atoms. Some of these elements' half-lives are mere fractions of seconds; they don't even stick around long enough for us to glimpse them, and we recognize them only from the decay particles they leave behind. For scientists hunting for new elements, the search is akin to analyzing a fissure left in the clouds by the speeding blur of a supersonic jet.

This may all be changing. For years, scientists have speculated that out beyond the unstable heavy elements, there may lie an "island of stability"—a rare region in which superheavy elements, even heavier than those yet discovered, may finally achieve much longer half-lives than those yet observed. Many chemists working in the field have hypothesized a series of "magic numbers," combinations of protons and neutrons that, if they could be brought together, might yield novel, stable nuclei. So far, the magic numbers include arrangements of 108, 110, and 114 protons, each combined with 184 neutrons. The reason for the speculated stability of such nuclei is that they would have the potential to form a structure known as the "bubble configuration," in which the superheavy nucleus has a hole in its center. These nuclei "have never been discovered yet, but the region that is being explored right now is really on the edge of bubble territory," remarked Witold Nazarewicz of the Oak Ridge National Laboratory in Tennessee. In nature, the heaviest element that occurs with any abundance is uranium, which contains only 92 protons. So how do scientists manage to create such superheavy nuclei? The answer, despite the advanced science involved, is something any layperson can understand, because it involves only simple arithmetic.

As anyone with decent mental math can tell you, the sum of 20 and 97 is 117. Recently, at the Joint Institute for Nuclear Research in Dubna, Russia, a team of American and Russian scientists took advantage of this fact by accelerating isotopes of calcium (which contain 20 protons) to 10 percent of the speed of light. They then bombarded these calcium atoms against isotopes of berkelium (which contain 97 protons). On the rare occasions when the two nucleus types collided head-on, they fused together to briefly create a new nucleus that contained 117 protons; for a brief moment, a new element was born. Like all superheavy nuclei, however, this nucleus quickly decayed. Nonetheless, even the decay particles of Element 117 were unique. One of them was a never-before-seen isotope of lawrencium (103 protons, 163 neutrons), which exhibited a half-life of 11 hours—far longer and more stable than any of the half-lives observed for previously examined isotopes of lawrencium. Physicist Christoph Dullman, who led the series of experiments, remarked, "Perhaps we are on the shore of the island of stability."

The discovery has important implications. If the island of stability does exist, new elements with highly stable half-lives—perhaps as long as thousands to even millions of years—could be synthesized. It is also possible that such elements already exist in nature, but that they are so rare that they have yet to be discovered. Now that there is evidence that supports their possible existence, the search for the island of stability looks more promising than ever. "All existing data for elements 116, 117, and 118 do confirm that lifetimes increase as one gets closer to the neutron number 184," said Nazarewicz. "This is encouraging."

Isotope Information

Isotope	Half-Life	Number of Protons
Calcium-47	4.5 days	20
Element-117	11 hours	117
Berkelium-245	4.94 days	97
Lawrencium-260	2.7 minutes	103

CONTINUE

1

As used in line 7, "spontaneous" most nearly means

A) instinctual.
B) straightforward.
C) automatic.
D) impulsive.

2

The author uses the comparison in lines 11-14 ("For scientists . . . supersonic jet") in order to imply that some elements

A) move extremely fast.
B) disappear quickly.
C) are studied by engineers.
D) are unusually heavy.

3

According to the passage, the process of creating superheavy nuclei

A) is in some respects easy to comprehend.
B) requires equipment only available in Russia.
C) has yet to be discovered.
D) must be completed within 11 hours.

4

Which choice provides the best evidence for the answer to the previous question?

A) Lines 1-4 ("Down at . . . course")
B) Lines 15-17 ("For years . . . stability")
C) Lines 37-39 ("The answer . . . arithmetic")
D) Lines 47-50 ("On the . . . protons")

5

The author implies that superheavy, stable elements

A) cannot be synthesized in laboratory settings.
B) could occur outside controlled environments.
C) are believed to only exist in theory.
D) are solely of interest to atomic physicists.

6

Which choice provides the best evidence for the answer to the previous question?

A) Lines 5-8 ("Due to . . . atoms")
B) Lines 33-35 ("In nature . . . protons")
C) Lines 54-58 ("One of . . . lawrencium")
D) Lines 64-65 ("It is . . . nature")

7

The main purpose of the passage is to

A) outline the progress in the search for superheavy elements.
B) indicate the potential medical uses of superheavy elements.
C) imply that superheavy elements may exist in outer space.
D) garner public support for inorganic chemistry research.

8

As used in line 44, "accelerating" most nearly means

A) increasing.
B) speeding up.
C) growing.
D) enhancing.

CONTINUE

9

According to the passage, the "bubble configuration" mentioned in line 28 is significant because it

A) allows superheavy elements to form the largest possible arrangements.
B) is arranged to include up to 184 protons.
C) provides stability for superheavy elements.
D) is the structure of several unstable elements listed in the periodic table.

10

Do the data in the table support Witold Nazarewicz's claim about "lifetimes" (line 70)?

A) Yes, because Element 117 has the highest number of protons.
B) Yes, because the number of protons is directly proportional to the half-life of the isotope.
C) No, because it fails to address the number of electrons necessary to support his claim.
D) No, because the table does not include the necessary information about neutron numbers.

11

It can be inferred from the data in the chart that

A) an isotope's half life is directly correlated to the isotope's nuclear mass.
B) an isotope's half life is directly correlated to the number of neutrons.
C) proton number does not correlate directly to an element's half-life.
D) the number of neutrons always exceeds the number of protons in super-heavy elements.

STOP

Questions 1-10 are based on the following passage.

This passage is adapted from a 2012 novella; the narrator is a teacher originally from the United Kingdom.

Twenty years ago, I was a teacher of English at Saint Andrew's School in Malawi, one of the smallest and poorest countries in Africa. The school occupied a large estate set back from the road leading from the city of Blantyre to Ndirande, a huddled township squeezed between the flanks of a mountain. The school buildings were solid and modern, the sports facilities were spacious and featured a large swimming pool. The students were the children of expatriates. Malawian children were educated, if at all, in villages, in the shade of baobab trees.

I had been in the country just four weeks when I was invited on a trip to the very southernmost tip of the country, to Sucoma. There was a small private reserve there which, occasionally, hosted selected visitors. We met in the late afternoon warmth: me, the headmaster and his wife, and the geography teacher and his wife, who was a native Malawian. Gripping her hand was a small girl gazing up in awe and silence at the white adults.

"This is Twambi, my niece," said the wife of the geography teacher.

"Here with you on a visit?" asked the headmaster's wife.

"No. My sister's husband died and she has three other children. So Twambi is with us. She only speaks Chichewa."

"Oh. *Bwanji*[1], Twambi." The headmaster took off his hat and bowed solemnly.

Twambi giggled and hid her face in her aunt's skirt. We piled into the jeep and set off on what turned out to be a three-hour, dusty, jolting drive along a deserted road which, more often than not, showed traces of tarmac. We arrived at the edge of the reserve as dusk was falling. We were brought to the lodges where we would spend the night, given a simple meal, and then shown to bed, for we were to wake at half past four in the morning in order to reach the hide beside the water hole before daybreak.

In the morning, the company's truck dropped us about half a mile from our destination and we made our way through the surprisingly chilly darkness and silence until we arrived. The hide was built on stilts and an alarmingly rickety ladder allowed us access to it. We sat beneath the thatched roof on tall stools and leaned forward to rest our elbows on the wooden shelf that ran the length of the structure. We peered through an opening, gazing at the clearing a few yards away. There lay the still water of the water hole. On the far edge of the pool was a sandy shore. Large trees framed the scene.

Stillness and silence. We held our breath intently. A rustle in the undergrowth and in procession small deer—nyala, perhaps—picked their way, delicately, to the water's edge and dipped their heads. Above them, an owl eased through the air and posed itself upon a heavy branch. The placid bird hooted softly. A heron, white and stately, as if by magic (for we had not seen it enter the scene) stood as rigid as a sentinel, and a fish eagle floated through the lightening air. The nyala paused, raised their heads, then turned and moved away through the bushes. They were replaced by other deer. A hammerkopf[2] called from the bushes, and this call seemed to be a cue, for a single line of warthogs, each with its tail pointing directly to the sky, trotted, almost comically, to the drinking place.

I do not remember all the animals we saw, although the Malawian guide with us whispered the name of each animal or bird that took its turn at the water's edge. The light strengthened. It was as if a climactic moment were approaching. A group of female kudu came down to the pool and drank. Then, in unison, they raised their heads and moved aside. At the top of the slope, silhouetted against the dawn, stood an adult male kudu. His head, raised proudly, showed off his towering, twisted, powerful horns. He stared across the pool, directly at the hide. Then, like royalty, he moved down to the pool, lowered his head, and drank. He raised his eyes, stared across the pool at us again, then turned and exited. The stage was bare. The sun had risen.

1. "Bwanji" means "Hello" in Chichewa, the native language of Malawi
2. A medium-sized brown stork native to Africa

CONTINUE

1

As used line 32, “jolting” most nearly means

A) surprising.
B) bumpy.
C) invigorating.
D) awakening.

2

According to the passage, the author was in Malawi to

A) teach native Malawian children.
B) work at a modern school.
C) experience Malawian culture.
D) observe local wildlife.

3

It can most reasonably be inferred from the passage that the reserve in Sucoma

A) has multiple water holes.
B) welcomes international support.
C) is not open to the entire public.
D) belongs to Saint Andrew’s School.

4

Which choice provides the best evidence for the answer to the previous question?

A) Lines 1-3 (“Twenty . . . Africa”)
B) Lines 14-15 (“There was . . . visitors”)
C) Line 49 (“There . . . hole”)
D) Line 52 (“Stillness . . . intently”)

5

The author uses the word “scene” in line 51 and the word “stage” in line 81 in order to

A) imply that watching the animals at the water hole is like watching a show.
B) suggest that a documentary could be made about the water hole.
C) hint that a moment of high drama is about to occur.
D) emphasize the untouched wildness of the Sucoma reserve.

6

According to the passage, the geography teacher’s wife has brought along a young girl who

A) has no living parent.
B) has suffered a loss.
C) is bilingual.
D) knows much about animals.

7

As used in line 81, “bare” most nearly means

A) devoid of activity.
B) inhospitable to life.
C) obvious.
D) unadorned.

8

It can be most reasonably inferred from the passage that a “hide” is

A) a large plot of land with diverse wildlife.
B) a type of water hole frequented by birds and mammals.
C) a place specifically built for observation.
D) an emergency shelter made of wood.

CONTINUE

9

Which choice provides the best evidence for the answer to the previous question?

A) Lines 12-14 ("I had been . . . Sucoma")
B) Lines 35-39 ("We were . . . daybreak")
C) Lines 45-48 ("We sat . . . yards away")
D) Lines 57-60 ("A heron . . . air")

10

The purpose of the last paragraph is to

A) dramatize the entrance and exit of the male kudu.
B) illustrate that the male kudu is larger than average.
C) suggest that the male kudu maintains order at the water hole.
D) imply that the guide misunderstands the male kudu's behavior.

Questions 1-11 are based on the following passage.

This passage considers how cities, in particular the city of New York, are shaped by their approaches to new attractions and entertainment centers.

Staten Island: Tourist Destination. That, in a nutshell, is the rationale behind the most ambitious construction and engineering project to grace the least-visited of New York's Five Boroughs. As I write, assembly is underway on the New York Wheel, a 630 foot-tall Ferris wheel that could give Staten Island a new identity and its businesses a new stream of tourist-provided cash. That's if the plan works out, which for good reason it may not.

I hope, though, that the New York Wheel lives up to the enormous expectations of the people who have conceived it, funded it, and believed in it. If successful, it will become a leisure destination like few others: visitors will ride the wheel in compartments large enough to house birthday parties and small corporate gatherings. There is some anticipation that in the years to come more people will visit the Wheel than will visit the Statue of Liberty—which would mean that there will be at least 3.5 million new annual visitors to Staten Island. (Well, at least there's enough anticipation that Staten Island has built a new four-story parking garage.) Finally, something other than the enjoyable but low-key Staten Island Ferry will define the Borough.

So why am I pessimistic? As an expert in urban studies (and a lifelong New Yorker), I have learned a thing or two about how the best-laid plans of the tourism and entertainment industries can go awry. Where attractions are concerned, there is no such thing as "too big to fail." In fact, when you look at New York's recent history of entertainment and development, the real rule of thumb should be something like "small enough to succeed."

Let's return to Staten Island for a minute. Right now, the best reason to visit the Borough isn't an attraction or a historic site or an entertainment center, though I have always had a soft spot for the Staten Island Children's Museum. Instead, perhaps the best reason to stop off in Staten Island is a bar and restaurant called the Phunky Elephant. Here you'll find a spacious dining room, live music, and a quirky, irresistible menu: I always get the charred corn salad and the house rigatoni with wild boar ragout. Few people know about the Phunky Elephant, but those who do feel uniquely and justifiably privileged.

The problem with the New York Wheel is simply that: everybody is going to know about it, and nobody is going to feel privileged to know it. It is often said that we are living in a knowledge economy, where the aptness of one's connections and the specialness of one's information are more important than the usual criteria of economic power—money and visibility. Something of the same sort has happened with urban planning in the past twenty years: the sites and spectacles that define the urban entertainment experience and draw some of the most respectable profits are, in large part, insider's weapons. And everyone has a different one.

Today, if you go to the most dramatically reinvented of all New York's Boroughs—Brooklyn—you won't find particularly many postcard-ready sights. You will find small boutiques, distinctive street fairs, idiosyncratic art galleries, and a restaurant scene of unparalleled vibrancy. Jersey City, Hoboken, and parts of Newark have revitalized themselves using similar fragment-and-conquer approaches. A Staten Island with a 630-foot wheel will give us something to stop and photograph. Will it give us anything to discover, anything like the wonderfully localized and diversified paths to experience that are part of every successful 21st-century city?

Year	Projected New York Wheel Visitors (millions)	Projected Statue of Liberty Visitors (millions)
2016	2.00	3.00
2017	3.00	4.00
2018	4.00	5.00
2019	5.00	4.00
2020	5.00	4.00
2021	5.00	6.00

1

The main purpose of the passage is to

A) point out the drawbacks to an ambitious construction project.
B) develop a theory on how to revitalize blighted urban centers.
C) establish guidelines for creating future tourist attractions in Staten Island.
D) dispel myths regarding the role of urban planning in the infrastructure of New York's Five Boroughs.

2

The second paragraph functions to

A) subtly mock those who believe in the potential of current Staten Island attractions.
B) counter claims that the New York Wheel's construction will generate an insufficient return on its investment.
C) provide an outline of the hoped-for benefits of the Wheel's construction.
D) argue that the Wheel will attract crowds that Staten Island's infrastructure cannot presently accommodate.

3

The tone of the parenthetical observation in lines 20-22 is best characterized as

A) wry.
B) dismayed.
C) nostalgic.
D) upbeat.

4

The author mentions the Staten Island Children's Museum (lines 37-38) in order to provide

A) an example of a widely-loved tourist attraction.
B) a best-case outcome for a large public works project.
C) an expression of a personal preference.
D) an instance of successful urban renewal.

5

As used in lines 45 and 48, "privileged" most nearly means

A) gifted.
B) wealthy.
C) exceptional.
D) confidential.

6

According to the passage, the New York Wheel could be unsuccessful because

A) nobody will want to take the Staten Island Ferry to ride it.
B) few people outside New York will know that it exists.
C) it will lack the allure of being a little-known attraction.
D) it will not feature the appealing hospitality of nearby destinations such as Jersey City and Hoboken.

7

Which choice provides the best evidence for the answer to the previous question?

A) Lines 12-16 ("If successful . . . gatherings")
B) Lines 29-30 ("Where attractions . . . to fail")
C) Lines 46-48 ("The problem . . . know it")
D) Lines 66-68 ("A Staten Island . . . photograph")

8

Which urban project would the author most strongly support as a means of attracting new tourists?

A) A monumental brass memorial in the style of the Statue of Liberty.
B) A strip of small but well-publicized restaurants specializing in eclectic dishes.
C) A giant outdoor art gallery meant to showcase paintings and handicrafts from all over the world.
D) A variety of small vendors, street performers, and cultural events.

CONTINUE

9

Which choice provides the best evidence for the answer to the previous question?

A) Lines 16-20 ("There is . . . Staten Island")
B) Lines 34-38 ("Right now . . . Museum")
C) Lines 40-43 ("Here you'll . . . boar ragout")
D) Lines 62-64 ("You will . . . vibrancy")

10

According to the projected data in the table, which year confirms the claim that more people will visit the New York Wheel than will visit the Statue of Liberty?

A) 2016
B) 2017
C) 2019
D) 2021

11

Do the data in the table provide support for the "anticipation" (line 16) of annual visitors to Staten Island?

A) Yes, because the New York Wheel estimate would be proportional to estimates for other Staten Island attractions.
B) Yes, because the estimates of annual visitors to each location listed are inversely proportional.
C) No, because the data suggest that Staten Island will see more than 3.5 million new visitors to its major attractions in 2019 and subsequent years.
D) No, because the Statue of Liberty is expected to become more popular than the New York Wheel by 2021.

STOP

Questions 1-11 are based on the following passage.

The author of this passage is an environmentalist and biologist who specializes in ocean and waterway ecosystems.

The threat of invasion has always loomed large in the human imagination. For hundreds of years, the possibility of invading armies attacking towns and cities was a real and ever-present danger. In contemporary culture, the fear of invasion has shifted towards the fantastical, with films, books, and television programs offering horrifying representations of a world overrun by zombies or aliens. By comparison, a species of freshwater fish hardly seems like a terrifying threat. Asian carp, however, pose a substantial risk to the ecological and socio-economic wellbeing of the Great Lakes region.

"Asian carp" is a label applied to four distinct species: bighead, silver, grass, and black carp. All of these species originated in rivers in China and Russia. In the 1970s, Asian carp were transported to the southern United States and introduced into ponds in hopes that they would help to control algae, plants, and snails. When flooding occurred, the fish were able to move from the ponds to small streams, and from those streams into the Mississippi River. The Mississippi was a carp paradise: it offered abundant food and no natural predators. As a result, the population of Asian carp increased rapidly. The different species have been moving steadily northwards ever since.

So far, the influence that Asian carp have exerted on aquatic ecosystems reveals the threats these fish pose. Able to eat up to 20% of their body weight per day, they consume huge masses of plankton and aquatic plants. One effect of this voracity is obvious: there is less food left for other aquatic species, and rapid population declines for other fish result. Other effects are more insidious: when the amount of aquatic plant matter is depleted, other species can no longer rely on plants to offer concealment from predators, or to serve as safe nurseries for eggs and spawn. Asian carp, on the other hand, tend to breed very successfully and can rapidly increase their numbers. They reduce biodiversity (in some areas, Asian carp now comprise up to 80% of the total fish population) and can also introduce new diseases and parasites.

It is clear that Asian carp pose a significant threat to the wellbeing of aquatic ecosystems. What is less apparent, but equally important to consider, the potential impact on human welfare. While Asian carp vary widely in size, some, especially the silver carp species, can grow to weigh up to 90 pounds. This species also displays a dangerous behavior when threatened: if startled, a silver carp will often leap into the air, sometimes attaining a height of close to 9 feet. If a fish of that size were to strike a person, especially at high velocity, serious injuries would result. This kind of injury is less bloody and dramatic than the shark attacks that spring to mind when we think of dangerous fish, but the frequent use of the Great Lakes for recreation means that a significant Asian carp population would create a high risk of injury. If recreational usage of the lakes for activities such as boating and water-skiing were to decrease as a result, a ripple effect would reach industries such as tourism and lead to declining employment.

Because of all these threats, a number of concerned individuals are actively countering the spread of Asian carp into the Great Lakes ecosystem. There are two ways by which Asian carp could enter the Great Lakes: they could spread through waterways or be introduced by human activity. The former possibility is being combated through close monitoring of areas with known Asian carp populations, especially during flooding, when it is easier for the fish to move into the streams and rivers that drain into the lakes. Risk reduction also hinges on eliminating the possibility that carp imported for food or as pets will be released into the wild. Legislation exists in the Great Lakes region that prohibits the transportation, sale, or possession of live Asian carp. Anyone who finds an Asian carp is required to report the fish's presence. Just as posting a guard atop a castle can ensure that distant invaders are sighted, this strategy aims to ensure that any Asian carp presence is noticed immediately—before a risk evolves.

CONTINUE

Great Lakes Vacation Industry and Carp Population

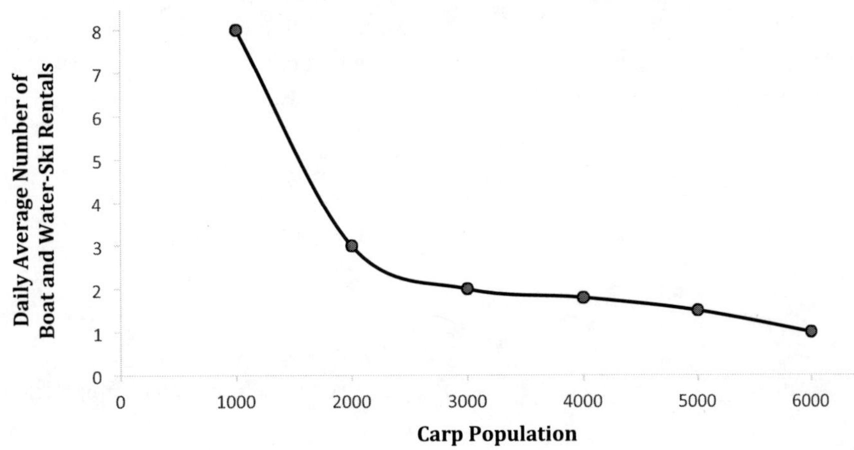

1

The first paragraph serves mainly to

A) summarize a problem and suggest a solution that will later be analyzed and encouraged.

B) provide an overview of the behavior of Asian carp in various environments.

C) inform the reader of the physical appearance and origins of Asian carp.

D) introduce an example of a concept that will be discussed in depth over the course of the passage.

2

According to the passage, Asian carp

A) were initially released into ponds as a solution to unwanted plant and animal growth.

B) were accidentally introduced into the Great Lakes area by means of trading boats from China.

C) were scarce in population in their native ecosystems but became ruthless predators in America.

D) were abundant yet benign in their native habitats, where they coexisted with many other species of fish.

3

Which choice provides the best evidence for the answer to the previous question?

A) Lines 1-4 ("The threat . . . danger")

B) Lines 16-19 ("In the 1970s . . . and snails")

C) Lines 26-30 ("So far . . . plants")

D) Lines 45-49 ("While Asian . . . threatened")

4

As used in line 42, "pose" most nearly means

A) cause.

B) present.

C) suggest.

D) arrange.

5

The author indicates that the growing population of Asian carp is harmful to native fish species because

A) the carp overcrowd ponds and lakes to the extent that some fish have stopped breeding as a result.

B) the carp are vicious carnivores that prey on small fish inhabiting the Great Lakes region.

C) the carp have discouraged environmental protection efforts in carp-dominated areas.

D) the carp deplete ecosystems of resources that other species use for food and protection.

6

Which choice provides the best evidence for the answer to the previous question?

A) Lines 5-10 ("In . . . threat")
B) Lines 21-25 ("The Mississippi . . . ever since")
C) Lines 31-35 ("there is . . . predators")
D) Lines 56-61 ("a significant . . . employment")

7

As used in line 72, "hinges on" most nearly means

A) is proved by.
B) is closely tied to.
C) takes into consideration that.
D) is defined by.

8

The author mentions "a guard atop a castle" (line 78) primarily in order to

A) explain the defensive strategies adopted by the carp using an unexpected metaphor.
B) create a contrast between the carp and the individuals who are working to eliminate them.
C) illustrate the way in which some people plan to reduce the carp population by making a comparison.
D) emphasize the discretion and urgency of scientists working to remove carp from the Great Lakes.

9

Which concept is supported by the passage and the information on the graph?

A) Asian carp are not only a threat to other animals in the Great Lakes region but also to the economic well-being of the area.
B) The growing population of Asian carp has come at the expense of plant and animal life in the Great Lakes.
C) Although scientists are aware of the threat Asian carp present to other fish, the danger that Asian carp present to humans has often been exaggerated.
D) While Asian carp can be detrimental to the safety of humans, they have nevertheless attracted new tourism to the Great Lakes.

10

How does the graph support the author's point that the carp population can also impact humans?

A) It demonstrates that the carp have become an unlikely but profitable tourist attraction.
B) It reveals that the number of humans attacked by carp is steadily increasing.
C) It shows that the growing number of carp has caused recreation activities in the Great Lakes to decline.
D) It illustrates that the increased population of carp has forced residents of the Great Lakes to migrate south.

11

Suppose the y-axis on the graph were to represent scuba gear rentals per day instead of boat and water ski rentals per day. Would this new graph support the author's claims?

A) Yes, because the author links growing carp populations to an overall decrease in water-based recreational activities.
B) Yes, because the author argues that water-based recreation can eventually adapt to larger carp populations.
C) No, because activities such as scuba diving would be more likely to disrupt Asian carp habitats.
D) No, because it is unclear to what extent the Great Lakes tourism industry profits from scuba gear rentals.

CONTINUE

Questions 1-10 are based on the following passage.

The following passage is taken from *How the Other Half Lives* (1890), a book by social reformer Jacob Riis that describes the tenements of New York and their inhabitants.

Long ago it was said that "one half of the world does not know how the other half lives." That was true then. It did not know because it did not care. The half that was on top cared little for the struggles, and less for the fate of those who were underneath, so long as it was able to hold them there and keep its own seat. There came a time when the discomfort and crowding below were so great, and the consequent upheavals so violent, that it was no longer an easy thing to do, and then the upper half fell to inquiring what was the matter. Information on the subject has been accumulating rapidly since, and the whole world has had its hands full answering for its old ignorance.

In New York, the youngest of the world's great cities, that time came later than elsewhere, because the crowding had not been so great. There were those who believed that it would never come, but their hopes were vain. Greed and reckless selfishness wrought like results here as in the cities of older lands. "When the great riot occurred in 1863," so reads the testimony of the Secretary of the Prison Association of New York before a legislative committee appointed to investigate causes of the increase of crime in the State twenty-five years ago, "every hiding-place and nursery of crime discovered itself by immediate and active participation in the operations of the mob. Those very places and domiciles, and all that are like them, are to-day nurseries of crime, and of the vices and disorderly courses which lead to crime. By far the largest part—eighty per cent, at least—of crimes against property and against the person are perpetrated by individuals who have either lost connection with home life, or never had any, or whose homes had ceased to be sufficiently separate, decent, and desirable to afford what are regarded as ordinary, wholesome influences of home and family. . . The younger criminals seem to come almost exclusively from the worst tenement house districts, that is, when traced back to the very places where they had their homes in the city here." Of one thing New York made sure at that early stage of the inquiry: the boundary line of the Other Half lies through the tenements.

It is ten years and over, now, since that line divided New York's population evenly. Today three-fourths of its people live in the tenements, and the nineteenth century drift of the population to the cities is sending ever-increasing multitudes to crowd them. The fifteen thousand tenant houses that were the despair of the sanitarian in the past generation have swelled into thirty-seven thousand, and more than twelve hundred thousand persons call them home. The one way out he saw—rapid transit to the suburbs—has brought no relief. We know now that there is no way out; that the 'system' that was the evil offspring of public neglect and private greed has come to stay, a storm-center forever of our civilization. Nothing is left but to make the best of a bad bargain.

What the tenements are and how they grow to what they are, we shall see hereafter. The story is dark enough, drawn from the plain public records, to send a chill to any heart. If it shall appear that the sufferings and the sins of the "other half," and the evil they breed, are but as a just punishment upon the community that gave it no other choice, it will be because that is the truth. The boundary line lies there because, while the forces for good on one side vastly outweigh the bad—it were not well otherwise—in the tenements all the influences make for evil.

CONTINUE

1

Riis describes the "half that was on top" (lines 3-4) as interested in

A) maintaining its advantageous position.
B) alleviating the struggles of other people.
C) prolonging its ignorance of social issues.
D) provoking civil unrest in American cities.

2

As used in line 13, "old" most nearly means

A) experienced.
B) used.
C) former.
D) aged.

3

According to Riis, why did one half take interest in the lives of the other half?

A) Tenement residents began protesting inequality.
B) Sanitarians exposed the foul conditions in tenements.
C) Individuals in the city led humanitarian efforts.
D) Increasing violence and strife was difficult to ignore.

4

Which choice provides the best evidence for the answer to the previous question?

A) Lines 7-10 ("There came a time . . . the matter")
B) Lines 26-29 ("Those very . . . to crime")
C) Lines 46-50 ("The fifteen . . . them home")
D) Lines 63-66 ("The boundary . . . for evil")

5

Lines 29-39 ("By far . . . city here") suggest that crime is the product of an individual's

A) relationship with criminal relatives.
B) innate tendency to be violent.
C) jealousy of those who are more well-off.
D) upbringing in a deprived home.

6

Based on the passage, which choice best describes the "boundary line" (line 40)?

A) It is a police response to rampant crime in the city.
B) It marks the geographical center of the city.
C) It is the result of human selfishness and indifference.
D) It continues to evenly divide the city's population.

7

As used in line 45, "drift" most nearly means

A) bank.
B) migration.
C) implication.
D) tendency.

8

The passage indicates that concerned urban reformers had what hope?

A) Wealthy individuals would provide financial assistance to those living in tenements.
B) Expanding connections to areas outside city limits would alleviate overcrowding.
C) New York City would never become overcrowded.
D) Municipal laws would improve conditions in tenements.

9

Which choice provides the best evidence for the answer to the previous question?

A) Lines 16-18 ("There were . . . vain")
B) Lines 36-39 ("The younger . . . city here")
C) Lines 50-51 ("The one . . . no relief")
D) Line 55 ("Nothing is . . . bargain")

10

What main effect does the final paragraph have on the tone of the passage?

A) It creates a conversational tone, relating the struggle of tenement residents in everyday language.
B) It creates a somber tone, focusing on the bleak prospects of those who live in the tenements.
C) It creates an irrational tone, using language that describes housing as a form of evil.
D) It creates an ominous tone, relating the results of one sanitarian's research.

STOP

Questions 1-10 are based on the following passage.

In these readings, two authors consider recent developments in the study of speech and language skills.

Passage 1

The question of how our language shapes our thought processes has long puzzled scientists. Since the 1940s, various theories have been put forth in an attempt to show that those who speak different languages quite literally see the world in different ways. Yet no theorist has been able to definitively prove that it is language, rather than one's cultural background, that more directly impacts perception.

Psycholinguist Panos Athanasopoulos of Lancaster University hopes to settle the debate. In a cleverly designed experiment, Athanasopoulos and his team worked with 15 participants. The first language of some participants is English; that of the rest is German. The choice of languages was intentional. English speakers tend to focus on what is happening in the present, rather than explicitly indicating what has happened in the past, or what will happen in the future. For instance, it is not odd to say in English, "The woman is driving," but a German speaker would include more information: "The woman is driving to the store." As a result of these linguistic tendencies, Athanasopoulos predicted that German speakers would be more "goal-oriented" in their thinking than English speakers.

To test his theory, Athanasopoulos had each of his participants view a video clip of someone walking, running, driving, or riding a bike. For each clip, the participants were then asked to determine if a given scene with an ambiguous goal (for instance, a man walking towards a car that may or may not be his) was more similar to a scene with no clear goal (a man walking along a beach) or more similar to a scene with an obvious goal (a man walking into a post office). Athanasopoulos found that English speakers only matched the ambiguous scenes with the goal-oriented scenes about 25% of the time, whereas the German speakers matched the ambiguous scenes with the goal-oriented scenes 40% of the time. The results are highly indicative that the native language of the participants had a clear impact on the nature of the participants' perceptions.

Passage 2

According to John McWhorter, the idea that language influences cognition is nothing short of a "hoax." He has declared as much with the title of his most recent book, *The Language Hoax: Why the World Looks the Same in Any Language* (2014), a quick read but a dense read, in certain respects. McWhorter, a scholar of linguistics at Columbia University, has declared that "Nothing has ever demonstrated that your language makes you process life in a different way. It just doesn't work." *The Language Hoax* expands upon this idea example-by-example: for instance, "Japanese has a term that covers both green and blue. Russian has separate terms for dark and light blue. Does this mean that Russians perceive these colors differently from Japanese people?" For McWhorter, it decidedly doesn't.

In certain respects, the idea that we all share the same language of cognition and observation is empowering. No human being on earth, under this theory, is shut off from a particular form of knowledge, expression, or emotion because said human being happened to be born into the "wrong" language.

Yet McWhorter's ideas—and McWhorter himself seems to sense this—are not impervious to criticism. Consider the Russian language: unlike English, Russian does not contain the articles "a" and "the"—a difference that is surely more consequential than a difference in shades of "blue." The most-studied divergences in language involve matters of structure rather than matters of naming: both a Russian and an American may see the same blue sky, but the habits of thought that each uses to process and internalize this sight may be incompatible. It could be that language-based thought structures are simply too great to be overcome, not that they are relatively tiny factors, swamped by more universal habits of thought.

CONTINUE

1

The primary role of the first paragraph of Passage 1 is to

A) cast doubt on a commonly held belief.
B) dispute a scientific principle.
C) redefine the parameters of a debate.
D) provide the theoretical context for an experiment.

2

As used in line 10, "settle" most nearly means

A) remedy.
B) rectify.
C) end.
D) suppress.

3

The description of Panos Athanasopoulos's experiment suggests that

A) culture has a strong effect on linguistic tendencies.
B) language influences how individuals assess specific situations.
C) country of birth is a strong indicator of an individual's willingness to make assumptions.
D) English and German have many similarities in terms of structure and vocabulary.

4

The author of Passage 2 would most likely respond to Panos Athanasopoulos's experiment with

A) disbelief, believing the methodology to be flawed.
B) skepticism, believing the link between lingual influences and behavior to be a fallacy.
C) support, believing language to be the most important determinant of an individual's behavior.
D) agreement, believing that differences in language structure may account for differences in thinking

5

Which choice provides the best evidence for the answer to the previous question?

A) Lines 49-51 ("Nothing has . . . work")
B) Lines 52-57 ("for instance . . . doesn't")
C) Lines 64-65 ("Yet McWhorter's . . . criticism")
D) Lines 69-74 ("The most . . . incompatible")

6

The author of Passage 2 regards the prospect that language does not influence cognition as

A) depressing.
B) liberating.
C) unusual.
D) shocking.

7

The example from *The Language Hoax* suggests that language does not influence cognition because

A) two languages can have the same word for one color but very different conceptions of that color.
B) two languages can have different words for different colors but the same opinion of those colors.
C) one language can be radically different from others, yet its speakers retain the ability to express their perceptions using other languages if they become fluent.
D) two languages can have different concepts of where one characteristic ends and another begins, yet speakers of both languages will perceive reality in the same way.

CONTINUE

8

Which choice provides the best evidence for the answer to the previous question?

A) Lines 42-44 (“According to . . . hoax”)
B) Lines 60-63 (“No human . . . language”)
C) Lines 66-69 (“Consider the . . . blue”)
D) Lines 74-77 (“It could . . . thought”)

9

As used in line 77, “swamped” most nearly means

A) inundated.
B) overpowered.
C) beset.
D) saturated.

10

The last sentence of Passage 2 indicates that the author questions whether

A) all languages provide equally useful tools for critical thinking.
B) the debate between those who see language’s influence on cognition as negligible and those who see it as critical will ever be resolved.
C) language is genuinely insignificant in the study of perception and cognition.
D) a comprehensive theory of human thought might be more important than theories that articulate the differences between individual languages.

Questions 1-10 are based on the following passage.

This passage is from Virginia Woolf, "Kew Gardens," originally published in 1919. Kew is the location of the Royal Botanic Gardens of the United Kingdom.

From the oval-shaped flower-bed there rose perhaps a hundred stalks spreading into heart-shaped or tongue-shaped leaves half way up and unfurling at the tip red or blue or yellow petals marked with spots of colour raised upon the surface; and from the red, blue or yellow gloom of the throat emerged a straight bar, rough with gold dust and slightly clubbed at the end. The petals were voluminous enough to be stirred by the summer breeze, and when they moved, the red, blue and yellow lights passed one over the other, staining an inch of the brown earth beneath with a spot of the most intricate colour. The light fell either upon the smooth, grey back of a pebble, or the shell of a snail with its brown, circular veins, or falling into a raindrop, it expanded with such intensity of red, blue and yellow the thin walls of water that one expected them to burst and disappear. Instead, the drop was left in a second silver grey once more, and the light now settled upon the flesh of a leaf, revealing the branching thread of fibre beneath the surface, and again it moved on and spread its illumination in the vast green spaces beneath the dome of the heart-shaped and tongue-shaped leaves. Then the breeze stirred rather more briskly overhead and the colour was flashed into the air above, into the eyes of the men and women who walk in Kew Gardens in July.

The figures of these men and women straggled past the flower-bed with a curiously irregular movement not unlike that of the white and blue butterflies who crossed the turf in zig-zag flights from bed to bed. The man was about six inches in front of the woman, strolling carelessly, while she bore on with greater purpose, only turning her head now and then to see that the children were not too far behind. The man kept this distance in front of the woman purposely, though perhaps unconsciously, for he wished to go on with his thoughts.

"Fifteen years ago I came here with Lily," he thought. "We sat somewhere over there by a lake and I begged her to marry me all through the hot afternoon. How the dragonfly kept circling round us: how clearly I see the dragonfly and her shoe with the square silver buckle at the toe. All the time I spoke I saw her shoe and when it moved impatiently I knew without looking up what she was going to say: the whole of her seemed to be in her shoe. And my love, my desire, were in the dragonfly; for some reason I thought that if it settled there, on that leaf, the broad one with the red flower in the middle of it, if the dragonfly settled on the leaf she would say "Yes" at once. But the dragonfly went round and round: it never settled anywhere—of course not, happily not, or I shouldn't be walking here with Eleanor and the children—Tell me, Eleanor. D'you ever think of the past?"

"Why do you ask, Simon?"

"Because I've been thinking of the past. I've been thinking of Lily, the woman I might have married. . . . Well, why are you silent? Do you mind my thinking of the past?"

"Why should I mind, Simon? Doesn't one always think of the past, in a garden with men and women lying under the trees? Aren't they one's past, all that remains of it, those men and women, those ghosts lying under the trees, . . . one's happiness, one's reality?"

"For me, a square silver shoe buckle and a dragonfly—"

CONTINUE

1

Which choice best describes what happens in the passage?

A) A man takes a solitary stroll through a garden.
B) A man ignores the nature around him and becomes lost in his thoughts.
C) A man is prompted by his surroundings to recall moments from his past.
D) A man expresses his marital unhappiness to his spouse.

2

Which choice best describes the developmental pattern of the passage?

A) A story about a specific location becomes an ode to nature.
B) An ongoing argument is recalled by two characters.
C) A specific example about love and loss facilitates a discussion of local scenery.
D) A scenic description gives way to a specific discussion.

3

As used in line 7, "clubbed" most nearly means

A) battered.
B) stunned.
C) hobbled.
D) thickened.

4

As used in line 11, "staining" most nearly means

A) tainting.
B) obfuscating.
C) influencing.
D) illuminating.

5

The main purpose of the second paragraph is to

A) provide an assessment of the story's setting.
B) explain the relationship between Lily and Simon.
C) describe the physical appearances of the people who regularly visit Kew Gardens.
D) introduce the vignette's main characters.

6

In the passage, the dragonfly serves to

A) indicate that Lily did not reciprocate the man's feelings.
B) suggest that creatures in the park are engaged in its visitors' personal lives.
C) display the man's somewhat frantic demeanor during his proposal to Lily.
D) provide imagery to show how the gardens were once arranged.

7

Which choice provides the best evidence for the answer to the previous question?

A) Lines 41-43 ("How the dragonfly . . . toe")
B) Lines 47-51 ("for some . . . anywhere")
C) Lines 53-54 ("Tell me . . . the past?")
D) Lines 56-57 ("Because . . . married")

CONTINUE

8

In his present emotional state, Simon is best described as

A) anxious over unresolved matters.
B) simultaneously ecstatic and disgruntled by everyday problems.
C) nostalgic despite his general appearance of contentment.
D) embittered because of past rejection.

9

Which choice provides the best evidence for the answer to the previous question?

A) Lines 12-17 ("The light . . . disappear")
B) Lines 27-31 ("The figures . . . bed")
C) Lines 34-37 ("The man . . . thoughts")
D) Lines 43-45 ("All the time . . . say")

10

It can most reasonably be inferred that the author sees the scenery in Kew Gardens as

A) incidental.
B) affecting.
C) enervating.
D) agitating.

STOP

Questions 1-11 are based on the following passage.

In the passages that follow, two authors consider new technology and how its development has shaped modern society.

Passage 1

Can you imagine going a full day without using technology? Few of us can; in fact, take away our cell phones for a couple of hours, and most of us will begin to feel something like existential panic. In ways that we immediately recognize, and in a few ways that we don't, technology commands the ways we communicate, the ways we gather information, even the ways we prepare our food.

The devices responsible—in the above cases, the cell phone, computer, and microwave—are just a few of the technologies that have been invented over the past 40 years. Often, it has taken a while for these inventions to catch on. The first cell phone call was placed on April 3, 1973; however, cell phones did not become mainstream until 2003. Personal computers were also created in the 1970s, but did not command a mass market until the early 1990s. Amazingly, while microwave ovens were first available to the public in the mid-1950s, it was not until the late 1970s that they became widely used.

Each of these pieces of technology has been successfully marketed in the same way: this product will help you meet your needs, make your life easier, and—best of all—save you time! In fact, we do have more leisure time than those in past generations, at least according to the Boston Federal Reserve. In a recent study, this institution found that since 1963, "leisure time for men increased by 6-8 hours per week and for women by 4-8 hours per week." Yet today, people regularly claim to be busy to the point of exhaustion. And according to sociology professor Judy Wacjman, technology itself may be responsible for this burnout effect. To quote Wacjman: "Technological utopians once dreamt of the post-industrial society as one of leisure. Instead, we are more like characters in *Alice in Wonderland*, running ever faster and faster to stand still."

Technology, it seems, is both a handmaiden and a temptress. While working hours may have decreased, the temptation to accomplish more work, or to go all-out finding new leisure pursuits, has been turbocharged. After all, utilize the right technology and you can have it all, or so we're told.

Passage 2

For the past five years, I have taught a university course that meets twice a week and that considers the psychological and ethical aspects of modern marketing practices. To gauge the psychology of my students, I always begin the semester with a veiled experiment—nothing unethical, though.

In the first class of the first week, I assign my students an article on the evils of modern technology: "The Flight from Conversation" by Sherry Turkle, a condemnation of the conversation-killing, dumbing-down effects of texting and social media, is always reliable. The students read, absorb, and are repulsed. They chime in with their own experiences of the inanity of technology—websites that include "ClownDating" and "Pictures of Hipsters Taking Pictures of Food," tone-deaf singing routines that somehow acquire 35 million views on YouTube, text messages without a single correctly-spelled word—and leave class devilishly amused at the prospect that society is falling apart.

However, next class, I switch gears and offer up an article that hails all the benefits technology imparts: the optimistic "Mind Over Mass Media" by Steven Pinker is my stalwart here. The students read, absorb, and this time laud the databases, the e-mails, the education platforms, the new and rapidly-delivered forms of entertainment that have enhanced their lives.

While I have never been surprised that my students have an ambivalent relationship to technology, I am surprised that such ambivalence has not waned. You would think they'd be used to all this by now. Instead, the strength of that love-hate push-and-pull only grows stronger with each passing semester. With the growth of technology has come the growth of a psychodrama that involves increasingly high emotions. We are still, as I see it, somewhat in disbelief at the scope that technology has assumed in only a few short decades of human history, and we need to bring it all down to a human level. We greet it with human negatives (disgust, annoyance) and human positives (loyalty, affection) without ever asking whether our emotions really add up.

CONTINUE

1

The author of Passage 1 cites the Boston Federal Reserve in line 26 in order to

A) disprove an earlier statement.
B) introduce a paradox.
C) refute a popular conception.
D) present a controversial idea.

2

The main purpose of the second paragraph of Passage 1 (lines 9-20) is to

A) address a common misconception.
B) provide a historical synopsis.
C) anticipate a counter-argument.
D) analyze a personal choice.

3

The author of Passage 1 characterizes technology as a "handmaiden and a temptress" in order to

A) demonstrate its potential both for progress and destruction.
B) argue that as much as technology saves time it also creates needs.
C) emphasize the association of modern communication technology with women's roles.
D) cast doubt on technology's purportedly humanitarian intentions.

4

As used in line 6, "commands" most nearly means

A) requires.
B) dictates.
C) gains.
D) instructs.

5

Passage 1 and Passage 2 differ in that

A) Passage 1 is concerned with technology's effect on leisure while Passage 2 is concerned with technology's effect on thought.
B) Passage 1 unequivocally condemns modern technology while Passage 2 is more ambivalent.
C) Passage 1 argues for a revised conception of technology while Passage 2 is satisfied with the status quo.
D) Passage 1 is deeply critical of technology while Passage 2 is more circumspect.

6

What would the author of Passage 2 most likely consider "it all" in line 43?

A) "texting" (line 54)
B) "ClownDating" and "Pictures of Hipsters Taking Pictures of Food" (lines 58-59)
C) "rapidly delivered forms of entertainment" (lines 69-70)
D) "high emotions" (line 78)

7

The author of Passage 1 would most likely attribute the popularity of new technologies to

A) economic prosperity.
B) spiritual decline.
C) great convenience.
D) alluring advertising.

CONTINUE

8

Which choice provides the best evidence for the answer to the previous question?

A) Lines 9-13 ("The devices . . . catch on")
B) Lines 21-24 ("Each of . . . you time")
C) Lines 24-29 ("In fact . . . week")
D) Lines 39-42 ("While working . . . turbocharged")

9

The author of Passage 2 offers his students a curriculum that can best be described as

A) unstable.
B) erudite.
C) investigative.
D) biased.

10

Which choice provides the best evidence for the answer to the previous question?

A) Lines 47-49 ("To gauge . . . though")
B) Lines 55-63 ("The students . . . apart")
C) Lines 67-70 ("The students . . . lives")
D) Lines 71-73 ("While I . . . waned")

11

As used in line 78, "high" most nearly means

A) elevated.
B) sophisticated.
C) intense.
D) lofty.

CONTINUE

Questions 1-10 are based on the following passage.

This reading is an excerpt from the essay "The Grand Unifying (Geological) Theory" by Eliza Morris.

The theory of plate tectonics posits that Earth's landmasses sit atop massive "plates," which shift with the passage of time. The theory was proposed in the early 1960s, as an answer to the problems with the theory of continental drift. Since that time, the plate tectonic theory has become widely accepted in the scientific community. Yet there remain dissenters, scientists who believe they see problems in the idea of plate tectonics. Though passions can run high over plate tectonics, dissent—even unpopular dissent—is part of the scientific process. Plate tectonics has a long and complicated history. In 1915, Alfred Wegener proposed a theory he called "continental drift." His ideas were based on his observation that Earth's continents could fit together neatly, like puzzle pieces—implying that they once fit together border-to-border. Wegener concluded that Earth's continents must have moved into their present positions over millions of years.

Wegener got it partially right—according to the theory of plate tectonics—when he said that the continents had moved. Yet Wegener, who was meteorologist and not a geologist, couldn't explain their movement. Scientists of the day pointed to one major hole in his theory: the oceanic crust is much too thick for continents to simply push their way through. It wasn't until the 1960s that scientists were able to propose a better hypothesis: that Earth's continents lie on top of vast plates, which are moved along by the spreading of the seafloor and the interaction of the different layers of the Earth.

Plate tectonics proposes what is generally referred to as the "conveyor belt principle." This states that as the seafloor spreads outward from the center, the material at the edges gets subducted into the Earth's mantle. The total surface area of the planet remains the same: as new material is introduced, older material is recycled. Another crucial component of plate tectonics is its explanation of volcanic and geologic activity. Scientists have noticed that mountains, deep-sea trenches, and volcanoes all tend to form where the massive plates converge.

This theory, however, is not without its detractors. In 1996, after a symposium in Beijing, a few scientists formed what they called "The New Concepts in Global Tectonics Group." Concerned with what they saw as shortcomings in the theory of plate tectonics, the leaders wrote: " . . . the Plate Tectonic Theory has swept aside much well-based data as though it never existed . . . result[ing] in the suppression or manipulation of data which does not fit the theory. In the course of time the method has become narrow, monotonous and dull . . . As new data has arisen there is a growing skepticism about the theory." Much of the evidence presented in the group's newsletter proposes an alternative hypothesis, which involves a system of "lineaments" which cover the surface of the Earth.

Most other critics of plate tectonics point out what they perceive as flaws in the theory, rather than proposing new theories to explain Earth's geology. Far from being a form of mere naysaying, this spirit of refutation is a vital part of how sound scientific practice operates. Indeed, the plate tectonics theory has undergone several important revisions since it was first proposed. Yet it's important to separate the working process of the scientific method (which thrives on the discarding of old, faulty data) from ideological dispute. According to the National Center for Higher Education, plate tectonics continues "to generate social controversy over [its] implications for policy or for personally-held religious views," much as the issues of global warming and evolution do. However, even in the face of the theory's shortcomings, and in reference to politically- or religiously-motivated dissent, the Center states that "plate tectonics [is] not scientifically controversial today."

CONTINUE

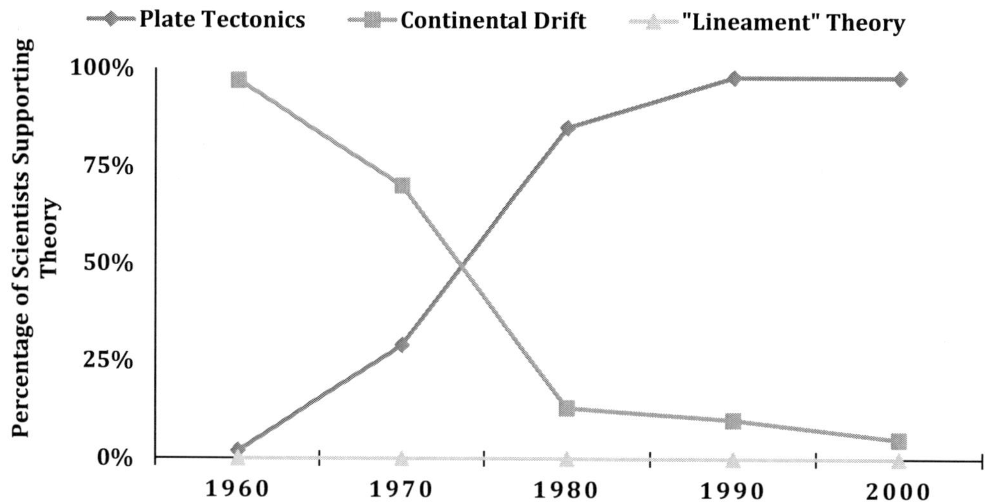

1

The passage indicates that the theory of continental drift is

A) not entirely inaccurate, but still incomplete.
B) unhelpful to the scientific process.
C) far-fetched but true.
D) still the best explanation for the movement of landmasses.

2

Which choice provides the best evidence for the answer to the previous question?

A) Lines 3-5 ("The theory . . . drift")
B) Lines 5-7 ("Since that . . . community")
C) Lines 17-19 ("Wegener . . . of years")
D) Lines 20-24 ("Wegener . . . movement")

3

As used in line 29, "vast" most nearly means

A) limitless.
B) profound.
C) immeasurable.
D) tremendous.

4

The main idea of the fourth paragraph (lines 43-57) is that

A) plate tectonic theory does not have very much support.
B) critics of plate tectonic theory argue that its proponents may be manipulating data to confirm their beliefs.
C) the scientific community is experiencing an ideological split that could threaten the objectivity of the scientific method.
D) a new explanation has superseded plate tectonic theory as the most popular landmass theory within the scientific community.

5

The passage suggests that some critics of the theory of plate tectonics may be

A) guilty of skewing data to confirm their own theories.
B) teaming up to attack the reputation of Alfred Wegener.
C) motivated by personal beliefs rather than scientific observations.
D) skeptical of the idea that landmasses are moving.

6

Which choice provides the best evidence for the answer to the previous question?

A) Line 43 ("This theory . . . detractors")
B) Lines 54-57 ("Much of the . . . Earth")
C) Lines 61-63 ("Far from . . . operates")
D) Lines 65-68 ("Yet it's . . . dispute")

7

As used in line 65, "separate" most nearly means

A) quarantine.
B) differentiate.
C) sever.
D) divide.

8

The main purpose of the final paragraph is to

A) distinguish between useful scientific debate and other, less scientific arguments against plate tectonic theory.
B) discuss the relative value of two disparate scientific organizations.
C) advocate for those who take issue with plate tectonics on ideological grounds.
D) criticize scientists who refute plate tectonics without offering a better alternative.

9

Data in the graph indicate that the greatest difference between support for plate tectonic theory and support for continental drift occurred during which year?

A) 1970
B) 1980
C) 1990
D) 2000

10

Data in the graph most strongly support which of the following statements?

A) From 1975 to 2000, plate tectonic theory replaced continental drift as the most popular explanation for the movement of landmasses.
B) Plate tectonic theory has consistently garnered more support than continental drift.
C) The scientific community grew considerably larger between 1980 and 2000.
D) In 2000, the combined support for continental drift and "lineament" theory was greater than support for plate tectonic theory.

STOP

CONTINUE

Chapter 2
Grammar Drills

Directions: For each drill, use about 8-9 minutes to read the passage and answer its questions. It is normal to finish either a minute before or after this time limit.

IES Workshops: You will **complete up to 4 grammar drills per workshop**. Please follow the time limits provided by your workshop teacher. Remember, you will complete these drills **during** workshop.

Good luck!

Questions 1-11 are based on the following passage.

Standard Time

If Train A leaves a station at 3:00 PM going 40 miles per hour, and Train B leaves the same station at 4:00 PM going 60 mph, at what time will Train B pass Train A?

If this math problem makes you groan, just be grateful that you didn't have to solve this problem in the early days of the [1] railroads in that era each municipality was responsible for determining its own time. This time was [2] based on the where the sun was at the time—also called "apparent solar time"—which meant, for example, that noon in New York City was late morning in Philadelphia. The most practical way for railway companies to coordinate was to schedule based on the time in the train's originating city. [3] However, they published timetables that allowed patrons to see the local time at each station relative to the train's time.

More than somewhat confusing and inconvenient for travelers, these time disparities were hazardous. [4] Most railway companies agreed that a standard time, and not a variety of local times, was desperately needed.

1

A) NO CHANGE
B) railroads—in that era—
C) railroads: in that era,
D) railroads, in that era,

2

A) NO CHANGE
B) based, on the position of the sun,
C) based in the positioning of the sun
D) based on the position of the sun

3

A) NO CHANGE
B) Accordingly,
C) Nonetheless,
D) By the same token,

4

At this point, the writer is considering adding the following sentence.

> There was no way to be absolutely certain where a train was while in transit, and head-on collisions were not uncommon.

Should the writer make this addition here?

A) Yes, because it states the main thesis of the passage and provides a supporting example.
B) Yes, because it elaborates on a claim made in the previous sentence.
C) No, because it would be better placed elsewhere in the passage.
D) No, because it introduces a concept that is irrelevant to the topic of the paragraph.

CONTINUE

The first group to adopt a standard time was the Great Western Railway in England. Using the time from the Royal Observatory at Greenwich, [5] the first time zone was effectively created by the company. Based on the sun's transit over one specific longitude, this time zone indicated a geographical range that would experience roughly the same 9:00, 10:00, 11:00, and so on. This was somewhat straightforward in a country as small as England, but inevitably would pose more challenges for a country as far and wide as the United States of America.

[6] In 1869, an American math teacher named Charles Ferdinand Dowd wrote a standard for railway time. He proposed that all trains run on the time in Washington D.C. This meant that travelers would only have to convert D.C. time to local time. Because of the distance across the United States, though, this meant that those traveling in the western reaches of the country would have to contend with a time disparity of hours. In order to solve this new problem, Canadian engineer Sanford Fleming created a new system (building off of Dowd's) that would make international scheduling much easier.

[1] In [7] that treatise on terrestrial time, Fleming asked his audience to imagine a dial in the center of the Earth, lying flat on the equator. [2] The hand would follow the Sun as it crossed each meridian, thereby showing where approximate noon was at any given time. [3] It would have 24 sections lining up with meridians (or lines of longitude) on the surface of the Earth.

5

A) NO CHANGE
B) effectively creating the first time zone.
C) the company effectively created the first time zone in the world.
D) the world effectively created the company's first time zone.

6

Which choice most effectively combines the underlined sentences?

A) An American math teacher, Charles Ferdinand Dowd in 1869 wrote a standard for railway time and proposed that all trains should run on the time in Washington, D.C.
B) In 1869, Charles Ferdinand Dowd, an American math teacher, proposed that all trains run on the time in Washington, D.C.; he put this in the standard for railway time.
C) Proposing that all trains run on the time in Washington, D.C., in 1869, Charles Ferdinand Dowd, an American math teacher, wrote a standard for railway time.
D) In 1869, an American math teacher named Charles Ferdinand Dowd wrote a standard for railway time, proposing that all trains run on the time in Washington, D.C.

7

A) NO CHANGE
B) its
C) his
D) their

CONTINUE

[4] The second part of the timepiece would be another clock in the middle that showed any given local time. [5] The purpose of using these two chronometers (time measuring devices) together was to give all users a common reference point. [6] If someone in Dublin was to make reference to the "mean solar hour," someone in New York City would understand what time it was for [8] them. [7] This meant that neat, orderly international scheduling was a distinct possibility, and that local time could still be used. [9]

However, asking everyone to buy a new timepiece was ultimately impractical. Instead, railroad engineer William F. Allen took the proposals, and developed his own concept of international time, which was based on a 24-hour clock and used meridians as reference points for the average solar hour. [10] From this Convention came the five time standards (or zones today) of the Americas: Atlantic, Eastern, Valley (now Central), Mountain, and Pacific. Each was based on a meridian. On November 18, 1883, the railways switched over to this "Railroad and Telegraph Time." [11]

8

A) NO CHANGE
B) him or her
C) it
D) us

9

To make this paragraph most logical, sentence 2 should be placed

A) where it is now.
B) after sentence 3.
C) after sentence 5.
D) after sentence 7.

10

Which choice most effectively sets up the information that follows in the passage?

A) His idea was presented at the General Time Convention of October 1883.
B) This meant that no one had to buy a new timepiece to adjust to Standard Time.
C) Allen was able to combine the proposals into a workable Standard.
D) Standard Time was not adopted in most places until the early 20th century.

11

The writer wants to add a concluding sentence that connects historical information to the present day. Which choice best accomplishes this goal for the whole passage?

A) Many people gravitated toward standard time, but there were notable exceptions such as Detroit, which was divided on whether to adopt it.
B) Although the benefit to commerce and travel was immediately obvious, some still took offense at the idea that they were to live their lives according to a train schedule.
C) It wasn't until March 19, 1918 that the Standard Time Act sanctioned these time zones, putting the United States—and most of the world—on the clock we know today.
D) We can learn a lot about shifts in society and cultural norms by studying how people have responded to them in the past.

CONTINUE

Grammar Drill 2

Questions 1-11 are based on the following passage.

Video Games

In 21st century American society, playing video games is one of the favorite pastimes of children. In 2002, the average child in the United States reportedly played video games for [1] 7 hours each week, with wide differences among different ages and between boys and girls. Unfortunately for the millions of video game players, an increasing body of research links violent video games to aggressive behaviors, attitudes, and cognitions. Those who play video games, however, would say they are cathartic expressions of aggression, thereby preventing violence rather than causing it—but opponents are not convinced. Can researchers document what is the long-presumed connection, if any, [2] around these variables and video game exposure?

1

Which choice most accurately reflects the data presented in the table?

A) NO CHANGE
B) 3 hours
C) 4 hours
D) 5 hours

2

A) NO CHANGE
B) by
C) between
D) about

Average Playtime Relative to Popular Children's Activities in the United States (2002)

Children's Activities	Average Playtime Each Week
Playing in the Park	5 hours
Reading an Extracurricular Book	4 hours
Participating in a Team Sport	3 hours
Playing Video Games	7 hours

CONTINUE

In 2004, researcher Douglas A. Gentile and others, using a General Aggression Model (GAM), looked at the possible connections between a number of variables and video game exposure. The GAM was initially developed by Anderson and colleagues to help **3** explain links between violent video gaming, aggressive behavior, attitude and, cognition. The GAM suggests specific results in relation to long-term exposure to violent content. For instance, it **4** takes for granted that repeated exposure to scenes of graphic violence may be desensitizing. So, over the long term, trait hostility may increase due to video game play. Additionally, violent game content may moderate or mediate the effect of violent games on one's aggressive behavior, depending on other factors.

The research team examined data from more than six hundred 8th and 9th graders from schools in the Midwest, including **5** urban private, suburban public, and rural public. Student data included anonymous surveys, descriptive data about video game habits, school performance, demographic data, and measures of trait hostility. Students were told to include as video games any computer games or consoles including Nintendo, Gameboy, and other handheld devices. Participants named their top three video games, rating them on

3

A) NO CHANGE
B) explaining linking between violent video games, aggressive behavior, attitude, cognition
C) explain links among violent video games, aggressive behavior, attitude, and cogniton
D) explaining links among violent video, games, aggressive behavior attitude, and cognition

4

A) NO CHANGE
B) nominates
C) guesses
D) postulates

5

A) NO CHANGE
B) urban private, suburban public; and rural public
C) urban private schools, suburban public, and rural public schools
D) schools being urban private, suburban public, and rural public

CONTINUE

how violent the games were. A video game violence exposure score was calculated for each subject. Then, subjects indicated [6] what they liked most about the artwork in the games. Besides violent video game exposure, additional variables were the amount of video game play, trait hostility, parental limits, arguments with teachers, grades, and physical fights.

The researchers found that, in general, youth preferred a moderate amount of violence, with significant sex differences on this variable—boys preferred more violence than girls did. [7] Most games that were rated among subjects' three favorite games fell into the category of having "some violence." Parents for the most part were not involved in their children's video game playing, [8] few parents set limits on the amount of game time. About one-fifth of the students had gotten into arguments with teachers almost weekly or almost daily, and were significantly more likely to have been suspended at some point than were those who preferred fantasy games. About one-third had been in a physical fight within the past year, with sex differences between boys and girls.

6

The writer wants to include relevant information about the subjects in the test. Which choice best accomplishes this goal?

A) NO CHANGE
B) how much violence they liked in their video games, using a 10-point scale.
C) what video games their friends and family liked and how violent those were.
D) whether they let other people borrow video games from them.

7

The writer is considering deleting the underlined portion. Should this sentence be kept or deleted?

A) Kept, because it adds another detail that supports the writer's overall claim.
B) Kept, because it gives a specific example of a game used in the study.
C) Deleted, because it strays from the author's argument by adding information about the subjects' parents.
D) Deleted, because it repeats information from the previous sentence.

8

A) NO CHANGE
B) and few set a limit on the number
C) with few parents setting limits on the amount
D) with a few parents setting limits on the number

CONTINUE

After the results had been calculated, the study substantiated the initial predictions. First, it showed that 9 how much violent video game content and amount of video game play correlated positively with having a physical fight, getting into an argument with a teacher, and trait hostility—and correlated negatively with school grades. Second, parental limits correlated negatively with trait hostility and arguments with teachers—and correlated positively with school performance.

What this study tells us is that exposure to video games could very well be causing violent behaviors. The team finally nailed down definitely that when adolescents expose themselves to more video games, they generally become more hostile. 10 Nevertheless, students who were once not hostile, but have high exposure to violent video games, are more likely to exhibit violent behaviors as a result than even highly hostile students who play little to no violent video games (38% compared to 28%, respectively). Looking at the data, it's not that there is a 100 percent likelihood that students will become more violent after playing violent video games, but that there is a definitive rise in violence, which implies that parents should pay close attention to what their kids are doing in their free time. The researchers conclude that 11 "clearly, media violence is not the sole cause of aggression, but it is likely that it is one of several causes leading to it."

9

NO CHANGE
B) violently playing video games and amount of video game playing
C) violent videos, game content, and how much time they spent playing video games
D) violent video game content and amount of video game play

10

A) NO CHANGE
B) Regardless,
C) In other words,
D) Likewise,

11

At this point, the writer wants to include a statement from the researchers that reflects the main finding of the experiment discussed in the passage. Which choice accomplishes that goal?

A) NO CHANGE
B) "perhaps we should be encouraging kids to play more traditional games like tag and tug-o-war."
C) "we would like to do a follow-up experiment to determine the effects of violence depicted in news outlets."
D) "it would be best for every school to warn both teachers and students about the effects of violence in video games."

CONTINUE

Questions 1-11 are based on the following passage.

Thyroid Misdiagnosis

[1] Some people experience the myriad debilitating symptoms of a low-functioning thyroid, a condition known as hypothyroidism. [2] Hypothyroidism manifests itself through such negative effects as weight gain, fatigue, depression, and impaired memory. [3] Because of the clearly unwanted nature of the disorder, patients who suspect they have it typically ask their doctors to run the appropriate medical tests in an attempt to obtain a speedy diagnosis and treatment plan. [4] Changes in related diagnostic criteria have emerged in recent years, and the conflicting nature of the diagnostic criteria has led to some people with hypothyroid disease not being able to receive the proper diagnosis. [5] The reality is that the diagnostic criteria for this increasingly widespread autoimmune disease continue to be complex and multi-faceted. [6] However, such individuals—and their doctors—may not be aware of the importance of comprehensive, up-to-date testing. [1]

The thyroid, a butterfly-shaped gland in the body, is susceptible to a [2] number of autoimmune conditions; the most prevalent of which is low function. To render the diagnosis, doctors often opt for a thyroid stimulating hormone (TSH) test to determine current levels and perhaps include other tests, based on a blood sample. If the thyroid produces a low amount of thyroid hormone, [3] that responds by increasing the amount of TSH in the body. Therefore, there is an inverse relationship

1

To make this paragraph most logical, sentence 6 should be placed

A) where it is now.
B) before sentence 3.
C) after sentence 3.
D) after sentence 4.

2

A) NO CHANGE
B) number of autoimmune conditions—the most prevalent of which is low function.
C) numbers of autoimmune conditions, including low function.
D) number of autoimmune conditions, the most prevalent is low function.

3

A) NO CHANGE
B) it
C) the pituitary gland
D) they

CONTINUE

between TSH levels and thyroid function. **4** Doctors usually work with an acceptable TSH range to determine a diagnosis.

A 20-year study began in the mid-1970s. Then in 1996, the National Academy for Clinical Biochemsitry reported that TSH levels above the maximum **5** 1.9 mIU/L (milli-international units per liter) were symptomatic of hypothyroidism. This study was conducted in the UK on close to 3,000 randomly selected adults. A second, larger study of more than 13,000 subjects was conducted between 1988 and 1994, but this one excluded subjects with conditions associated with thyroid disease. **6** This study ran during some of the same years as the first study. Its researchers proposed new acceptable TSH ranges of between 0.3 and 2.5 mlU/L. In 2002, the National Academy for Clinical Biochemistry evaluated the then available research data, and had recommended the same change in the TSH threshold, from 2.0 to 2.5 mlU/L, saying that "it is likely that the upper limit of the serum TSH reference range will be reduced to 2.5 mIU/L."

4

At this point, the writer is considering adding the following sentence

> The lower the TSH level, the higher the level of thyroid functioning, as it produces thyroid hormone.

Should this sentence be added here?

A) Yes, because it introduces the concept of an inverse relationship.
B) Yes, because it illustrates the concept in the previous sentence.
C) No, because it simply restates the topic of the paragraph.
D) No, because it would be better placed elsewhere in the passage.

5

Which choice most closely reflects the information in the table?

A) NO CHANGE
B) 0.1
C) 0.5
D) 4.5

6

The writer is considering deleting the underlined portion. Should this sentence be kept or deleted?

A) Kept, because it is the only link between the two studies mentioned in this paragraph.
B) Kept, because it introduces a third study discussed later in this passage.
C) Deleted, because it adds unnecessary information at this point in the paragraph.
D) Deleted, because it directly contradicts the claim in the previous sentence.

Acceptable TSH Range (mIU/L), Various Standards

ORGANIZATION	*YEAR*	*MINIMUM*	*MAXIMUM*
NATIONAL ACADEMY FOR CLINICAL BIOCHEMISTRY	1996	0.1	1.9
AMERICAN SOCIETY OF CLINICAL ENDOCRINOLOGISTS	1997	0.25	2.25
AMERICAN THYROID ASSOCIATION	1997	0.125	3.875
NATIONAL ACADEMY FOR CLINICAL BIOCHEMISTRY	2001	0.5	4.5
AMERICAN SOCIETY OF CLINICAL ENDOCRINOLOGISTS	2003	0.3	2.7
AMERICAN SOCIETY OF CLINICAL ENDOCRINOLOGISTS	2012	0.4	3.85

The American Society of Clinical Endocrinologists (AACE) issued a statement in 2003 in support of changing the upper limit of the acceptable TSH range. They stated, "Now AACE encourages doctors to consider treatment for patients who test outside the boundaries of a narrower margin based on a target TSH level of [7] 0.25 to 2.25." The same document [8] sited a previous range of 0.5 to 4.5 mIU/L as an acceptable TSH range in 2001. The AACE acknowledged in the press release the possibility that patients with "mild thyroid disorder" may have gone untreated in the past, due to the use of TSH thresholds that, in effect, failed to properly identify patients with hypothyroidism.

However, in 2012, the AACE, in conjunction with another organization, the American Thyroid Association, [9] again reversed and nullified its recommendation, changing the upper limit of the range to 3.85 mIU/L, replacing the 2.7 mIU/L threshold identified in the earlier studies and press releases.

7

The writer wants to include information from the table that accurately reflects the acceptable TSH level as reported by American Society of Clinical Endocrinologists in 2003. Which choice accomplishes this goal?

A) NO CHANGE
B) 0.125 to 3.875
C) 0.4 to 3.85
D) 0.3 to 2.7

8

A) NO CHANGE
B) citing
C) sighted
D) cited

9

A) NO CHANGE
B) again reversed
C) reversed and nullified
D) again went back on

As a result of these conflicting recommendations regarding acceptable TSH levels, and the ensuing consequences for thyroid patients, [10] Dana Trentini stated that thyroid advocates and many integrative physicians are fighting to narrow that range." Dr. Weston Saunders and patient advocates like Mary Shomon suggest that subclinical symptoms that do not fit the current diagnostic criteria not be brushed aside or overlooked by doctors or patients. Shomon says patients must learn to advocate for themselves, and find another doctor, if their doctor will not listen to them. Shomon, like Trentini, recognizes that many of the various so-called acceptable TSH ranges fail to properly identify many who suffer from hypothyroidism.

To solve the misdiagnosis issue, some doctors request a full thyroid panel in addition to the required TSH test, which provides a more comprehensive understanding of the [11] patient's thyroid level's. A full thyroid panel helps to determine both proper diagnosis and an effective treatment plan. In the future, individuals who have the symptoms of any thyroid disorder need to be active in requesting that the proper diagnostic criteria be fulfilled.

10

A) NO CHANGE
B) Dana Trentini, states "thyroid
C) Dana Trentini states that, "thyroid
D) Dana Trentini states, "thyroid

11

A) NO CHANGE
B) patient's thyroid levels.
C) patients thyroid level's.
D) patients thyroids' levels.

CONTINUE

Questions 1-11 are based on the following passage.

Pluto's Surface

—1—

As technology affords scientists the ability to peer further and further into space, they jump at the opportunity to search for exoplanets of all kinds. Each planet discovered has valuable information to contribute to the fields of meteorology, geology, climatology, hydrology—the list goes on. An understanding of our neighbors in our own solar system also [1] <u>help</u> scientists to comprehend the composition of these exoplanets. They can use observed phenomena of nearby celestial objects to gain insight into planets we may never reach in our lifetimes. The newest knowledge of our solar system comes from observations of Pluto. After pictures were taken of its surface, astronomers began working to determine the age of Pluto's surface. The [2] <u>age of any given planet's</u> (or dwarf planet's) surface has more to do with geophysical processes than with the age of the planet itself. [3] <u>For instance, the Earth is a little over 4.5 billion years old, but a new island emerged from the Pacific Ocean in 2015.</u> Effectively determining the age of distant objects, though, requires a little more work on the part of astronomers.

1

A) NO CHANGE
B) has helped
C) are helping
D) helps

2

A) NO CHANGE
B) age of any given planets
C) ages of any given planets'
D) ages of any given planet's

3

The writer is considering deleting the underlined portion. Should the sentence be kept or deleted?

A) Kept, because it introduces the writer's overall thesis about land formation.
B) Kept, because it supports the claim in the previous sentence with a concrete example.
C) Deleted, because it mentions the Earth while the rest of the passage is about Pluto.
D) Deleted, because it is contradicted in the following two sentences.

CONTINUE

—2—

Two factors that astronomers can use are the number and depth of craters on a given surface, because they show the frequency and intensity of impacts. If a celestial object is highly likely to experience impacts but there are very few craters, then **4** astronomers must turn to the geophysical activity of the object itself. In the case of Mars, evidence of asteroid impacts is often smoothed over by eruptions or landslides: depending on the size of the crater and its properties, it is possible for astronomers to use the time of the eruptions and landslides to estimate the age of a given area. **5** In the case of Pluto, asteroid impacts would occur as it crosses the Kuiper Belt. The Kuiper Belt is an asteroid belt similar to the one between Mars and Jupiter, but many times larger. Just as they do for Mars' estimates, astronomers use the time lapse of geophysical processes to estimate the age of Pluto's surface.

—3—

In calculating the frequency of such an impact on Sputnik Planum, Trilling started with an established estimate of how many 100 km KBOs exist in one square degree of the Kuiper Belt. **6** He then calculated how long Pluto would take to cross the Kuiper Belt when using the volume and circumference of both orbits. By using both results, he concluded that Pluto was highly likely to be impacted by large KBOs during its journey through the Kuiper Belt.

4

The writer wants to add information that connects the first part of the sentence to the discussion that follows in the paragraph. Which choice best accomplishes this goal?

A) NO CHANGE
B) it will be difficult to determine the age of the surface.
C) perhaps it is not that likely to experience impacts after all.
D) astronomers must use other features to map the topography.

5

Which choice most smoothly and effectively combines the underlined sentences?

A) Asteroid impacts occur as Pluto crosses the Kuiper Belt; an asteroid belt similar to but larger than the one between Mars and Jupiter.
B) Pluto crosses the Kuiper Belt, an asteroid belt similar to but many times larger than the one between Mars and Jupiter, and asteroids impact it.
C) In Pluto's case, the Kuiper Belt is where asteroid impacts occur, and this is similar to but larger than the one between Mars and Jupiter.
D) In the case of Pluto, asteroid impacts would occur as it crosses the Kuiper Belt, which is an asteroid belt similar to the one between Mars and Jupiter, but many times larger.

6

A) NO CHANGE
B) Using the volume and circumference, both orbits helped him determine how long it would take Pluto to cross the Kuiper Belt.
C) Then, using the volume and circumference of both orbits, he calculcated how long it would take Pluto to cross the Kuiper Belt.
D) Then, calculating how long it would take Pluto to cross the Kuiper Belt, he determined this by using volume and circumference of both orbits.

CONTINUE

—4—

In 2015, Dr. David Trilling of the Department of Physics and Astronomy at Northern Arizona University, Flagstaff, used photos of the surface of Pluto to determine the maximum possible age of a section of the dwarf planet's surface, called Sputnik Planum. Images of it were taken at two different resolutions, and researchers were surprised to find that in neither image resolution 7 did craters appear; craters would have to be bigger than 2 kilometers to show up at the lower resolution, and a Kuiper Belt Object (KBO) would have to be at least 100 km in diameter to leave a crater that size.

—5—

The lack of large craters could usually be explained by familiar geophysical processes like those of Mars. 8 Since Mars has a crust made mostly of volcanic basalt rock, though, Pluto has a surface comprised of frozen nitrogen, and its geophysical activity involves freezing and melting—cryo-geophysical processes—similar to those observed on Ganymede, a moon of Jupiter; even then, Ganymede has frozen water. Trilling presents several cryo-geophysical scenarios that could have erased the craters from Sputnik Planum. The first is viscous relaxation, which means that the tops of the craters were warmer than the bases, and the ridges melted, slowly filling in the craters. The second is 9 convective overturn: essentially the opposite of viscous relaxation, this process would mean that the bases of craters were warmer, thereby

7

A) NO CHANGE
B) do craters appear in them
C) have they seen craters in them
D) do they find craters

8

A) NO CHANGE
B) While
C) However,
D) DELETE the underlined portion and adjust capitalization as needed.

9

A) NO CHANGE
B) convective overturn, essentially the opposite
C) convective overturn, essentially. The opposite
D) convective overturn essentially the opposite

CONTINUE

melting the tops over time. The third is cryovolcanism. In this scenario, the impact of the KBOs would create cracks in subsurface reservoirs, allowing melt to seep into the craters. [10]

—6—

However, this is a conservative estimate, to say the least. In fact, a more recent estimate based on new images of Sputnik Planum puts the surface age at only around 180,000 years. If we plan on reconciling these greatly varying estimates, we need to know more about the actual surface of Pluto and the dwarf planet's relationship to the Kuiper Belt. Perhaps we will—possibly from a Pluto Rover. But Trilling's methodology may yet be essential to understanding the surfaces of rocky exoplanets.

Question [11] asks about the previous passage as a whole.

10

Which choice provides the most effective conclusion for this paragraph?

A) The likelihood of any of these processes occurring is low, to say the least, because they each depend on the unique composition of the planet.

B) There may even be a fourth cryogeophysical process, but no researcher can know for sure until we get first-hand observations from Pluto.

C) The potential time frame for any one of these processes to fill in a crater puts the estimate of Sputnik Planum's age at less than 10 million years old.

D) Whatever process is responsible for smoothing over craters on Pluto, all have been recorded both on Earth and on Ganymede.

Think about the previous passage as a whole as you answer question 11.

11

To make this passage most logical, paragraph 3 should be placed

A) where it is now.

B) before paragraph 2.

C) after paragraph 4.

D) after paragraph 6.

STOP

Questions 1-11 are based on the following passage.

Pain Coping

Cognitive coping techniques can help to mask the physical experience of pain, new research from a university in Croatia has found. These findings could potentially be useful in the medical field for patients [1] <u>that are</u> undergoing invasive procedures, such as those in dentistry or surgery, that are usually accompanied by noxious pain.

"Our study has important practical considerations," said Natasa Jokic-Begic, lead author of the study at Zagreb University's Department of Psychology. "Health professionals could teach the patients who are about to undergo a painful medical procedure how to use cognitive strategies that would help them cope with pain."

The perception of pain, also known as *nociception*, can be broken down into two parts: biological and psychological. Biological pain originates at the source of the stimulus, and manifests itself as an unpleasant physical sensation; the stinging of a paper cut and the throbbing of a bruise are both examples of this phenomenon. Psychological pain, [2] <u>moreover,</u> arises when the original stimulus sends electrical signals from the point of impact to the brain via the peripheral nervous system. This is then interpreted by us as "ouch!" In

1

A) NO CHANGE
B) who is
C) which are
D) DELETE the underlined portion.

2

A) NO CHANGE
B) nevertheless,
C) for example,
D) on the other hand,

CONTINUE

short, physical pain is inevitable and results from actual or potential tissue damage, whereas psychological pain is **3** located only at the origin of the pain stimulus.

Jokic-Begic and her colleagues selected 96 undergraduates from the university's psychology department and divided them into three groups. Each group was subjected to acute pain by undergoing the Cold Pressor Test, **4** in which participant's hands are submerged in a bath of water that is maintained at 2 degrees Celsius. The participants were instructed to remove their hands from the water once the pain became unbearable.

5 The control group followed the standard procedure for the Cold Pressor Test. The researchers ran this part of the test without any modifications. The second group performed a "distraction task" while their hands were immersed. Participants were asked to list several nouns beginning with a specified letter, switching letters after every minute as instructed by the investigator. The third and final group was asked to choose and read one or more positive statements that either confronted or redefined the pain experienced. These statements had been written beforehand by the researchers, and included **6** phrases such as "This hurts, but I have control" and "The water is pleasantly cool." Participants were allowed to say the statements out loud or silently, and were encouraged to come up with self-statements in addition to the ones provided.

3

Which choice most smoothly and effectively concludes both this sentence and paragraph?

A) NO CHANGE
B) subjective and varies upon our perception of the pain's intensity.
C) a result of one's past psychological trauma.
D) based purely on imagined aches and pains.

4

A) NO CHANGE
B) the hands of participants
C) participants' hands
D) in which participants' hands

5

Which choice most smoothly and effectively combines these two sentences?

A) The control group followed the standard procedure for the Cold Pressor Test without any modifications.
B) Without any modifications, the researchers had the control group following the Cold Pressor Test exactly the way it was designed.
C) The researchers ran the Cold Pressor Test, without modification, for the control group; they used the standard procedure.
D) Running the test without any modifications, the control group followed a standard procedure.

6

A) NO CHANGE
B) phrases, such as "This
C) phrases such as: "This
D) phrase's such as "This

CONTINUE

The researchers found that the cognitive pain coping strategies as used on the second and third groups of participants [7] would have a significant influence on their tolerance of pain. In the Cold Pressor Test, the experimental groups (those distracted or using coping strategies) lasted [8] more than 4.5 minutes longer on average compared to the control group who only lasted 3 minutes on average. This proves that the experimental groups were able to extend their pain tolerance threshold using psychological techniques. No difference in pain tolerance time was found between the two experimental groups, indicating that distraction and redefining statements were equally effective in pain suppression.

[9] This is not to say that the participants in the experimental groups did not feel pain—far from it. At the

7

A) NO CHANGE
B) influenced to a significant extent
C) had a significant influence
D) having significant influence

8

Which choice accurately and effectively uses the information provided in figure 1?

A) NO CHANGE
B) between 4 to 4.5 minutes
C) almost 5 minutes longer
D) between 1 to 2 minutes

9

The writer is considering deleting the underlined portion. Should the writer make this deletion?

A) Yes, because it indicates that the author included faulty data from the experiment.
B) Yes, because it undermines the main thesis of the passage.
C) No, because it provides an effective transition from the previous paragraph.
D) No, because it gives an example of a factor that makes the experiment unique.

Figure 1

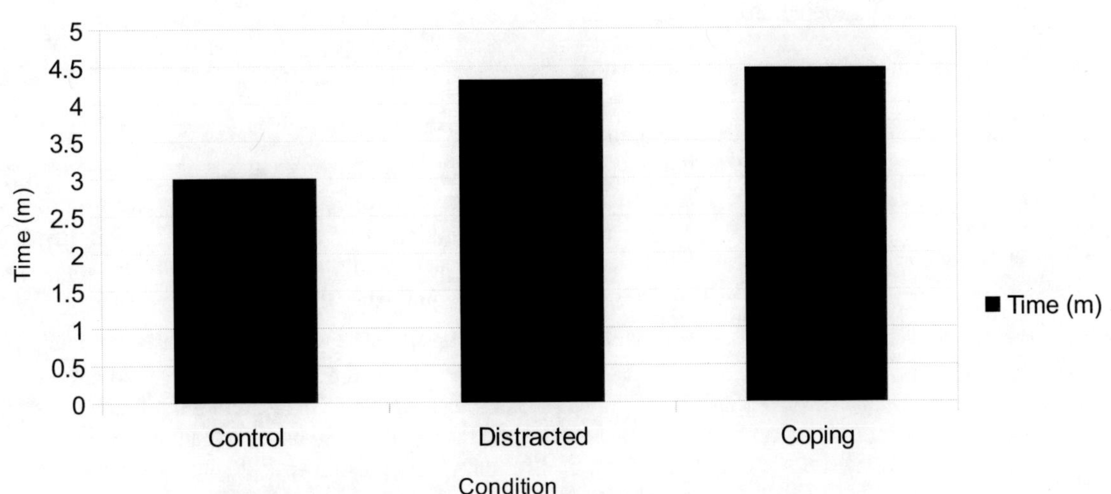

Average length of time that participants left their hands in a cold-pressor test across three conditions: control, a distraction task, or a coping task

CONTINUE

Figure 2

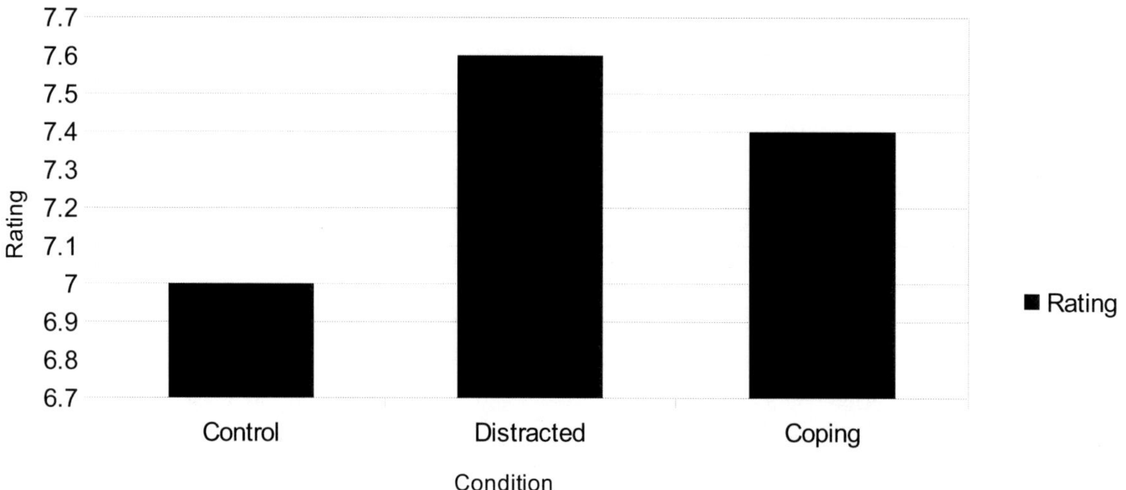

Average participant ratings of pain at the end of a cold-pressor test across three conditions: control, a distraction task, or a coping task.

end of the study, each group was asked to rate their pain on a scale of 0-10. The intensity of the pain did not vary much, with members from **10** <u>the control group feeling significantly less pain.</u> However, participants from experimental groups perceived the time their hands were submerged as much shorter than the participants in the control group did. This suggests that while all groups felt pain equally, members of the experimental groups had their attention diverted enough for their recognition of the pain to be delayed.

Though this study could represent a breakthrough in the field of pain management, Jokic-Begic is still not completely convinced. **11**

10

At this point, the writer wants to add information from figure 2 that supports the main idea of the paragraph. Which choice most effectively completes the sentence with relevant information from the figure?

A) NO CHANGE
B) all groups responding with a pain level between 7 to 7.6.
C) the distraction group feeling significantly more pain.
D) the experimental groups feeling less pain than the control group.

11

The writer wants to conclude the paragraph with a suggestion from the lead researcher that includes a solution to a specific shortcoming of the study as presented in the passage. Which choice best accomplishes this goal?

A) "There are some limitations to our study."
B) "We recommend that future studies be based on a sample of the general population to obtain the variability in baseline pain tolerance."
C) "That they were all young and healthy could have biased the results toward higher pain tolerance."
D) "The study was conducted under laboratory conditions...the participant's feeling of safety could have influenced pain tolerance time."

CONTINUE

Questions 1-11 are based on the following passage.

Voter Turnout

—1—

According to a 2018 *Washington Post* article, nearly half of the United States voting age population did not cast a ballot in the 2016 presidential election. This statistic puts the US far behind nearly every other democratic nation in terms of voter turnout. There are many explanations for why that happens. What we need is not to look back and ask why, but to look forward and ask how can this problem be solved in the future.

—2—

Quick fixes have been suggested to address this problem of voter [1] turnout such as: automatic voter registration, getting rid of laws requiring voter ID, making Election Day a national holiday, and [2] reminding people to research political candidates in advance. None of these solutions seems to fit the needs of all citizens, however, and as a result they have not been implemented to any success. In a recently published study, political scientist John Holbein, assistant professor at Brigham Young University, offers a unique solution: teaching children social skills.

1

A) NO CHANGE
B) turnout: such as automatic voter
C) turnout, such as, automatic voter
D) turnout: automatic voter

2

Which choice provides an additional supporting example that is most similar to the examples already in the sentence?

A) NO CHANGE
B) holding elections on the weekend.
C) providing information on a candidate's voting record.
D) polling voters for their political affiliation sooner.

CONTINUE

—3—

Holbein's research attempted to answer two related questions. First, assuming that efforts that target adults have small effects, would focusing on children be more effective? Second, [3] there is a relationship between voter participation and social skills? Holbein explains the reason that these are important questions, saying, "voting is a foundational act of democracy," making implementing this mantra into children's minds appear to be a good first priority. He further suggests that inequalities in both voting and policies tend to go hand in hand.

—4—

The notion advanced by Holbein that childhood interventions can improve adult outcomes [4] is hardly new, and the impact of these interventions has been studied for decades. In the early 1990s, a project called "Fast Track" was one of the first to demonstrate the impact of childhood interventions. This study set its focus on high-risk children in four different communities, looking at factors such as the utilization of general and mental health services (between the ages of 12 and 20), arrests, and reduced delinquency rates. Published in 2015, that research delineated the effects of treatment. [5] Improvements in problem solving, emotion regulation, and prosocial behavior were also noted as greatly beneficial.

3

A) NO CHANGE
B) is there a relationship between voter participation and social skills?
C) is there a relationship between voter participation and social skills.
D) are there a relationship between voter participation and social skills.

4

A) NO CHANGE
B) are
C) was
D) were

5

At this point, the writer is considering adding the following sentence

> Improvements in social and self-regulation skills from ages 6 to 11 led to the greatest reduction in crime committed during adolescence.

Should the writer add this sentence here?

A) Yes, because it states one potential benefit of the treatment described earlier in the paragraph.
B) Yes, because it provides a specific example of a social skill that was important to the research.
C) No, because it discusses crime while the rest of the paragraph is about voter participation.
D) No, because it would be better placed elsewhere in this passage.

CONTINUE

—5—

To determine whether these data correlated to greater civic engagement as well, [6] 20 years of data from Fast Track were built upon by Holbein. His program began in 1992 and included 891 children. Half of the children were put into the "treatment" group, and the other half were placed in the "control" group. Children in the first group got special social skills training, which included communication and emotional understanding, as well as social problem-solving, self-control, and friendship.

—6—

When Holbein matched the Fast Track participant data and his own study's data [7] by state voting records, he noticed that those receiving the training were much more likely to have voted. The rate of voting in the treatment group was 6.6 percent higher [8] than the control group. Accounting for factors such as socioeconomic status, age, gender, and race, this number rose to 7.3 percent.

6

A) NO CHANGE
B) Holbein's research built on Fast Track's 20 years of data.
C) Holbein conducted his own research, building on 20 years of data from Fast Track.
D) Fast Track helped Holbein build his own research, with 20 years of data.

7

A) NO CHANGE
B) of
C) from
D) to

8

A) NO CHANGE
B) than those of the control group.
C) than that of the control group.
D) DELETE the underlined portion and adjust punctuation as necessary.

—7—

Holbein offers several explanations as to how social skills may lead to increases in political participation. One's ability to empathize can lead to recognizing social problems, resulting in a greater motivation to participate in politics. In addition, social skills such as emotional regulation, self-control, and grit can help people overcome various barriers in the voting process such as registering, scheduling time to travel, locating the polling place, and learning about the issues and the candidates.

—8—

Most importantly, he notes that current civics education classes are usually **9** dry and boring; they lack the necessary ingredients to create a compelling story and an active and engaged citizen. Instead, Holbein recommends a school program to promote general social skills. The best way to **10** abet such skills is to involve children in volunteering programs. In particular, he suggests ones that provide civic experiences that are hands-on and that increase personal self-control and empathy. In turn, he says, these experiences are likely to result in higher political participation later in life.

Question 11 asks about the previous passage as a whole.

9

Which choice maintains the style and tone of the passage?

A) NO CHANGE
B) nothing to write home about
C) prosaic and wearisome
D) real drags

10

A) NO CHANGE
B) assist
C) nurture
D) tend

Think about the previous passage as a whole as you answer question 11.

11

The writer wants to insert the following sentence.

> He also suggests that his findings on the impact of social skills on voting have important implications for public policy.

To make the passage most logical, the sentence should be placed immediately after the last sentence in paragraph

A) 1.
B) 4.
C) 7.
D) 8.

CONTINUE

Questions 1-11 are based on the following passage.

Stress Eating

What do ice cream, pizza, and donuts have in common? If your mind went to 3AM on a night before a big deadline, you're not alone. According to the American Psychological Association (APA), 38% of American adults report having engaged in unhealthy eating behaviors as a response to stress. For nearly half of these people, stress eating has become a routine: 49% of adults who stress eat [1] do it on at least a weekly basis. While [2] it may or may not be clear that stress eating is a common occurrence, knowledge about the mechanisms that make it so effective is much more elusive. Furthermore, with so many Americans engaging in stress eating to cope with the strains of daily life, it has become even more important to understand the implications of sustaining such an unhealthy habit.

New research has found that eating high-fat foods, such as those commonly consumed during stress eating, actually has a strong [3] anxiolytic or anxiety-reducing, effect. Neurobiologists from the Southern Medical University in Guangzhou, China recently conducted a study to observe the effects that different diets can have on mood. Inspired by a previous finding that linked the enzyme SIRT1 to major depressive disorder, the scientists sought to further explore the relationship between SIRT1 and other psychological afflictions.

1

A) NO CHANGE
B) do so
C) does this
D) did that

2

A) NO CHANGE
B) its
C) they're
D) it's

3

A) NO CHANGE
B) anxiolytic or, anxiety-reducing, effect.
C) anxiolytic, or anxiety-reducing, effect.
D) anxiolytic or anxiety-reducing affect.

CONTINUE

[1] The study was comprised of four groups of mice, organized by both type and duration of diet. [2] Group 1 was fed a high fat diet (defined as 60% kcal fat) and sustained the diet for four weeks, while Group 2 was fed a high fat diet for twelve weeks. [3] In one such test, mice were placed in an open **4** field, when their movements around the area were tracked. [4] Groups 3 and 4 were fed standard diets (10% kcal fat) and sustained the diets for four and twelve weeks, respectively. [5] The effects of these diets were measured in a series of behavioral tests. [6] More movement and exploratory activity indicated a sense of comfort, while refusal to move from the center of the space was a sign of anxiety and stress. **5**

4

A) NO CHANGE
B) field, in which
C) field, where
D) field where,

5

To make this paragraph most logical, sentence 3 should be placed

A) where it is now.
B) after sentence 1.
C) after sentence 5.
D) after sentence 6.

CONTINUE

The results were surprising: reduced anxiety was found in mice who had been fed high-fat diets. Mice in Group 1 expressed lowered levels of SIRT1 compared to the control groups (Groups 3 and 4) and covered **6** almost 400 cm on average during the open field test. However, the positive effects were fleeting; Group 2, which ate a high-fat diet for twelve weeks, did not exhibit anxiolytic effects by the end of their trials. Group 2's performance on the open-field test was **7** actually comparable to that of the control groups, thus showing that they were unable to reap the benefits of a high-fat diet in the long term. Moreover, their diet seemed to have an adverse effect on their movements: even when mice in the group conveyed a desire to explore, they were hindered due to their rapid weight gain.

6

Which choice best reflects the information provided in the graph?

A) NO CHANGE
B) almost 1000 cm
C) more than 1000 cm
D) exactly 400 cm

7

The writer wants the information in the underlined portion to correspond as closely as possible to the information in the graph. Which choice best accomplishes this goal?

A) NO CHANGE
B) significantly less than
C) more interesting than
D) significantly better than

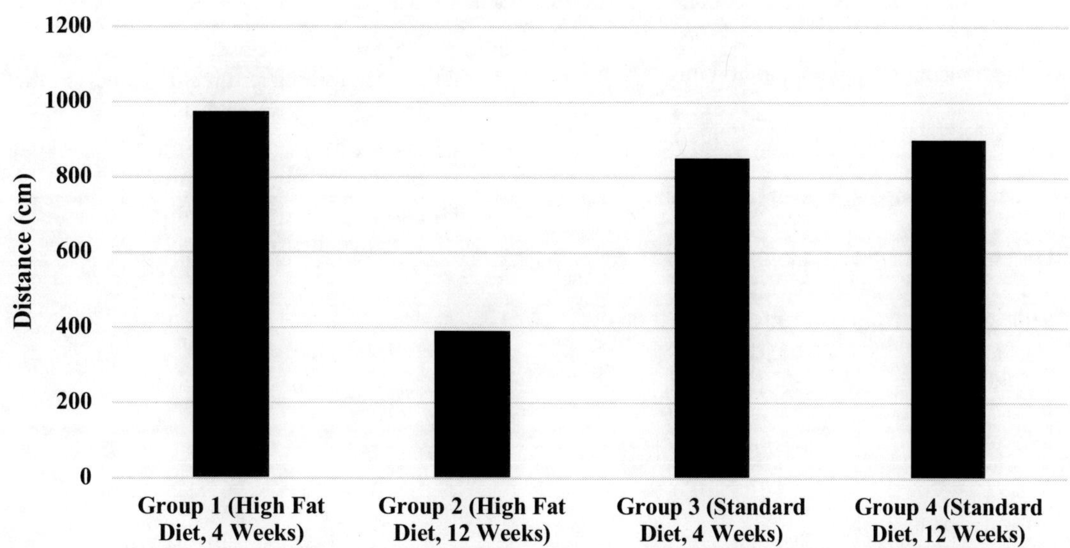

From this study, it is evident that fatty foods work with our brain to lower levels of anxiety, but that our bodies quickly **8** adapted with the change in diet, causing the initial changes in our brain to be reverted. **9** However, eating foods high in unwanted substances has adverse effects on our weight, which can lead to other negative long-term effects like depression. So while it may seem like a good idea to binge while you're feeling stressed, it might work against you as a long-term coping strategy.

But how certain can we be about the results of this study? This research was conducted using mice, which share many genetic traits with humans but are ultimately very different. Therefore, a mitigation of SIRT1 may have completely divergent consequences in humans. **10** The type of fat alone can have vastly differing effects on one's condition: trans fats and saturated fats have been shown to be the most harmful, while polyunsaturated fats and monounsaturated fats can, in fact, benefit both the mind and body. To build on this research, a future study should consider measuring the outcome of diet manipulation in humans, taking the type of fat consumed into consideration. Only with this additional information **11** we can truly have a chance to determine the affects of diet on our mental and physical health.

8

A) NO CHANGE
B) adopt by
C) adopted by
D) adapt to

9

A) NO CHANGE
B) Furthermore,
C) Nevertheless,
D) For instance,

10

Which choice, if added here, would add enough relevant detail to address a shortcoming of the study as presented in the passage?

A) In addition, the human diet is much more complex than that of mice, with many more nutritional nuances that were not addressed in the study.
B) This drawback is common among studies performed on animals.
C) It will be important to run a similar test on humans to verify some of these findings.
D) In fact, it may be enlightening to re-run this research with different types of fat.

11

A) NO CHANGE
B) we can truly determine the effects of diet on our mental and physical health?
C) can we truly determine the effects of diet on our mental and physical health?
D) can we truly determine the effects of diet on our mental and physical health.

CONTINUE

Questions 1-11 are based on the following passage.

Rat Poison

—1—

Second-generation rodenticides, which are used because they're known to be much stronger and deadlier to animals than first-generation rodenticides, do have legitimate uses—for example, if you have an island that is infested with rats and you want to restore its ecosystem. Meanwhile, mostly low-income children and many birds and mammals continue to be poisoned. Pro-raptor efforts such as RATS ("Raptors Are The Solution"), the Hungry Owl Project, and San Francisco's "Don't Take the Bait" consumer campaign [1] <u>is</u> offering education and alternatives to these poisons.

—2—

Many raptors (a bird of prey such as an owl or a falcon that hunts on rodents and other small animals) in the US today [2] <u>was a victim</u> of what is known as "second generation anticoagulant rodenticides," according to the Audubon Society's magazine in 2013. Such poisons, found in such brand names as Havoc, Talon, Generation, Hot Shot, and d-Con, are being used by homeowners, farmers, and exterminators due to the consuming hatred that many people have for mice and rats. According to the article, "the general attitude among the public is, 'if a little poison's good, a lot's better.' But even a

1

A) NO CHANGE
B) are
C) had been
D) was

2

A) NO CHANGE
B) are becoming victims
C) are victims
D) is a victim

CONTINUE

little second-generation rodenticide kills non-target wildlife." If people do not start becoming more judicious with their use of [3] rat poison, then birds, humans, and other wildlife will certainly pay a grave price.

—3—

Many people remain oblivious to the dangers associated with the widespread use of the second-generation rodenticides. It's generally better to use first-generation poisons first, so you have a backup, because if you use your strongest choice first, you have no backup. [4] All a person has to do with a first-generation bait is leave it out for a week. It is just as efficient as a second generation one. In contrast, second-generation rodenticides kill [5] slowly over time, but by the time the rodent expires it contains multiple lethal doses and is deadly to other organisms while the poison is in its system.

—4—

As overuse by consumers is becoming a larger threat to the environment, the EPA has declared second-generation rodenticides too dangerous for public use, ordering their removal from the general market. [6] Accordingly, courts allowed 3 large manufacturers to defy the order, and many stores still have large stocks of these chemicals. At Tufts Cummings School of Veterinary Medicine, [7] clinical, assistant professor, Maureen Murray, has many birds who, as a result of this poisoning, do not have enough red blood cells to deliver oxygen to their bodies.

3

A) NO CHANGE
B) rat poison: birds, humans, and other wildlife
C) rat poison, then birds, humans and, other wildlife
D) rat poison—birds, humans, and other wildlife—

4

Which choice most smoothly and effectively combines these two sentences?

A) All a person has to do with a first-generation bait is leave it out for a week: it's just as efficient as a second generation one.
B) All a person has to do with a first-generation bait is leave it out for a week; and it's just as efficient as a second generation one.
C) Leaving it out for a week, all a person has to do with a first-generation bait is be just as efficient as a second generation one.
D) To be as efficient as a second generation one, a person has to leave a first-generation bait out for a week.

5

A) NO CHANGE
B) slow and over time
C) slow
D) slowly

6

A) NO CHANGE
B) However,
C) Consequently,
D) Therefore,

7

A) NO CHANGE
B) clinical, assistant, professor Maureen Murray
C) clinical assistant professor Maureen Murray
D) clinical assitant professor Maureen Murray,

CONTINUE

—5—

According to a study by the EPA conducted from 1999 to 2003, at least 25,549 children who were under the age of 6 had eaten enough rodenticide to show symptoms of poisoning. Each year, 15,000 calls to the Centers for Disease Control (CDC) come in from parents whose children have eaten a rodenticide. [8] Sometimes small children and pets ingest other harmful materials such as old batteries that leak acid. Since rodents often distribute baits around the home and property, measures to place bait where a child cannot get it often fail.

—6—

As of the time this study was conducted, New York and California [9] have been the only two states to have looked at the problem of rodenticide poisoning. In the state of California, these poisons showed up in 78 percent of mountain lions, 79 percent of fishers, 92 percent of San Diego County raptors, and 84 percent of San Joaquin kit foxes. In New York state, they were found in 81 percent of great horned owls and 49 percent of a dozen different species of necropsied raptors.

8

The author is considering deleting the underlined sentence. Should the author delete it?

A) Yes, because it introduces loosely related information, blurring the focus of the paragraph.
B) Yes, because it undermines the claim that rodenticide is the biggest threat to children's health.
C) No, because it is another example of a reason that people may have to call the CDC.
D) No, because it develops the claim made in the previous sentence.

9

A) NO CHANGE
B) had been
C) was
D) has been

CONTINUE

—7—

After researching these harmful chemicals, New York City's local Audubon Society asked the public to refrain from using Brodifacoum and Difethialone—the most toxic second-generation rodenticides that are poisonous to birds. They also ask people not to use them during nesting season, or only as a last resort. But the organization's director, Glenn Phillips, stopped short of demanding a total ban, arguing that New York City still has a "huge rat problem." The best solution, it appears, is to use second-generation rodenticides in moderation, and  to attempt to keep them away from vulnerable groups like children.

Question 11 asks about the previous passage as a whole.

10

The writer wants a conclusion that recalls a major concern mentioned in the passage. Which choice best accomplishes this goal?

A) NO CHANGE
B) to apply newer technology to counter the rodent issue.
C) to inform other cities to consider moderation as well.
D) to focus on the unseen issues that are contributing to the growing rodent population.

Think about the previous passage as a whole as you answer question 11.

11

To make this passage most logical, paragraph 1 should be placed

A) where it is now.
B) after paragraph 2.
C) after paragraph 5.
D) after paragraph 6.

STOP

Questions 1-11 are based on the following passage.

Generation Gap

Humans are tribal creatures. We have been so since the first hunter-gatherer groups banded together as a means of protection and identity, and one only has to look at our loyalties to groups from political parties to sports teams to know that this still persists in modern society. But [1] <u>how does this tendency to "stay to one's own"—the very core of tribalism manifest in our use of technology?</u> Cell phones, in particular, were created as a means of connecting us to others around the world. But several studies examining the usage of cell phones among different cohorts, or generations, [2] <u>had found</u> that instead of bridging the gap between generations, phones have [3] <u>only brought some families closer together.</u>

Several groups of researchers have noted the trend and have sought to find whether there is truth in the stereotypes regarding different cohorts' usage of cell phones. They focused particularly on the cell phone habits of two prominent generations: Baby Boomers (born in the 1940's–1960's) and Millennials (born in the 1980's–1990's). Baby Boomers have gained a reputation among younger generations for being "technologically illiterate," whereas Millennials are frequently criticized for their apparent attachment to, or borderline obsession with, their phones.

1

A) NO CHANGE
B) how does this tendency to "stay to one's own"—the very core of tribalism—manifest in our use of technology?
C) does this tendency to "stay to one's own"—the very core of tribalism—manifest in our use of technology.
D) does this tendency to "stay to one's own" the very core of tribalism manifest in our use of technology?

2

A) NO CHANGE
B) has found
C) have found
D) were finding out

3

Which choice most smoothly and effectively concludes both this sentence and this paragraph?

A) NO CHANGE
B) connected people on opposite sides of the globe.
C) facilitated growth in business technology.
D) reinforced the tribal barriers that separate age groups.

CONTINUE

The studies compiled data from several different **4** <u>databases. They included</u> the Pew Research Center's research on the topic of cell phone use. The data included information describing both the amount of time spent on mobile devices and the type of content perused during that time. The researchers then compared the findings between the two generations. Millennials were found to spend 3.1 hours per day on their smartphones, while Baby Boomers were noticeably less active, spending only 1.2 hours on their phones per day. 19% of millennials are also more likely to use their phones as a source of mobile news. Comparatively, **5** <u>only 13%</u> of Baby Boomers use their phones in the same way.

4

Which choice most effectively combines the sentences at the underlined portion?

A) databases, which were including
B) databases, including
C) databases but also included
D) databases, and including

5

Which choice provides accurate information from the data in figure 1?

A) NO CHANGE
B) less than 13%
C) about 30%
D) only 19%

Figure 1

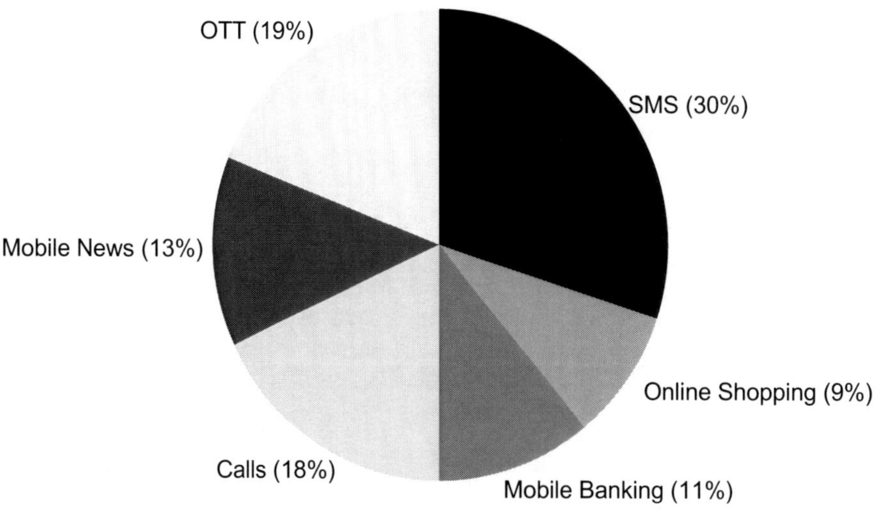

CONTINUE

The researchers also found interesting patterns in the use of SMS (texting) and OTT ("over the top": audio, video, and other media that are delivered via the Internet) that furthered the distinction between the two generations. SMS, or traditional texting, is popular among Boomers, with 30% of them using the service as their primary mode of communication. On the other hand, only **6** <u>10%</u> of Millennials use their phones in this way, and are more likely to use OTT platforms such as Facebook Messenger, Snapchat, and Google Hangouts.

6

Which choice provides accurate information from the data in figure 2?

A) NO CHANGE
B) 11%
C) 19%
D) 24%

Figure 2

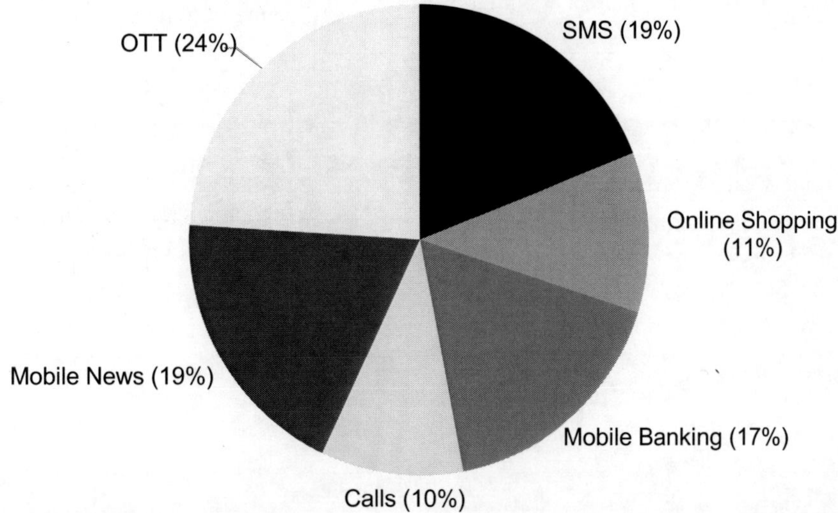

CONTINUE

What could be causing these striking differences and how do they **7** affect these groups' perceptions of one another? For one, Boomers and Millennials were raised in completely different technological environments. In the 1950s, when most Boomers were children, the **8** acclaimed forms of media were television and the radio. This preference still stands today, as the researchers found that Boomers watch TV, read newspapers, and listen to the radio for 4.3 hours per day in addition to using their cell phones. **9** There are many more television programs today than there were in the 1950s. In contrast, Millennials, who came of age in the 80's and 90's and therefore had access to devices such as computers and MP3 players, quickly took to smartphones as they **10** had been immersed in similar technologies since childhood.

As smartphones have become more integrated into daily life and have begun to act as essential tools in **11** communication; Boomers are consequently feeling "left behind." As a result, Boomers have grown to reject assimilation into more tech-savvy communities, which can lead to grave consequences. Understanding these trends is the first step in reconciling the two generations' misperceptions of each other.

7

A) NO CHANGE
B) effect these groups' perceptions
C) affect these group's perceptions
D) effect these group's perception's

8

A) NO CHANGE
B) illustrious
C) famed
D) prominent

9

The writer is considering deleting the underlined sentence. Should the writer make this deletion?

A) Yes, because it contradicts the writer's claim that Boomers are less likely to use smartphones.
B) Yes, because it detracts from the focus of the paragraph by adding loosely related information.
C) No, because it elaborates on the finding conveyed in the previous sentence.
D) No, because it provides evidence in support of the writer's central thesis.

10

A) NO CHANGE
B) immersed
C) were immersing
D) having been immersed

11

A) NO CHANGE
B) communication, Boomers
C) communication Boomers,
D) communication Boomers

CONTINUE

Questions 1-11 are based on the following passage.

Gravitational Waves

Scientists have discovered that neutron stars could be the source of heavy metals, as indicated in recently published research. They claim that these heavy metals were formed when two [1] super-dense, super-small stars called neutron stars—the product of two ultra dense stars colliding—smashed together. On August 17, 2017, astronomers detected these two stars merging in galaxy NGC 4993, more than 130 million light-years away. In this case, the collision of the two massive stars occurred at a velocity of 1/3 of the speed of light, creating gravitational waves. The waves from such a crash, which astronomers say happens only once every 100,000 years, were picked up by scientific instruments on Earth, making scientists able to witness the event for themselves—and the scientific event has been heralded as one of the biggest of 2017.

What's much more interesting than two stars colliding in the night, though, is that this crash possibly resulted in the creation of enormous gold, platinum and silver stores. There is new evidence [2] to a strong link between these heavy metals and dark matter, but at this point it's equally as unlikely as it is likely. The proposal is that during a collision, a black hole settles in the middle of the involved star (or stars). Once inside, the black hole [3] stays there, like white blood cells killing

1

A) NO CHANGE
B) super-dense and super-small stars, called neutron stars, which are the product of
C) super-dense super-small stars, called neutron stars; the product of
D) super-dense, super-small stars (called neutron stars), the product of

2

A) NO CHANGE
B) of
C) in
D) with

3

Which choice best sets up the analogy that follows in this sentence?

A) NO CHANGE
B) eats up the center of the star
C) is hard to capture in photographs
D) is forcefully ejected

CONTINUE

intruders in our immune system. 4 Then the star begins to spin more quickly, resulting in some of its contents flying out. These contents include heavy metals that have a hard time holding their place in the star as a result of such speeds.

The same scientists who were awarded a Nobel Prize for discovering gravitational waves announced that they had detected the collision first, and they alerted astronomers world-wide. 5 For example, as many as fifteen percent of all scientists pointed their telescopes at the sky in unison to record the unprecedented 6 observations, detecting gamma rays, X-rays, radio waves, and visible light (waves predicted by Einstein's theory of relativity). The waves compressed and stretched spacetime and they moved outwards like ripples.

What made this event so unusual was that while the waves were created 130 million years ago, they arrived at Earth at the very moment when astronomers finally had the equipment to detect them. 7 Extraordinary timing such as this is an example of the phenomenon "serendipity". The highly-sensitive instruments register shifts in spacetime that are smaller than a proton. Observatories located in Louisiana and Washington in the US and in Pisa, Italy noticed the waves and were able to use triangulation to locate the source. Only two seconds later, a high-energy burst of light was recorded by gamma-ray telescopes.

4

Which choice most smoothly and effectively combines the sentences at the underlined portion?

A) Spinning more quickly, some contents of the star, such as heavy metals, have a hard time holding their place and flying out.
B) Then the star begins to spin more quickly, resulting in some of its contents flying out—specifically heavy metals that have a hard time holding their place in the star as a result of such speeds.
C) Then, spinning more quickly, the star begins to lose heavy metals, that have a hard time holding their place in the star as a result of such speeds.
D) Then the star begins to spin more quickly; resulting in some of its heavy metals, that have a hard time holding their place in the star, going flying.

5

A) NO CHANGE
B) Nonetheless,
C) Regardless,
D) As a result,

6

A) NO CHANGE
B) observations, they detected
C) observations that were detecting
D) observations, which were detecting

7

The writer is considering deleting the underlined sentence. Should this sentence be kept or deleted?

A) Kept, because it clarifies the scientific importance of the events.
B) Kept, because it elaborates on a claim made in the previous sentence.
C) Deleted, because it merely reformulates statements made earlier in the passage.
D) Deleted, because it introduces loosely related information, blurring the focus of the paragraph.

CONTINUE

In the ensuing days, radio waves, X-rays, and visible, infrared and ultraviolet light were all captured by telescopes. Outstripping all previous astronomical finds, [8] many papers announced results and ruled out hundreds of theories about the event providing alternatives to dark energy, which had been a somewhat perplexing explanation that most astronomers commonly offered as to why the universe is expanding at an accelerated rate.

The rate at which the universe is expanding has puzzled astronomers for years, but these observations finally gave researchers an opportunity to take new measurements of that acceleration. Previous data obtained from watching neutron stars said that the universe was expanding at 73 kilometers per second for each parsec (a standardized space distance of about 3.26 light years). Measurements using ancient light [9] offers an expansion rate of 67 km/s per megaparsec. It turns out that a new measurement indicates 70 km/s per megaparsec, midway between the other two readings. [10] Scientists hope that this event is just the first of many and that they will be able to gain more information from future collisions, like what makes up neutron stars and [11] how they are formed in the first place. Duncan Brown, a member of the research collaboration and astronomer at Syracuse University, says, "we're going to be puzzling over the observations we've made with gravitational waves and with light for years to come."

8

A) NO CHANGE
B) the results of the event were announced in many newspapers, and theories were ruled out about
C) the event resulted in many papers announcing results and ruling out hundreds of theories
D) hundreds of theories about the event were announced in many papers as a result, and ruled out

9

A) NO CHANGE
B) offering
C) has offered
D) offer

10

At this point, the writer is considering adding the following sentence.

> This finding provides valuable insight, but in order to resolve the discrepancy, additional neutron stars will have to be observed.

Should this sentence be added here?

A) Yes, because it addresses both the importance and limitations of the data mentioned earlier.
B) Yes, because it gives a specific example of a similar study done by other researchers.
C) No, because it downplays the importance of the observations discussed in the passage.
D) No, because it would be better placed elsewhere in the passage.

11

Which choice best reflects a topic of interest established earlier in the passage?

A) NO CHANGE
B) why so many people find them interesting.
C) whether they pose a direct threat to our solar system.
D) what do they have to do with dark matter.

Questions 1-11 are based on the following passage.

Data Fail

Predictive analytics, a trendy field of statistics, [1] has pervaded all aspects of modern life from economics to politics to advertising. This technology utilizes artificial intelligence that tracks previous interactions to predict the likelihood of future occurrences. Information about these past actions can be acquired through data mining, in which patterns are [2] extracted by large data sets. [3] The skill required for this task is taught at most universities: Microsoft, for example, bought business social media platform LinkedIn for $26 billion dollars primarily to access its database of over 400 million profiles. So each time you like something on Facebook or click on a link in an email, you can be sure that predictive analytics is recording your actions for future use.

Predictive analytics can be useful for companies that want to maximize profits and efficiency, or [4] for consumers searching for and seeking a tailor-made and seamless shopping experience. But the technology is not without its limitations. In an attempt to predict the number of future flu outbreaks,

1

A) NO CHANGE
B) have pervaded
C) are pervading
D) had pervaded

2

A) NO CHANGE
B) abstracted from
C) extracted with
D) extracted from

3

Which choice most effectively sets up the example and the information that follows?

A) NO CHANGE
B) This data is often bought and sold among companies without our knowledge
C) As artificial intelligence advances, it is becoming a very lucrative market
D) Companies are buying failing social media companies in order to resell them at a profit

4

A) NO CHANGE
B) be useful to consumers that want
C) for consumers seeking
D) DELETE the underlined portion

CONTINUE

Google Flu Trends did not take into account human error, and grossly overstated the number of cases in the 2012-2013 flu season. More humorously, Microsoft's "Cleverbot" was intended to "learn conversational understanding" through data mining of online conversations. However, it began to generate offensive racial comments, and was pulled shortly thereafter. [5] Because predictive analytics sacrifices nuance for accuracy, it ultimately falls short of both.

[6] Moreover, people still had faith in the power of data, and it was only after Donald Trump's unexpected win in the 2016 U.S. presidential election that the techniques behind predictive analytics were questioned. All major vote forecasters had predicted that Hillary Clinton, Trump's opponent, would win in a landslide, citing 70-99% chances of her victory. In an attempt to understand this anomaly, [7] the major polling companies that had made predictions of Clinton's success were contacted by journalists. Amanda Cox, editor of The Upshot, and Sam Wang, of the Princeton Election Consortium, were surprised at the failure of their platforms to predict an accurate outcome, blaming faulty data sourcing such as inaccurate representation in polls and surveys. According to Wang, "state polls were off in a way that has not been seen in previous presidential election years." He further speculated that [8] journalists may have overhyped the likeliest outcome, causing discrepancies between their answers to the polls and their votes in the election itself.

5

The writer is considering deleting the underlined sentence. Should this sentence be kept or deleted?

A) Kept, because it supports the author's claim that predictive analytics is an underdeveloped technology.
B) Kept, because it clarifies the problem that underlies predictive analytics as described in the passage.
C) Deleted, because it contradicts the writer's claim that predicitive analytics is already highly advanced.
D) Deleted, because it undermines the writer's thesis that predictive analytics is highly nuanced.

6

A) NO CHANGE
B) Regardless,
C) Consequently,
D) Thus,

7

A) NO CHANGE
B) Clinton's success, that was predicted by major polling companies were contaacted by journalists
C) journalists contacted the major polling companies that had made predictions of Clinton's success.
D) contact was made between journalists and the major polling companies that had predicted Clinton's success.

8

Based on this passage, which choice provides the most logical transition between the beginning and end of this sentence?

A) NO CHANGE
B) a significant number of voting machines were rigged,
C) polling companies accidentally duplicated their data sets,
D) people might have changed their minds in the election booth,

CONTINUE

Data scientists, on the other hand, were not at all surprised. Erik Brynjolfsson, a professor at MIT, cited misunderstanding of the nature of probability analytics as [9] primary factors of the 2016 election results. "Data science is a tool that is not necessarily going to give you answers, but probabilities." Even if Clinton had had a 99% chance of winning the election, the 1% outcome would still have been a possibility. In addition, election models only accounted for data in a limited time frame, usually dating back two decades. When that data set is expanded to include earlier decades, the predictions change drastically.

Dr. Pradeep Mutalik, a research scientist at the Yale Center for Medical Informatics, had calculated that the vote models used prior to the election would be off by 15 to 20 percent, [10] comparing election modeling to weather forecasting. He stated, "even with the best models, it is difficult to predict the weather more than 10 days out because there are so many small changes that can cause big changes. In mathematics, this is known as chaos."

After the failure of predictive analytics to determine the outcome of one of America's most important events, it might seem like a good idea to let go of the technology completely. However, a better solution entails changing our approach to interpreting the data, rather than relying blindly on it. Instead of treating predicted outcomes as certain, it would be wiser to remember that they are just [11] that, probabilistic predictions.

9

A) NO CHANGE
B) factoring out
C) a primary factor in
D) a factor primarily of

10

Which choice best connects the sentence with the information that follows in the paragraph?

A) NO CHANGE
B) proving that election modeling is actually accurate.
C) supporting previous theories on voter turnout.
D) confirming that updated technology is essential.

11

A) NO CHANGE
B) that; probabilistic predictions.
C) that. Probabilistic predictions.
D) that: probabilistic predictions.

CONTINUE

Grammar Drill 12

Questions 1-11 are based on the following passage.

Korean Pine

It is no secret that there is an ongoing scramble to protect endangered species, [1] or it might come as a surprise to some that trees are among the targets for preservation. In fact, some people go to great lengths to prevent local trees from getting cut down; for instance, the so-called "tree massacre" events of Sheffield, 2015, (during which a company was engaged by the city to cut down many old, healthy trees) prove that saving trees can even be a flashpoint for government officials and [2] one's constituents.

Humans seeking to remove trees for their own personal benefit are not the only culprit of tree extinction, however: climate change and nature itself also play major roles. In cases of widespread disease afflicting entire populations, such as fungus chipping away at Torreya numbers in Florida, solutions have centered on cross-breeding individual trees to create a more resilient species, or [3] to raise them carefully in nurseries. While the Torreya, and other species in extreme peril of extinction, may need to be rehabilitated away from its natural environment, many experts are looking at ways to promote the growth of trees *in situ* [4]. Doing so requires that the trees and their characteristics be monitored during growth seasons in order to evaluate how they adapt.

1

A) NO CHANGE
B) for
C) but
D) and

2

A) NO CHANGE
B) their
C) they're
D) its

3

A) NO CHANGE
B) by raising
C) on raising
D) with sometimes raising

4

At this point, the writer is considering adding the following information.

(or while the tree is alive and in its natural habitat)

Should the writer make this addition?

A) Yes, because it explains a term and its relevance to the passage.
B) Yes, because it describes a specific type of climate discussed in the passage.
C) No, because it blurs the focus of the passage with irrelevant information.
D) No, because it would be better placed elsewhere in the passage.

One of the first studies to do so [5] has taken place from June to August of 2015, targeting the Korea Pine as its subject. At 8 different sites around Northeastern China, between 10 and 20 individual trees were chosen [6] as a representative for all trees of each particular region. The traits of the trees necessary to their survival—also known as functional traits—were measured and sampled, and then analyzed against environmental factors that fell into one of three broad categories: geography, temperature, or moisture.

Measured functional traits included density, thickness, and dryness of leaves, root length, and the phosphorus and nitrogen content of both the leaves and the roots. [7] Phosphorous and nitrogen are critical to plant respiration and growth. These were compared to the geographic factors of latitude (how far north or south the tree was located), longitude (how far east or west the tree was), and altitude. Temperature factors included mean for the whole year, mean for the growth season, and mean for the coldest month. Moisture factors similarly employed means for precipitation of the whole year and the growth season, as well as the potential for moisture to return to the atmosphere [8] from both the land and plants. This process is known as *evapotranspiration.*

By the end of August, several significant relationships were established. The only environmental factors that showed negligible or unclear correlations were longitude and mean annual temperature. Both latitude and altitude showed a

5

A) NO CHANGE
B) have took
C) will take
D) took

6

A) NO CHANGE
B) to be representations, or samples, of
C) for representing and samples of
D) as representatives for

7

The writer is considering deleting the underlined portion. Should this sentence be kept or deleted?

A) Kept, because it introduces how phosphorous and nitrogen are important to plants.
B) Kept, because it describes the plant respiration process.
C) Deleted, because it would be better placed elsewhere in the paragraph.
D) Deleted, because it introduces information that disrupts the transition into the next sentence.

8

Which choice most effectively combines these sentences at the underlined portion?

A) from both the land and the plants, this process is known as *evapotranspiration.*
B) from both the land and the plants; this process is known as *evapotranspiration.*
C) from both the land and the plants, and this is called *evapotranspiration.*
D) from both the land and the plants, known as *evapotranspiration.*

CONTINUE

remarkable connection to all functional traits: as either increased, so too did the dryness of the leaves and the nitrogen content of the leaves and the roots. In the same way, a decrease in leaf density, leaf thickness, root length, and phosphorus content in both leaves and roots **9** coincide with increases in latitude and altitude.

10 Latitude and altitude have similar effects. These two elements are essential to the growth and function of plants, and their interplay over latitude and altitude is quite telling of the adaptation strategies of the Korean Pine. The decreasing phosphorus content demonstrates that the species tends to reduce **11** energy consumption while respiring (storing and making use of nutrients already present in the plant) the further north it is. The increase of nitrogen in leaves indicates that the Korean Pine also has longer-lasting leaves in more northern sites. These two factors show that the Korean Pine tends to adopt a slow-growth strategy in colder climates.

Overall, the results show that it is quite possible to predetermine the best places to regenerate populations of Korean Pine, and may even have implications for targeted nutrient treatment in the soil.

9

A) NO CHANGE
B) coincided
C) coinciding
D) coincides

10

Which choice provides the most effective introduction to this paragraph?

A) NO CHANGE
B) The specific findings on nitrogen and phosphorous content have a broader implication.
C) Sometimes, researchers hit a lucky break in their studies.
D) It is too early to tell what the fate of the Korean Pine will be.

11

A) NO CHANGE
B) energy consumption, while respiring, storing, and
C) energy, consumption, respiring, and storing
D) energy consumption, respiration, storing, and

STOP

Questions 1-11 are based on the following passage.

DNA & Diet

In our current age of information, dieting can seem impossible. It's almost as if we know too much about the influencers of weight loss—gut bacteria, diet type, diet length, stressors, DNA, and personality can each play a role. So, how do we figure out which information to use when determining the best method to lose weight? A recent study says we should forget all of the things we currently know about dieting, and focus on the basics: eating less and sticking to whole foods.

In the study, researchers split 632 overweight or obese people into three groups based on DNA: sensitive to fat, sensitive to carbohydrates, or sensitive to neither. Participants were then told to eat either low-carbohydrate or low fat, based on their predetermined genetics; half of the "neither" group went to each dieting condition. At the end of the study, the researchers recorded how much weight was lost by participants of all groups, and found surprisingly similar numbers regardless of participants' sensitivities. The low-carb, or carbohydrate sensitive, group lost [1] 10.5 pounds, while [2] the fat sensitive group lost 11.5 pounds, on average.

1

Which choice most accurately reflects the information provided in the charts?

A) NO CHANGE
B) 13 pounds
C) 14.5 pounds
D) 15 pounds

2

Which choice provides the most accurate interpretation of the data in the charts?

A) NO CHANGE
B) the salt sensitive group
C) the dairy sensitive group
D) those not sensitive to fat or carbohydrates

Chart 1

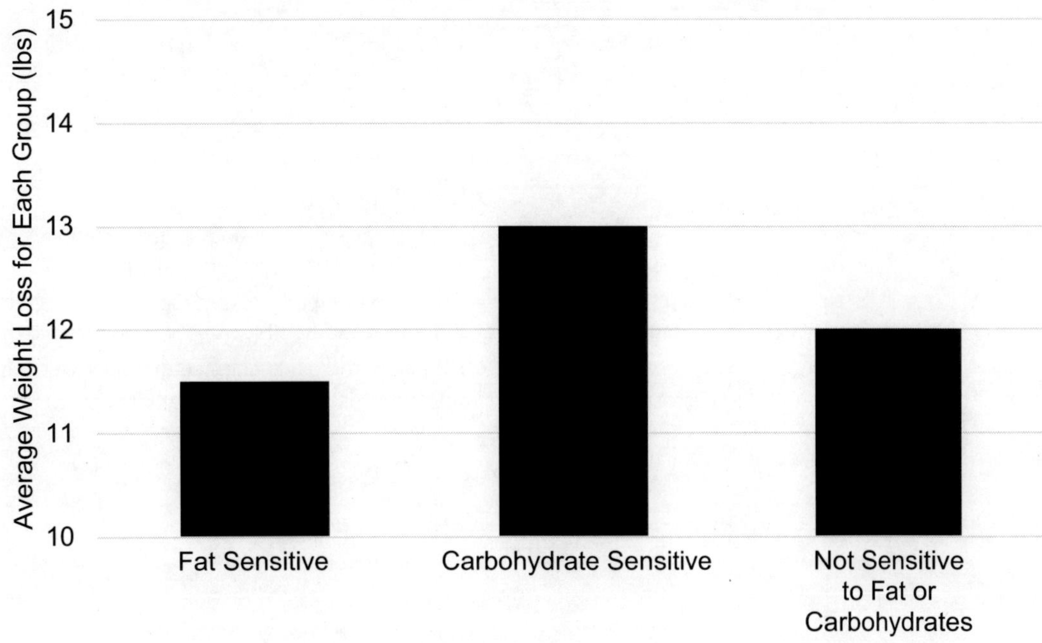

CONTINUE

Chart 2

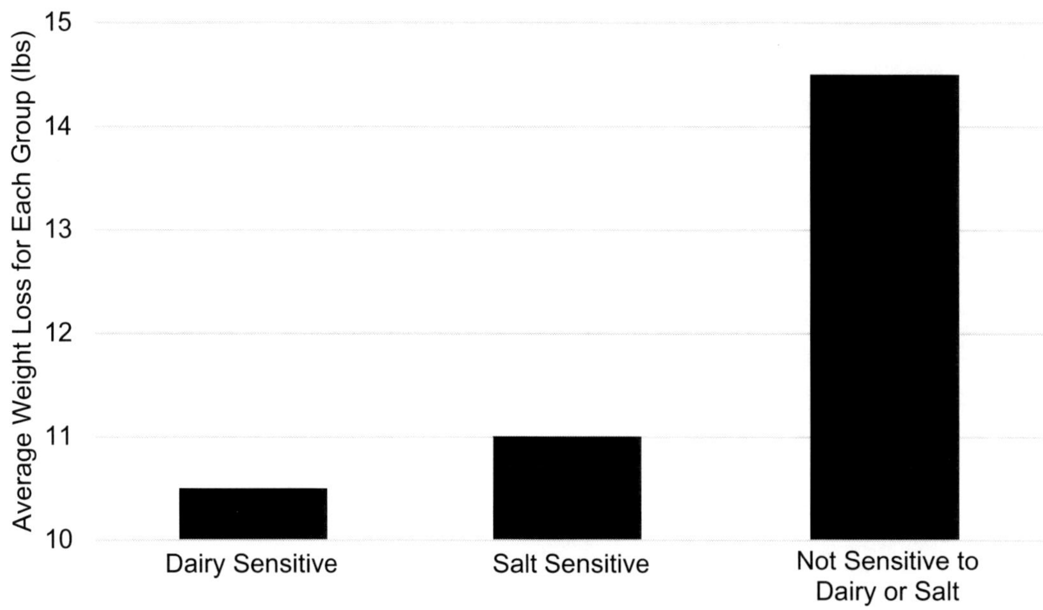

[3] Surprisingly, this study proved that there was one way for everyone to lose weight. This is a result we often see in the real world of dieting—a person sets out to lose weight and becomes disengaged with the diet and therefore ends up losing no weight or binge-eating out of frustration. What was surprising, though, was that nothing about the [4] participants DNA testing predicted who would win at dieting and who would lose, even in a controlled experimental setting.

3

Which choice provides the most effective introduction to this paragraph?

A) NO CHANGE
B) Not surprisingly, in both groups, some people lost no weight or gained weight in the process.
C) Many participants also improved in musculoskeletal strength and flexibility.
D) Some participants claimed that they were able to perform daily tasks with more ease.

4

A) NO CHANGE
B) participation
C) participant's DNA
D) participants' DNA

CONTINUE

The researchers did everything they could to make the diets successful. They told participants not to count calories (a part of dieting known to cause aversion), held group meetings to keep everyone on track, [5] but they also encouraged the dieters to enjoy their food. Furthermore, the study included several helpful tips for dieting in general, including preparing food at home, eating more vegetables and less processed food, and directed participants to never let themselves to get too hungry (or too full).

Still, nothing the researchers attempted during the study predicted weight loss, although it's possible that psychological issues caused stress which led to increased eating, especially of high-fat and high-sugar foods. So, what can be made of this seemingly "null" result? [6] Interestingly, it's the failure of the experiment that gives it its significance. By not finding a good predictor of "diet success" in DNA, [7] support was provided to researchers for aforementioned idea that it's time to go back to the basics with dieting.

5

A) NO CHANGE
B) so they encourage and motivate
C) and even encouraged
D) and encouraging

6

A) NO CHANGE
B) Unfortunately,
C) Therefore,
D) Consequently,

7

A) NO CHANGE
B) the researchers provided support
C) providing support
D) they provide support

Research methods have a major flaw when it comes to **8** human studies by controlling out "extraneous variables," or those that help isolate an independent variable, results are less reflective of the real world. Any time a researcher controls a factor to ultimately make participants more similar, the resulting study lacks in diversity. And while this is optimal for determining cause and effect relationships, it is quite sub-optimal for approximating life-like conditions. **9** If research studies are made more like extra-laboratory conditions, the outcomes are less certain due to the independent variables that the study intends to test. On the other hand, if research studies are more controlled and less life-like, they test the independent-dependent variable relationship, but approximate life much less. **10** Controlling experiments to a high degree may provide an answer about relationships between variables, but lack representation of the real world.

In the case of dieting, the solution is probably simply to take the parsimonious route. While it is important to consider each individual on a case-to-case basis rather **11** then to assume we're all the same, it is equally important to follow the golden rules of dieting: eat more vegetables and less sugar and processed food, while maintaining a regime of not overeating or starving yourself.

8

A) NO CHANGE
B) human studies, by controlling out
C) human studies: by controlling out
D) human study in controlling

9

At this point, the writer is considering adding the following sentence.

> As life has diversity, so too should experiments, but that in itself poses a dilemma.

Should the writer add this here?

A) Yes, because it introduces and defines a term used later in the passage.
B) Yes, because it sets up the relationship between the next two sentences.
C) No, because the tone of the sentence is too conversational.
D) No, because it reformulates the idea in the previous sentence.

10

The writer is considering deleting the underlined portion. Should this sentence be kept or deleted?

A) Kept, because it reinforces the writer's central claim in the passage.
B) Kept, because it sets up a transition into the next paragraph.
C) Deleted, because it merely reformulates the ideas expressed in the previous sentence.
D) Deleted, because it introduces loosely related information, blurring the focus of the paragraph.

11

A) NO CHANGE
B) as
C) but
D) than

CONTINUE

Questions 1-11 are based on the following passage.

Nothing is Certain

For many, going to the doctor's office is tedious: scheduling an appointment requires more effort than we are used to in today's technologically advanced world, and the bureaucratic process is time consuming. Indeed, [1] these factors make this seemingly simple task a daunting one. What causes this is almost a mystifying idea for the millennials: the healthcare industry still runs on paper. Although many hospitals and doctor's offices are now using Electronic Medical Records (EMR), it turns out that less than 10 percent of hospitals report being able to exchange patient records using their digital systems. Instead, they are relying [2] about faxes to exchange patient information and to send referrals to other doctors. [3] Surprisingly, this means that about half of the medical related faxes that are sent never make it to their intended destination.

According to researchers, this is mostly due to the "lack of timeliness" and "delays in completion" within current referral systems. Under the current system, [4] referrals, or recommendations your doctor makes for the care he thinks you require that is out of his area of expertise—are likely to be lost by way of [5] employee underperformance: busy office workers can forget to refill fax machines and can easily misplace an inconspicuous piece of paper. When such mishandling occurs, it can be hard to track or even identify.

1

A) NO CHANGE
B) this factor makes
C) that factor makes
D) factoring

2

A) NO CHANGE
B) to faxes in
C) on faxes to
D) to faxes by

3

A) NO CHANGE
B) Unfortunately,
C) Moreover,
D) Instead,

4

A) NO CHANGE
B) referrals—or
C) referrals or
D) referrals and

5

Which choice provides the most logical transition to the examples that follow?

A) NO CHANGE
B) malicious intervention
C) simple human error
D) intentional negligence

CONTINUE

This lack of communication between health systems, and the complexities of those communications, **6** is of concern to patients and health care professionals alike. It's important to be able to get a patient to an appointment, not just for the health of the patient, but for a health care system to be reputable for the sake of revenue generation. The reputations of hospitals, insurance companies, and medical device and pharmaceutical companies depend upon patients getting to doctors as efficiently as possible. In this way, the health care system can be described as a tightly-knit ecosystem: **7** everything works exactly the way it is intended to, without outside intervention.

According to a paper published in the Journal of General Internal Medicine, unreceived specialist referrals pose a major risk: they often translate into medical errors. Some referrals never arrive at their destination because of failures in technology or in processing. Researchers attempted to determine whether the move from a paper-based referral to an online system with automated track features would lead to an increase in the scheduling of appointments among the patients who were referred. They hoped to minimize the cumbersome **8** process. This would increase the number of appointments and make the process run much more smoothly and efficiently.

The study was designed as part of a staggered implementation of a project designed to improve levels of quality, comparing a control group, consisting of referrals made via faxes, to an intervention group, consisting of referrals

6

A) NO CHANGE
B) are
C) have been
D) being

7

Which choice most accurately reflects both the comparison in this sentence and the main idea of the paragraph?

A) NO CHANGE
B) wild and untamed.
C) this "ecosystem" includes nurses, physicians, technicians, assistants, clerks, and many more.
D) everyone will suffer whenever any part of the communication chain breaks down.

8

Which choice most effectively combines these sentences at the underlined portion?

A) process, increase the number of appointments, and would make the process run much more smoothly and efficiently.
B) process; therefore, there woud be an increasing of number of appointments, and making the process run smoothly and efficiently.
C) process, therefore increasing the number of appointments and making the process run much more smoothly and efficiently.
D) process because increasing the number of appointments is a smoothly efficient process.

CONTINUE

made via the internet. In the intervention group, generalists and specialists shared the referral application, which provided automated notifications to the specialty offices, as well as enhanced communications. Researchers compared scheduling both before and after implementation, as well as the time elapsed between the referral and the appointment.

Among the 40,487 referrals that occurred, only 54% resulted in specialty visits among the control group. In contrast, 83% resulted in specialty visits among the intervention group. Furthermore, median time to an appointment dropped from 168 days to 78 days when the intervention was implemented. [9] They then found that referrals under the intervention condition were "more than twice as likely to have scheduled visits."

The researchers suggest that by making the referral system more efficient, improvements in quality of both care and costs can occur. Similar approaches in other aspects of the medical industry, such as electronic messaging systems, have been reported as useful in facilitating communications between primary and secondary care. Such online systems are almost three times as likely to lead to a visit being scheduled, implying that this health care technology may be able to nearly [10] decimate the problem of failed scheduling. As a result, the researchers anticipate [11] shorter waiting times and greater efficiency and accuracy for appointments in the future.

9

A) NO CHANGE
B) Doctors
C) Patients
D) The researchers

10

A) NO CHANGE
B) eradicate
C) kill off
D) expunge

11

Which choice provides the most logical conclusion to this paragraph and passage as a whole?

A) NO CHANGE
B) that people will enjoy interacting with the healthcare system.
C) there will be fewer visits to emergency rooms and urgent care centers.
D) patients' lives will be forever changed for the better.

CONTINUE

Questions 1-11 are based on the following passage.

Alzheimer's Diet

—1—

For over 100 years, scientists **1** had been attempting to better understand one of the most mysterious disorders of the mind in the world: Alzheimer's Disease. **2** Alzheimer's disease is characterized by a progressive loss of memory, leading ultimately to death. It was first discovered in 1906 by a doctor of the same name.At its conception, the disease was understood only in terms of its phenotypical—non-genetic—symptoms: cognitive decline, confusion, loss of memory, and paranoia. The first Alzheimer's patient died soon after her symptoms were discerned and—upon autopsy—it was discovered that her brain showed severe shrinkage, as well as abnormal deposits in what was left of its mass, compared to the brain of an individual not plagued with Alzheimer's now-hallmark symptoms.

—2—

One of the possible biological markers is a protein called 'tau.' In a normally functioning brain, tau poses no threat. But in an Alzheimer's-affected brain, tau begins to act abnormally, and becomes tangled up, possibly explaining the abnormal deposits Dr. Alzheimer discovered. **3** Another, second hypothesis is that proteins called amyloids are disrupting neuronal connections by getting in the way of the synapse, or space through which neurons send communication back

1

A) NO CHANGE
B) have been attempting
C) attempted and tried
D) DELETE the underlined portion

2

Which choice most smoothly and effectively combines the underlined sentences?

A) In 1906, a doctor of the same name discovered it, Alzheimer's disease is characterized by progressive loss of memory and ultimately to death.
B) Alzheimer's disease is characterized by a progressive loss of memory, leading ultimately to death; it was discovered in 1906 by a doctor of the same name.
C) First discovered in 1906 by a doctor of the same name, Alzheimer's disease is characterized by a progressive loss of memory, leading ultimately to death.
D) Alzheimer's disease, being that it was discovered in 1906 by a doctor of the same name, is characterized by a progressive loss of memory, leading ultimately to death.

3

A) NO CHANGE
B) Besides this first possibility is a second possibility
C) Another hypothesis, is
D) A second hypothesis is

CONTINUE

and forth. As neighboring neurons are blocked by amyloid (and thus blocked from communicating), [4] they shorten and eventually stop sending information throughout the brain. [5] Even though many do not understand how neurons and proteins interact, people become confused, and subsequently forgetful of important information that allows them to perform everyday functions like get to work. Both of these hypotheses have been studied in parallel for many years without either one being [6] disproven, and implying that they likely both play a part in causing the disorder.

—3—

Interestingly, neither tau nor amyloid researchers have yet been able to show exactly how their respective protein has caused the disorder, [7] and both have proved some connection between their research and the Alzheimer's genotype, or genetic markers. Because of this, and because of how devastating and prevalent the disorder is, it is paramount to find some underlying mechanism by which to hold off its onset. To do this, scientists are turning to dietary possibilities, the first of which is called the MIND (Mediterranean intervention for neurodegenerative disorders diet). To follow this diet, one must follow a strict regimen of eating more leafy greens, vegetables, nuts, berries, legumes, whole grains, fish, poultry, and olive oil— while eating less red meat, butter, cheese, fried food, and sweets. The diet is still in [8] its' early days of testing, but it has been shown to fight inflammation, one of the symptoms coupled with cognitive decline.

4

A) NO CHANGE
B) it shortens
C) shortening
D) they short out

5

Which choice most effectively transitions from the previous sentence and sets up the information that follows in this sentence?

A) NO CHANGE
B) In typical Alzheimer's cases,
C) While other degenerative diseases attack different bodily systems,
D) Without effective communication among critical memory areas of the brain like the hippocampus,

6

A) NO CHANGE
B) disproven and implied, that they
C) disproven; implying that they
D) disproven, implying that they

7

A) NO CHANGE
B) although
C) however,
D) DELETE the underlined portion

8

A) NO CHANGE
B) it's early day's
C) early days'
D) its early days

CONTINUE

—4—

In the future, researchers hope to be able to use this diet as an early intervention for people who are at-risk for developing Alzheimer's disease. If individuals who have known instances of Alzheimer's in their family begin modifying their eating habits based on this diet as early as their 40th birthday, it is possible that they can prevent either tau or amyloid or both from attacking their neurons and disrupting vital connections. While this seems to be working with patients who have [9] adapted the MIND diet, the scientific community is still far from proving the direct connection that would link it to Alzheimer's prevention. There is yet much to be learned about genetic causes of the disorder, but this information could prove to be a crucial factor in linking the competing hypotheses and ultimately solving the puzzle.

9

A) NO CHANGE
B) adaptations of
C) adopted
D) adepted

CONTINUE

—5—

With the introduction of innovative brain scanning techniques that can, while a patient is alive, provide a still image of the brain or reveal brain chemical or electrical processes in real time, researchers now have a better understanding of what an Alzheimer's-affected brain looks like from inception of the disorder throughout its entire progression. **10** The most effective brain scanning technique for Alzheimer's is fMRI, which was developed in 1990 by Seiji Ogawa. What has been found is similar to the shrinkage and deposits originally discovered by Dr. Alzheimer, but further exploration also shows abnormal transmission of neurotransmitters in the brain and possible biological markers of the disease.

Question 11 asks about the previous passage as a whole.

10

The writer is considering deleting the underlined sentence. Should the writer make this deletion?

A) Yes, because it would be better placed elsewhere in the passage.
B) Yes, because it blurs the focus of the paragraph with loosely related information.
C) No, because it specifies the best type of brain scanning technique.
D) No, because it defines a term that is essential to the rest of the passage.

Think about the previous passage as a whole as you answer question 11.

11

To make this passage most logical, paragraph 5 should be placed

A) where it is now
B) after paragraph 1
C) before paragraph 3
D) after paragraph 3

Questions 1-11 are based on the following passage.

Chronic Bronchitis

Air pollution is a favorite topic of conversation among those who are concerned about the future of the environment and global warming, as carbon dioxide is both the leading air pollutant and the leading cause of rising temperatures. A second [1] affect of air pollutants, though, is the impact they have on those who breathe them in. Bronchitis, a common clinical condition defined by [2] chronic cough and mucus production can be caused by the same viral culprits that give us the flu. There is also a second—less well known but infinitely more present—cause of bronchitis: breathing in particulate matter, more commonly known as air pollutants. [3]

While the relationship between short-term air pollution exposure and acute respiratory symptoms is well established, limited data suggest a relationship between long-term ambient pollution exposure and COPD (chronic obstructive pulmonary disorder), of which chronic bronchitis is a [4] phenotype—a physical symptom that manifests itself as a result of contracting any of the disorders that fall under the umbrella of COPD such as bronchitis or emphysema.

1

A) NO CHANGE
B) infection
C) effect
D) affectation

2

A) NO CHANGE
B) chronic cough and mucus production,
C) chronic cough, and mucus production
D) chronic cough, and mucus production,

3

At this point, the author is considering adding the following sentence.

> A recent study by the National Institute of Health seeks to determine just how much of an effect everday air pollution can have on both acute (short-term) and chronic (long-term) bronchitis.

Should this be added here?

A) Yes, because it connects the discussion earlier in the paragraph to the discussion that follows in the passage.
B) Yes, because it introduces the group of researchers discussed in the next paragraph.
C) No, because it would be better placed elsewhere in the passage.
D) No, because it restates information that was provided in the previous two sentences.

4

A) NO CHANGE
B) phenotype; a physical symptom
C) phenotype. A physical symptom
D) phenotype, and a physical symptom

CONTINUE

There is a paucity of data on the possible relationships between classically defined chronic bronchitis and long-term exposure to particulate matter, [5] pieces of dust that remain in the atmosphere as a result of gas fumes or dirt that are unknowingly ingested every day. To address [6] these in a larger study, using specific outcome definitions and advanced exposure assessments, the NIH investigated the association between residential exposure to small and large particulate matter, and both incident (newly diagnosed cases) and prevalent (previously occurring cases) chronic bronchitis in a nationwide cohort of more than 50,000 U.S. women.

Outcome Assessment Chronic bronchitis was defined according to the classical symptom-based definition of chronic cough productive of phlegm for at least 3 months out of a year for a minimum of 2 consecutive years. Participants were asked about the presence of cough and phlegm independently, and the duration of each symptom was specified using questions derived from the British Medical Research Council adult respiratory symptom standardized questionnaire. Women with cough and phlegm symptoms, both present for at least 3 months per year out of the previous 2 years, [7] are considered to have chronic bronchitis.

5

The author is considering deleting the underlined portion and adjusting the punctuation as necessary. Should the author do this?

A) Yes, because it relays information already presented earlier in the paragraph.
B) Yes, because it introduces information that is only loosely related to the main idea of the paragraph.
C) No, because it elaborates on a concept that is central to the main idea of the passage and study.
D) No, because it introduces the author's central thesis of the overall passage.

6

A) NO CHANGE
B) a relationship
C) these relationships
D) it

7

A) NO CHANGE
B) were
C) had been
D) is being

CONTINUE

[1] At baseline, 1,351 (3.1%) women met symptom-based criteria for chronic bronchitis, whereas 4,698 (10.6%) participants reported ever having had a physician diagnosis of chronic bronchitis. [2] No statistically significant associations were found between incident chronic bronchitis and any of the air pollution exposures. [3] For prevalent chronic bronchitis, a statistically significant positive association was seen with large particulate matter. [4] Similar **8** magnitudes of association with prevalent chronic bronchitis were seen for nitrous oxide and small pieces of particulate matter, but were not statistically significant. [5] Large particulate matter was also statistically significantly associated with chronic cough, chronic phlegm, and chronic cough or phlegm. **9**

8

A) NO CHANGE
B) severities
C) vastness
D) volumes

9

The author wants to add the following sentence.

> Prevalent chronic cough was reported by 3,749 (8.5%) and chronic plegm by 2,776 (6.3%) participants at baseline.

This sentence should be placed

A) before sentence 1.
B) after sentence 1.
C) after sentence 3.
D) after sentence 5.

CONTINUE

This is the largest study to [10] check up on the association between classically defined chronic bronchitis and long-term ambient air pollution exposure using a validated national exposure model. The team did not find an association between incident chronic bronchitis and any of the air pollution measures. [11] Moreover, exposure to higher concentrations of large particulate matter was significantly associated with all prevalent outcomes: chronic bronchitis, chronic cough, chronic phlegm, and chronic cough plus phlegm. The researchers also found that nitrous oxide exposure was significantly associated with chronic cough and chronic cough or phlegm. These findings provide evidence that long-term ambient air pollution exposure, especially to large particulate matter, is a risk factor for chronic bronchitis and the chronic respiratory symptoms of cough and phlegm that define it.

10

A) NO CHANGE
B) investigate
C) audit
D) analyze and evaluate

11

A) NO CHANGE
B) Indeed,
C) Consequently,
D) However,

STOP

Questions 1-11 are based on the following passage.

STEM PISA

In 2012, the media coverage that followed the results of tests administered by the Program for International Student Assessment (PISA) alarmed many Americans. The U.S. ranked 35th in mathematics, and 27th in science. Politicians, educators, parents, and students voiced a growing fear that American students are rapidly falling behind in STEM subjects (science, technology, engineering, and mathematics), and that this **1** widening, growing gap will lead to an economically crippling shortage of sufficiently educated applicants for jobs in STEM-related fields. It would seem logical then that to fill this growing demand for STEM workers, schools and educators in the US should devote more of their limited time and resources to STEM subjects.

However, the idea that American STEM educators suddenly cannot produce competent employees to fill jobs in STEM-related fields depends on assumptions worth interrogating. **2** Therefore, the results of the PISA tests are not shockingly low, and when considering the current job market for American STEM workers, the educational system in the U.S. is actually providing an ample number of graduates with STEM degrees each year.

1

A) NO CHANGE
B) wider and expanded gap
C) widens the gap
D) widening gap

2

A) NO CHANGE
B) In fact,
C) However,
D) Nevertheless,

CONTINUE

Every three years the Program for International Student Assessment tests 15-year-old students from a growing number of educational systems around the world in various subjects, including reading, math, and science. In 2012, out of 65 educational systems, the U.S. ranked 35th in math, and 27th in science. If this number sounds low, consider that many of the educational systems at the top of the list represent [3] nations that prioritize learning above all else. There are a number of reasons we can expect more affluent populations to perform better in schools; factors such as greater school funding, additional resources such as tutors, and a higher likelihood of having a parent or guardian who went to college [4] place students in affluent populations at an advantage. Educational systems like [5] Hong Kong can reasonably be expected to outperform the U.S. system, and many have for decades.

Since the PISA tests were initiated in 2000, the U.S. has never outranked Hong Kong, Belgium, or tens of other smaller educational systems. American PISA scores in STEM subjects are not the best in the world, but they are not decreasing rapidly, nor are they [6] shockingly low—considering that the U.S. provides education to a large and economically diverse population.

3

The author wants to introduce two factors that put the rankings of the U.S. into perspective. Which choice best accomplishes this goal?

A) NO CHANGE
B) much smaller and wealthier populations.
C) older, more cohesive educational systems.
D) many allies and trading partners of the U.S.

4

A) NO CHANGE
B) places
C) placed
D) placing

5

A) NO CHANGE
B) that of Hong Kong's
C) the Hong Kong system
D) those of Hong Kong

6

A) NO CHANGE
B) shockingly low; considering that the U.S.
C) shockingly low. Considering that the U.S.
D) shockingly low, and considering that the U.S.

CONTINUE

The Department of Commerce reported in 2010 that 7.6 million people were working in jobs related to STEM. 4.7 million of those workers had college degrees, and only [7] 2.9 million of those graduates majored in STEM. This means that 1.4 million STEM workers went to college but majored in something else. In 2014 the Census Bureau reported that only 26% of those with [8] bachelor's degree's in STEM related fields, actually work in those fields now. Majoring in a STEM subject in college does not guarantee that students can or will find jobs in STEM, and not all STEM workers with college degrees majored in a STEM-related subject. The economic principle of supply and demand tells us that if there is a shortage of STEM workers, their services would be in high

7

Which choice offers an accurate interpretation of the data in the graph and logically follows the pattern established in the first half of the paragraph?

A) NO CHANGE
B) 18%
C) 38%
D) 3.3 million

8

A) NO CHANGE
B) bachelors degrees in STEM related fields,
C) bachelor's degrees in STEM related fields
D) bachelors degrees; in STEM related fields,

Educational Backgrounds of STEM Workers, 2010

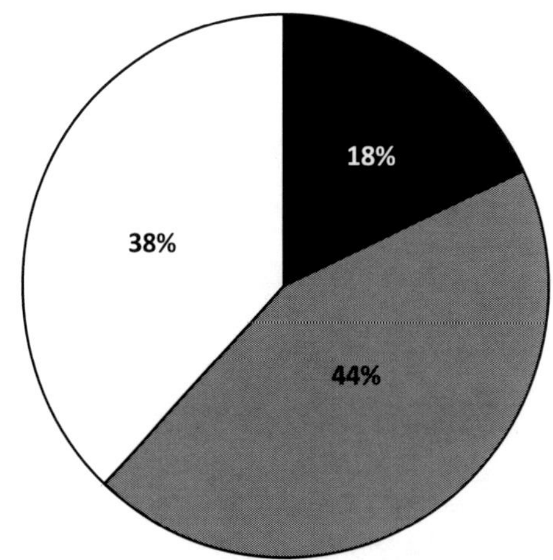

CONTINUE

demand and their wages would rise. [9] But largely stagnant wages in many sectors of the STEM workforce suggest otherwise.

Many of the most specialized and educated STEM workers, such as engineers, have experienced relatively stagnant wages in recent decades compared to non-STEM workers, and also in comparison to STEM workers as a whole. This means that many of the STEM workers with degrees in non-STEM subjects have salaries that are growing more quickly than [10] that of engineers who possess advanced educations in STEM subjects.

There is room for improvement in the American educational system, STEM subjects included. Certainly, American students could achieve higher-ranking PISA scores if the appropriate resources [11] had been devoted to that end. However, there is not a sudden shortage of highly-educated applicants for jobs in STEM fields, nor does our educational system struggle to produce an adequate number of graduates with advanced degrees in STEM fields. There is arguably a case to be made, rather, that salaries for many of the most desirable STEM jobs in the U.S. are lower than they might be if the market were less saturated than it is now.

9

The author is considering deleting the underlined sentence. Should this sentence be kept or deleted?

A) Kept, because it transitions from this paragraph into the discussion that follows.
B) Kept, because it specifies a STEM field that has experienced stagnant wages.
C) Deleted, because it merely reformulates an idea from the previous sentence.
D) Deleted, because it directly contradicts the writer's overall thesis about the growth of STEM fields.

10

A) NO CHANGE
B) engineers who
C) those of engineers who
D) the job prospects of engineers who

11

A) NO CHANGE
B) were
C) were being
D) was

CONTINUE

Questions 1-11 are based on the following passage.

Drowsy Driving

In October 2017, the National Highway Traffic Safety Administration released statistics on vehicle crashes from 2011 to 2015. More specifically, these statistics revealed that drowsy driving poses a significant risk: out of 6,296,000 crashes, 90,000 involved drowsy driving. Furthermore, according to a CDC Morbidity and Mortality Report from 2013, a survey conducted from 2009 to 2010 indicated that 1 in 25 drivers had reported falling asleep at the wheel in the prior 30 days. [1] In 2017, there were 10, 880 deaths related to driving under the influence of alcohol according to the NHTSA. What this means is that drowsy driving is extremely common and extremely dangerous. Laws against it have helped in some areas, but individual detection and prevention [2] is equally important in reducing the number of crashes involving drowsy driving.

To start, many car manufacturers have been developing technologies that could alert drivers to impending collisions or abnormal driving behavior, such as drifting in the lanes. While this may help lessen the number of accidents, there is certainly quite a way to go: most of these technologies are available only in luxury or brand-new cars. [3] This makes new safety technology inaccessible to those who are less affluent.

1

The author is considering deleting the underlined sentence. Should this sentence be kept or deleted?

A) Kept, because it provides a helpful point of comparison for the earlier statistics.
B) Kept, because it introduces the author's central claim about the dangers of drunk driving.
C) Deleted, because it contradicts the ideas in the previous sentence.
D) Deleted, because it interrupts the logical order of ideas with loosely related information.

2

A) NO CHANGE
B) are
C) were
D) had been

3

Which choice provides the most logical conclusion to this paragraph while also anticipating the discussion that follows?

A) NO CHANGE
B) Furthermore, it may be one thing for technology to detect driver or car behavior, but quite another to predict it.
C) Examples of such car manufacturers are Volvo, Audi, and Mercedes.
D) There was an experiment in France that was done to explore whether it was possible to predict drowsy driving with artificial neural networks.

An experiment was run at Aix-Marseilles University in France to test several factors commonly measured to determine drowsiness. The premise of the experiment was to feed independent variables about [4] drivers participating in the experiment into one of two artificial neural networks (ANNs). One would determine whether the driver was drowsy, and the other would predict how soon the driver would become drowsy. The output of the ANNs would then be matched against the evaluations of video footage by two scorers. However, because drowsiness occurs on a scale, the ANNs would be trained with participant information and driving time.

[1] Both ANNs would have access to the information about driving performance, physiological information, and behavioral data. [2] All 21 participants were questioned on susceptibility to motion sickness and drowsiness, age, amount of sleep, driving frequency, and circadian type (essentially whether they were predisposed to prefer morning or evening). [3] This information would then be used as participant information. [4] Driving information—or car input—was based on 7 different factors, including position in lane and speed. [5] For the physiological input, heart and respiration rates (and their variations) were measured. [6] The behavioral input included blink duration and frequency, percentage of eye closure, rapid eye movement between fixed points, and head rotation. [5]

4

A) NO CHANGE
B) drivers that participate
C) participating drivers
D) drivers who participate

5

In order to make this paragraph most logical, sentence 1 should be placed

A) where it is now.
B) after sentence 3.
C) after sentence 5.
D) after sentence 6.

CONTINUE

Participants were put in a driving simulator set in a room with a temperature of about 75° Fahrenheit. The experiment was run just after lunch **6** (right about the time you would want to take a nap), and lasted one hour and forty or fifty minutes. They would drive on a "highway" for about an hour and a half, during which they would encounter no traffic, except for a sudden burst of 22 cars on the right of the highway. This was intended to alter the driver's drowsiness. They would then continue, turning off the "highway" to reach a city, and then drive through the city for about 5 minutes.

In all cases, the ANNs performed best if **7** they also had access to both driving time and participant information. Behavioral input also seemed to correlate to the top performances. **8** Indeed, if driving time or participant information was not included, the behavioral input or combined input led to the best results in the ANNs. In both detection and prediction, the car input by itself led to poor results. Ultimately, the researchers found that a comprehensive ANN can predict drowsiness around 5 minutes before it happens.

6

The author is considering deleting the underlined portion. Should the author do this?

A) Yes, because it introduces irrelevant information.
B) Yes, because it contradicts the author's thesis.
C) No, because it defines a key concept.
D) No, because it elaborates on the significance of the timing.

7

A) NO CHANGE
B) it
C) one or the other
D) the drivers

8

A) NO CHANGE
B) At any rate
C) However,
D) Nevertheless,

CONTINUE

These results show that current technology may be measuring some of the wrong—or simply insufficient—aspects of drowsy driving. For instance, technology that relies on lane drift or departure as indicators may not be accurately monitoring drowsiness: the driver may be distracted by a spilled beverage or [9] problems at school or work. At best, the researchers conclude, car behavior by itself is more suited to detecting severe drowsiness, but likely would not be able to monitor it over a longer period of time. Moreover, while driving time was found to be an important factor, it could never be used by itself to predict drowsiness: it would be unable to take into consideration any event that would wake up a driver.

In the future, it would be necessary to replicate this experiment before basing any new technology on [10] it's findings. The participants were a fairly small group, and ranged from 20 to 27 years old. The experiment also took place in a controlled setting, so it would also be prudent to test the ANNs on people who are [11] truly driving—perhaps not on busy streets, but maybe on a closed course. The researchers themselves also suggest that, since it is difficult to measure the very things they used for behavioral input in an actual car, there should in fact be a focus on developing models that use driving and physiological information.

9

Which choice provides a second supporting example similar to the one already in this sentence?

A) NO CHANGE
B) traffic lights.
C) intrusive thoughts.
D) a rowdy child in the backseat.

10

A) NO CHANGE
B) there findings
C) its' findings
D) its findings.

11

A) NO CHANGE
B) truly driving but perhaps
C) truly driving perhaps,
D) truly driving; perhaps

CONTINUE

Questions 1-11 are based on the following passage.

Pluto's Fall

In 2006, the International Astronomical Union (IAU) defined planets as celestial bodies that pass three tests, namely that they "are in orbit around the sun"; they have sufficient mass to assume "a nearly round shape," also called hydrostatic equilibrium; and they have "cleared the neighborhood" around their orbits. [1] For example, dwarf planets pass only the first two tests.

Because of the implementation of this definition, Pluto was suddenly [2] discounted to dwarf status—not even a planet—in 2006, after enjoying 75 long years of planetary-status inclusion. This change has proven to be controversial: [3] astronomers, planetary scientists, and the public alike are taking sides concerning Pluto's proper classification. What is the hard science that lies behind these events? Do scientists have an objective basis for their differences of opinion? Is the planet Pluto the victim of a shady conspiracy and personal vendetta, or merely the casualty of changes and advancements in the field? A May 2016 article published in *The Guardian* attempts to unravel the details of the possibly shady demotion of the ninth planet, which was discovered in 1930 by astronomer Clyde Tombaugh.

1

A) NO CHANGE
B) Indeed,
C) To that end,
D) However,

2

A) NO CHANGE
B) demoted
C) weakened
D) decreased

3

The author is considering deleting the underlined portion and adjusting punctuation as necessary. Should the author do this?

A) Yes, because it merely reformulates an idea from the previous sentence.
B) Yes, because it would be better placed elsewhere in the paragraph.
C) No, because it elaborates on a statement from earlier in the sentence.
D) No, because it defines a term that is important in the rest of the passage.

After Tombaugh discovered Pluto, another astronomer named Brian Marsden reportedly set out to discredit him. According to the article, a planetary scientist named Stern reports that after Tombaugh died in 1997, "Marsden went on a jihad to diminish his reputation by removing Pluto from the list of planets." Marsden apparently found his opportunity at the 2006 meeting of the IAU in Prague, in which attendees agreed to have a vote to demote Pluto. Interestingly, the vote that determined Pluto's fate consisted of only 4% of the total attendance or about 400 members. Stern criticized the vote, saying that astronomers do not have the specialized scientific knowledge that planetary scientists have: "just as you shouldn't go to a podiatrist for brain surgery, you shouldn't go to an astronomer for expert advice on planetary science."

Claiming their objectiveness, **4** they maintain that when they voted, they used three tests that evolved over years of committee discussions leading up to the 2006 vote. Of the tests it had to pass, **5** "clear the neighborhood around its orbit" is a requirement that Pluto failed, meaning that when a planet forms, it must achieve what is known as gravitational dominance, with no other bodies of similar size under its gravitational influence except for **6** it's satellites.

4

A) NO CHANGE
B) we
C) both astronomers
D) members of the IAU

5

A) NO CHANGE
B) the requirement to "clear the neighborhood around its orbit" is something Pluto failed,
C) Pluto failed the requirement that it "clear the neighborhood around its orbit,"
D) failure to "clear the neighborhood around its orbit" happened to Pluto,

6

A) NO CHANGE
B) their satellites
C) its satellites
D) its satellite's

CONTINUE

Stern objects to the process and criteria used to demote Pluto at the IAU meeting. "Science isn't about voting," he says. "We don't vote on the theory of relativity. **7** We only vote on planets. The image of scientists voting gives the public the impression that science is arbitrary." His objection to the third test is shared by Dr. Gerald van Belle, an astronomer who attended the IAU voting session. Of a planet clearing the neighborhood around its orbit, van Belle says, "I have yet to encounter a succinct mathematical definition of this concept." Van Belle calls the third test an "ill-defined, dynamic argument." Stern argues that Neptune does not even pass the third test and should also be demoted if this **8** were the standard used to define all planetary objects.

Meanwhile, other astronomers **9** like Brown, a professor of planetary astronomy at CalTech, see things much differently. "Pluto," according to Brown, "is essentially this insignificant chunk of ice that really is of no consequence in the solar system." In this way, whether Pluto had passed the three tests or not, it would never be worthy in his eyes of planetary status. **10** Brown is unapologetic in his stance, and has written a memoir entitled, "How I Killed Pluto, and How It Had It Coming."

7

Which choice provides a second example most similar to the one in the previous sentence?

A) NO CHANGE
B) We take part in the democratic process.
C) We sometimes vote in elections.
D) We don't vote on evolution.

8

A) NO CHANGE
B) would of
C) should be
D) had been

9

A) NO CHANGE
B) like, Brown, a professor
C) like Brown a professor
D) like Brown, a professor,

10

At this point, the writer is considering adding the following sentence.

> He neglected to mention how he feels about Neptune's planetary status.

Should the wrtier make this addition here?

A) Yes, because it addresses an important distinction between Neptune and Pluto.
B) Yes, because it elaborates on a concept introduced earlier in the passage.
C) No, because it disrupts the paragraph's discussion with unnecessary information.
D) No, because it contradicts the idea that Pluto is a dwarf planet.

CONTINUE

In a 2008 press release published by the Planetary Science Institute based in Tucson, Arizona, scientists agreed to disagree. "We all have a conceptual image of a planet. Therefore, we need a term that encompasses all objects that orbit the Sun or other stars." Larry Lebofsky, who works there as Senior Education Specialist, thinks of this as a teachable moment for all scientists who wish to maintain objectivity in their respective fields. **11** For the foreseeable future, everyone, including the scientists, has something to learn.

11

The author wants a conclusion that reinforces the idea of the previous sentence. Which choice best accomplishes this goal?

A) NO CHANGE

B) Indeed, it seems that a standard planetary definition remains unsolved.

C) Perhaps as technologly advances, the IAU will agreen on standard characteristics for planetary classification.

D) Without objectivity, scientists and the IAU will lose credibility with the public at large.

Questions 1-11 are based on the following passage.

Diabetic Lifestyle Improvements

—1—

When someone is newly diagnosed as prediabetic or diabetic, he or she is often at a loss about how to proceed. Such a diagnosis can be daunting, overwhelming, and confusing. Patients may have a variety of thoughts, feelings, and emotions, due in part to the plethora of seemingly contradictory advice they receive. In an unpublished study, user experience researcher Aimee Richardson [1] seeking to discover how well the diabetes section of a medical website, www.MyDoctorOnline.com, supported the needs of those who are diagnosed as pre-diabetic. Her research sought to identify gaps in the website's [2] ability to fulfill patient needs. Richardson focused on exploring both specific content and site organization.

—2—

Subjects in the study had varied needs: some were younger, diagnosed years ago, and had developed strategies to keep their illness under control; others were older, newly diagnosed, and were overwhelmed by all the potential changes they'd need to make. Richardson sought to understand how one website might meet the needs of these different patients. To test the effectiveness of the website, [3] Richardson conducted her research using three different methodologies with five subjects: in-person interviews, a task-based usability study using the "think-aloud" protocol, and a desirability list (adjective test).

1

A) NO CHANGE
B) had seeked to discover
C) was seeking to discover and find
D) sought to discover

2

Which choice most effectively combines the sentences at the underlined portion?

A) ability to fulfill and meet patient needs, specific content, and site organization.
B) specific content and site organization, which would tell her whether or not it met the needs of patients.
C) exploration of patient needs, specific content, and site organization.
D) ability to fulfill patient needs, exploring both specific content and site organization.

3

A) NO CHANGE
B) three different methodologies were conducted during Richardson's research
C) Richardson's conduct of research included three different methodologies
D) research was conducted by Richardson, using three different methodologies

CONTINUE

—3—

Task-based studies were either open-ended and exploratory, meaning the respondent can choose any answer (not limited to a few options), [4] but close-ended, meaning the respondent was prompted to choose an answer from a set list (i.e. "yes or no" or a scale of 1–10). The tasks were presented in such a way as not to "lead" the subject to give an answer that would be desirable for the findings the researcher aimed to get. Moderators qualitatively [5] computed how much assistance subjects needed to complete each task. In one open-ended task, users were prompted to "explore the pre-diabetes website," during which they were asked to walk the moderator through [6] one's thought process. One of the close-ended tasks instructed subjects to look at the tools section of the site, where they were told, "Let's say you wanted to walk more. How would you do this?" Related measures included *Time on Task* and *Number of Errors*, two typical measurements in any test that quantify data from the participant and make their data easily comparable to those of others.

—4—

The [7] adjective test, or desirability list, that Richardson used, was based on one created by Microsoft in 2002. Users are asked to select the five adjectives that best describe the site. To counteract the positive bias that subjects typically display, 2/3 of the presented adjectives were negative, while the remaining 1/3 were positive. Examples of adjectives used in the Microsoft

4

A) NO CHANGE
B) or
C) nor
D) and

5

A) NO CHANGE
B) quantified
C) gauged
D) calculated

6

A) NO CHANGE
B) his or her
C) their
D) they're

7

A) NO CHANGE
B) adjective, test or desirability list that Richardson used,
C) adjective test, or desirability list, that Richardson used
D) adjective test or desirability list that Richardson used,

test include empowering, approachable, and disconnected. Richardson's modified version consisted of 15 adjectives, nine of which were negative and six of which were positive.

—5—

Her findings suggested that the pre-diabetes section of the MyDoctorOnline.com website could be significantly improved by providing the exact content that patients were looking for. The website satisfaction rating of 6.5 out of 10 suggests that there is room for improvement. Regarding the use of the exercise tracking tool on the website, patients did not see any value in using it to graph their progress. On balance, patients indicated that the site was helpful and easy to use.

—6—

8 <u>"Patients want to know what they can do right now to make a difference with small, actionable steps."</u> They expected the website to provide motivation and support, offering realistic testimonials from other patients, and tips and strategies that other patients had used successfully. They asked for the option to connect with each other online through the website. Patients suggested that the organization of content on the website could be improved, so they can find the information they are looking for quickly. Users had a great desire to know more (6.2 out of 7 points). Most patients did not understand that the most important change they could make was to lose **9** <u>weight: some thought exercise was most important, others thought it was their diet.</u>

8

Which choice provides a quote that most effectively establishes the discussion that follows in this paragraph?

A) NO CHANGE
B) "I do not see the point in graphing my progress."
C) "There is room for improvement regarding the aesthetics of the website."
D) "This site is not helpful at all."

9

A) NO CHANGE
B) weight, some thought exercise was most important, while others thought it was their diet.
C) weight: some thought exercise was most important, while others thought it was their diet.
D) weight; and some thought exercise was most important while others thought it was their diet.

CONTINUE

—7—

Ultimately, the study's findings imply that medical websites such as MyDoctorOnline.com can be useful, so long as website owners conduct appropriate user experience research to identify and meet their patients' specific, varied needs. **10** In order for these sites to be most beneficial, studies like Richardson's should be part of a preliminary process, incorporating users' advice and expectations into the final design of the site.

Question 11 asks about the previous passage as a whole.

10

Which choice concludes both the paragraph and the passage by stating the overall significance of the study as presented in the passage?

A) NO CHANGE
B) MyDoctorOnline.com is currently still in beta testing.
C) Some users of this website still have mixed feelings about usefulness of the exercise tracking tool.
D) Richardson's study is currently unpublished, which is indicative of an overall problem in STEM publishing that ignores user-end analytics.

Quesion 11 asks you to consider the passage as a whole.

11

The writer wants to insert the following sentence.

> In addition to these three methods, overall website satisfaction ratings on a 0-10 scale were collected.

To make the passage most logical, the sentence should be placed immediately after the last sentence in paragraph

A) 1.
B) 2.
C) 3.
D) 4.

STOP

Questions 1-11 are based on the following passage.

Cooperative Economics

One of the least favorable utterances for a child to hear is "you have to share." But what of adults? Do humans carry the reluctance to share beyond adolescence? And if so, how does that manifest itself when what's being shared isn't just a toy? Researchers at the University of Reading, United Kingdom, set out to answer these questions in a study published in PLOS ONE in 2017. Based on primate studies of the same **1** thing, the team hypothesized that humans would be more likely to share a monetary reward with others who performed well if they were of a higher status than the "sharee," or person receiving a portion of the "sharer's" reward. This has implications for **2** careers—the first is that if you help your superior receive bonuses, he or she is likely to share them with you because you are perceived as competent. The second is that you are likely not expected to **3** share your rewards mutually in return because of your subordinate status.

1

The writer want to revise the underlined portion of the sentence to be more specific to the information earlier in the paragraph. Which choice best accomplishes this goal?

A) NO CHANGE
B) nature
C) ecosystem
D) environment

2

A) NO CHANGE
B) careers: such as
C) careers, and also
D) careers: the first is

3

A) NO CHANGE
B) be sharing your rewards back in return
C) mutually share your rewards in returning
D) share your rewards in return

CONTINUE

4 The researchers used 44 male and 44 female Canadian undergraduate students. These participants were randomly split into arbitrary high- or low status positions. They were then broken up into three fictional collaborating groups: their coworker was either of higher, lower, or equal status. Furthermore, the fictional coworker was always assigned as being equally or more competent than 5 them. In the first study, the reward was hypothetical, meaning the participant did not have any tangible money to share with the partner and received no actual reward for the job performed. At the end of the study, the team found that participants shared more money with the more competent, lower-status individuals; this means that monetary reward increased as a function of competence and status.

In a subsequent study, designed using real monetary rewards, the researchers sought to further their hypothesis by including claims regarding the difference between male and female sharing behavior. They believed that males would share more than females would, regardless of the sex of the partner. The experiment was set up the same as the first one, except that tangible money was used as an incentive. As expected, an interaction between sex and status was found, meaning that while the results mimicked study one (participants shared more with high-competence, low-status partners), males shared significantly more than females. 6 Furthermore, there was an interaction between status and competence level, meaning that when participants were assigned to a higher status (furthering

4

Which choice most effectively combines the underlined sentences?

A) The researchers, using 44 male and 44 female Canadian undergraduate students, who were split randomly into arbitrary high- or low-status positions.
B) 44 male and 44 female Canadian undergraduate students were used by researchers, being randomly split into arbitrary high- or low-status positions.
C) The researchers used 44 male and 44 female Canadian undergraduate students, randomly splitting them into arbitrary high- or low-status positions.
D) Randomly split into arbitrary high- or low- status positions, 44 male and 44 female Canadian undergraduate students, were used by researchers.

5

A) NO CHANGE
B) they
C) the participant's
D) the participant

6

A) NO CHANGE
B) However,
C) Nonetheless,
D) Therefore,

the status divide between the participant and his/her partner) they shared more, but when the competence level of the partner was low, this generous sharing behavior disappeared. 7 Additionally, when the lower status partner failed to meet expectations, the higher status partner shared very little or nothing at all.

There are clear-cut real world implications here. When performing a job, often we cannot obtain a result on our own 8. Naturally, if a person provides assistance, that person will expect a reward. But prior to this study, it would not be understood what mechanisms underlie the sharing behavior, therefore giving no explanation as to why competent partners may sometimes be more highly rewarded than at other times. Now, based on the findings from the study, we can better understand how to collaborate for maximum productivity and therefore maximum reward.

[1] As for why males share more than females, the researchers had a few hypotheses. [2] First, males form large, stable groups of peers whom they largely view as equals, regardless of rank. [3] In female-centric groups, the interactions are usually in unrelated, equally-ranked dyads (or two-person groups). [4] Because of this, males see lower-status peers in a more positive light, and therefore are more likely to want them to succeed. [5] Furthermore, males are more inclined to behave in such a nature as to keep a group intact, whereas females, who were not part of a large group to begin with, have no such motivators. 9

7

The author is considering deleting the underlined portion. Should this sentence be kept or deleted?

A) Kept, because it clarifies the claim made in the previous sentence.
B) Kept, because it summarizes the author's central claim.
C) Deleted, because it merely reformulates an idea from the previous sentence.
D) Deleted, because it contradicts the results of the study discussed in this paragraph.

8

The author is considering adding the following.

—for example, if a person writes a book, it is likely that he or she will need help editing the final product

Should the writer add this here?

A) Yes, because it provides an example to support a previous claim.
B) Yes, because it demonstrates the essence of the writing process.
C) No, because it directly contradicts a statement made in the previous sentence.
D) No, because it introduces loosely related information, blurring the focus of the paragraph.

9

The writer plans to add the following sentence.

Females, on the other hand, view rank as a competition and prefer to maintain their higher status, therefore wanting to keep lower-ranked peers below them.

This sentence should be placed

A) before sentence 1.
B) after sentence 1.
C) before sentence 5.
D) after sentence 5.

CONTINUE

In the future, it would be beneficial to expand beyond using just college students as participants, incorporating [10] people who are already in the job sector. This could eliminate some of the hypothetical nature of the task, as it has been shown many times in the past that people have a tendency to report beliefs about themselves that [11] is contradictory to their actions in a non-hypothetical situation.

10

Which choice provides an example that both expands upon the suggestion made earlier in this sentence and connects this study to a practical application?

A) NO CHANGE
B) more graduate students as participants.
C) a greater range of nationalities and ethnicities.
D) those who did not attend any type of university.

11

A) NO CHANGE
B) are
C) was
D) were

CONTINUE

Questions 1-11 are based on the following passage.

Top Down

In 2016, German researchers sought to find out what neural mechanisms underlie the brain's response to moving targets. In everyday life, we experience the world as stable—even though the eye, head (brain), and body are [1] constantly in motion—with the help of saccades coupled with some other, unknown phenomenon.

Saccades, or quick jumps that the eye makes between visual fixation points, have been extensively studied in previous research, but their role in stabilizing our world has never been fully understood. At this point, scientists know that when we look at something in our visual field, we don't stare directly at a point on the [2] object, rather, we are constantly scanning (via saccades) over the entire visually-available area of the object—top to bottom and left to right—in order to get a complete picture into our field of view. On their own, these eye jumps would not seem sufficient to justify how we hold attention on one thing even in the midst of frequent retinal image displacements.

One theory that could explain why our world remains stable is that our brains "anticipate" the consequences of saccades, meaning that the information in our brain moves faster than the physical movement of [3] their eyes. If true, this would mean that sight is experienced as "top-down," or internally guided based on prior knowledge, willful plans, or

1

A) NO CHANGE
B) constantly in motion with the help of
C) constantly in motion: with the help of
D) constantly in motion, with the help of

2

A) NO CHANGE
B) object; rather,
C) object; but
D) object,

3

A) NO CHANGE
B) his or her
C) our
D) one's

CONTINUE

current goals, rather than "bottom-up," or constructed as we go, using no prior knowledge. If this is true, it would cause our brain to more quickly recognize information in the visual field as "whole pictures," rather than as broken-up into pieces.

This theory holds weight in the field of neuroscience for two reasons. The first is that the brain has a **4** propriety for putting incomplete pictures together even in two-dimensional planes. The **5** brains need to do this is so that it can make sense of the world and make perceiving and understanding the world quicker and easier, therefore requiring fewer resources. The second reason is that the brain uses heuristics **6** —or stereotypes based on previous experience that help us come to quick-and-easy solutions—to anticipate consequences based on environmental cues that much of the time we don't even realize are present. Both of these concepts help us to remain safe from dangerous situations and free from repeating events that **7** had negative outcomes for us in the past.

4

A) NO CHANGE
B) propensity
C) proficiency
D) proposition

5

A) NO CHANGE
B) brain's need's to do
C) brains needing to do
D) brain's need to do

6

The author is considering deleting the underlined portion. Should the author do this?

A) Yes, because it merely repeats information from the previous sentence.
B) Yes, because it directly contradicts an earlier description of the brain.
C) No, because it states the author's central claim of the entire passage.
D) No, because it clarifies a concept that is important to understanding this paragraph.

7

A) NO CHANGE
B) having
C) have
D) has

CONTINUE

Based on previous brain anticipatory behavior research, the study, conducted by Tao Yao, Stefan Treue, and B. Suresh Krishna, [8] attempt to finally answer the question of exactly what mechanism our brain uses to prevent our field of view from becoming an unstable mess. In their research, [9] employing electrical brain recording techniques, using Macaque monkeys as subjects. They first had the monkeys stare at a fixation point (usually a cross) in order to stabilize the eye and prevent saccadic movements. Once saccadic movements were fully repressed, activity in the brain was measured as a "baseline" of activity in order to later be compared to activity during saccades. Next, monkeys were trained to orient their field of vision to a "target" random dot pattern, or RDP, to stimulate a saccadic eye movement. [10] At the same time as the target was presented, a distractor was presented, equidistant from the original fixation point but in the opposite visual field. The distractor would be used as a comparison when the team later analyzed the data. Again, activity in the brain, referred to as a "memory trace," was mapped via the electrical recording device.

8

A) NO CHANGE
B) have attempted
C) attempting
D) attempts

9

A) NO CHANGE
B) the team's members employing electrical brain recording techniques,
C) the team's members employed electrical brain recording techniques,
D) electrical brain recording techniques were used by the team's members,

10

At this point, the author is considering adding the following sentence.

> The team recorded separate data for male and female Macaque test subjects.

Should this sentence be added here?

A) Yes, because it clarifies why the researchers applied a random dot pattern as discussed in the study.
B) Yes, because it defends a controversial choice made by the researchers.
C) No, because it contradicts infomation provided earlier in this paragraph.
D) No, because it distracts from the author's discussion on how the experiment was conducted.

CONTINUE

Not surprisingly, the researchers found evidence of anticipatory activity in the brain. When the monkeys knew that they would soon be attending to an item in their left field of view (representing the aforementioned "target"), neurons corresponding to the left field of view in the brain fired more strongly than neurons corresponding to the right field of view (representing the aforementioned "distractor") fired. **11** What's more impressive, though, is that the neurons fired prior to the saccade happening, meaning that the saccade itself didn't cause the activity—anticipation of focusing on a new target did.

11

At this point, the author would like to add a statement that evaluates the significance of the findings mentioned in this paragraph. Which choice best accomplishes this goal?

A) That the neurons in the target's direction experienced stronger stimulation implies that more neurons were recruited to attend to that field of vision.

B) Future research on this topic is needed, as the research team only had a combined 124 trials of data to examine, and the subjects were monkeys, not humans.

C) The team members indicate that they are optimisic about their results, even in this preliminary stage of research.

D) There is still more to learn about top-down versus bottom-up processing in the visual systems of animals other than primates.

Questions 1-11 are based on the following passage.

Taste Perception

Human beings and other mammals depend on their taste buds to guide their choice of foods. A sometimes overlooked sense, [1] taste's importance as a contributor to our perception of the world. Crucially, foods that taste good to us stimulate the reward center in our brain, causing us to crave those foods. [2] Therefore, if a food does not taste good, it stimulates an aversive pathway in the brain that causes long-term learned behavior—simply put, we don't want to eat, or even smell, that food ever again if it activates the severe end of the aversion spectrum. Scientists (and cooks) know that we are attracted to foods that are sweet, for instance, as these are usually high in energy and likely to activate the aforementioned reward pathway. A taste that is bitter, however, can warn of a potentially harmful substance. Another taste of particular interest to researchers is salt—which doesn't fit into any of the specific categories identified in taste buds.

[3] After their linking salt to the bitter taste receptors, scientists have perhaps explained why humans do not find high levels of salt appetizing. Most animals will [4] gobble salt up to a point, after which it becomes unappealing, making salt unique. Animals should want to consume salt: dietary salt, or sodium chloride (NaCl), is used by every cell in the body and

1

A) NO CHANGE
B) the importance of taste is as a
C) taste is an important
D) taste is being an important

2

A) NO CHANGE
B) Fortunately,
C) Conversely,
D) Moreover,

3

A) NO CHANGE
B) They linked
C) Linking
D) Upon their linking of

4

Which choice best maintains the style and tone of the passage?

A) NO CHANGE
B) guzzle
C) ravage
D) consume

CONTINUE

is thought to be an essential ion. [5] However, it does become harmful in excess. This most likely indicates an evolutionary cause of salt's "unappealing in high quantities" property. Researchers have identified taste receptor cells that are able to detect low levels of sodium salts (necessary for a homeostasis in all cells throughout the body) through the epithelial sodium channel (ENaC), but cells responsible for aversion to high salt levels [6] was unknown.

Past studies show that bitter and sweet tastes are represented in several distinct [7] areas, or "fields," of the taste cortex. Ryba and Zuker's teams recently explored whether activating such cortical fields in mice would evoke taste, even without the presence of an actual sweet or bitter compound. This idea is hardly new. [8] For years, scientists have been activating neurons in the brain and evoking responses correlating with the activated area. Take, for example, the "music" processing center of the brain, which has been studied for a long time. If a neuron in that specific area is activated in a conscious human, the person will report having heard a sound even when none was present.

5

Which choice most smoothly and effectively combines the underlined sentences?

A) Becoming harmful in excess, this likely indicated an evolutionary causing of its "unappealing in high quantities" property.
B) However, becoming harmful in excess, most likely indicating an evolutionary cause of salt's "unappealing in high quantities" property.
C) It does become harmful in excess, however; this is mostly indicating an evoluationarily cause of its "unappealing in high quantities" property.
D) However, it does become harmful in excess—most likely indicating an evolutionary cause of its "unappealing in high quantities" property.

6

A) NO CHANGE
B) were
C) would have been
D) is

7

A) NO CHANGE
B) areas—or "fields,"
C) areas, or "fields"
D) areas, "or fields,"

8

The author is considering deleting the underlined sentence. Should this sentence be kept or deleted?

A) Kept, because it describes the methods used exclusively for testing the sense of taste.
B) Kept, because it sets up the relevance for the example about music processing in the brain that follows.
C) Deleted, because it directly contradicts the assertions made earlier in this paragraph.
D) Deleted, because it introduces completely irrelevant information.

CONTINUE

In the taste study, they used a technique called optogenetics to selectively activate the bitter or sweet cortical fields. [9] To implement optogenetics, you must first inject a virus that carries the gene for a specific light-sensitive protein into either the bitter field or the sweet field. Light can then activate the neurons that accept this virus and produce a protein in response. To activate the protein and stimulate the false "taste" sensation, the scientists implanted some customized optical fibers near the site of the injection.

Once equipped with the light-sensitive optogenetic mechanism, the mice were given the option to choose one of two chambers. Entrance into one chamber would cause a stimulation in the "bitter" area of the brain, while entrance into the other would cause a stimulation in the "sweet" area. Mice naturally developed a preference for the chamber that was coupled with stimulation of the sweet cortical field area. As expected, mice [10] who's bitter cortical field was activated when they choose that chamber learned to avoid it, quickly.

9

At this point, the author is considering adding the following sentence.

This technique was first functional in the early 2000s.

Should the writer make this addition here?

A) Yes, because it provides crucial background information for the study.
B) Yes, because it highlights how recently optogenetics was developed.
C) No, because it introduces loosely related information, blurring the focus of the paragraph.
D) No, because it detracts from the author's discussion of the history of optogenetics.

10

A) NO CHANGE
B) whose
C) with
D) that

CONTINUE

[1] Even when animals had no experience with bitter or sweet tastes, researchers discovered that they could trigger behaviors corresponding to those tastes by activating cortical fields. [2] The way human beings think of taste is in the brain, as Zuker says: "dedicated taste receptors in the tongue detect sweet or bitter and so on, but it's the brain that affords meaning to these chemicals." [3] The salt-related findings suggest that humans and other mammals have specialized salt receptor cells to make salt appealing. [4] Bitter-tasting cells are activated by high salt concentrations, and our cells have evolved to help prevent consumption levels that could severely affect our health. [5] This finding shows evidence of support for the view that one's sense of taste is hardwired into the brain. 11

11

To improve the cohesion and logic of this paragraph, sentence 5 should be

A) placed where it is now.
B) placed before sentence 2.
C) placed before sentence 4.
D) DELETED from the paragaph.

CONTINUE

Questions 1-11 are based on the following passage.

End of Men

After thousands of years, Hanna Rosin argues in a 2010 *Atlantic* article that "patriarchy is coming to an end." Once dominating economic territories, [1] men becoming the minority of the workforce in 2010, for the very first time in US history. As proof that the shift is continuing, currently 40% of men and 60% women have or are obtaining a college degree. Furthermore, the shift towards women [2] were prominent in middle management. According to the Bureau of Labor Statistics, women now hold 51.4 percent of managerial and professional jobs—up from 26.1 percent in 1980. They make up 54 percent of all accountants and hold about half of all banking and insurance jobs. [3] Exactly half of America's physicians are now women, as are 45 percent of associates

1

A) NO CHANGE
B) the minority of the workforce were men in 2010
C) the workforce in 2010 had a minority of men
D) men became the minority of the workforce in 2010

2

A) NO CHANGE
B) is
C) are
D) have been

3

Which choice most accurately and effectively reflects information from the graph?

A) NO CHANGE
B) About a third
C) Many
D) More than half

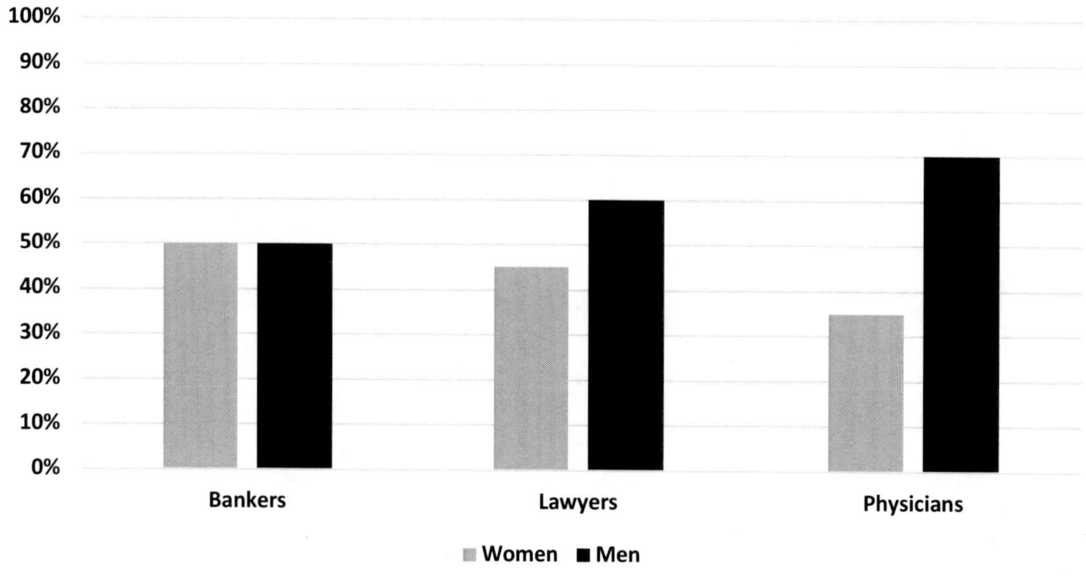

CONTINUE

in law firms—and both those percentages are rising fast. Is post-industrial, modern society better suited to women than to men, and what are the vast cultural consequences of this historically unprecedented role reversal?

To attempt to understand the force behind this phenomenon, post-Darwinians argue that skills such as communicating and thinking have become more important than stamina and physical strength in our post-industrial economy. In times **4** where the majority of jobs required physical labor, it would have made sense that men would dominate, but that is simply not the case any longer. Machines have taken over many of the hard-labor jobs, making way for women to no longer be thought of as "unsuited." **5** In fact, since 2000, manufacturing has lost more than a third of its total workforce. Even skilled jobs, such as for electricians, builders, or real estate agents, are scarce. Only two of 15 job categories predicted to grow by 2020 are dominated by men—computer engineer and janitor. Women get all the others, creating an economy that is friendlier to women than to men.

4

A) NO CHANGE
B) that
C) which
D) when

5

The writer is considering deleting the underlined portion. Should this sentence be kept or deleted?

A) Kept, because it shows how women are bringing innovation into manufacturing.
B) Kept, because it supports the writer's discussion about the changes in a post-industrial economy.
C) Deleted, because it contradicts the claim that women are becoming a majority of the workforce.
D) Deleted, becuase it blurs the focus of the author's discussion with completely irrelevant content.

As proof that the trend is sustainable, organizations like the Organization for Economic Cooperation and Development **6** reports that a country's economic success is correlated to both the political and economic power of women in that society. In war-torn countries like Liberia and Rwanda, women are rising to leadership roles, becoming a "maternal rescue team" to **7** their countries and attempting to improve their fortunes. The more flexible and more nurturing behaviors associated with women are seen as more adaptive and better suited to successful fulfillment of **8** social roles in today's world. In 2008, these "more-feminine" management styles were quantified and researched. Using data from the top 1,500 US companies between 1992 and 2006, researchers at the University of Maryland and Columbia Business School found that women in top positions performed better. They cited skills such as collaboration and creativity—as part of an innovation-intensive strategy—as especially strong contributors to such performance.

6

A) NO CHANGE
B) reporting
C) report
D) had reported

7

A) NO CHANGE
B) they're
C) her
D) one's

8

A) NO CHANGE
B) social role's in todays world
C) social roles in todays world
D) social role's in today's world

Even though the top tiers of US society remain male-dominated, Rosin describes this as what she sees as the "last gasp of a dying age," with many powerful forces pushing for change. With this painful role reversal, male support groups are increasingly springing up in America's rust belt and other similar places. Traditional family roles are being turned upside-down. Thus, some support groups assist with the lack of employment, **9** since others teach relationship and social skills. Many of the men who wind up in these groups are casualties of the lack of manufacturing jobs—a true sign of the shifting times, as manufacturing jobs used to be one of the most abundant sectors to turn to when in need of work.

Instead of being nostalgic for the past, society should embrace this change and figure out how to capitalize on it moving forward. As the perception of the ideal business leader shifts, the old "command and control" model is seen as passé. Nowadays, leaders need to channel their charisma, act like good coaches, **10** and encouraged hard work and creativity. **11**

9

A) NO CHANGE
B) because
C) while
D) DELETE the underlined portion

10

A) NO CHANGE
B) encourage hard work
C) and encourage hard work
D) and hard work

11

The author wants to conclude this paragraph and passage with additional examples of desirable traits in leaders. Which choice best accomplishes this goal?

A) Skills like reading body language and facial expression have become important—as have "sensitive leadership" and social intelligence.
B) As these trends continue, as women increasingly take on leadership positions, there may, some speculate, be a time when traditional roles are completely reversed.
C) While it is usually easy to cultivate these skills, it is very rare for any single one of these to be innate skills in any given person.
D) However, these traits are nothing new, and have, in fact, been proven to be detriments in some fields that still require heavy-handed leadership.

STOP

Questions 1-11 are based on the following passage.

Myth of ADD

In modern society, most people have some knowledge of attention deficit/hyperactivity disorder (ADD/ADHD). It sprang into existence swiftly and quickly gained prevalence: the media has been reporting a sharp uptick in diagnoses over recent decades. [1] Moreover, Webb *et al*, authors of "Misdiagnosis and Dual Diagnoses of Gifted Children and Adults," suggest that the actual occurrence of AD(H)D is much lower than the rate of diagnosis. They also see a significant increase in stimulant medication prescriptions, such as Ritalin, to treat the condition. Misdiagnosis would be bad enough on its own [2]—many physicians and psychologists are hesitant to diagnose children with psychological disorders at all—but combine being diagnosed improperly with taking potentially harmful drugs and you have a recipe for disaster. To protect kids from these issues in the future, we must come to a consensus as to whether the disorder exists and how exactly to determine that a diagnosis should be made.

1

A) NO CHANGE
B) However,
C) Indeed,
D) On top of this,

2

The writer is considering deleting the underlined portion and adjusting punctuation as necessary. Should the writer do this?

A) Yes, because it contradicts the claim that the rate of misdiagnoses is dropping.
B) Yes, because it contains information completely irrelevant to the overall passage.
C) No, because it cites a specific psychologist speaking out against misdiagnosing children.
D) No, because it elaborates on a claim made in this sentence.

CONTINUE

Professor Jerome Kagan, a preeminent developmental psychologist, in a 2012 Der Spiegel interview, faults an eager pharmaceutical industry with selling the medications to treat what he describes as a sham [3] illness, it is an invention. Every child who's not doing well in school is sent to see a pediatrician, and the pediatrician says: 'It's ADHD; here's Ritalin.' In fact, 90 percent of these 5.4 million kids don't have an abnormal dopamine metabolism. The problem is, if a drug is available to doctors, they'll make the corresponding diagnosis."

Others besides Kagan question the AD(H)D diagnosis. Dr. Richard Saul, in a 2014 *Time* article, also says the condition does not exist as understood by the general public and defined in the DSM V (Diagnostic and Statistical Manual of Mental Disorders, 5th Edition). Saul says that, since 1937, doctors have been prescribing medications to cover up the symptoms. The DSM's definition and criteria have changed on several occasions since the diagnosis was first coined. He adds that the current criteria [4] is so loose and variable that, at one time or another, the entire population of the US would meet the diagnostic requirements. He lists [5] many numerous alternative diagnoses that, under appropriate circumstances, would be a far better fit. He has found that his patients are either exhibiting "normal" behavior, or symptoms of what, after an extensive evaluation, turns out to be something other than AD(H)D.

3

A) NO CHANGE
B) illness "it is an invention.
C) illness: "it is an invention.
D) illness: it is an invention.

4

A) NO CHANGE
B) are
C) was
D) were

5

A) NO CHANGE
B) a large amount
C) an abundant amount
D) numerous

On the other hand, health writer Eileen Bailey asserts that this phenomenon exists, observing that "in 2002, 75 scientists from around the world **6** discuss the continuing inaccurate portrayal of AD(H)D and, in response, signed an AD(H)D International Consensus Statement." They asserted that there was "no question" that the disorder involved a deficiency in abilities that causes serious harm to those with the disorder.

7 There is no consensus among physicians on how to go about diagnosing AD(H)D. First, psychologists and physicians have to agree on a number of traits that represent the disorder; then, they need to determine which ones are crucial for the diagnosis, and what other criteria need to be present (length of time, severity of symptoms, effect on daily life); third, any underlying disorders that may mimic or cause AD(H)D need to be ruled out; lastly, and **8** most difficulty, it needs to be determined whether there is a biological component that can be traced to the disorder. If a biological marker can be pinpointed, diagnosing becomes much easier: in come neuroscientists, using those with the AD(H)D diagnosis as subjects, to try to determine which areas of the brain may be associated with this condition. As nothing has been found to solidify the existence of the disorder, arguments for and against its actual existence continue.

6

A) NO CHANGE
B) discusses
C) discussed
D) discussing

7

Which choice most smoothly and effectively introduces this paragraph?

A) NO CHANGE
B) The process of diagnosing AD(H)D was first delineated in the 1960s.
C) AD(H)D was first described in 1902 as a "defect" in the morality of children.
D) As a whole, scientists appear divided as to whether AD(H)D exists, because the process of diagnosing is tricky.

8

A) NO CHANGE
B) most difficult
C) more difficulty
D) most difficultest

CONTINUE

Four recent neuroscience studies attempted to identify and correlate brain-related phenomena to AD(H)D to support the existence of the disorder. Although the study wasn't particularly helpful in finding a brain-related AD(H)D marker, something interesting did come of the study: in reviewing the methods used in each of these studies, a pattern emerged. The subjects identified **9** that has AD(H)D were presumed to have been diagnosed with the condition by a process consistent with the DSM V recommendations. It is unclear that any effort was made to explore how each initial diagnosis was made, or whether **10** the diagnosis was in fact correct. In other words, these studies do not refute or confirm the AD(H)D diagnosis, but instead accept it as a given. If they want to have better success in defining the biological basis of the disorder, neuroscientists and others who wish to build a case to support the existence of AD(H)D must take steps to ensure that the DSM V criteria are properly applied. It is going to be impossible to determine whether there exists a correlation between any brain-related issue and AD(H)D, if they do not know that the diagnosis is accurate and the patient does, in fact, have AD(H)D.

Because of the exhaustive nature of the task of ruling out so many other possible causes, a correct diagnosis winds up being a challenge. Some experts say that it cannot be properly made after one 15-minute appointment with a general practitioner who looked at a questionnaire that was filled out by school staff and **11** parents, which is what often happens.

9

A) NO CHANGE
B) as having
C) among those who have
D) by having had

10

The author wants to add an additional problem similar to the one provided earlier in the sentence. Which choice best accomplishes this goal?

A) NO CHANGE
B) the subjects' family members had AD(H)D as well
C) the DSM V recommendations should change
D) other psychological disorders were apparent

11

A) NO CHANGE
B) parents—this is, often, what happens
C) parents. Which is what often happens
D) parents; which is what often happens

CONTINUE

Questions 1-11 are based on the following passage.

Redefining Health

[1] Some think of health merely as the absence of disease, but it is more than that. [2] Health means well-being, including social, psychological, and physical well-being. [3] Unfortunately, many traditional models of health seem to focus on medical conditions, such as heart disease, cancer, and diabetes. [4] The World Health Organization (WHO) has defined health as a "state of complete physical, mental and social well-being and not merely the absence of disease or infirmity." [5] What's more, redefining and reevaluating health can allow for more accurate assumptions of lifespan, allowing doctors to predict how long patients will live with their current lifestyle or if they make lifestyle changes (for better or for worse). **1**

At the University of Chicago, Dr. Martha McClintock and her team **2** attempt to classify the health of senior citizens by using a comprehensive, longitudinal approach, supported by the National Institutes of Health's (NIH's) National Institute on Aging (NIA). They published their findings in 2016 in the Proceedings of the **3** National Academy of Sciences, in McClintock's research study, more than 3,000 US adults from the ages of 57 to 85 were sampled and interviewed. The sample included US older adults who lived at home, no matter what their current health status was. Questionnaires covering 54 diverse health variables were administered. Five years later,

1

The author is considering adding the following sentence.

> According to this definition, we should be evaluating health differently for a clearer picture of older adulthood.

This sentence should be placed

A) before sentence 1.
B) after sentence 1.
C) after sentence 4.
D) after sentence 5.

2

A) NO CHANGE
B) attempted to classify
C) attempts to classify
D) attempting to classify

3

A) NO CHANGE
B) National Academy of Sciences but in McClintock's research
C) National Academy of Sciences; and in McClintock's research
D) National Academy of Sciences. In McClintock's research

CONTINUE

the same participants were contacted again. They were either re-interviewed or noted for their inability to participate, due to either death or incapacity.

The researchers constructed two models. First was a traditional "medical model," using 19 of 54 variables from what is known [4] by a data-driven latent class analysis (LCA) from the National Social Life, Health, and Aging Project (NSHAP). The variables included a variety of medical issues and organ functions, such as liver disease, kidney disease, diabetes, stroke, lung disease, cancer, and heart disease. A second model, a "comprehensive model," included 35 measures from the LCA. The redefined approach included variables covering aspects of well-being and health that were not present in the traditional model. The variables associated with the second model included frailty (such as urinary incontinence, anemia, bone fracture, and gait speed), sensory function (such as hearing, vision, and taste), psychological health (such as self-esteem, loneliness, depression, and stress), and health behaviors (such as smoking, drinking, and sleeping).

[5] About half of the people who were classified as healthy based on the medical model had a number of vulnerabilities that were identified by the comprehensive model. These vulnerabilities impacted the chances that they would become incapacitated or die within 5 years—something anyone would certainly want to know. Additionally, some of the people [6] that had chronic disease had a number of strengths that allowed

4

A) NO CHANGE
B) for
C) to
D) as

5

Which choice most smoothly and effectively introduces the paragraph?

A) Not surprisingly, the comprehensive model gave a much better picture of health.
B) Regardless, there is still so much that science does not understand about ageing.
C) Sadly, there is no guaranteed way to stave off disease indefinitely.
D) Moreover, the comprehensive model employed metrics that the traditional model did not.

6

A) NO CHANGE
B) who had
C) whom have
D) which have

CONTINUE

them to be reclassified as healthy under the comprehensive model. **7** However, older adults who were clinically obese but were physically and mentally healthy in other respects actually had the lowest risk of dying or of becoming incapacitated.

8 The better factors that lead to good or bad health are understood, the better people can feel and live when they're older, and that's beneficial to everyone. An analysis of the entire comprehensive model of health and well-being showed several unique variables that were able to predict both **9** incapacity and mortality. Strong markers for future health problems included having a broken bone any time after age 45, poor social engagement and sensory function, and poor mental health. In contrast, greater mobility generally was a predictor of well-being. Dr. Luigi Ferrucci, who is an NIH geriatrician overseeing aging and **10** health research, saying "If I had to rank behaviors in terms of priority, I'd say that exercise is the most important thing associated with living longer and healthier. Exercise is especially important for lengthening active life expectancy, which is life without disease and without physical and mental/thinking disability."

7

A) NO CHANGE
B) Although
C) For instance,
D) Since

8

The author is considering deleting the underlined portion. Should the author do this?

A) Yes, because it blurs the focus of ideas with loosely related information.
B) Yes, because it directly contradicts the discussion that follows.
C) No, because it elaborates on the example in the previous paragraph.
D) No, because it specifies steps that individuals can take to become healthier.

9

A) NO CHANGE
B) incapacity or morality
C) incapacitate and mortality
D) incapacity and mortal

10

A) NO CHANGE
B) health research says, "If
C) health research, says, "If
D) health research says "If

CONTINUE

Chart 1
Percentages of US Population Relevant to Classifications Based on the Medical Model

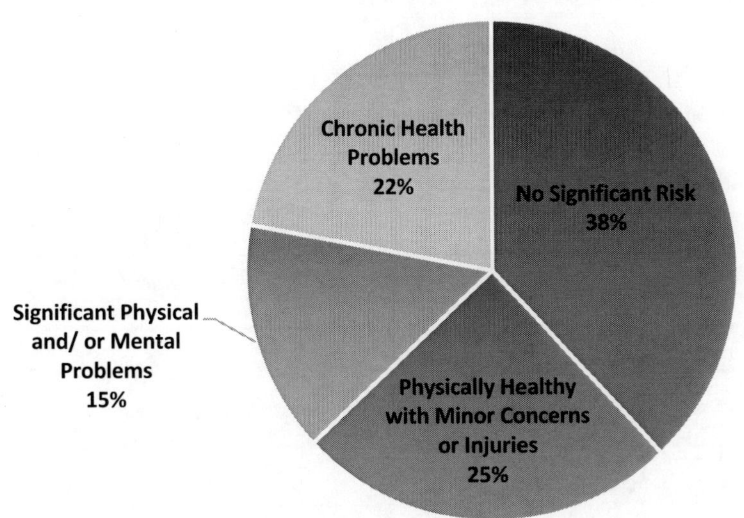

Chart 2
Percentages of US Population Relevant to Classifications Based on the Comprehensive Model

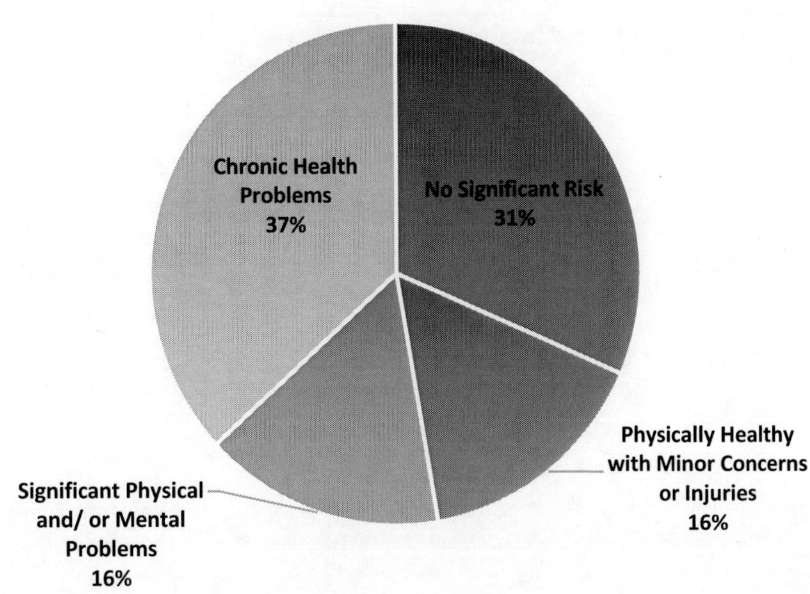

CONTINUE

Moreover, McClintock's researchers found that several specific medical diagnoses such as cancer and hypertension were not as important as mental health (loneliness), mobility, sensory function (hearing), and bone fractures, when it comes to defining vulnerable health classes. She says that "the new comprehensive model of health identifies constellations of health completely hidden by the medical model and reclassifies about half of the people seen as healthy as having significant vulnerabilities."

While the medical model puts **11** only 38 percent of US citizens into classes considered to be of good health (no significant risk and physically healthy with minor concerns or injuries), the comprehensive model shows that roughly half of the population belongs to less healthy classes, ones independently associated with higher mortality rates. These findings are consistent with research by other scientists at the NIA—and with the suggestions made by some parents who typically advise their children to stay away from bad habits, get plenty of sleep, exercise regularly, and eat well.

11

Which choice provides the most accurate information from the charts?

A) NO CHANGE
B) roughly two-thirds
C) about a quarter
D) about one third

CONTINUE

2 Grammar Drill 27 2

Questions 1-11 are based on the following passage.

Wildfires

To those who don't know differently, the image conjured of fall in California might be one of a peaceful and sunny day coupled with a calming breeze. To those who have experienced the [1] annoyance of the Santa Ana winds during this season, however, the understanding is that it is no such thing. [2] The Santa Ana winds are strong, extremely dry down-slope winds. They originate inland and affect coastal Southern California and northern Baja California. They originate from cool and dry high-pressure air masses in the Great Basin. These winds have been clocked at 150 mph, with some approximations showing even higher speeds. Add those gusts to a hot and dry climate, and you have discovered the recipe for wildfire season. Although wildfire season has always been a blight to Californians, it's only getting worse thanks to the ever-growing [3] affects of climate change. In December 2017, videos of infernos next to Californian cities went viral on social media, giving us evidence that a more vicious wildfire season may become our new reality.

It's a given that we do our best to prepare for these intense fire [4] seasons, however, forest management groups, industry groups, and political groups can't quite seem to agree on how exactly to do so. At present, there are three choices: thin out the forests, conduct controlled burns, or let wildfires run their natural courses. Most people are (reasonably) suspicious of

1

Which choice most accurately expresses the destructive power of the Santa Ana winds while maintaining the style and tone of the passage?

A) NO CHANGE
B) excitement
C) wrath
D) irritability

2

Which choice most smoothly and effectively combines the underlined sentences?

A) The Santa Ana winds are strong, extremely dry down-slope winds, originating from the cool and dry high-pressure air masses in the Great Basin and affecting coastal Southern California and Baja California.
B) The Santa Ana winds, being strong, extremely dry down-slope winds, originating from the cool and dry high-pressure air masses in the Great Basin, affecting coastal Southern California, and Baja California.
C) Originating from the Great Basin's cool and dry high-pressure air masses, coastal Southern California and Baja California are affected by the Santa Ana winds, which are strong, extremely dry down-slope winds.
D) Coastal Southern California and Baja California are affected by the Santa Ana winds, which are hot, and extremely dry, being that they come from: the Great Basin's inland dry and cool high-pressure air masses.

3

A) NO CHANGE
B) affected by
C) effects of
D) effectiveness of

4

A) NO CHANGE
B) seasons; however,
C) seasons, however;
D) seasons however

the last option, which leaves us with two different methods for managing fire by altering the composition of the forest, known as fuel treatment. Now, how does it work?

Before the 1990s, there weren't really any published experiments comparing fuel treatments and [5] their effects on a fire's behavior. A group of experts changed that in 1995 by running such an experiment in a region of the western United States called the Sierra Nevada.

These experts chose a plot of mixed-conifer land that was 3000 meters by 9000 meters (only slightly larger than the combined area of 3780 standard soccer fields), and was [6] large enough to accomodate several fires. Their plan was to test 7 different methods of reducing or reconfiguring the fuel in forests. An 8th section of land was set aside as a control group, where no treatment would be done. After the treatments, the team simulated wildfires in order to test which fuel treatment had been most effective.

5

A) NO CHANGE
B) its effects on a fire's behavior
C) it's effect's on fire behavior
D) their effect's on a fire's behavior

6

The writer want to include an additional advantage of the land specifically chosen for the experiment. Which choice best accomplishes this goal?

A) NO CHANGE
B) forested mostly by mixed-conifer trees.
C) located in the Sierra Nevada of the western United States.
D) representative of the majority of the topography in the region.

CONTINUE

[1] The 7 treatments included prescribed burning, pile-and-burn, and cut-and-scatter, in addition to four other methods that used canopy thinning (biomassing) alone or in combination with the first three treatments. [2] These areas, called fuel breaks, would be used to determine which treatments were most likely to prevent a wildfire from crossing empty areas. [3] In essence, the treatments **7** not only reduced the fuel in the space between the forest floor and the bottom of the canopy, or moved the fuel closer to the forest floor so that the canopy would be less likely to catch fire. [4]Additionally, two strips of land (one 90 meters wide and one 390 meters wide) that were free of most brush and trees over 3 meters tall were created in each treatment area. [5] The researchers then ignited fires on two different days with extremely dry and hot weather. **8**

The results they found revealed a few patterns. In both scenarios, the land treated with prescribed burning experienced a fire that spread slower and was less intense **9** than in any other area. Additionally, all four treatments that included biomassing saw the most intense fires, and the two treatments incorporating cut-and-scatter had the fastest spreading fires. The treatments that used pile-and-burn and cut-and-scatter alone, as well as the control, had fire spreading into the canopy on the day with a more extreme temperature. Moreover, on

7

A) NO CHANGE
B) either
C) neither
D) both

8

To make this paragraph most logical, sentence 2 should be placed

A) where it is now.
B) before sentence 1.
C) after sentence 3.
D) after sentence 4.

9

A) NO CHANGE
B) then in any other area
C) as the fire was in any other areas
D) than, other areas

the same day every fire—except those in the areas treated with prescribed burning—created spot fires beyond the smaller fuel break, but none created spot fires beyond the larger break.

[10] Since this experiment used predictive models that assumed that the fuel was homogenous throughout each area and that the fires would not exhibit extreme behavior, it still produced a few important takeaways. The first, and perhaps most obvious, is that the fuel should be reduced or moved out of the canopy, or both. The second is that prescribed burning shows the most promise as an effective fuel treatment to prevent wildfires from reaching their full potential. The third, and perhaps most important, is that combinations of fuel treatment and fuel breaks lead to the best results.

To many, it may seem frightening to literally fight fire with fire, but more and more people in fire-prone areas are gradually accepting this preventative measure. Public outreach and education [11] is absolutely critical to implementing any of these land management schemes. Changing public opinion must happen soon if we don't want the firestorms of December 2017 to become the new normal.

10

A) NO CHANGE
B) Because
C) Even
D) Although

11

A) NO CHANGE
B) has been
C) was
D) are

CONTINUE

Questions 1-11 are based on the following passage.

Rogue Waves

—1—

Ever since humanity took to the high seas, there [1] has been tales of monstrous waves appearing out of nowhere, tales of towering walls of water that could dwarf the Great Sphinx of Giza or rival the Colossus of Rhodes. But with the rise of the objectivity of science, many of these stories were cast into doubt, much like those of Greek Gods and Goddesses were. Most scientists and mathematicians studying the behavior of ocean waves did not think it possible that, even in severe storms, there would ever be a wave taller than 15 meters. [2] Well into the 20th century, however, stories of these "rogue waves" persisted.

—2—

A number of questions were immediately raised in the scientific community: [3] how do we graph and predict rogue waves. How common are they? And how do we make ships that can weather them?

—3—

The answer to the first question begins in 1983 with Howell Peregrine, then a mathematician at the University of Bristol, who developed a solution to the nonlinear Schrödinger equation. The Schrödinger equation—derived in 1925 by Erwin Schrödinger—describes changes in systems of matter, such as molecules, atoms, and subatomic particles, over a period

1

A) NO CHANGE
B) have been
C) were
D) was

2

Which choice most smoothly and effectively concludes this paragraph and supports the main idea of the passage?

A) NO CHANGE
B) Few scientists took rogue waves seriously because they tended to dismiss sailors' experiences.
C) Sailors are rather famous for being superstitious.
D) When it comes to elusive phenomena, scientists tend to feel rather "at sea", so to speak.

3

A) NO CHANGE
B) we graph and predict rogue waves?
C) how do we graph and predict rogue waves?
D) we do graph and predict rogue waves.

CONTINUE

of time. Its nonlinear variant is crucial to the study of waves. Peregrine's solution (also called a breather or soliton) was unique in that [4] he could describe a wave that seems to come from nowhere and to disappear just as quickly. The first study of the Peregrine breather in a water wave tank took place in 2010, three years after Peregrine himself passed away. Shortly thereafter, in 2012, another group of researchers studied the Peregrine breather in a water wave tank at the Technical University of Berlin.

—4—

The latter group [5] using a model of a chemical tanker to determine whether it was possible to employ Peregrine breathers in studying the effects of rogue waves on a ship. A suspension system was used to keep the model in a fixed location in the wave tank, so that the waves would hit the bow (front) of the model first. The model was also fitted with force transducers, [6] and measuring the pressure on the model from the waves: two were put on either side of the deck, and one was placed underneath on the keel. The movements of the ship were tracked by an optical system of four infrared cameras in a 7 by 10 meter frame, and by 9 strategically-placed wave gauges. Two water gauges were used to measure the effects of the waves on the bow, and were placed on the foredeck and weather deck. Once the model was in place, the researchers generated several waves based on the Peregrine breather and recorded the impact on the ship.

4

A) NO CHANGE
B) it
C) they
D) one

5

A) NO CHANGE
B) had used
C) were using
D) used

6

A) NO CHANGE
B) that would be measuring
C) which would measure
D) measuring and quantifying

CONTINUE

—5—

The researchers found that the forces on the ship had affected major vertical bending moments (vbm). In order to understand vbm, picture a large sponge. 7 If it is bent in half, the top side will grow wider while the bottom side will grow proportionately narrower; the top side is in compression, and the bottom side is in tension. When a ship has an extreme bending moment near its mid-length, according to the Society of Naval Architects and Marine Engineers, there are usually two outcomes: the ship will be in a sagging condition or in a hogging condition. The former happens when a wave trough 8 makes contact at mid-length, and the latter occurs when a wave peak makes contact at mid-length. The chemical tanker's bending moment caused the ship to go through hogging and sagging conditions in rapid succession, but this did not cause the ship to go into structural failure.

—6—

These findings show that it is entirely possible to use the Peregrine breather to study the impact of rogue waves on ships, and it opens up avenues to apply the findings to engineer ships. 9 Indeed, recent years have seen a growth in the industry's interest in the problem of rogue waves—especially since it has been discovered that they're fairly common. In addition, scientists have been working on building a world-wide network of buoys that could broadcast the presence of rogue waves to all nearby vessels. All of these efforts will be invaluable to finally conquering this monster of the oceans.

7

The writer is considering deleting the underlined portion. Should the writer do this?

A) Yes, because it contains information irrelevant to this paragraph.
B) Yes, because it would be better placed elsewhere in this passage.
C) No, because it illustrates a concept from the previous sentence.
D) No, because it introduces a new term that will be important later.

8

At this point, the writer is considering adding the following.

(the "valley" between two waves)

Should the writer add this here?

A) Yes, because it illustrates a difficult concept by using a simile.
B) Yes, because it defines a term that may be unfamiliar to the audience.
C) No, because the quotation marks indicate a sarcastic tone.
D) No, because it blurs the focus of this sentence with unrelated information.

9

A) NO CHANGE
B) However,
C) Nevertheless,
D) For example,

—7—

On the afternoon of December 31st, 1994, in the North Sea off of the coast of Norway, the Draupner oil rig was subject to a barrage of hurricane-force winds and 12 meter waves. Around 3:00, all workers were told to remain inside for the worst of the storm. Later, when engineers were scrutinizing the logs of a wave-height detector, it was discovered that the rig had actually been hit by a wave over 19 meters tall! They had just attained the world's first [10] empirical indisputable measurement of rogue waves.

Question [11] asks about the previous passage as a whole.

10

A) NO CHANGE
B) empirically, indisputably
C) indisputably empiricism
D) empirical, indisputable

Think about the previous passage as a whole as you answer question 11.

11

In order to make this passage most logical, paragraph 7 should be placed

A) where it is now.
B) before paragraph 1.
C) after paragraph 1.
D) after paragraph 3.

STOP

Questions 1-11 are based on the following passage.

Preventing Alzheimers

Today, Alzheimer's disease threatens more people than [1] cancer, affecting potentially one in three people. Fortunately, "we are closer than ever to the abolition of Alzheimer's," says Joseph Jebelli, a researcher and author of *In Pursuit of Memory: The Fight Against Alzheimer's*. Jebelli contends that, far from being something to be feared, this illness is not only treatable, but also preventable. In his book, he discusses the preventive roles of [2] stress, reduction, dieting, exercise, brain training, and sleep. He also highlights related experimental research, his own experience with Alzheimer's in his family, and his work as a neuroscientist.

[1] Jebelli also observed that his grandfather was not a smoker, ate a healthy diet, and lived a mostly stress-free existence. [2] Having inherited a fortune, his grandfather did not actually need to work. [3] Looking at his grandfather and other individuals he had met, Jebelli sought to identify whether Alzheimer's is "an equal opportunity disease." [4] While stress reduction, diet, exercise, brain training, and sleep all show preventive promise, brain training appears to be among the most interesting to emerge (although the author remains cautiously optimistic about preventive steps that anyone can take). [3]

1

A) NO CHANGE
B) that of cancer
C) cancer is doing
D) cancer does

2

A) NO CHANGE
B) stress reduction, diet, exercise, brain training, and sleep
C) stress reduction, diet and exercise, brain training; and sleep
D) stress, reduction, diet, exercise, brain training, and, sleep

3

The author would like to add the following sentence to the paragraph.

> The author shares the journey of his grandfather through progressive stages of the disease, noting his daily hikes in the foothills outside of northern Tehran, Iran.

This sentence should be placed

A) before sentence 1.
B) after sentence 1.
C) after sentence 3.
D) after sentence 4.

CONTINUE

Jebelli became interested in the work of Ryuta Kawashima, who, in 2001, started researching the impact of video games on the human brain. Four years later, Kawashima created the *Nintendo Brain Training* game. In Japan, in nursing homes by the thousands, people began using this video game **4** in attempting stave off dementia. Kawashima thinks his game works; it's in use by more than 30,000 people in Japan. Said Kawashima during a visit by Jebelli, "Patients who were doing nothing before, just sleeping and sitting in a wheelchair, were doing simple arithmetic problems." Upon further discussion, it turns out that Kawashima indeed knows something about the neuroscience of the brain: the build-up of tau and beta-amyloid proteins, beginning at age forty, coincides with the onset of Alzheimer's symptoms. **5** Moreover, brain training must start before that age.

Over 13,000 people were studied through research funded by the Alzheimer's Society in September 2009. In the study, subjects had to participate in the cognitive training for ten minutes a day, every weekday, for half a year. **6** No improvement among those under age fifty was found with cognitive training. However, improvements with such activities as shopping, memorizing lists, and overseeing finances for those over sixty were found with such training. There are researchers who claim that the benefits can last as long as five years. Jebelli says that the jury is out on whether such training can prevent the onslaught of the illness, however.

4

A) NO CHANGE
B) in an attempt to
C) as attempting to
D) by attempting to

5

A) NO CHANGE
B) Furthermore,
C) Therefore,
D) However,

6

The author is considering deleting the underlined portion. Should this sentence be kept or deleted?

A) Kept, because it specifies methods used in the study.
B) Kept, because it conveys some of the findings of the study.
C) Deleted, because it contradicts the writer's thesis.
D) Deleted, because it contains irrelevant information.

CONTINUE

In another study, 700 people over age 65 in the U.S. played checkers and cards as well as completed crossword puzzles and other puzzles; they were studied over a five-year period. The research suggested that the subjects were "47 percent less likely to develop Alzheimer's." Jebelli cites [7] his personal fondness for crossword puzzles.

At Tohoku University in Japan, Kawashima leads a group of forty neuroscientists in research funded by the game's profits. Simulating human conditions of deprivation and stimulation, researchers move mice between cages to mimic the experience of brain training. So far, the results show that the brains of old mice and genetically modified mice get bigger.

Says Kawashima, "We know that the prefrontal cortex is activated by brain training." This part of the brain is involved in decision-making, attention, and memory. It stands to reason that when we stimulate that part of the brain, its basic functions must improve.

One of the Tohoku researchers [8] believe that the results they are seeing are due to a neuroscientific concept known as "brain reserve." The [9] geriatric researcher James Mortimer came up with this concept decades ago, positing that each individual's brain has a set amount of resistance to mental decline, regardless of the amount of structure damage occurring. In what became known as the "Nun Study," Mortimer's co-researcher, D. A. Snowdon, was able to predict which nuns would develop Alzheimer's with 80 percent

7

The author wants to add an observation from Jebelli relevant to the study presented in this paragraph. Which choice best accomplishes this goal?

A) NO CHANGE
B) a distaste for assisted living facilities.
C) physical activity as crucial to overall health.
D) concerns about the study's small sample size, however.

8

A) NO CHANGE
B) have believed
C) believing
D) believes

9

A) NO CHANGE
B) geriatric researcher, James Mortimer
C) geriatric researcher James Mortimer,
D) geriatric, researcher James Mortimer,

accuracy. Snowdon, believing that such brain reserves are developmental, suggested that the best thing parents can do for their children is to read to them.

Kawashima has concerns that any [10] positive effects by brain training may be due to the Hawthorne effect: changes due to the fact that subjects know that they are being observed. These cautions should frame our understanding of any related research and results that attempt to correlate prevention of Alzheimer's with brain training. More research must be done to investigate the long term effects of brain training, and any other Alzheimer's research that shows promise, as the disease is as devastating to loved ones of people with Alzheimer's [11] as it is to those suffering it themselves.

10

A) NO CHANGE
B) positive affects of
C) positive affects from
D) positive effects of

11

A) NO CHANGE
B) as they are to
C) than they are to
D) than it is to

CONTINUE

Questions 1-11 are based on the following passage.

Marangoni Effect

—1—

Oil spills are a growing problem worldwide, and few good solutions currently exist to address them. They are an example of the omnipresent phenomenon of the mixing and spreading of two or more liquids. Other examples include ocean pollution; the brackish water of estuaries; processing of food, beverages and cosmetics; and polymer processing. Scientists have not been able to clearly describe how two miscible liquids mix and spread. Typically, since two liquids will have two different surface tensions, the results are often counterintuitive: a liquid drop on a second liquid [1] will absorb the other liquid right away. In other words, it does not immediately spread and mix, but instead generates a "Marangoni-driven connective flow." Often referred to as the "Marangoni effect," this [2] phenomenal is the mass transfer along an interface between two fluids due to a surface tension gradient.

1

Which choice both elaborates on the claim in this sentence and sets up the next sentence?

A) NO CHANGE
B) remains as a static lens for a period of time.
C) immediately begins to dissolve.
D) is repelled away within seconds.

2

A) NO CHANGE
B) phenomenon
C) phenomena
D) phenomenally

CONTINUE

—2—

An associate professor in the mathematics department of the New Jersey Institute of [3] Technology Shahriar Afkhami, can answer this question. Professor Afkhami is currently heading a research team at NJIT that is working to make enhancements to a computational model that will help us better understand the Marangoni Effect. The computational model was initially [4] evolved by Ivana Seric, who is one of his former Ph.D. students. The original research team, led by Princeton University's Professor Howard A. Stone, used advanced flow visualization techniques to [5] take and predict what happens when a single alcohol drop is placed on water, as well as a number of Marangoni-driven factors that were not previously known, including spreading time, length scale, and surface mixing time.

—3—

How would the process of cleaning up an oil spill be advanced if scientists understood these dynamics better? Recently, a model has been developed that predicts the finite spreading time and the length scale, the convection flow speed, and the finite timescale. By establishing a model that describes the quasi-steady state for this flow, [6] surface cleaning approaches that don't contaminate the water may be enabled by the researchers with spilled oil, as one of many applications.

3

A) NO CHANGE
B) Technology Shahriar Afkami can
C) Technology Shahriar Afkami, can
D) Technology, Shahriar Afkami, can

4

A) NO CHANGE
B) grown
C) developed
D) expanded

5

A) NO CHANGE
B) capture
C) seize
D) kidnap

6

A) NO CHANGE
B) the researchers' surface cleaning approaches may not contaminate the water
C) the researchers may enable surface cleaning approaches without contaminating the water
D) contaminating the water won't happen with the researchers' surface cleaning approaches

CONTINUE

—4—

The "tears of wine" that form along the rim of a wine glass may serve as an illustration of the Marangoni effect, occurring when two miscible liquids with different surface tensions meet. The liquid with greater surface tension (water) pulls on the surrounding liquid with greater force than do solutes, such as alcohol, that [7] were having lower surface tension. When "tears of wine" are formed, the alcohol evaporates and lifts the wine up the glass. In the process, it raises the concentration of the water in the liquid, as well as the overall surface tension. When the material contracts, the liquid starts to pool on the glass walls as droplets. When they become heavier than the force of the effect, they fall down into the wine.

—5—

In their research, Afkhami and the team focused on the spreading mechanisms and flows of a droplet that was fully soluble in a liquid bath. [8] They collected data such as finite diffusion times and length scales that occurred where the two liquids interface, and created videos that showed how the two materials mix together.

7

A) NO CHANGE
B) had
C) has
D) have

8

A) NO CHANGE
B) He
C) One
D) It

CONTINUE

—6—

The results suggest that even when a miscible solute causes a solutal Marangoni flow, it will mix with the bulk liquid and not significantly change the properties of the surface. [9] Moreover, the solutal Marangoni flow is capable of delivering the materials as well as cleaning the surface of the liquid without contaminating the surface. Through facilitating better understanding the dynamics of liquid-liquid flows, this theoretical model can potentially enable an approach to [10] cleaning surfaces, including oil spills. These approaches could clean surfaces without contaminating the surface of the water with additional chemicals.

Question [11] asks about the previous passage as a whole.

9

A) NO CHANGE
B) However,
C) Specifically,
D) Regardless,

10

Which choice most smoothly and effectively combines these sentences at the underlined portion?

A) cleaning surfaces: including oil spills that can be approached without contaminating the surface of the water with additional chemicals.
B) cleaning surfaces, including oil spills; this can be done without contaminating the surface of the water with additional chemicals.
C) cleaning surfaces including oil spills that can be cleaned without contaminating the water with additional chemicals.
D) cleaning surfaces, including oils spills, without contaminating the surface of the water with additional chemicals.

Think about the previous passage as a whole as you answer question 11.

11

To make this passage most logical, paragraph 2 should be

A) where it is now.
B) before paragraph 1.
C) after paragraph 3
D) before paragraph 6.

CONTINUE

Questions 1-11 are based on the following passage.

Flu Vaccine

In January of 2018, the WHO (World Health Organization) published a report on how well the annual flu vaccine in America was working during the 2017-2018 season to date. According to the report's findings, the season's flu shot offered poor protection against the worst strain. The WHO is not sure what caused this alarming fact, [1] however the organization has set out to determine how to prevent it from happening in the future. The first place to start is to evaluate the process that goes into selecting what goes into the flu vaccine—a process that has led to a lot of uncertainty about how effective it may be in any given year.

The worldwide annual process of determining which flu strains to target [2] begins with public health agencies making an educated guess about which flu strain is going to circulate, based on clinical and laboratory studies, and surveillance. This prediction is made long before the flu season begins in the US, possibly a reason it has not had [3] many efficacy as hoped. Soon after, the Food and Drug Administration makes the final determination of how to go about making the vaccines. Once the FDA determines what will go into it, the flu virus that will be used in the flu vaccine is grown in chicken eggs.

[4] These problems specifically relate to a strain of the virus known as H3N2, the same strain that dominated the 2017-2018 season. They believe H3N2 coverage has lacked

1

A) NO CHANGE
B) but
C) however,
D) nevertheless,

2

A) NO CHANGE
B) begin
C) had begun
D) began

3

A) NO CHANGE
B) much more
C) less
D) as much

4

Which choice most smoothly and effectively introduces this paragaph?

A) The World Health Organization, working in tandem with the National Institutes of Health and the Centers for Disease Control and Prevention, has launched a thorough investigation into the matter.
B) Recently, researchers have pinpointed issues with their standard approach that they believe are the causes of lowered rates of effectiveness with the resulting shot.
C) The Food and Drug Administration was founded in 1906, established by a presidential administration that was eager to protect the general public from medicines of dubious origin, quality, efficacy, and safety.
D) Back in 2010, the H1N1 strain, known as "swine flu", surprised the world by manifesting the most severe symptoms in young adults—historically, a recipe for disaster on a global scale.

because “in the process of adapting the virus to grow in eggs… further changes to the [H3N2] virus [are introduced], which may impair the effectiveness of the vaccine.” Apparently, the H3N2 virus is mutating to **5** adept to the eggs, while the flu virus is growing to be used as a vaccine, and the result is a mismatch between the vaccine and the H3N2 strain. That doesn’t mean one should forego **6** the flu shot, say scientists, as the flu shot is about reducing, not eliminating, a person’s risk.

In order to determine just how much efficacy and protection against the flu has been lost, **7** a recent Morbidity and Mortality Weekly Report was released by the Centers for Disease Control and Prevention that included their study of the 2017-2018 flu season data. On average, the effectiveness of the

5

A) NO CHANGE
B) adopt to
C) adopt by
D) adapt to

6

A) NO CHANGE
B) the flu shot, say scientists
C) the flu shot: say scientists,
D) the flu shot say scientists;

7

A) NO CHANGE
B) the Centers for Disease Control and Prevention’s study of the 2017-2018 flu season data was included in the Morbidity and Mortality Weekly Report that was recently released.
C) the Centers for Disease Control and Prevention released a recent Morbidity and Mortality Weekly Report that included their study of the 2017-2018 flu season data.
D) a study of the 2017-2018 flu season data, from the Centers of Disease Control and Prevention, was included in the recent Morbidity and Mortality Weekly Report that they released.

CONTINUE

flu shot for influenza B ranges between [8] <u>0 and 70 percent</u>. However, during years in which the circulating flu virus is the H3N2, that number drops drastically. Scientists tracked flu cases of 1,700 adults and children in the US and learned that the flu shot was 36 percent effective, reducing someone's chances of getting ill with the flu and having to see a doctor by about one-third. Moreover, in 2017-2018, the vaccine was only 25 percent effective against this year's most common strain of the flu. In Canada, an earlier report came up with similar findings, with the flu vaccine being only 17 percent effective against this strain.

8

The writer wants to include an estimation from the graph's data to support the claim in the sentence. Which choice best accomplishes this goal?

A) NO CHANGE
B) 30 and 40 percent
C) 20 and 30 percent
D) 50 and 60 percent

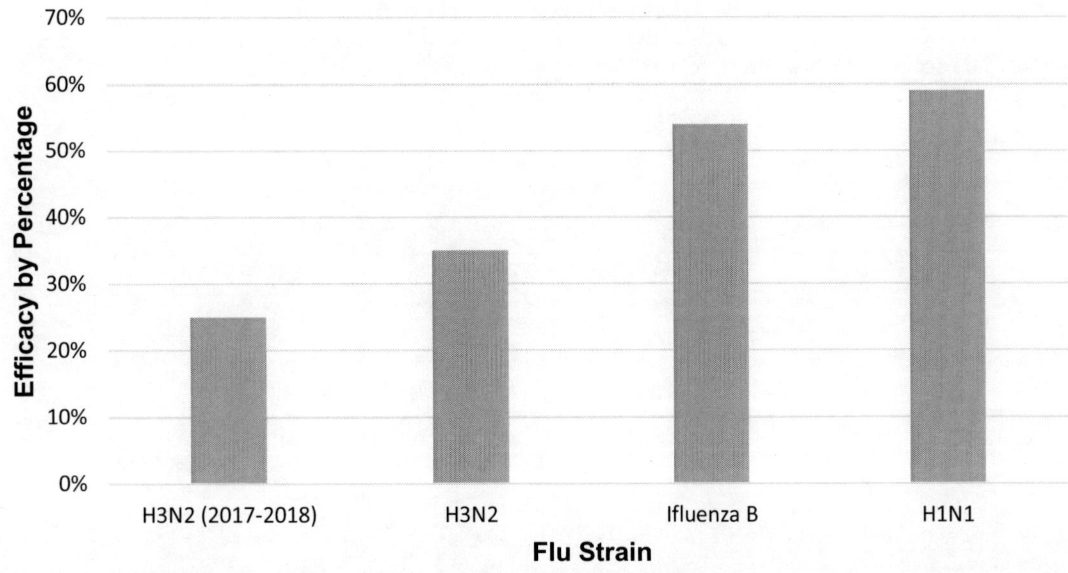

CONTINUE

Concurrently, a study of flu vaccine efficacy was conducted by Edward Belongia, epidemiologist at the Marshfield Clinic Research Institute in Wisconsin. He found that, during H3N2 seasons, vaccines were 33 percent effective, **9** collaborating data from the CDC. When influenza B seasons were compared, the effectiveness rate jumped to 54 percent, and 67 percent during seasons of H1N1.

Some of the researchers **10** that discovered this egg-related vaccine problem expect to find, in the future, other reasons that the annual flu vaccine underperforms. The production method that uses eggs might not tell the entire story. For example, it is thought that this virus strain mutates at a faster rate than other strains, making it more challenging to design a vaccine that matches what is circulating. The flu virus and scientists' response to it can be very complicated. Pending the arrival of the long-awaited universal flu **11** vaccine—a seemingly elusive dream—it's important to understand how current production methods may cause the vaccine to be less effective with certain strains.

9

A) NO CHANGE
B) corroborating
C) corroborated
D) collaborated

10

A) NO CHANGE
B) who
C) which
D) whom

11

At this point, the author is considering revising the underlined portion to the following.

vaccine—a seemingly elusive dream of a vaccine that would offer protection from all flu viruses at once—

Should the author add this here?

A) Yes, because it further explains the significance of a concept introduced in this sentence.
B) Yes, because it names the pharmaceutical groups working toward a universal vaccine.
C) No, because it introduces a concept that is not discussed in the rest of the passage.
D) No, because it blurs the focus of this paragraph with loosely related information.

CONTINUE

Questions 1-11 are based on the following passage.

Crown of Thorns

Coral reefs are known to be relatively delicate ecosystems. They need just the right ocean temperature, just the right amount of nutrients, and just the right populations of cohabiting species to sustain [1] our existence. The primary threats to coral reefs today come from climate change in the forms of ocean acidification and warming, as well as worsening storms. Another threat, which has become more common, is the outbreak [2] —or the sudden and extreme increase of a population—of a starfish called "Crown-of-Thorns" that attaches to coral and [3] directly digest the tissue.

1

A) NO CHANGE
B) their
C) its
D) his or her

2

The author is considering deleting the underlined portion and adjusting punctuation as needed. Should the author do this?

A) Yes, because the underlined portion repeats information from the previous sentence.
B) Yes, because the information is entirely irrelevant to the paragraph.
C) No, because the underlined portion describes the starfish more thoroughly.
D) No, because the information defines a term that may be unfamiliar to readers.

3

A) NO CHANGE
B) directing digestion of
C) directly digesting
D) directly digests

CONTINUE

But is there an effective way to prevent Crown-of-Thorns outbreaks? No one is entirely sure what directly causes them, **4** and the starfish itself is horrifically unattractive, even frightening. For many years, the foremost explanation for these outbreaks was the "larval dispersal hypothesis," which suggested that the starfish's larvae **5** was carried on the strong, wide-ranging currents of the Pacific Ocean. This would mean that distant populations of Crown-of-Thorns starfish have genetic similarities, **6** which is then giving researchers a testable hypothesis to determine the accuracy of this theory.

4

Which choice provides the most relevant detail?

A) NO CHANGE
B) so there are still outbreaks every so often, unfortunately.
C) and the Crown-of-Thorns starfish are found all across the Pacific Ocean.
D) making prevention strategies difficult to come by.

5

A) NO CHANGE
B) were
C) is
D) are being

6

A) NO CHANGE
B) this gives researchers
C) giving researchers
D) and giving researchers

CONTINUE

[1] Excited by this possibility, a group of researchers set out to determine exactly what sort of genetic similarities there could be between and among disparate populations. [2] From 2005 to 2008, specimens were collected from the North Central, Northwest, and South Central Pacific—23 sites in all—which had both outbreak 7 or non-outbreak populations. [3] The DNA of these samples was extracted and sequenced, and thereafter analyzed several ways: DNA was compared both between regions and within each region. [4] For example, a specimen from the Northwest Pacific would be part of the regional group to be compared to those of the North and South Central regions, but that same specimen would also be compared to other North West specimens. [5] In all, the researchers obtained 656 specimens, including one which had been collected in 1982 in Hawai'i. 8

7

A) NO CHANGE
B) and
C) nor
D) and also

8

In order to make this paragraph most logical, sentence 5 should be placed

A) where it is now.
B) before sentence 1.
C) after sentence 1.
D) after sentence 2.

CONTINUE

The team found that there were 341 haplotypes (DNA variations that are typically inherited as a set) that were specific to the regions of origin. Furthermore, significant variations were not found between outbreak and non-outbreak populations from the same area, and populations shared fewer and fewer similarities the more distant another population was. Taken together, these data led researchers to be fairly certain that genetic variations were due to local [9] variations—not migration.

The findings on the genetic similarities and differences indicate that local environmental factors are [10] within the outbreaks. Several studies suggest that those local factors could involve a deluge of nutrients during the wet season, while other studies suggest that the declining populations of predators allow the starfish to multiply unchecked. Whatever the factor or combination of factors, the findings mean that [11]

9

A) NO CHANGE
B) variations; not
C) variations. Not
D) variations; but not

10

A) NO CHANGE
B) upon
C) behind
D) under

11

Which choice most logically and effectively concludes this passage?

A) diving around coral reefs should be heavily restricted for the foreseeable future.
B) we will lose nearly all of the coral reefs in the world within the next decade.
C) management and prevention strategies should be tailored to local needs.
D) people should try to incorporate this starfish into traditional cuisines.

STOP

Questions 1-11 are based on the following passage.

Desk Jobs

[1] From *homo sapien* harpoons to the Samsung Galaxy phone, mankind has created tools to help itself complete tasks more efficiently. [2] As the "tool" is perfected, it [1] took on more basic responsibility of physical action or computation. [3] While the tool frees the operator to think on a higher level and quickens production, it also creates a primarily sedentary worker. [4] In combination with the millions of American manufacturing jobs being steadily outsourced, the evolution of technology has resulted in an economy dominated by desk jobs. [5] To combat this, American companies must develop more balanced work environments for their employees, as they recognize the major health risks posed by deskbound positions. [2]

1

A) NO CHANGE
B) takes
C) had taken
D) have taken

2

To make this paragraph most logical, sentence 5 should be placed

A) where it is now.
B) after sentence 1.
C) after sentence 2.
D) after sentence 3.

CONTINUE

The average American spends 13 hours a day in his or her chair, with only a remaining few spent actually moving or standing. Dr. James [3] Levine an endocrinologist and Co-Director of the Mayo Clinic program Obesity Solutions, has discovered through years of studying the sedentary lifestyle that sitting most directly slows down the metabolism. This causes weight gain along with the associated health [4] issues; cardiovascular problems, diabetes, cancers, and arthritis. Individuals who exercise rigorously, for an hour or so a day, can be afflicted by the same repercussions on a lesser scale, if their other waking hours remain largely inactive. [5] For example, small changes in habit may have the most success in battling the health risks of desk jobs.

Among the simplest measures that American companies can take to activate the everyday routines of office workers is the standing desk (or even walking meetings). Online blogger Gina Trapani works from home and made a New Year's resolution to switch to a standing desk in 2011. A full year later, she had no plans to switch back. [6] Gina stands for the majority of the day. She reports that she has increased her motion from pacing and fidgeting. In her first few weeks of using the standing desk, she lost 3 to 5 pounds.

3

A) NO CHANGE
B) Levine—an endocrinologist
C) Levine, an endocrinologist
D) Levine an endocrinologist,

4

A) NO CHANGE
B) issues: cardiovascular problems—
C) issues, cardiovascular problems;
D) issues: cardiovascular problems,

5

A) NO CHANGE
B) Thus,
C) Nevertheless,
D) Moreover,

6

Which choice most effectively combines the underlined sentences?

A) Gina stands for the majority of the day, reporting that she has increased her motion from pacing and fidgeting.
B) Gina stands for the majority of the day and additionally reported that she has increased her motion from pacing and fidgeting.
C) Gina stands for the majority of the day, having reported that she has increased her motion from pacing and fidgeting.
D) Gina stands for the majority of the day, and she also reported that she has increased her motion from pacing and fidgeting.

Additionally, certain companies have found that onsite wellness centers can incentivize by providing a communal environment. The proximity alone can be enough motivation to exercise, while many programs also offer reductions in health premiums for those dedicated to exercise. Company gyms—like those at Verizon, Discovery, and Cisco—can serve as **7** a meeting place that invigorate the daily routine and as relaxed settings that build co-worker relationships.

8 FitBit, for example, is a wrist device that keeps track of daily calories burned, steps taken, and overall time spent active. The Fitbit Wellness Division partners with corporations to create programs that focus on rewarding participation. Since Texas medical center Houston Methodist partnered with Fitbit Wellness in 2014, **9** it has distributed over 11,000 trackers among 4,000 employees. One of the first step challenges organized by Houston Methodist tasked workers with "over-stepping their superiors," initiating engagement and socialization between the CEO's and staff.

7

A) NO CHANGE
B) meeting places
C) places for meetings
D) a place to meet

8

Which choice most effectively introduces the topic of this paragraph?

A) Now, because of new technology, companies have more efficient ways to track the health of their employees.
B) For certain individuals, this onsite option is unattractive.
C) It is easy for hospitals to underestimate the benefits of having a company gym.
D) More creative workplace health initiatives have utilized other methods like friendly competition.

9

A) NO CHANGE
B) they have
C) it had
D) they had

CONTINUE

Over time, a healthy work environment benefits the employer and the individual equally. Overweight men and women miss a greater number of work days per year due to illness or injury on average, and healthy employees have higher productivity than those who continue to work while sick. **10** About 79% of them offer health improvement plans, and 54% of those are incentive-driven exercise programs. Dr. Ron Goetzel, a Senior Scientist at the Institute for Health and Productivity Studies, stresses that "companies are a microcosm of society." Using this logic, **11** <u>the same components that make up a balanced community must be present in a workplace to sustain successful employees.</u>

10

At this point, the writer is considering adding the following sentence.

> American employers are beginning to recognize the relationship between wellness and performance.

Should the writer make this addition here?

A) Yes, because it develops a point made in the previous sentence about about overweight employees.

B) Yes, because it clarifies the statement made in the following sentence about workplace health programs.

C) No, because it distracts from the paragraph's focus on the benefits of a healthy work environment.

D) No, because it contradicts the point made earlier in the paragraph that overweight employees are problematic for many companies.

11

Which choice most clearly ends the passage with a restatement of the writer's primary claim?

A) NO CHANGE

B) workplace health programs will ultimately be too costly to implement.

C) health initiatives for employers will also be neccessary to sustain the overall company.

D) companies can utilize improved social programs to engage and motivate their employees.

CONTINUE

Questions 1-11 are based on the following passage.

Stocks

Investing in the stock market can be described as the art of making money by doing nothing—and the less you do, the more money you make. I'm not joking about this (entirely). I am not trying to depict investors, investment bankers, and financial managers as unfairly-rewarded [1] "do-nothings"; movies such as *The Wolf of Wall Street* and blogs such as Goldman Sachs Elevator have been doing that for years (and still haven't ruined the romance of big-time investing). I'm actually giving [2] them a sound piece of advice, whether you're an activist investor with hundreds of millions at your disposal or a college student with a couple thousand dollars in an E-Trade account. Buy stocks and sit on them.

The principles of approaching investments as an exclusively long-term game [3] is nothing new. [4] Warren Buffett is widely regarded as the most successful investment businessman of the twentieth century. He famously noted that "the stock market is designed to transfer money from the active to the patient." For much of his career, Buffett's investment approach was to pour money into noted brands and well-structured companies and watch them gain strength over time. The idea is to find sound investments that may not

1

A) NO CHANGE
B) "do-nothings," movies
C) "do-nothings" movies
D) "do-nothings movies";

2

A) NO CHANGE
B) one
C) you
D) this

3

A) NO CHANGE
B) are
C) was
D) beings

4

Which choice most effectively combines the underlined sentences?

A) Widely regarded as the most successful investment businessman of the twentieth century, Warren Buffett was noted in famously saying that "the stock market is designed to transfer money from the active to the patient."
B) Warren Buffett famously noted that "the stock market is designed to transfer money from the active to the patient" and is therefore, widely regarded as the most successful investment businessman of the twentieth century.
C) Although widely regarded as the most successful investment businessman of the twentieth century, Warren Buffett famously noted that "the stock market is designed to transfer money from the active to the patient."
D) Warren Buffett, who is widely regarded as the most successful investment businessman of the twentieth century, famously noted that "the stock market is designed to transfer money from the active to the patient."

CONTINUE

do much day to day, but that will excel decade to decade. As Buffett noted elsewhere, "it's far better to buy a wonderful company at a fair price than a fair company at a wonderful price."

All investors dream of putting money on a stock and watching it double, triple, or skyrocket in a few days. The truth is that this seldom **5** happens; in forty years of investing, it never once happened to me. **6** (Late in 2014 I bought shares of the biomedical company Incyte, which doubled in value roughly five days after I made my purchase.) But the belief that it could happen is what propels many non-specialists into the activity known as "day trading"—investing based not on long-term investment quality but on making daily buys and sells in the hopes of accumulating a profit.

Day traders make investments based not on company fundamentals, but on market volatility. If a good company is poised to lose value, day traders will sell; if a terrible company is poised to gain value, day traders will buy. **7** At any rate, some day traders focus exclusively on relatively terrible companies and have had enormous luck doing so. Consider the story of **8** Tim Grittani who— began trading a few thousand dollars worth of penny stocks in 2011 and had amassed $1 million by 2014.

5

A) NO CHANGE
B) happens, in forty years
C) happens in forty years;
D) happens, in forty years,

6

The writer is considering deleting the underlined sentence. Should the sentence be kept or deleted?

A) Kept, because it reinforces the reasoning for long term investments.
B) Kept, because it anticipates the following information about day trading.
C) Deleted, because it offers an irrelevant detail that is not focused on the discussion of investment.
D) Deleted, because it contradicts the writer's argument in the previous sentence.

7

A) NO CHANGE
B) However,
C) Nevertheless,
D) In fact,

8

A) NO CHANGE
B) Tim Gittani; who
C) Tim Gittani, who
D) Tim Gittani. Who

CONTINUE

The pitfalls [9] with day trading, penny stocks, and excessive day-to-day financial posturing are evident to many. Perhaps these realities are not evident enough, though, in a world transformed by the Internet and increasingly prone to media-driven fantasies. Accessible investment platforms such as E-Trade do not really make investment expertise more accessible, and such expertise may not even be the point. Since 2008, hedge funds, which rely on professional day trading as a fundamental business strategy, have underperformed the stock market at large; late in 2011, [10] over 80% of hedge funds were operating at a loss. You would do better to pick household name companies you like and trust, put some money on them, and stick around—which is what I have done, buying stock in telecommunications companies, chemical companies, companies that provide auto parts, companies that manufacture toilet paper. Exciting? No. But seeing firsthand how the stock market transfers money "from the active to the patient" [11] has their own quiet thrill.

9

A) NO CHANGE
B) of
C) in
D) to

10

The writer wants to add information that reinforces the claim from the previous sentence about the underperformance of hedge funds. Which choice best accomplishes this?

A) NO CHANGE
B) less than 5% of hedge funds were operating at a loss.
C) over 80% of hedge funds produced profit.
D) more than 50% of hedge funds were profitable.

11

A) NO CHANGE
B) have their
C) has its
D) were its

CONTINUE

Questions 1-11 are based on the following passage.

Right Brain Left Brain

—1—

Are you right-brained or left-brained? Both Internet and print media have long been smitten with the notion that there are two types of people in the world: the right-brained, who are more creative, empathetic, and [1] spatially-minded, and the left-brained, who are more rational, analytic, and linguistically gifted. It's certainly an appealing idea. If it were true, a simple quiz could tell us our strengths and weaknesses—a valuable personal insight in just five minutes! But the brain is the most mysterious and intricate machine that science has yet encountered. Could such a simple, sweeping claim be true?

—2—

For the answer, we must travel back to the 1960s, when a team of researchers under Roger Sperry conducted a series of studies on epilepsy patients, who had been treated with a surgical procedure that severed the left and right hemispheres of the brain from each other by cutting the corpus callosum. Their clever tests found that, in isolation, the two hemispheres had different levels of involvement in a variety of tasks, such as math, language, and drawing. [2] However, the studies showed that there are notable differences between the hemispheres, at least when they're unable to communicate with each other.

1

A) NO CHANGE
B) spatially-minded; and the
C) spatially-minded, and the—
D) spatially-minded—and the

2

A) NO CHANGE
B) Additionally,
C) Regardless,
D) As a result,

CONTINUE

—3—

Popular psychology took this idea and ran with it. Before long, the complex differences that Sperry and his team had enumerated [3] was distilled into a more easily digestible concept, the "left/right" dichotomy we're familiar with today. Artists are right-brained, and economists are left-brained. It caught on like wildfire.

—4—

However, since the 1960s, the vast majority of relevant research has [4] either undermined but also directly contradicted this notion. A recent study at the University of Utah, analyzing over 1,000 brains, found no evidence that the subjects were more attuned to their right or left hemispheres. "It is not the case that the left hemisphere is associated with logic or reasoning more than the right," said [5] Dr. Jeff Anderson—lead author— of the study. "Also, creativity is no more processed in the right hemisphere than the left."

—5—

How would one even define the amorphous terms used by the myth's proponents, such as "creative" and "rational?" Creativity is particularly hard to measure in a laboratory setting. You can't just give your subjects a paintbrush, and have the researchers judge the paintings on a scale from one to ten; [6] art is, by definition, subjective.

3

A) NO CHANGE
B) were
C) is
D) will be

4

A) NO CHANGE
B) either undermined nor directly
C) neither undermined or directly
D) either undermined or directly

5

A) NO CHANGE
B) Dr. Jeff Anderson lead author
C) Dr. Jeff Anderson, lead author
D) Dr. Jeff Anderson, lead author,

6

The writer wants a concluding sentence that reinforces the main idea of the paragraph. Which choice best accomplishes this?

A) NO CHANGE
B) regardless, art is still predominantly for creative-minded people.
C) you can, however, have researchers judge the relevancy of the artwork.
D) thus, the concept of defining standards for art is easier than it seems.

CONTINUE

—6—

Even math, something that most people would firmly place under the "rational" column, is quite the mixed bag. [7] It includes a number of discrete skills, such as counting, calculating, estimating, and memory, each arising from processes that take place in both hemispheres. "Damage to either hemisphere can cause difficulties with math," according to Dr. Kara Federmeier, a professor at the University of Illinois. "This kind of pattern, in which both hemispheres of the brain make critical contributions, holds for most types of cognitive skills. It takes two hemispheres to be logical—or to be creative."

—7—

There is some solid research that outlines striking differences between the hemispheres. But such differences are rarely straightforward enough for popular science, and often vary wildly from person to person. [8] Likewise, Broca's area, a structure that controls much of our ability to speak, exists only on the left hemisphere—unless you're left handed, in which case it's just as likely to show up on your right side. Before you conclude that the left hemisphere has more aptitude for language, keep in mind that other activities (such as reading [9] and comprehending speech, are much more widely distributed between the two halves.

7

The writer is considering deleting the underlined sentence. Should the sentence be kept or deleted?

A) Kept, because it introduces the claim about the human brain provided in the following sentence.
B) Kept, because it further develops the claim about math in the previous sentence.
C) Deleted, because it offers an irrelevant detail that interrupts the discussion of math's creative aspects.
D) Deleted, because it repeats information about math that was provided earlier in the passage.

8

A) NO CHANGE
B) Consequently,
C) For example,
D) Similarly,

9

A) NO CHANGE
B) and comprehending speech)
C) but comprehending speech,
D) or, comprehending speech,

CONTINUE

—8—

Given the wealth of data opposing the myth of the "left/right" brain dichotomy, why does it enjoy such vigorous persistence, showing up everywhere from Oprah's "O" Magazine to CNN headlines? Part of it may be that, even if it's not good science, it's an excellent metaphor. We all know people who fit cleanly into the left-brain or right-brain personality types, and perhaps it's easier and more practical to think of them in this way. But by putting people in boxes, [10] we risk ignoring the human being underneath the type. No personality test, whether it's a Buzzfeed quiz or a Myers-Briggs assessment, can truly capture the fascinating complexity of the mind. As Neil deGrasse Tyson said, "Don't call me left brained, right brained. Call me human."

Question [11] asks about the previous passage as a whole.

10

A) NO CHANGE
B) journalists
C) researchers
D) Delete the underlined portion.

Think about the previous passage as a whole as you answer question 11.

11

To make the passage most logical, paragraph 2 should be placed

A) where it is now.
B) after paragraph 4.
C) after paragraph 5.
D) after paragraph 8.

Questions 1-11 are based on the following passage.

Food Deserts

Imagine a child arriving home for dinner to find a tub of Kentucky Fried Chicken on the table, rather than a home cooked meal with plenty of fruits and vegetables (and this occurs three times a week on average). [1] Imagine living in a community where a raw cantaloupe could be considered exotic for its scarcity. For many geographic areas in the United States with limited access to fresh and nutritious food, the fried chicken phenomenon is a reality. Yet even the biggest fans of KFC need a balanced diet.

[1] The U.S. Department of Agriculture has termed areas such as these "food deserts." [2] In these areas, the average diets often are high in sugar, fat, and salt—the calling card of processed comestibles. [3] More than 29.7 million Americans currently live in neighborhoods that qualify as food deserts, where fast food restaurants and convenience stores are the nearest, and primary, options for nourishment. [4] The consulting and research company, Mari Gallagher, labels these as "fringe retailers." [5] Community and health organizations, like this one, are searching for ways to improve the diets of America's food deserts in an effort to eliminate the high levels of obesity and chronic diseases that they foster. [2]

1

The writer is considering deleting the underlined sentence. Should the sentence be kept or deleted?

A) Kept, because it explains a term that is important to the content that follows.
B) Kept, because it adds more relevant information to the primary focus of the paragraph.
C) Deleted, because it repeats information that is mentioned previously.
D) Deleted, because it introduces information that blurs the focus of the paragraph.

2

To make this paragraph most logical, sentence 4 should be placed

A) where it is now.
B) before sentence 1.
C) before sentence 2.
D) after sentence 5.

CONTINUE

The circumstances hindering the residents of food deserts are unique in each community. The distance of a mile or two in an urban area that relies heavily upon various types of public transportation **3** were more comparable to the distance of 10 miles in a rural community. While an overwhelming number of qualifying sites are low income, factors such as education, ethnicity, and dietary restrictions must also be taken into account. **4** Fortunately, proposing broad solutions to the problem of inadequate nutrition is quite complex and challenging.

The 2011 presidential budget requested over 400 million dollars for a Healthy Food Financing Initiative (HFFI) to be launched. This program aims to open supermarkets and wholesome food retailers in food deserts across the nation. In addition to providing fresh food to nutritionally starved areas, the program purports that supermarkets can stimulate the economy of a disadvantaged area by creating jobs. For example, in 2010, the neighborhood supermarket in Highland Falls, New York closed its doors. **5** Securing a major financial loan from an international bank, a local couple was eventually able to re-open the abandoned store, with 16,000 square feet of new or improved produce vending space—creating 27 jobs. Highland Falls is just one example of the many success stories that this government initiative boasts since **6** it's inception.

3

A) NO CHANGE
B) was
C) is
D) are

4

A) NO CHANGE
B) Furthermore,
C) That is,
D) Thus,

5

Which choice provides the most logical introduction to the sentence?

A) NO CHANGE
B) Applying innovative business practices,
C) Then using financing from HFFI,
D) Popular with the town's chamber of commerce,

6

A) NO CHANGE
B) its
C) their
D) they're

CONTINUE

That said, research does not firmly suggest that establishing a new grocery store in a food desert will change the diets of those people living in it. A study conducted by population health professor Steven Cummins observed the population of a food desert in Philadelphia after a new supermarket was opened. The study showed no changes in BMIs [7] or the consumption levels of produce, and participants did not switch to better provisions. Rather, the community perception of access to food was [8] changed; the inhabitants, only had the sense that their area had improved.

However, there may be another solution. Citizens seeking to initiate their own change may help to fill the gaps between fresh food availability and affordability. Community farms and gardens provide one method [9] to augmenting diets in disadvantaged, urban areas with the nutrients that fringe retailers do not offer. Since 2011, the Shawnee area of Louisville, Kentucky has hosted [10] *The People's Garden* an outpost of the local non-profit Louisville Grows. The organization has produced more than 3,000 pounds of produce to be circulated among local markets since 2012. Farms like these viscerally connect individuals to the foods that they are eating, inviting them to be active, educated participants in the process of food arriving on the dinner table. With hope, homegrown initiatives can supplement [11] government programs. This can satisfy a need for community specific solutions and helping to alleviate America's hankering for healthy options.

7

At this point, the writer is considering adding the following to the sentence.

(body mass index)

Should the writer make this addition here?

A) Yes, because it defines an abbreviated term relevant to the study's findings.
B) Yes, because it further explains the writer's concern for the increasing trend of food deserts.
C) No, because it introduces a concept that is irrelevant to the paragraph's focus.
D) No, because it repeats information that is discussed elsewhere in the paragraph.

8

A) NO CHANGE
B) changed, the inhabitants
C) changed: the inhabitants
D) changed—the inhabitants—

9

A) NO CHANGE
B) with
C) of
D) in

10

A) NO CHANGE
B) *The People's Garden*, an outpost
C) *The People's Garden*, an outpost,
D) *The People's Garden*; an outpost,

11

Which choice most effectively combines the sentences at the underlined portion?

A) government programs, satisfying
B) government programs, but can satisfy
C) government programs; and satisfy
D) government programs: which can satisfy

STOP

Questions 1-11 are based on the following passage.

The Gist of Pipilotti Rist

Pipilotti Rist is a Swedish video artist [1] that has been producing work since the late 1980's. She studied video [2] by the School of Design in Basel, Switzerland. Over the course of her career, Rist has exhibited in both group and solo shows across the globe. Her artwork [3] focused on images of women and objects associated with women, such as flowers and makeup. Electric hues of pink and purple regularly color her films, while the individual images often appear to be softened.

[1] In 2008, Rist exhibited at the Museum of Modern Art in New York City. [2] Installed in the museum's atrium, Rist's show consisted of a sixteen-minute film played on a loop. [3] The effect was immersive, almost as though the viewer had been placed at the bottom of a bowl. [4] In this way, Rist created an artistic womb in which to nurture the museum's visitors. [4]

1

A) NO CHANGE
B) who
C) whom
D) whose

2

A) NO CHANGE
B) for
C) at
D) with

3

A) NO CHANGE
B) focuses on
C) focusing on
D) focuses into

4

The writer plans to add the following sentence to this paragraph.

> Due to the scale of the projection, the viewer was surrounded by floor-to-ceiling images on all sides.

To make the paragraph most logical, the sentence should be placed

A) after sentence 1
B) after sentence 2
C) after sentence 3
D) after sentence 4

CONTINUE

Unlike passive and uninterested television spectators, Rist's viewers actively choose to bring themselves into her art. Thus, to accommodate her audience, Rist routinely transforms the physical spaces of her installations into areas that viewers can comfortably **5** inhabit. Her 2011 exhibit at the Australian Centre for Contemporary Art, *I Packed the Postcard in My Suitcase*, demonstrates this idea. **6** So, Rist projected her videos both onto the ceiling and onto arranged piles of fabric on the floor. Viewers could lie down and absorb the images, which drifted by like passing clouds.

Some critics found the warmth of the environment generated by *I Packed the Picture in My Suitcase*, and the pleasantry of Rist's imagery, to be cloyingly friendly. But pleasantry is not a prevailing state for Rist. Rather than providing mellow sensations all the time, she has actively challenged contemporary culture; she appropriates videos from mass media and uses a great deal of popular and contemporary music in her pieces. Her video *Sip My Ocean*, **7** then, is set to an interpretation of Chris Isaac's pop song "Wicked Game." **8** This whimsical tactic likens her to a producer of experimental music.

5

A) NO CHANGE
B) inhibit.
C) habitat.
D) exhibit.

6

Which choice provides the most logical introduction to the sentence?

A) NO CHANGE
B) But,
C) Consequently,
D) There,

7

A) NO CHANGE
B) therefore,
C) also,
D) for example,

8

Which choice most effectively concludes the paragraph?

A) NO CHANGE
B) Here as elsewhere, Rist appropriates contemporary culture for the purposes of re-evaluation and critique.
C) Frustration with songs that seem faddish has led some art critics to become frustrated with Rist's entire project.
D) Generally, Rist knows how to find the most beautiful aspects of mass-marketed entertainment.

CONTINUE

Rist's awareness of popular culture is complemented by her participation in the intellectual or "conceptual" turn that art-making has recently taken. **9** Increasingly the concept, or idea behind the creation of artwork supersedes that idea's physical manifestation. The Rist video *Open My Glade (Flatten)* depicts a blonde woman, her body bare from the shoulders up. She is heavily made up with red lipstick and blue eye shadow. She **10** stood before a pane of glass and proceeds to rub her face back and forth across it, streaking it with makeup. Here, **11** Rist records the creation of something emotional and visceral, rather than distantly ideological or academic. She makes art accessible to the viewer.

9

A) NO CHANGE
B) Increasingly, the concept or idea behind the creation of artwork
C) Increasingly, the concept or idea behind the creation of artwork,
D) Increasingly, the concept or idea, behind the creation of artwork

10

A) NO CHANGE
B) had stood
C) has stood
D) stands

11

Which choice most effectively combines the sentences at the underlined portion?

A) although Rist records the creation of something emotional and visceral, rather than distantly ideological or academic, and makes art accessible to the viewer.
B) Rist records the creation of something emotional and visceral, rather than distantly ideological or academic, making art accessible to the viewer.
C) Rist records the creation of something emotional and visceral, rather than distantly ideological or academic in contrast to making art accessible to the viewer.
D) Rist records the creation of something emotional and visceral, rather than distantly ideological or academic; which makes art accessible to the viewer.

CONTINUE

Questions 1-11 are based on the following passage.

Lucky as an Owl

Owls, often associated with Athena, goddess of wisdom and war, can be regarded 1 to be totems of protection. It is said that the feather of an owl can repel illness and negative influences. In some countries, a dead owl nailed to a barn door is believed to 2 attract wild animals which spend the entire night staring at the figure. The silent passage of the owl through the forest night can be seen as a metaphor for the observation of ourselves by the gods, who make no comment but note all that we do (or do not do) in our passage through life. It is an unnerving metaphor perhaps, but also possibly a comforting one.

I am not the only one to believe this. The 3 Zuni, a Native American tribe, of the Pueblo peoples believe that placing an owl feather in a 4 babies crib guards the baby from evil spirits. Essentially, the hooting of an owl signifies the coming of death upon an individual. But 5 they left an owl feather in the crib was an attempt to confuse the owl so that death would not descend upon the infant. For me, it is unclear whether or not this custom indicates that the owl was truly a positive, benevolent force. Regardless, the prevalence of this practice means that, for the Zuni, the owl was benign.

1

A) NO CHANGE
B) as
C) like
D) for

2

Which choice best supports the point made about owls in the previous sentence?

A) NO CHANGE
B) bring wealth and fortune to a family.
C) ward off both wolves and robbers.
D) signify reverence for the power of large birds.

3

A) NO CHANGE
B) Zuni a Native American tribe of the Pueblo peoples,
C) Zuni—a Native American tribe of the Pueblo peoples,
D) Zuni, a Native American tribe of the Pueblo peoples,

4

A) NO CHANGE
B) babies'
C) babys'
D) baby's

5

A) NO CHANGE
B) if they had left
C) leaving
D) when they leave

CONTINUE

I remember coming home after school to my Grandmother's house and [6] to see a large stuffed owl suspended from twine and attached to the frame of the front door. I am not really the superstitious type. I do not believe that adorning my car with a trinket of Saint Christopher will safeguard me from accidents or that [7] driving a car is ever really a safe activity. [8] Therefore, when I used to walk under her door, I felt all of my troubles melt away like snow. I felt invincible, protected, safe. Perhaps this feeling can really be explained by the comforts that Grandma had to offer [9] me: a warm snack, afternoon cartoons, and her little quips and anecdotes about her life in bucolic Tuscany. "Owls are good luck, dear. They keep the wolves away from the sheep. Just look at the eyes. Like daggers into a dark spirit's soul. No malicious force would dare cross an owl." Grandma would "hoot" at the owl any time she felt as though she were being watched. That strange yet familiar feeling of discomfort, which signified an intangible though unwelcome presence in the room, successfully faded with each "hoot."

6

A) NO CHANGE
B) I saw
C) I see
D) seeing

7

Which choice offers a second supporting example that is most similar to the example earlier in the sentence?

A) NO CHANGE
B) a rabbit's foot is lucky.
C) birds of prey are typically malicious.
D) knocking on wood to avoid bad luck is ineffective.

8

A) NO CHANGE
B) In light of this,
C) Nonetheless,
D) Likewise,

9

A) NO CHANGE
B) me, a warm snack, afternoon cartoons, and,
C) me: a warm snack, afternoon, cartoons, and
D) me—a warm snack, afternoon cartoons, and,

CONTINUE

Grandma passed away thirty years ago; since then, I [10] <u>had kept</u> my own version of her owl hanging wherever I have lived, from my childhood bedroom to my dorm room to [11] <u>it's</u> current resting place, my own home. Sometimes I "hoot" at the owl, remembering her. You may smile in a patronizing fashion at this, but my Grandma's old habit has worked so far.

10

A) NO CHANGE
B) have kept
C) will keep
D) would keep

11

A) NO CHANGE
B) its'
C) its
D) their

CONTINUE

Grammar Drill 39

Questions 1-11 are based on the following passage.

Earth Invades Mars!

The process of terraforming, or planetary engineering, was first proposed by science fiction writer Will Stuart in the [1] year 1940's, but has since been adopted as practical theory among modern scientists. Leading this group, Carl Sagan advocated the idea of terraforming Venus in *Science* journal (1961) and [2] later Mars in *Icarus* journal (1973). The process itself involves scientifically altering the environment of another planet to make it suitable for human habitation and biological growth, [3] without the use of elaborate life support systems. The practice is presently hypothetical and depends on a wide range of factors, including the current and historical geology, atmosphere, and chemical composition of the world in focus.

1

A) NO CHANGE
B) 1940's
C) 1940 years
D) year and decade 1940

2

A) NO CHANGE
B) then later transforming Mars for
C) later Mars's transformation for
D) later doing Mars in

3

The writer is considering deleting the underlined sentence. Should the writer do this?

A) Yes, because science fiction novels seldom feature realistic life support systems.
B) Yes, because it simply re-phrases an idea presented slightly earlier.
C) No, because it gives a pertinent detail that clarifies the concept of terraforming.
D) No, because it highlights a limitation of past terraforming projects.

CONTINUE

[1] These factors make certain planets appear better candidates for modification **4** <u>than others.</u> [2] Data from robot-operated spacecraft **5** <u>has</u> allowed scientists to determine that Mars was previously much more temperate and moist than its existing cold, dry climate would suggest. [3] By introducing certain greenhouse gases with low freezing points, planetary engineers would endeavor to thicken the existing atmosphere of Mars. [4] As a result, the surface might become sufficiently warm to once again generate liquid water and, eventually, to sustain biological ecosystems. [5] **6** At one point, liquid water flowed across the surface of the planet, forming the great canyons and mountains observable today.

Among the greenhouse gases with the potential for powerful heating effects are chlorofluorocarbons (or CFCs), which are human-generated organic compounds consisting of carbon, chlorine, and fluorine. Manufacturers have chiefly used these substances in refrigerants and aerosol products. In the late 1970's, scientists began arguing that such compounds **7** <u>has</u> significantly depleted the Earth's ozone layer; production of CFCs has since been heavily regulated. These compounds, so devastating to Earth's atmosphere, may be a paradoxical part of the recipe for transforming Mars into a Garden of Eden. The desired warming effect has already been marginally produced on Earth, and crudely demonstrates that humans are **8** <u>capable about altering</u> the climate on a planetary scale.

4

A) NO CHANGE
B) than it does others.
C) than others used to be.
D) than others are feasible to modify.

5

A) NO CHANGE
B) had
C) have
D) will have

6

To make this paragraph most logical, sentence 5 should be placed

A) where it is now.
B) after sentences 1.
C) after sentence 2.
D) after sentence 3.

7

A) NO CHANGE
B) had
C) were
D) will be

8

A) NO CHANGE
B) capable to alter
C) a capability to alter
D) capable of altering

CONTINUE

The initial goal of introducing greenhouse gases into the Martian atmosphere [9] is raising the mean temperature of the planet above the freezing point of water. Other stages of terraforming might involve the introduction of microbes to the Martian surface. These small organisms, while too tiny to see with the naked eye, produce many of the Earth's gases; some microbes do not need oxygen to survive. With very little liquid water, vast communities of microbes might subsist on the Martian soil. Through such soil consumption, these microscopic organisms [10] would expel quantities of gases large enough to help further insulate the planet. [11] Thus water would flow profusely, in a manner very similar to its origin on Earth.

9

A) NO CHANGE
B) is razing
C) is to raise
D) are raising

10

A) NO CHANGE
B) have expelled
C) do expel
D) expel

11

Which choice best supports the statement made in the previous sentence?

A) NO CHANGE
B) We could then study these organisms for clues to survival in extreme environments,
C) Thus life would begin on Mars,
D) The gas would cease to be harmful,

CONTINUE

Questions 1-11 are based on the following passage.

Mystery Shoppers: Commerce Goes Undercover

For some people, shopping is a tedious [1] chore, for others, it may be a source of enjoyment. For a third group, shopping is actually a job. The incognito business tactic known as "mystery shopping" has become an increasingly popular method of assessing customer satisfaction. While winning new customers is important, most business models stress the importance [2] in making sure of customer loyalty through repeated positive interactions; mystery shopping can help a business to gauge how consistently those positive interactions are taking place.

1

A) NO CHANGE
B) chore, which for
C) chore; but for
D) chore; for

2

A) NO CHANGE
B) of ensuring
C) in reassuring
D) of insuring

CONTINUE

[1] Individuals who work as mystery shoppers function a bit like undercover detectives: by posing as people [3] <u>who buy a product or using</u> a service for personal purposes, these stealthy consumers are able to simulate a typical customer service interaction. [2] Mystery shoppers can be hired [4] <u>providing</u> assessments of customer service, vendor expertise, or product placement and display. [3] After this interaction, they will then provide a report either to the specific business or to a third-party customer assessment firm. [4] Depending on what aspect is under assessment, a mystery shopper may be given a specific task. [5] For example, someone hired to assess staff knowledge about a digital camera brand may be given a series of questions to ask and then be required to score how effectively the staff answered each inquiry. [6] Mystery shoppers need to be keenly observant, as small details are often [5] <u>crucial, a shopper</u> for instance, may be required to note an employee's manner of greeting customers or the position of an employee's name badge. [6]

3

A) NO CHANGE
B) buying a product or to use
C) buying a product or using
D) buy a product or use

4

A) NO CHANGE
B) provide
C) in providing
D) to provide

5

A) NO CHANGE
B) crucial: a shopper
C) crucial: a shopper,
D) crucial, a shopper,

6

To make this paragraph most logical, sentence 3 should be placed

A) where it is now.
B) after sentence 1.
C) after sentence 4.
D) after sentence 6.

CONTINUE

The mystery shopping industry has experienced steady growth in recent years, **7** <u>although customer surveys are still the most popular form of customer service quality control.</u> According to Fred Philips, the head of the store observation department for a major mystery shopping **8** <u>firm; todays</u> purchasers "have more disposable income and they want more service. They're not so price conscious, but they're more service

7

Which choice most effectively sets up the information in the following sentence?

A) NO CHANGE
B) yet research suggests that it will grow even more.
C) due largely to worsening customer service practices.
D) thanks in part to increasingly exacting customer service standards.

8

A) NO CHANGE
B) firm; today's
C) firm, todays
D) firm, today's

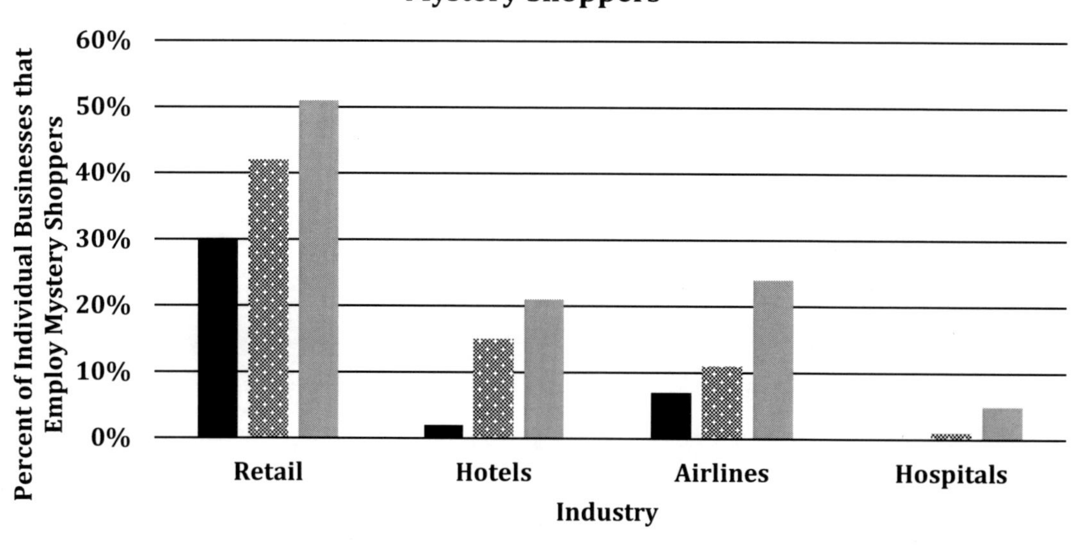

CONTINUE

conscious." There [9] has also been a steady expansion of mystery shopping practices outside of the retail industry. While hotels and airlines [10] employ identical numbers of mystery shoppers, hospitals use mystery shoppers significantly less often.

Many of the problems detected by mystery shoppers can be traced [11] on deficient employee knowledge and poor training. Mystery shoppers, indeed, are instrumental in pointing the way to specific enhancements. For some mystery shoppers, contributing to improved standards of customer service provides job satisfaction. An anonymous shopper who has worked in the industry for nearly ten years explains that he is motivated "to assist in providing a better shopping experience." For others, the thrill of maintaining secrecy can make working as a mystery shopper an interesting job.

9

A) NO CHANGE
B) were also
C) have also been
D) having also been

10

Which choice offers an accurate interpretation of the data in the chart?

A) NO CHANGE
B) have steadily increased in use of mystery shoppers, hospitals have also begun to employ mystery shoppers.
C) are not using mystery shoppers as much as hospitals, they use mystery shoppers much more than retail businesses.
D) have seen a recent downtrend in mystery shopper use, they are still using mystery shoppers more than hospitals.

11

A) NO CHANGE
B) to
C) for
D) in

STOP

Questions 1-11 are based on the following passage.

Keeping Your Cool with Hot-Desking

"Hot-desking" refers to a system of workplace organization in which different individuals utilize the same workspace (either a desk or a physical office) on a rotating basis. This contrasts with traditional systems of organization in which workers are assigned permanent spaces, often according to status or seniority. Technology, particularly a reliance on mobile devices, [1] make it possible for employees to move more easily between different workspaces and has facilitated the rise of hot-desking. Desires for more flexible working hours, as well as the option to work from home or from another remote location, can be much more readily accommodated within a hot-desk workplace.

[2] Hot-desking, offers a number of advantages, which businesses often cite when deciding whether to adopt this model. It accounts for the reality of a high proportion of workers not being physically present in the office at [3] once, according to a study conducted in 2013, approximately 30% of the individual offices in American workplaces are vacant at any given time. Employee vacancies may be due to travel, meetings (both in conference rooms and off-site), or decisions to work from home.

1

A) NO CHANGE
B) made
C) have made
D) has made

2

A) NO CHANGE
B) Hot-desking:
C) Hot-desking
D) Hot-desking—

3

A) NO CHANGE
B) once; according
C) once—according
D) once, so according

CONTINUE

Hot-desking therefore allows businesses to maintain spaces that are proportional to the number of individuals likely to be occupying a given office at the same time, rather than **4** about the total number of employees. The option to lease a smaller space then becomes a possibility, and this possibility is especially attractive in major city centers, **5** where rent can become a significant operational cost.

6 Despite the economic benefits for employers, there may be other advantages to hot-desking. This method of office organization both makes it easier for employees to work remotely **7** while creating an office culture that encourages this practice. It may also boost creativity and collaboration, and encourage greater levels of interaction between employees with different jobs. **8** But there are drawbacks to hot-desking.

4

A) NO CHANGE
B) with
C) on
D) to

5

A) NO CHANGE
B) which
C) when
D) that

6

Which choice best connects the sentence with the previous paragraph?

A) NO CHANGE
B) In addition to economic benefits for employers,
C) Besides the savings for employees,
D) Though operational costs vary from city to city,

7

A) NO CHANGE
B) while it creates
C) and creates
D) and creating

8

The writer is considering deleting the underlined sentence. Should the writer do this?

A) Yes, because it detracts from the writer's main point in this paragraph.
B) Yes, because it makes a claim about hot-desking that is not supported by the passage.
C) No, because it supports the passage's argument that hot-desking is ultimately detrimental.
D) No, because it illustrates a general principle discussed in this paragraph.

CONTINUE

[1] However, critics point out that many individuals tend to prefer the stability, routine, and sense of control associated with having an individualized, permanent workspace. [2] Workspace distribution in many offices has also often been traditionally tied to status within the organization. [3] If employees feel threatened or competitive due to unfamiliar workspace arrangements, 9 they're feelings can heighten interpersonal conflict, leading to disruptions and reduced efficiency. [4] By allowing employees to work in many different spaces, including spaces outside of the office, hot-desking 10 may possibly also make it more difficult for employers to monitor productivity. [5] For example, a promotion to a more senior role might be accompanied by a move to a larger or more desirable office. [6] Yet whether it is a benefit or a drawback, hot-desking, in many modern offices, is here to stay. 11

9

A) NO CHANGE
B) their
C) his or her
D) there

10

A) NO CHANGE
B) may
C) might have
D) may perhaps

11

To make this paragraph most logical, sentence 5 should be placed

A) where it is now.
B) after sentence 1.
C) after sentence 2.
D) after sentence 3.

CONTINUE

Grammar Drill 42

Questions 1-11 are based on the following passage.

Pantomime Time

It is quite difficult to explain to anyone who is not British what exactly Pantomime is. Foreigners are bemused by this particular theatrical genre, which [1] appears annually from Christmas to March every year. Clearly it is [2] popular, it plays to packed houses. Going to see a "Panto" at Christmas [3] have often been the first (and, in many cases, the only) time a child is ever taken to the theater. The whole family goes, for a holiday treat, so there has to be something about the show that will appeal to each member of the family. The theme always concerns a poor and good hero making his way to success and riches against all odds. An element of magic [4] could be important, since it allows for a "transformation" scene, which is always the dynamic, sparkling climax to the first half of the Pantomime. Children (and very often adults) sit agape when such a spectacle unfolds before their eyes.

[1] A proper "Panto" [5] is a thoroughly rehearsed performance: "something for everyone" necessitates the inclusion of acrobatics, dancing, music, and, above all, glamor and comedy. [2] [6] In other words, these two last elements are created through role reversal and cross dressing—techniques that may strike audiences beyond Britain as strange, but that are Pantomime essentials. [3] "He" is always played by a woman,

1

A) NO CHANGE
B) every year appears from Christmas to March, annually.
C) annually appears from Christmas to March.
D) it appears annually from Christmas to March.

2

A) NO CHANGE
B) popular: it
C) popular when it
D) popular it

3

A) NO CHANGE
B) were often
C) was often being
D) has often been

4

A) NO CHANGE
B) would be
C) was
D) is

5

Which choice best introduces the information that follows?

A) NO CHANGE
B) is an eclectic affair
C) performs nearly every night
D) carefully coordinates a sophisticated set of performers

6

A) NO CHANGE
B) However,
C) To avoid confusion,
D) DELETE the underlined portion and begin the sentence with a capital letter.

CONTINUE

who strides across the stage dressed as a man. [4] The comedy is provided by the character of the Dame, always played by a deep-voiced man in a big wig, billowy costume, and exaggerated makeup. [5] This role reversal is one of the ways in which the Pantomime takes on the surrealism of a dream and motivates the audience to suspend the logic of everyday life. [7]

[8] The most extraordinary element of Pantomime is the participation of the audience. They are encouraged to sing along with the cast, call out when the hero is in danger, join in the moments of slapstick comedy on stage, boo the villain, and sigh contentedly when the hero finally wins the heroine. A tremendous sense of relationship builds up between the characters on the stage [9] to the real life of the audience: topical

7

The writer plans to add the following sentence to this paragraph.

> The Hero is the Pantomime character who imparts glamor to the whole show.

To make this paragraph most logical, the sentence should be placed

A) after sentence 1.
B) after sentence 2.
C) after sentence 3.
D) after sentence 4.

8

Which choice most effectively combines the underlined sentences?

A) The audience is encouraged to sing along with the cast, call out when the hero is in danger, join in the moments of slapstick comedy on stage, boo the villain, and sigh contentedly when the hero finally wins the heroine, this audience participation is the most extraordinary element of Pantomime.
B) The audience's participation, which is encouraged to sing along with the cast, call out when the hero is in danger, join in the moments of slapstick comedy on stage, boo the villain, and sigh contentedly when the hero finally wins the heroine, is the most extraordinary element of Pantomime.
C) The most extraordinary element of Pantomime is the participation of the audience, which is encouraged to sing along with the cast, call out when the hero is in danger, join in the moments of slapstick comedy on stage, boo the villain, and sigh contentedly when the hero finally wins the heroine.
D) The most extraordinary element of Pantomime, which is encouraged to sing along with the cast, call out when the hero is in danger, join in the moments of slapstick comedy on stage, boo the villain, and sigh contentedly when the hero finally wins the heroine, is the participation of the audience.

9

A) NO CHANGE
B) and
C) for
D) as

CONTINUE

jokes, innuendos, and characters coming down from the stage and mixing with the audience are all favored "Panto" techniques. [10] The final moments of a Pantomime bring this interactive element to a climax. The Dame appears in front of the curtain and a huge sheet printed with song lyrics descends.

The Dame and the audience now work together one last time, chatting, interacting, and [11] they sing together lustily. Then, prompted by a drum roll, those onstage return to their seats. The Dame exits, and the curtains part to reveal the final scene, where the villains are thwarted and the hero and heroine are united, rich at last and greeted with the audience's happy applause.

10

The writer is considering deleting the underlined sentence. Should the sentence be kept or deleted?

A) Kept, because it introduces and identifies the relevance of the following sentences.
B) Kept, because it points out that audience participation is only important in one part of the play.
C) Deleted, because it blurs the focus of the paragraph by shifting to a summary of the play's ending.
D) Deleted, because it weakens the writer's point about Pantomime being a cheerful genre.

11

A) NO CHANGE
B) sing
C) singing
D) they would sing

CONTINUE

Questions 1-11 are based on the following passage.

Finding the Missing Lynx

[1] The lynx has roamed the earth for over two million years, and has wandered at times into human folklore. Throughout Europe and Northern America, there [2] have arose myths that emphasize the elusive and mysterious powers of this relatively small wildcat. Folk tales speak of an alliance between the lynx and the Morning Star: it was believed that the animal's remarkable powers of vision were linked with the purity of that star's light. From this association stemmed the belief that the animal's sight could pierce solid objects and reach what might be hidden from others. Indeed, the rugged independence of the lynx made it a figure of power, and its very isolation [3] (since these wildcats avoid human settlements) gave it an almost mystical status.

1

Which choice most effectively introduces the main idea of the paragraph?

A) NO CHANGE
B) The lynx is not only a beautiful creature but also a daunting and unusual one.
C) Through the ages, the human imagination has been drawn to elusive and ferocious animals.
D) Animal activists are in an uproar over declines in lynx populations.

2

A) NO CHANGE
B) were raised
C) have arisen
D) are arising

3

At this point, the writer is considering deleting the following portion of the sentence.

(since these wildcats avoid human settlements)

Should the writer make this deletion?

A) Yes, because it is redundant.
B) Yes, because it contradicts a previous statement.
C) No, because it clarifies the preceding statement.
D) No, because it mentions the impact of humans on the lynx.

CONTINUE

There are currently four distinct variations of lynx in the Northern hemisphere: Iberian, Eurasian, Canadian, and Bobcat. All species mate in late winter; cubs are born within two months and stay with their mothers for about a year before setting off on their own. The appearance of the typical lynx is both [4] elegant and practical. Its fur can range in color from gold to white. The lynx's ears are often tipped with black hair; its tail is short and its paws are padded for walking on snow. High-altitude forests and rocky heights, far from human habitation, [5] has long been the animal's natural habitat.

While it is true that the Lynx is a carnivore, [6] it does not, as a rule, attack domestic beasts. Nor does it attack humans, though humans, sadly, have often hunted it.

At present, the lynx is third, after the brown bear and the gray wolf, on the list of endangered species for North America and Europe. [7] Its can still be found in the more remote areas of Norway and Sweden and in several of the Baltic countries, but it is already almost extinct elsewhere. In Britain, the lynx population was wiped out in the seventeenth century. In 1995, a report on the state of wildlife in Washington revealed that there were fewer than 250 lynx roaming the state. By 2000, in 49 of the 50 United States, the lynx was recorded as being threatened with extinction [8] and about to disappear. So much, perhaps, for its abilities of clairvoyance.

4

Which choice most effectively combines the two sentences at the underlined portion?

A) elegant and practical in that its fur can range in
B) elegant and practical, with fur that can range in
C) elegant and practical by having fur that can range in
D) elegantly and practically ranged with fur in

5

A) NO CHANGE
B) have
C) had
D) will have

6

A) NO CHANGE
B) it does not as a rule,
C) it does not, as a rule
D) it does not; as a rule,

7

A) NO CHANGE
B) It's
C) They
D) It

8

A) NO CHANGE
B) and going to disappear.
C) and unable to live anymore.
D) DELETE the underlined portion.

CONTINUE

Yet the existence of these conscientious lists of endangered species **9** reflect the new concern and attention that the lynx is garnering. There have been some attempts to re-establish the lynx in especially rugged parts of Europe. **10** In addition, in Colorado and the Rockies there has been a tentative reintroduction. Perhaps the lynx will flourish in such habitats, with only campers and mountain climbers for human company. **11**

9

A) NO CHANGE
B) reflects
C) are reflecting
D) reflected

10

The author is considering deleting the underlined sentence. Should the sentence be kept or deleted?

A) Kept, because the additional information supports the main idea of the paragraph.
B) Kept, because the lynx is more important in the United States than in Europe.
C) Deleted, because mentioning areas outside Europe distracts from the author's argument.
D) Deleted, because it reiterates information that appears in an earlier paragraph.

11

At this point, the writer is considering adding the following sentence.

> At present, the lynx is not common in zoos and wildlife parks, but could soon become a popular fixture at such attractions.

Should the writer make this addition here?

A) Yes, because it reinforces the author's other ideas about wildlife conservation.
B) Yes, because it indicates that contemporary ecologists are interested further study of the lynx.
C) No, because it undermines the passage's claim that the lynx will soon become extinct.
D) No, because distracts from the paragraph's discussion of efforts to reintroduce the lynx.

CONTINUE

Questions 1-11 are based on the following passage.

Economic Cycles

In the limited space of an urban environment, bicyclists and automobile drivers can at times feel at odds with one another. Cars can pose a serious threat to cyclists: one study performed in 2008 and 2009 found that  over 2,000 cyclists had been recently injured in Toronto and Vancouver. Risk can be a deterrent for many potential cyclists, even though bicycles are an environmentally friendly and physically invigorating form of urban transit.

1

Which choice provides the most accurate and relevant information from the graph?

A) NO CHANGE
B) the safest city for cyclists is Calgary.
C) more injuries and fatalities from cycling occur in Canada than in any other country.
D) at least 1,000 cyclists are killed each year in Toronto, Vancouver, Ottawa, and Winnipeg.

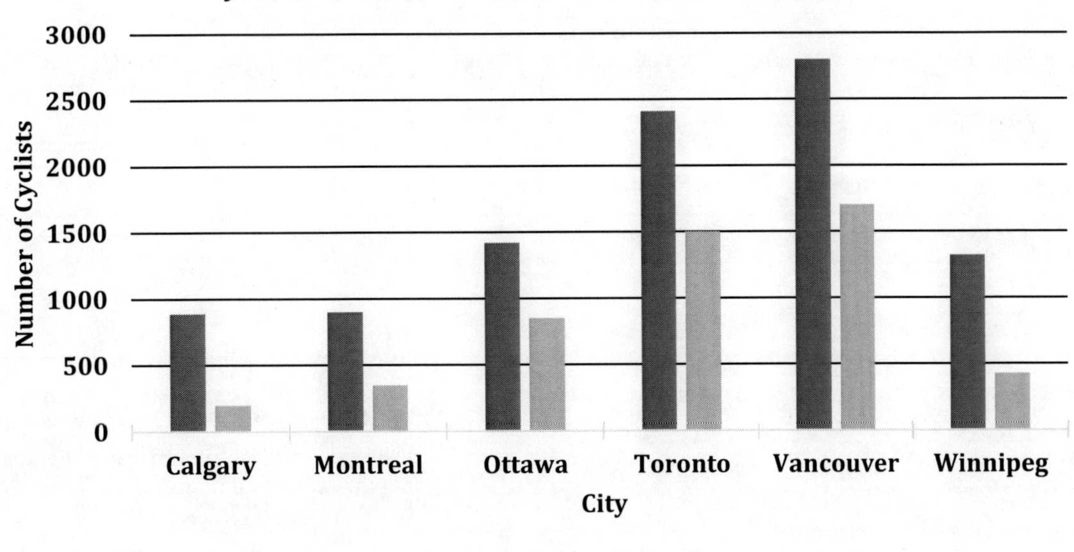

CONTINUE

John [2] Forester, a cyclist and urban planner asserted decades ago that the safest and most effective way for cars and bicycles to share the road is for cyclists to behave like car drivers and take up part of the main roadway. In many cities in the U.S., this practice remains the norm. However, not all cyclists agree with Forester, and sometimes roadway sharing can lead to accidents: for example, [3] drivers who are used to seeing bikers on the road are more likely to pay attention and yield to those cyclists.

Today, many cyclists prefer commuting options such as bike lanes separated from main [4] roadways, and such lanes are built at the expense of valuable car parking spaces. Business owners [5] being worried that converting parking spaces into bike lanes is economically unwise, since limited parking would cause consumers to migrate to new businesses or to just stay home. [6] Yet this worry turns out to be unfounded. It turns out that cyclists spend roughly the same amount as drivers. In fact, as a 2012 survey of New York City residents revealed, cyclists

2

A) NO CHANGE
B) Forester, a cyclist and urban planner,
C) Forester—a cyclist and urban planner
D) Forester: a cyclist and urban planner,

3

Which choice provides the most relevant detail?

A) NO CHANGE
B) a cyclist in a dedicated bike lane may become complacent and crash due to lack of attention.
C) a cyclist who decides to coast through a stop sign to save energy runs the risk of colliding with an oncoming car.
D) it is a fairly common occurrence for speeding cars to crash into the median of a highway.

4

A) NO CHANGE
B) roadway's, and
C) roadway's, though
D) roadways, though

5

A) NO CHANGE
B) worried
C) were worrying
D) worry

6

Which choice most effectively combines the two underlined sentences?

A) Yet this worry turns out to be unfounded, it turns out that cyclists spend roughly the same amount as drivers.
B) Yet this worry is unfounded: cyclists spend roughly the same amount as drivers.
C) Yet this worry about cyclists is unfounded, spending roughly the same amount as drivers.
D) Yet this worry has turned out to be unfounded, so cyclists spend roughly the same amount as drivers.

CONTINUE

outspend drivers by $20 per capita. [7] Although, as one study in Melbourne, Australia, demonstrated, even if each cyclist [8] were to spend less money in one trip than each driver, merchants still would see net revenue increases, since approximately six bicycles can park in the space allotted to one car.

Research such as this indicates that both cyclists and automobile drivers can have a positive impact on neighborhood economics. The challenge for U.S. cities [9] are to provide safe passage for cyclists within existing infrastructure so that bicycles can travel without facing the perils of parking cars, intermittently stopping buses, and other automobile-related hazards. Bike lanes may be the answer: a 2010 study of the Vancouver area found that using separate bike lanes presented only 10% of the risk of cycling on main roadways.

In New York City, the years 2006-2010 saw major progress in bike infrastructure; [10] with the city now containing more than 400 miles of bike lanes today. By adding even more protected lanes, the city can both protect its cyclists [11] as well as work towards a major transportation target—bicycle usage that accounts for 6% of all trips within the city.

7

A) NO CHANGE
B) Furthermore,
C) Since
D) Whereas,

8

A) NO CHANGE
B) spend
C) had spent
D) having spent

9

A) NO CHANGE
B) are providing
C) is the provision of
D) is to provide

10

A) NO CHANGE
B) the city currently contains
C) the city contains
D) the city containing

11

A) NO CHANGE
B) and
C) plus
D) also

STOP

Questions 1-11 are based on the following passage.

Mutual Attraction: New Magnetic Metals

— 1 —

Many aspects of modern technology [1] rely on the use of magnets. Magnetic Resonance Imaging (MRI) technology uses magnets to obtain anatomical images, which facilitate diagnosis and treatment. Magnets inside credit cards allow these thin pieces of plastic to communicate valuable financial information. Computer memory storage requires magnets, and wind turbines transform wind into electricity using magnets. Yet only three of all known metals are permanently magnetic at room temperature: iron, nickel, and cobalt. Others can hold only a weak charge for a short period of time, so manufacturers rely [2] almost only exclusively on these three elements.

— 2 —

While it is possible to turn a non-magnetic object containing iron, nickel, or cobalt into a magnet by passing a magnet over the object, the new technology requires a more specialized approach. The researchers coated thin pieces of copper and manganese with a special one-nanometer layer of organic molecules called "buckyballs." [3] Buckyballs are spheres made of 60 carbon atoms. The interaction between the metal and buckyball layers [4] transfer some electrons from the metal to the organic layer, and this change makes the metal magnetic.

1

A) NO CHANGE
B) relies
C) to rely
D) relying

2

A) NO CHANGE
B) almost exclusively in only
C) only exclusively in
D) almost exclusively on

3

The writer is considering deleting the underlined sentence. Should the sentence be kept or deleted?

A) Kept, because it supports the writer's claim that magnetizing metals is a simple process.
B) Kept, because it defines a term that is important in this paragraph.
C) Deleted, because it blurs the paragraph's focus by discussing a loosely related detail.
D) Deleted, because it provides information that is found earlier in the passage.

4

A) NO CHANGE
B) transferring
C) transfers
D) that transfer

CONTINUE

—3—

The research team was indeed able to produce magnets, though these were relatively weak. Copper produced a stronger effect than manganese, yet was ten times weaker than nickel and thirty times weaker than iron. However, the significance of this research lies in the permanence of the magnetism, rather than [5] their strength, since [6] it shows that it is possible for scientists to [7] work around a supposedly intrinsic property of metals. One of the study's lead authors, Tim Moorsom, likens this breakthrough to mixing iron and carbon to produce steel, which is lighter and more flexible than iron, and therefore can be used in a different range of applications. This magnetizing technique, if it can be successfully applied to metals beyond copper and manganese, may prove to be just as useful when it comes to computing innovations.

—4—

Fatma Al Ma'Mari, another of the study's lead authors, [8] predict that computing will soon require new types of materials, including new magnets, to provide greater storage and processing abilities. [9] However, these small, efficient components may even make computers more environmentally friendly. Improved computing and storage ability combined with improved energy and material efficiency would be a positive step for technologies that are increasingly necessary for many industries.

5

A) NO CHANGE
B) its
C) its'
D) it's

6

A) NO CHANGE
B) this study
C) they
D) the team

7

A) NO CHANGE
B) make accommodations for
C) fight against
D) evade

8

A) NO CHANGE
B) predicts
C) have predicted
D) predicting

9

A) NO CHANGE
B) Thereafter,
C) Furthermore,
D) So,

CONTINUE

— 5 —

A recent **10** breakthrough in materials, science may help to change this situation. In a 2015 study led by scientists at the University of Leeds, a research team was able to generate weak magnetism in two non-magnetic metals, copper and manganese. These elements are relatively abundant and the team's innovative technology could expand the range of possible metals used for magnetic applications.

Question 11 asks about the previous passage as a whole.

10

A) NO CHANGE
B) breakthrough in materials science, may help
C) breakthrough, in materials, science may help
D) breakthrough in materials science may help

Think about the previous passage as a whole as you answer question 11.

11

To make the passage most logical, paragraph 5 should be placed

A) where it is now.
B) after paragraph 1.
C) after paragraph 2.
D) after paragraph 3.

CONTINUE

Questions 1-11 are based on the following passage.

More Than One Way to Bounce a Dead Cat

In 2014, electronics retailer RadioShack was well on [1] there way to corporate catastrophe. The company's stock price had declined [2] from almost \$3 per share in 2013 to a paltry \$0.50 per share just two years later. Yet there was a break from all this bad news when RadioShack stock experienced a brief period of recovery and, temporarily, reached a price of \$1.00-1.50 per share in the summer of 2014. From there, the stock abruptly reversed course and [3] plummeted; the company itself filed for bankruptcy in February of 2015.

1

A) NO CHANGE
B) its
C) it's
D) their

2

Which choice most accurately and effectively represents the information in the graph?

A) NO CHANGE
B) from its highest point to a paltry \$0.50 per share just a year later.
C) from almost \$5 per share in 2012 to a paltry \$1.50 just two years later.
D) from almost \$5 per share in 2012 to a paltry \$0.50 per share just two years later.

3

A) NO CHANGE
B) plummeted, the
C) plummeted, but the
D) plummeted, with the

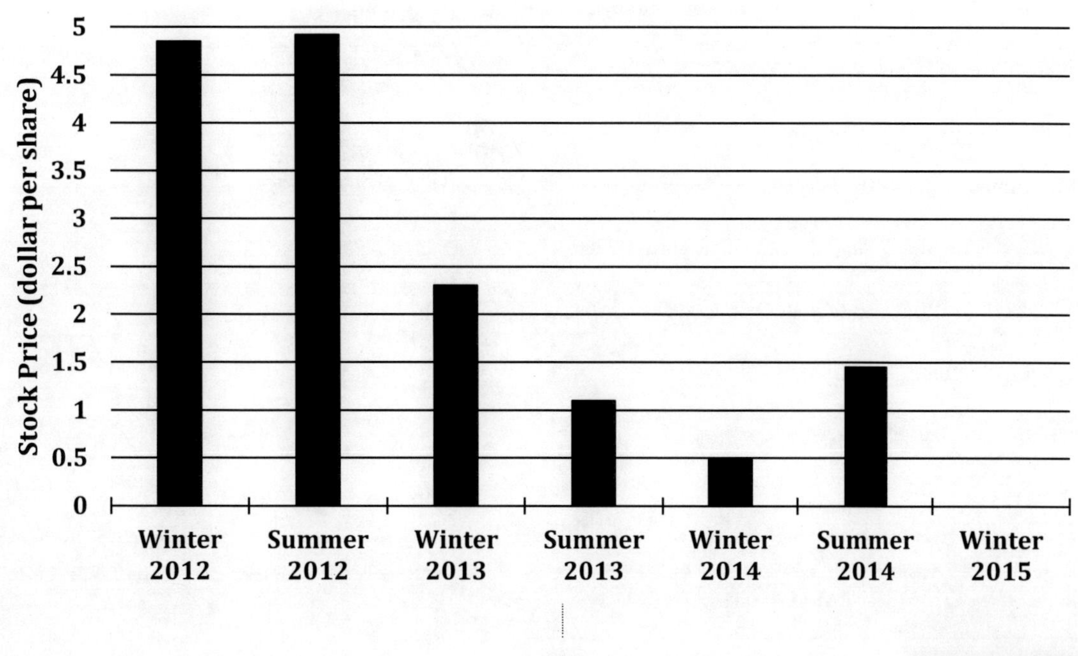

CONTINUE

What happened to RadioShack in this brief reversal of ill fortune [4] were what economists call a "dead cat bounce." This phenomenon takes its name from the idea that even something as lifeless and useless [5] than a dead cat will bounce if dropped from a high enough elevation. [6] The reasons for such a bounce are various. In business, a spate of good press, a sudden investment, or the normal ups and downs of the stock market may "bounce" a company slightly higher; however, such a bounce should not obscure the overall and irreversible downtrend that, by definition, must accompany a "dead cat bounce."

Yet it is not uncommon for commentators [7] interpreting a "dead cat bounce" as a genuine business turnaround. One source of such mistaken interpretation is simply wishful thinking: after all, the glory days of a dying business can have a nostalgic value that clouds better judgment. Many Americans, [8] for instance, fondly remember how RadioShack flourished decades ago by selling electronic equipment to homeowners, hobbyists, and computer startups. Nobody would really want such a business to fail, even if it ultimately does. There is also the idea, equally prevalent but equally false, that a dead cat bounce represents an opportunity to profit. In truth, if you buy stock in a company that is experiencing such a bounce, you are buying into a small, hard-to-gauge uptick and a larger pattern of decline.

4

A) NO CHANGE
B) being
C) is
D) are

5

A) NO CHANGE
B) for
C) to
D) as

6

The writer is considering deleting the underlined sentence. Should the writer do this?

A) Yes, because it merely reformulates the thought in the previous sentence.
B) Yes, because it undermines the writer's claims about the prevalence of dead cat bounces.
C) No, because it introduces the following sentence.
D) No, because it reinforces the writer's point that dead cat bounces are preventable.

7

A) NO CHANGE
B) to interpret
C) that interpret
D) when interpreting

8

A) NO CHANGE
B) however,
C) likewise,
D) regardless,

CONTINUE

[9] Dead cat bounces are notoriously difficult to spot. First, consider the market at large, and see if there is still healthy demand for the kind of goods and services a company provides: if such demand [10] will dry up, expect little more than a dead cat bounce. Second, look at the on-the-ground operations: a company that is single-mindedly downsizing its operations or changing leadership in a panic is probably headed nowhere but down. And third, [11] to keep in mind that turnaround success stories are much-publicized yet ultimately rare, while dead cat bounces—even though the press never reports most of them—abound.

9

Which choice most effectively sets up the paragraph?

A) NO CHANGE
B) So how can you decide whether a company is experiencing the beginning of a turnaround or simply a dead cat bounce?
C) So how can a company avoid experiencing a dead cat bounce, and acquire the investments necessary for a true business rebound?
D) Most people don't understand the fundamental strategies involved in making sound short-term investments.

10

A) NO CHANGE
B) dried
C) had dried
D) has dried

11

A) NO CHANGE
B) keeping
C) keep
D) make sure that you keep

Questions 1-11 are based on the following passage.

Aspiring to a Spire: Domfront's New Church

To most people, the phrase "country village in France" instantly conjures up the [1] image of a group of houses in the middle of verdant pasture, or nestled in the protective curve of rolling hills, or perched on the peak of a stony outcrop. There will be a bakery for warm fresh baguettes, a small, low-roofed café with its parasol tables where [2] urbanites from Paris scoff at this provincial life. There will be a war memorial, and a church, the bells of which will chime the day away.

Domfront, where I live in Lower Normandy, has all these features with one omission: the central church. Established in the early Middle Ages, Domfront does not seem to have had much success with religious structures, despite the fact that the town [3] lie on the pilgrimage road from Paris to the Abbey of Saint Michel on the coast. In the beginning, there were three Gothic churches here; all are now picturesque ruins [4] currently.

1

A) NO CHANGE
B) image with
C) image that
D) images in which

2

Which choice provides the most relevant detail?

A) NO CHANGE
B) the villagers smoke and chat and read their newspapers.
C) the townsfolk discuss the gentrification of their rural existence.
D) tourists find respite from a long day of sightseeing.

3

A) NO CHANGE
B) lay
C) lays
D) lies

4

A) NO CHANGE
B) today
C) presently
D) DELETE the underlined portion

CONTINUE

[1] In modern times, the village's efforts centered on Saint Julien's plaza, where the small Chapel of Saint Julien once stood. [2] This chapel was 5 raised in the eighteenth century and rebuilt fifty yards away on a wider area. [3] The townspeople should not have 6 bothered, without the enlarged and reconstructed edifice fell into a state of near-collapse by the end of the nineteenth century. [4] Yet Domfront decided to approach the Church of Saint Julien anew after World War I. [5] The resurrected structure would be distinguished by its neo-Byzantine design: the church would be built not in the traditional shape of a Latin cross, 7 but the square shape characteristic of Byzantine churches, a much more space-efficient layout. [6] To cut down the cost, the planners also decided to build the church using concrete, not cut stone. [7] Nonetheless, Domfront has persisted in 8 it's church-building.

9

5

A) NO CHANGE
B) risen
C) razing
D) razed

6

A) NO CHANGE
B) bothered, since
C) bothered, but
D) bothered for,

7

A) NO CHANGE
B) but also
C) but in
D) but even

8

A) NO CHANGE
B) its
C) its'
D) their

9

To make this paragraph most logical, sentence 7 should be placed

A) where it is now.
B) before sentence 1.
C) before sentence 4.
D) before sentence 6.

It took nineteen years to complete the building [10] (in part because the planners decided to add a fifty-one meter spire after the central dome was already built). Domfront's Church of Saint Julien consequently became a prominent part of the local scenery, easily seen from miles away. However, in the end, the weight of the spire was punishing to the concrete supports. The church had to be closed for safety reasons in the 1990s, just seventy years after it was completed.

Yet all was not lost. In 2013, Domfront completed a final round of repairs and the bells of Saint Julien [11] rung once more. The Domfront citizenry was ecstatic! The local pastry shop created special cakes for the occasion, and the local café hosted light festivities. If history is kind, the church will last forever.

10

The writer is considering deleting the parenthetical statement. Should the writer do so?

A) Yes, because it does not provide a specific example.
B) Yes, because it distracts from the main idea of the sentence.
C) No, because it provides additional detail supporting the main idea of the sentence.
D) No, because it continues the description of Byzantine architecture begun in the previous paragraph.

11

A) NO CHANGE
B) rang
C) rings
D) will ring

Questions 1-11 are based on the following passage.

Giving Your Two Scents

The British poet and novelist Rudyard Kipling wrote that "scents are surer than sights or sounds/ To make the heart strings crack." He intuitively understood what modern science and commerce have demonstrated: scents can trigger powerful psychological associations. Tastes are equally compelling. [1] Despite this, it is obvious that different flavors will drive consumer preferences for products such as food and beverages, flavor is also crucial to a growing number of non-edible goods, from dental floss to lipstick.

[1] The power of flavor and fragrance to influence consumer experiences [2] drive a global industry worldwide. [2] In the nineteenth century, it gradually became possible to synthesize aroma chemicals, allowing for the reproduction of characteristic tastes and smells. [3] Consumer goods associated with the flavor and fragrance industry now include pet food, vitamins, and laundry detergent, not to mention food, beverages, and perfumes. [4] Among these sensation-oriented products, which grow ever more varied, exotic and complex combinations of scents and tastes [3] has become increasingly more commoner. [5] Since then, more and more products have begun to appear in scented or flavored varieties. [4]

1

A) NO CHANGE
B) While
C) Given that
D) DELETE the underlined portion and begin the sentence with a capital letter.

2

A) NO CHANGE
B) drives a global industry worldwide.
C) drive a global industry.
D) drives a global industry.

3

A) NO CHANGE
B) have become increasingly more common
C) has become increasingly commoner
D) have become increasingly common

4

To make this paragraph most logical, sentence 5 should be placed

A) where it is now.
B) after sentence 1.
C) after sentence 2.
D) after sentence 3.

CONTINUE

Flavor and fragrance are usually only small components of a finished product, typically accounting for between one and five percent of manufacturing attention, yet consumers will often **5** cite taste or smell as a top reason for preferring one brand **6** against another. The fragrance and flavor industry thus **7** occupying a position at the intersection of psychology and **8** science, it relies on a highly sophisticated set of processes to accurately reproduce and combine scents and flavors, and on an understanding of what individuals find appealing about certain smells and tastes. It is also both global and culture-specific: there will be very different expectations of what might smell "fresh" or "cozy" in different regions of the world. The complexity of the industry means that the jobs within it are wide-ranging and rely on different skill sets. While chemists perform the technical work of synthesizing flavor and fragrance compounds, focus group coordinators test how consumers are likely to respond to new combinations and marketing specialists develop strategies for branding and promotion.

5

A) NO CHANGE
B) site taste
C) sight taste
D) siting taste

6

A) NO CHANGE
B) than
C) to
D) at

7

A) NO CHANGE
B) occupies
C) occupy
D) occupy's

8

A) NO CHANGE
B) science: it relies
C) science; which relies
D) science, they rely

CONTINUE

The flavor and fragrance business [9] were experiencing steady growth since 2011 and is projected to continue to grow at least through 2017. The global sector of this industry is now estimated to have [10] an annual value of 25 billion dollars each year. [11] The reasons for steady growth include the constant consumption of scented and flavored products; for example, laundry detergent is used every time clothes are washed. Expenditures on these products also tend to vary relatively little during periods of economic fluctuation. For as long as the prospect of a pleasant scent or delicious taste can entice consumers, the market for flavor and fragrance is likely to thrive.

9

A) NO CHANGE
B) have experienced
C) has experienced
D) had experienced

10

A) NO CHANGE
B) an annual yearly value of 25 billion dollars.
C) an annual value of 25 billion dollars per year.
D) an annual value of 25 billion dollars.

11

A) NO CHANGE
B) Huge things about
C) Big causes behind
D) Main things leading up to

STOP

Questions 1-11 are based on the following passage.

The Digital Generation

Can you remember a world before the Internet? For many individuals born in the mid-1980s or later, the answer is no. "Digital natives" is a term that has been used to refer to people [1] that have lived the entirety of their lives surrounded by the digital technology that has come to define much of contemporary culture. Marc Prensky, an educational consultant, coined the term in 2001. The term was adapted from the notion of a "native speaker" of a [2] language, that is someone who was never formally "taught" a language but acquired it naturally through early exposure. Likewise, a whole generation has grown up in a world where computers, videos, video games, and social media are [3] all over the place. In contrast, older people are known as "digital immigrants" [4] :these individuals have been introduced to digital tools and technologies later in life and have had to adapt.

1

A) NO CHANGE
B) who
C) whom
D) DELETE the underlined portion.

2

A) NO CHANGE
B) language that is
C) language that,
D) language:

3

A) NO CHANGE
B) universal.
C) commonplace.
D) invasive.

4

The writer is considering deleting the underlined portion of the sentence. Should the writer do this?

A) Yes, because it repeats information already mentioned in the paragraph.
B) Yes, because it sets up a new topic at the end of the paragraph.
C) No, because it sets up the argument that older people lack direct experience with technology.
D) No, because it explains a term discussed earlier in the sentence.

CONTINUE

Much of the interest in the notion of a generation of digital natives has involved questions of conflict [5] between this group and today's large population of digital immigrants. Education has often been a dominant issue. [6] Commentators who are friendly to digital natives argue that students now require the use of media and technology in classroom settings in order to learn effectively. However, many educators were never trained to incorporate technology. Educators may thus feel unsure about their competence. As a result, they may be perceived as increasingly [7] out of reach with the needs and expectations of a new generation of students.

5

A) NO CHANGE
B) between your
C) among this
D) amongst

6

Which choice most effectively combines the underlined sentences?

A) While commentators friendly to digital natives argue that students now require the use of media and technology in classroom settings in order to learn effectively, many educators were never trained to incorporate technology.
B) Commentators friendly to digital natives argue that students now require the use of media and technology in classroom settings in order to learn effectively; likewise, many educators were never trained to incorporate technology.
C) Contrasted with commentators friendly to digital natives arguing that students now require the use of media and technology in classroom settings in order to learn effectively, educators were never trained to incorporate technology.
D) When commentators friendly to digital natives argue that students now require the use of media and technology in classroom settings in order to learn effectively, many educators were never trained to incorporate technology.

7

A) NO CHANGE
B) out of touch
C) out of style
D) out of place

CONTINUE

Other conflicts between digital natives and those who acquired digital aptitudes later in life may arise in workplaces, [8] whereas increased reliance on technology and digital communication can put digital natives at an advantage and lead to tension with older staff members. Debates between parents and children [9] with reliance on and appropriate usage of cellphones, video games, and social media offer further examples of a potential gap in understanding.

[1] While recognizing and analyzing an apparent generational divide is valuable, [10] heavy reliance on the concept of the "digital native" risks oversimplification. [2] Not everyone born in the same era has had equal access to digital technologies. [3] Because access to technology is often tied to relatively high income and education, the digital native paradigm risks excluding individuals from certain socio-economic backgrounds. [4] Current research into digital media behaviors draws on a wide range of viewpoints. [5] This breadth of perspective is likely to provide an optimal understanding of how individuals have been affected by growing up in an electronic and online world. [11]

8

A) NO CHANGE
B) in which
C) where
D) from

9

A) NO CHANGE
B) in
C) on
D) about

10

A) NO CHANGE
B) being heavily relied
C) relying too heavily
D) heavy relying

11

The writer wants to add the following sentence to this paragraph.

> Thus individuals of the same age may differ radically in digital competence.

To make the paragraph most logical, the sentence should be placed

A) after sentence 1
B) after sentence 2
C) after sentence 3
D) after sentence 4

CONTINUE

Questions 1-11 are based on the following passage.

Cognitive Science Comes of Age

— 1 —

The set of mental processes through which the brain acquires knowledge [1] are known as cognitive functioning. These processes include perception, reasoning, problem solving, and the creation of memories. A number of [2] disruptions, such as strokes or head injuries, may lead these functions to become impaired. Individuals suffering from cognitive impairment may display problems recalling familiar information and may also find it difficult [3] completing simple tasks; they may also exhibit poor judgment or experience personality changes.

— 2 —

[4] In a world of rapidly expanding technology, medical professionals can employ any one of a number of different tests. These tests typically involve asking individuals to perform tasks related to one or more cognitive processes and then determining whether the individuals' abilities fall [5] to a normal range. [6] For example, in the Clock-Drawing Test, elderly patients will either be presented with a blank sheet of paper and be asked to draw a clock-face from memory, or be given a sheet with a circle printed on it and be asked to fill in the appropriate numbers. Some variations of the test will also require individuals to draw the hands of the clock positioned to indicate a specific time.

1

A) NO CHANGE
B) were
C) is
D) was

2

A) NO CHANGE
B) disruptions—such as strokes or head injuries,
C) disruptions such as strokes, or head injuries
D) disruptions such as, strokes or head injuries,

3

A) NO CHANGE
B) to complete
C) for the completion of
D) in completing

4

Which choice best introduces the paragraph?

A) NO CHANGE
B) As a testament to their ingenuity,
C) In order to identify cognitive impairment,
D) To find effective treatments for dementia,

5

A) NO CHANGE
B) for
C) throughout
D) within

6

A) NO CHANGE
B) Given that,
C) Finally,
D) To be clear,

CONTINUE

— 3 —

Among the general population of today's advanced countries, aging is the primary cause of cognitive impairment. Cognitive impairment that significantly affects an elderly individual and disrupts [7] their daily life may be termed dementia, and the prevalence of dementia increases with age: a 2015 study suggests that 5% of individuals [8] aged 71 to 79 years experience dementia; for individuals aged 80 to 89 years, that figure rises to 68%. Many other elderly individuals experience milder forms of cognitive impairment, which involve symptoms that are similar but not severe enough to indicate dementia.

7

A) NO CHANGE
B) one's
C) his or her
D) everybody's

8

Which choice offers the most accurate and relevant information from the data in the chart?

A) NO CHANGE
B) aged 71 to 79 years experience incontinence; for individuals aged 80 to 89 years, that figure rises to 22%.
C) aged 71 to 79 years experience dementia; for individuals aged 80 to 89 years, that figure rises to 24%.
D) aged 80 to 89 years experience dementia; for individuals aged 71 to 79 years, that figure rises to 41%.

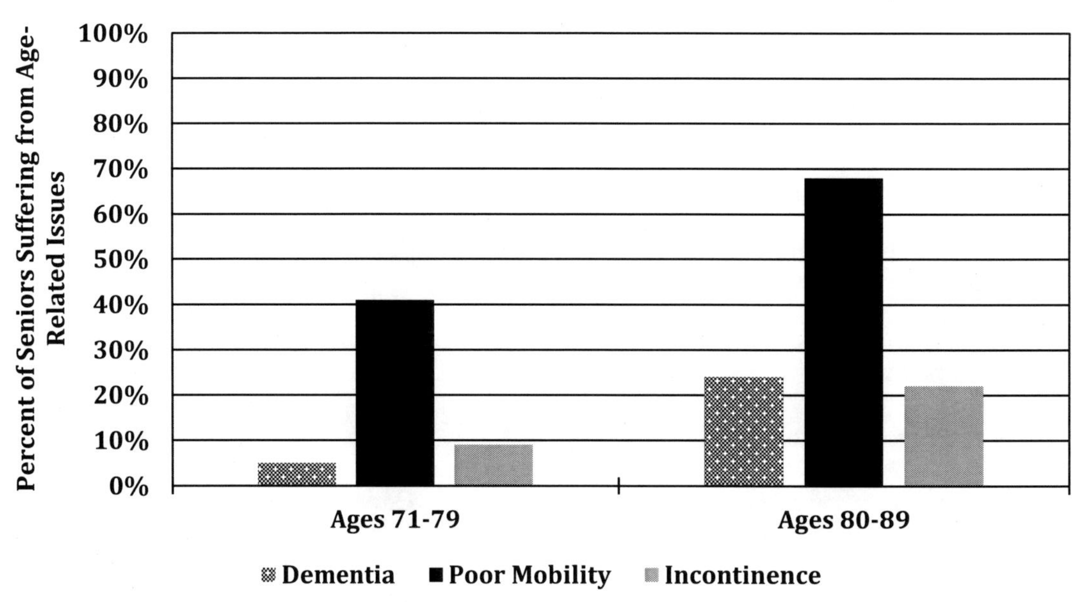

CONTINUE

—4—

Despite the seeming lucidity of these procedures, various problems [9] are posed by the current methods of assessing cognitive functioning. There is the possibility of mis-diagnosis or inconclusive diagnosis, since uncontrollable factors that may lead to poor performance on a cognitive assessment test [10] can complicate test results. Conducting a full cognitive assessment is also often a lengthy process and requires a highly-trained supervisor, both to administer the assessment and to interpret and score the tests.

—5—

Fortunately, recent research has yielded cognitive assessment tools that are more accessible, such as brief questionnaires. The results of the questionnaires often require review by a physician, but these forms can offer a useful method for quickly identifying individuals likely to be suffering from cognitive impairment.

Question [11] asks about the previous passage as a whole.

9

A) NO CHANGE
B) is posed
C) posing
D) are being posed

10

The writer is considering adding the following information.

—acute pain, chronic pain, and psychological distress (such as depression or anxiety)—

Should the writer make this addition here?

A) Yes, because it provides support for the writer's claim that many factors cause dementia.
B) Yes, because it elaborates on the writer's reference to uncontrollable factors.
C) No, because it would be better placed elsewhere in the passage.
D) No, because it provides detail that does not explain the main point of the paragraph.

Think about the previous passage as a whole as you answer question 11.

11

To make the passage most logical, paragraph 3 should be placed

A) where it is now.
B) after paragraph 1.
C) after paragraph 4.
D) after paragraph 5.

Questions 1-11 are based on the following passage.

The Rise and Fall of Vaudeville

Vaudeville, an American theatrical pastime, still exists today as the more commonly known "variety show." This form of theater began in the late 1800s and reached its peak popularity around 1910. In the early years of the twentieth century, Americans needed an escape from the unpleasant realities of urban crowding and menial labor. Audiences flocked to Vaudeville theaters, often drawn by [1] there burlesque set [2] pieces, they featured scantily clad female performers. However, as theater promoters sought new opportunities, standard Vaudeville evolved into a more genteel version known as "Polite Vaudeville."

This new form of Vaudeville did not have any uniform structure, other than an eclectic set of acts mashed together under one playbill. Performances included musicians, singers, dancers, set-piece comedians, magicians, male and female impersonators, acrobats, jugglers, and occasionally one-act plays. Most of these forms [3] being interactive in nature, often provoking the audience to cheer or jeer at the performances and the performers. Importantly, Polite Vaudeville began to emphasize "family entertainment" as a marketing strategy. [4] The American family became important for Polite Vaudeville, and with that change, this form of theater also changed its focus.

1

A) NO CHANGE
B) its
C) it's
D) their

2

A) NO CHANGE
B) pieces, some of them featured
C) pieces, which featuring
D) pieces, which featured

3

A) NO CHANGE
B) are
C) were
D) were to be

4

The writer is considering deleting the underlined sentence. Should the writer do this?

A) Yes, because it merely reformulates the thought in the previous sentence.
B) Yes, because it directly contradicts the writer's point about Polite Vaudeville.
C) No, because it sets up the argument that will follow.
D) No, because it introduces an additional difference between older Vaudeville and Polite Vaudeville.

CONTINUE

[5] As the audience transitioned into this parents-with-children demographic, many performances took the lionization of the American Dream as their topic. Illustrating and celebrating the theme of upward mobility through individual hard work, [6] and defeating all odds, most set pieces for Polite Vaudeville had to be "peppy" with an often superficial struggle of a protagonist. [7] Then, the hero would rise to the occasion, overcome an arbitrary and trivial obstacle, and then go on to save his family, his farm, or some other cherished aspect of his life.

These performances were (and are) easy to criticize, since they promised victory and relief to Americans who faced harsh social and economic conditions on a daily basis. However, some rare Vaudeville performances were more political and took derisive jabs at the institutions that [8] emulated the American Dream. Irrespective of their specific content and its virtues, Polite Vaudeville performances all invited audiences to think, comment, and even participate.

5

Which choice most effectively transitions from the previous paragraph and introduces the information that follows?

A) NO CHANGE
B) As a result of the economic struggles most Americans faced,
C) Despite the shift in audience from adults to families,
D) Largely due to the influence of the government,

6

A) NO CHANGE
B) most set pieces for Polite Vaudeville had to be "peppy," featuring the often superficial struggle of a protagonist who defeats all odds.
C) a protagonist and a superficial struggle to defeat all odds often were featured in these "peppy" set pieces for Polite Vaudeville.
D) most set pieces for Polite Vaudeville, "peppy" and featuring an often superficial struggle of a protagonist defeating all odds.

7

A) NO CHANGE
B) Typically,
C) Consequently,
D) Nevertheless,

8

A) NO CHANGE
B) helped
C) achieved
D) perpetuated

CONTINUE

But [9] <u>all that</u> would not last. Some *dramaturges* [10] suggest that, as cinema's popularity [11] <u>promulgated</u>, the interactive nature of performances like those of Polite Vaudeville declined. This theatrical ebb led to a disconnect between the audience and the performance, replacing what was once engaging theater with the spectacle of movie-goers passively staring at a celluloid screen.

9

The writer wants to more specifically identify what changed about entertainment in America. Which choice best accomplishes this goal?

A) that style of theater
B) the cynical and jaded attitude of the audience
C) the prevalence of audience involvement
D) disaffection with the American Dream

10

At this point, the writer is considering adding the following information.

—theater experts—

Should the writer make this addition here?

A) Yes, because it defines an obscure term in the sentence.
B) Yes, because it illustrates the reason for the change.
C) No, because it interrupts the flow of the sentence by supplying irrelevant information
D) No, because it weakens the focus of the passage by discussing a subject other than Polite Vaudeville.

11

A) NO CHANGE
B) grew
C) fostered
D) opened

CONTINUE

Questions 1-11 are based on the following passage.

A High-Tech Helping Hand

For a person who is missing a limb due to illness, accident, or a congenital condition, a prosthetic limb is a tool for independent living. Modern prosthetics can be highly specialized to fit the needs of specific wearers, and the expertise of biomedical engineers is fundamental to prosthetic limb design.

Conventional prosthetic limbs require careful measurements of an individual patient to ensure that the device fits the body as [1] closer than possible. Engineers have typically been concerned [2] for aspects of prosthetics such as the weight and function of artificial joints. Lightweight design is essential for prosthetic limbs because they contain no muscles of their own and require extra effort from remaining muscles to [3] move, such exertions can be tiring for the wearer. Some prosthetic limbs are controlled through [4] will power and frequent practice. For example, an artificial hand can grip an object through the manipulation of shoulder muscles. While these types of devices have their merits, they [5] clearly do not resemble true human parts.

1

A) NO CHANGE
B) closely for
C) close as
D) closely as

2

A) NO CHANGE
B) with
C) on
D) about

3

A) NO CHANGE
B) move, these
C) move; and such
D) move; such

4

Which choice provides the most relevant detail?

A) NO CHANGE
B) careful movement of distant muscle groups.
C) vigorous exercise of a single limb.
D) electromagnetic impulses from the brain.

5

Which choice best sets up the topic of the following paragraph?

A) NO CHANGE
B) have not been seriously considered by engineers.
C) can also be less precise than some users would like.
D) are also prone to malfunction and breakage.

Modern technological advancements are allowing engineers to experiment with more precise and sophisticated devices. Biomedical engineers who understand the neuromuscular structures of the body [6] has developed ways to link a device and [7] its wearer without relying on external motors or cables that respond to more distant muscles. Myoelectric prosthetic devices respond to the electrical impulses in the muscles of a truncated limb, which in some cases are still able to contract as though the limb were intact. Based on this electrical activity, the artificial limb can move naturally.

6

A) NO CHANGE
B) had developed
C) have developed
D) developing

7

A) NO CHANGE
B) its'
C) it's
D) their

One challenge facing engineers in prosthetics research and development is how to provide nervous system feedback on a prosthetic limb's activity. **8** Human limbs can quickly register information about temperature and texture, and this kind of sensory information is what allows a person to shake someone's hand without crushing it or to hold a cup without letting it fall. In response to such considerations, biomedical engineers are conducting new research to test prosthetic limbs that, in addition to listening **9** to the bodys' electrical impulses to detect whether and how to move, can also give feedback to the body the way an organic limb does. **10** It would use electrical activity to tell the brain how much pressure an artificial limb is exerting on an object. A biomedical engineer **11** that works on such advanced prosthetic limbs is naturally required to work closely with users to identify needs and to test out possible solutions; only through subtlety and sensitivity will a new and improved generation of prosthetic devices be developed.

8

The writer is considering deleting the underlined sentence. Should the sentence be kept or deleted?

A) Kept, because it highlights the superiority of natural body systems.
B) Kept, because it details an ability that the engineers are attempting to recreate in prosthetic limbs.
C) Deleted, because it undermines the writer's notion that all capabilities can be recreated in prosthetic limbs.
D) Deleted, because it merely provides experimental details that are not relevant to this paragraph.

9

A) NO CHANGE
B) to the bodies
C) at the body's
D) to the body's

10

A) NO CHANGE
B) This technology
C) They
D) The scientists

11

A) NO CHANGE
B) works
C) working
D) will work

STOP

Questions 1-11 are based on the following passage.

Low Visibility, High Wages

For many people, the words "high-salary job" bring to mind the [1] figure of doctors, lawyers, business executives, and international celebrities. [2] Far less people, upon hearing these same words, would think of air traffic controllers. However, in 2015, the average air traffic controller earned a salary of roughly $126,000, according to the jobs and employment statistics site Glassdoor.com. This number is comparable to the average salary for lawyers, [3] which was estimated at $131,000 in 2013.

1

A) NO CHANGE
B) figures of
C) figure with
D) figures with

2

A) NO CHANGE
B) Far lesser
C) Far fewer
D) Fewer by far

3

A) NO CHANGE
B) which they estimated
C) which being estimated
D) having estimated it

Air traffic controllers are not the only professionals who earn considerable salaries while working more or less out of sight. (After all, when was the last time you saw a television drama about air traffic controllers?) In its current rankings of the "Best Paying Jobs," U.S. News and World Report lists both a fair number of expected careers (doctors, lawyers, software specialists) **4** despite a fair number of unexpected choices. Pharmacists, nurses, construction managers, and physical therapists are among the professionals who earn relatively high salaries **5** by expecting to see their chosen industries grow increasingly important in the years ahead. **6** Some of these industries also experienced remarkable, though short-lived, expansion during the 1990s.

Why exactly do individuals in these careers command such high wages? In many cases, employers are paying for valuable specialized knowledge and training and are selecting from an already small pool of talent. Air traffic controllers, for instance, must complete courses at the Federal Aviation Academy in order to begin work. **7** Surprisingly, without the expertise provided by air traffic controllers— **8** who will actually spend less time on their formal studies than some software engineers will—the day-to-day workings of major airlines would be imperiled.

4

A) NO CHANGE
B) including
C) beyond
D) and

5

A) NO CHANGE
B) which makes them expect
C) so that you expect
D) and who can expect

6

The writer is considering deleting the underlined sentence. Should the writer do this?

A) Yes, because it is not clear exactly what industries the writer could be referring to.
B) Yes, because the sentence detracts from the passage's emphasis on the job market during the past few years.
C) No, because the sentence offers an important exception to the writer's overall thesis.
D) No, because the sentence provides historical and economic context that is referenced in subsequent paragraphs.

7

A) NO CHANGE
B) In contrast,
C) Similarly,
D) Furthermore,

8

The writer wants to add detail that explains the practical duties of air traffic controllers. Which choice best accomplishes this goal?

A) NO CHANGE
B) who coordinate flights so that runway space is used efficiently and collisions do not occur
C) who hold themselves to the highest standards of attention to detail
D) who are respected by other air transit professionals, including airline pilots

CONTINUE

[1] Granted, those who seek fame would probably not find work in air traffic control especially fulfilling: the workstations of many air traffic controllers are located in tall cement towers near airport runways, well removed from the public eye. [2] The same is true of many high-paying healthcare roles, since nurses, pharmacists, and physical therapists all **9** focus primarily on customers and patients, not on public relations or hot-button causes. [3] In today's economy, very few aspiring entertainers will attain the multimillion-dollar salaries of the Hollywood **10** elite, because few aspiring businessmen will achieve the multibillion-dollar net worth of magnates such as Bill Gates and Michael Bloomberg. [4] However, sometimes sacrificing opportunities for fame to opportunities for security is an excellent choice. [5] People who harbor such visions of fame and power still need to provide for themselves and their families on a day-to-day basis. [6] For these individuals, the best course in life may be to find a high-paying job that is rather predictable and out-of-the-way, but could impart the life skills and the sense of responsibility needed to reach for something bigger. **11**

9

A) NO CHANGE
B) apportion energy to
C) devote themselves to
D) are mostly about

10

A) NO CHANGE
B) elite, although few
C) elite; few
D) elite, few

11

To make this paragraph most logical, sentence 4 should be placed

A) where it is now.
B) before sentence 1.
C) before sentence 3.
D) before sentence 6.

Grammar Drill 54

Questions 1-11 are based on the following passage.

Art in the Great Outdoors

Because I have always enjoyed the world of nature, I have often found museums to be cold and constricting. Growing up, I viewed class trips to museums as unpleasant ordeals: I [1] remember distinct one visit to the Museum of Modern Art in New York, when I refused to explore any of the indoor exhibitions and [2] planted myself on a bench in the sculpture garden until it was time to leave. [3] No matter how pristine, no matter how beautiful, museums induce a claustrophobia. I cannot overcome it, not even now that I have graduated from college.

1

A) NO CHANGE
B) remember direct
C) distinctly remember
D) remember directing

2

A) NO CHANGE
B) had planted
C) have planted
D) was planting

3

In context, which choice best combines the underlined sentences?

A) I cannot overcome it, even now that I have graduated from college, no matter how pristine, no matter how beautiful, museums induce a claustrophobia.
B) No matter how pristine, no matter how beautiful, museums induce a claustrophobia that I cannot overcome, not even now that I have graduated from college.
C) No matter how pristine, no matter how beautiful, museums induce a claustrophobia without overcoming it, not even now that I have graduated from college.
D) Museums induce a claustrophobia yet I cannot overcome it, not even now that I have graduated from college, no matter how pristine, no matter how beautiful.

CONTINUE

[4] Until then, I discovered a few years ago that closed-in museums are not the only places where great art can be experienced. I was searching the Internet to plan a weekend trip [5] when I came across an advertisement for Grounds for Sculpture, which describes itself as "a 42-acre sculpture park and museum located in Hamilton Township, New Jersey." There are indoor exhibitions, [6] but, as I soon discovered these, are designed mostly to [7] compliment the major offerings in outdoor art, which grow "by approximately fifteen sculptures annually." My eventual visit did not disappoint: hills, trees, and flowers work in tandem with sculptures by both figurative and abstract artists to create a landscape of stirring beauty.

Grounds for Sculpture is not the only outdoor sculpture park in America. It did not take me long to discover another, similar attraction in my area of the country, the Storm King Art Center, which is located in New York State's Hudson Valley. This second "outdoor museum" is sprawling, almost sublime. Visit during the fall, and [8] visitors will find massive abstract sculptures [9] by Barnett Newman and David Smith in settings of rousing natural beauty; the fiery colors of autumn foliage accentuate the stark and powerful shapes of the artworks that populate Storm King.

4

A) NO CHANGE
B) In the past,
C) Fortunately,
D) Certainly,

5

A) NO CHANGE
B) where
C) in which
D) by which

6

A) NO CHANGE
B) but as I soon discovered these,
C) but as, I soon discovered, these
D) but, as I soon discovered, these

7

A) NO CHANGE
B) complement
C) complete
D) corroborate

8

A) NO CHANGE
B) you
C) one
D) the public

9

The writer is considering deleting the underlined phrase. Should the writer make this deletion?

A) Yes, because Barnett Newman and David Smith are not the only important artists featured at the Storm King Art Center.
B) Yes, because the artwork of Barnett Newman is not analyzed elsewhere in the passage.
C) No, because the reference to David Smith sets up the author's later discussion.
D) No, because the author expresses a preference for these artists earlier in the passage.

I realize that some people may write off destinations such as Grounds for Sculpture and Storm King Art Center as gimmicky tourist attractions, places somehow "inferior" to more traditional museums. But those people couldn't be more wrong. After all, David Smith designed many of his metalwork sculptures specifically for outdoor display; **10** he even set up several of his creations in a field on his own property, in arrangements that recall the installations at Storm King. As I see it, sculpture parks such as the ones I admire serve valuable purposes. These attractions **11** agitate a new audience for art, winning over reluctant museum-goers such as myself. Just as importantly, these attractions help us to understand dimensions of great art that traditional museums may not be equipped to address. David Smith's sculptures should be surrounded by nature; let's visit them in their proper habitat.

10

Which choice provides information that best supports the claim made earlier in the sentence?

A) NO CHANGE
B) the curators at Storm King have had considerable success finding aesthetically pleasing arrangements for even his largest works.
C) among his favorite motifs are shapes that recall leaves and ferns, but that were crafted using stainless steel.
D) there is no logical reason why placing Smith's sculptures outdoors should compromise their status as celebrated works of art.

11

A) NO CHANGE
B) institute
C) constitute
D) create

CONTINUE

Questions 1-11 are based on the following passage.

Going Crazy with MSG

Monosodium Glutamate (MSG) is an additive used to enhance the flavor of food. It has a reputation for being used most commonly in Chinese restaurant cuisine, and even spawned the idea of "Chinese Restaurant Syndrome," **1** it is a reaction to consumption of the ingredient. But many do not realize that MSG is also present in thousands of commonly packaged pantry items such as canned soups, flavored potato chips, and salad dressings. After World War II, this substance rose in popularity in the American market and developed a reputation for being detrimental to one's health. Some experts claim that daily ingestion of MSG can initiate headaches, depression, and fatigue—among other concerning effects. **2** To disassociate their dining experience from the MSG craze, both domestic and international restaurants have posted "No MSG" notices. These appear in their windows and even on their menus.

In an effort to combat this negative media attention, many scientists, aided by the Food and Drug Administration (FDA), **3** had worked to **4** dull the unsavory reputation of MSG. Functionally, MSG is the salt component of an amino acid called Glutamic Acid. Amino acids form proteins, and thus can be found naturally in foods containing protein. **5** Specifically, high levels of the amino acid Glutamate occur biologically in tomatoes, mushrooms, and Parmesan cheese.

1

A) NO CHANGE
B) being
C) that is
D) DELETE the underlined portion.

2

Which choice most effectively combines the underlined sentences?

A) Both domestic and international restaurants have posted "No MSG" notices in their windows and even on their menus, this strategy is employed to disassociate their dining experience from the MSG craze.
B) To disassociate their dining experience from the MSG craze, "No MSG" notices have been posted by both domestic and international restaurants in their windows and even on their menus.
C) To disassociate their dining experience from the MSG craze, both domestic and international restaurants have posted "No MSG" notices in their windows and even on their menus.
D) "No MSG" notices have been posted in the windows and even on the menus of both domestic and international restaurants to disassociate their dining experience from the MSG craze.

3

A) NO CHANGE
B) have worked
C) working
D) are going to be working

4

A) NO CHANGE
B) get done with
C) disqualify
D) dispel

5

A) NO CHANGE
B) However
C) Fortunately
D) Broadly speaking

CONTINUE

[1] So how did the regular use of MSG begin? [2] Japanese scientist Kikunae Ikeda first recognized MSG as a flavor enhancer in 1908 while creating soup stock out of seaweed that contained high MSG concentrations. [3] The substance now bought by companies and kitchens all across the United States is a clear crystal—like salt or sugar. [4] In some cases, misuse of the product may be to blame for adverse reactions. [5] If a restaurant 6 had sprinkled MSG on top of a dish, as opposed to mixing it in during cooking, a customer would ingest a whole serving in one bite. [6] He subsequently found a method of isolating the ingredient through bacterial fermentation, 7 patents the process, and begins producing MSG commercially. [7] This overexposure will tax the body and induce an adverse reaction, comparable to the reaction to consuming a high concentration of salt or sugar. 8

6

A) NO CHANGE
B) were to sprinkle
C) will sprinkle
D) sprinkle

7

A) NO CHANGE
B) patenting the process, and began to produce
C) patented the process, and began producing
D) patented the process, and beginning produced

8

To make this paragraph most logical, sentence 6 should be placed

A) where it is now.
B) after sentence 1.
C) after sentence 2.
D) after sentence 3.

CONTINUE

Unfortunately, scientists have stood in the way of an honest assessment of MSG. Neuroscientist John Olney's recent study, which involved injecting laboratory mice directly with MSG, only perpetuated MSG misconceptions. Proportionally, the quantities given to the mice would be fit for a horse rather than a human. Additionally, the substance was released under the skin while humans only introduce MSG to **9** its bodies via the digestive system. This "meticulous, double blind study" was conducted by scientists from reputable institutions around the world but only addressed the worst-case misuse of MSG that occurs in some restaurants. Furthermore, those who consumed the placebos in this study **10** reported symptoms as inconsistently as those ingesting the MSG—largely disproving any clear scientific basis for the MSG outcry. Olney's study does not legitimately prove that MSG is harmful, **11** yet the public continues to believe that MSG, rather than overeating, is responsible for mass discomfort.

9

A) NO CHANGE
B) it's
C) there
D) their

10

Which choice offers an accurate interpretation of the data in the graph?

A) NO CHANGE
B) were significantly less likely to experience symptoms than
C) experienced even higher rates of depression than
D) were marginally less susceptible to an increase in headaches than

11

The writer wants a conclusion that conveys how the flaws in John Olney's study have been overlooked by those in the restaurant industry. Which choice best accomplishes this goal?

A) NO CHANGE
B) and the FDA is currently working with restaurants to inform the public about MSG's harmful effects.
C) but those in the restaurant industry continue to liberally use MSG in their dishes.
D) and still, restaurateurs strive to distance themselves from the stigma of MSG.

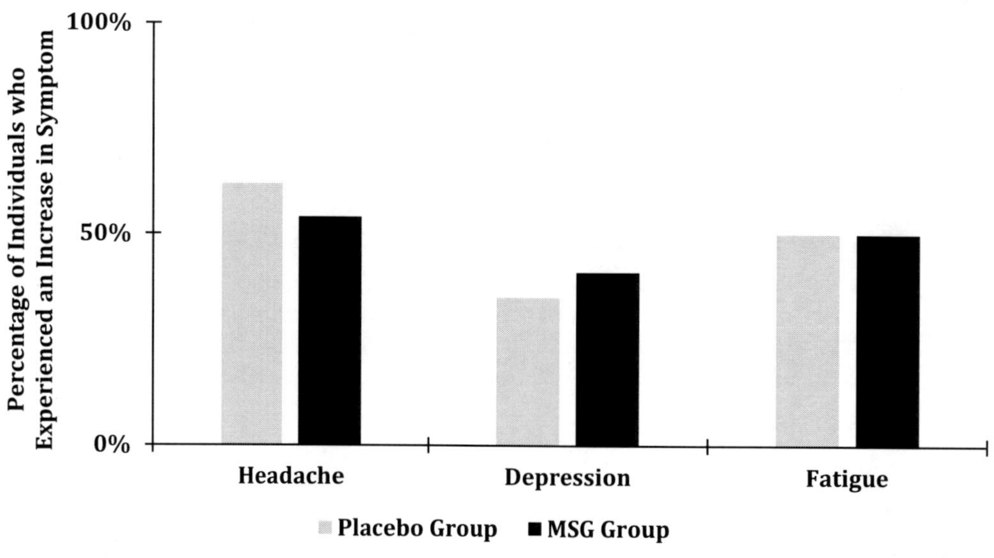

CONTINUE

Questions 1-11 are based on the following passage.

Save the Bananas!

— 1 —

Bananas are one of the world's largest fruit crops and are consumed in great volume in the United States. Of the many species that can be found in the wild, Cavendish bananas are most commonly cultivated and sold for human consumption. [1] These are the seedless, perfectly yellow variety that American shoppers have come to recognize on supermarket [2] shelves, they currently represent about forty-five percent of global banana production. All Cavendish bananas are in fact clones of one another. One side effect of this cloning is that Cavendish bananas do not have sufficient genetic variation to subsist in the face of major fungal or bacterial diseases.

1

A) NO CHANGE
B) This is
C) That is
D) That were

2

A) NO CHANGE
B) shelves they
C) shelves; they
D) shelves; it

CONTINUE

—2—

However, this favorable resistance would only last until an old foe of the Cavendish took a new form. Tropical Race 4, an evolved strain of a disease that heavily affects the [3] Cavendish— surfaced in Asia in 1992. The fungus has slowly spread to the Philippines, Australia, and most recently Africa. [4] Nevertheless, Tropical Race 4 can live in the soil for decades and [5] will contaminate bananas as soon as they are re-introduced. Some prominent agricultural companies have implemented crop rotation as one method of managing the diseased soil. Growers who use this method will often plant a distinct crop with anti-fungal capabilities. Farmers in China have demonstrated the efficiency of this practice by alternately planting bananas and Chinese leeks on the same land.

—3—

The Cavendish was cultivated as [6] a replacement for the previously popular banana species, the Gros Michel, which reigned supreme within American and European agricultural markets through the late 1950's. However, Panama Disease began spreading through Gros Michel crops in South America and the Caribbean [7] —creating a banana plague that almost bankrupted major importers of the crop. On account of its resistance to the incurable Panama disease, [8] growers resolved to adopt the Cavendish as the most comparable substitute in taste and appearance.

3

A) NO CHANGE
B) Cavendish,
C) Cavendish;
D) Cavendish:

4

A) NO CHANGE
B) Consequently,
C) Moreover,
D) Regardless,

5

A) NO CHANGE
B) can contaminate
C) may contaminate
D) contaminating

6

A) NO CHANGE
B) replacements
C) replacing
D) having replaced

7

The writer is considering deleting the underlined portion (ending the sentence with a period). Should the writer make this deletion?

A) Yes, because it digresses from the main point of the paragraph.
B) Yes, because the information discussed is irrelevant to the passage as a whole.
C) No, because the underlined portion offers new insight into the causes of Panama Disease.
D) No, because the underlined portion provides information necessary to the paragraph's main idea.

8

A) NO CHANGE
B) the Cavendish was adopted by growers as
C) growers determined that the Cavendish was
D) Cavendish bananas are

CONTINUE

—4—

Still, developing strains of bananas that will be resistant to Tropical Race 4 is a more viable, collective solution. The Taiwan Banana Research Institute, for instance, cultivates tissue-culture plants and deposits them in soil thoroughly polluted with Tropical Race 4. Scientists form these engineered plant specimens by harvesting and cleaning healthy suckers [9] from existing banana plants. Disinfected pieces of the suckers are planted on a laboratory medium and made to grow several shoots. After assessing the shoots for known diseases and viruses, technicians discard those that test positive and prepare the problem-free specimens for planting.

—5—

This meticulous selection and growth procedure [10] assures that the banana plants are free of harmful fungi and bacteria, which are harder to combat through crop rotation. It can also produce plants that exhibit slight variations from their mother plant, mutants like the Giant Cavendish banana. Generated by the Taiwan Banana Research Institute, the Giant Cavendish is much more resistant to Tropical Race 4 and may serve as a viable substitute for the common Cavendish banana.

Question [11] asks about the previous passage as a whole.

9

At this point, the writer is considering adding the following parenthetical statement.

(lateral shoots of the underground stem)

Should the writer make this addition here?

A) Yes, because it demonstrates the writer's extensive knowledge of botany.
B) Yes, because it defines a term that is introduced in the paragraph.
C) No, because it is not necessary to the main point of the paragraph.
D) No, because it conflicts with points made elsewhere in the writer's discussion of cultivating banana tissue.

10

A) NO CHANGE
B) insures
C) ensures
D) reassures

Think about the previous passage as a whole as you answer question 11.

11

To make the passage most logical, paragraph 2 should be placed

A) where it is now.
B) before paragraph 1.
C) before paragraph 4.
D) before paragraph 5.

STOP

CONTINUE

Chapter 3
Math Drills

Directions: For each **Math-No Calculator** drill, use 25 minutes to answer the questions. For each **Math-Calculator** drill, use 28 minutes to answer the questions.

IES Workshops: You will **complete 1 math drill per workshop**. Please follow the time limits provided by your workshop teacher. Remember, you will complete this drill **during** workshop.

Good luck!

Math Test - No Calculator

25 MINUTES, 20 QUESTIONS

DIRECTIONS

For each question from 1-15, choose the best answer choice provided in the multiple choice bank and fill in the appropriate circle in the provided answer key. Alternatively, for questions **16-20**, answer the problem and enter your answer in the grid-in section of the answer key. Refer to the directions given before question 16 as to how to enter your answers for the grid-in questions. You may complete scratch work in any empty space in your test booklet.

NOTES

A. Calculator usage **is not allowed** in this section.
B. Variables, constants, and coefficients used represent real numbers unless indicated otherwise.
C. All figures are created to appropriate scale unless the question states otherwise.
D. All figures are two-dimensional unless the question states otherwise.
E. The domain of any given function is all real numbers *x* for which the function, $f(x)$, is a real number unless the question states otherwise.

REFERENCE

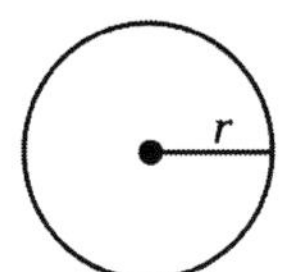

$A = \pi r^2$
$C = 2\pi r$

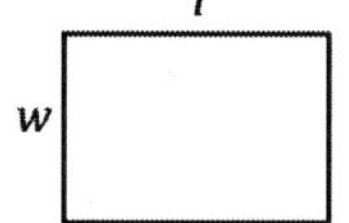

$A = lw$

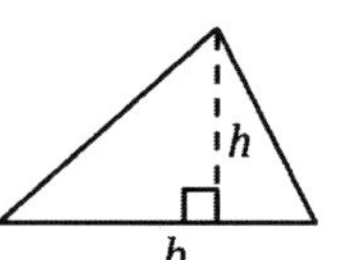

$A = \frac{1}{2}bh$

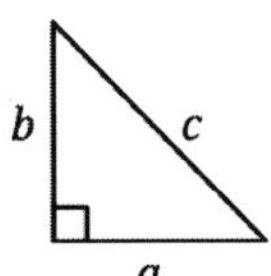

$c^2 = a^2 + b^2$

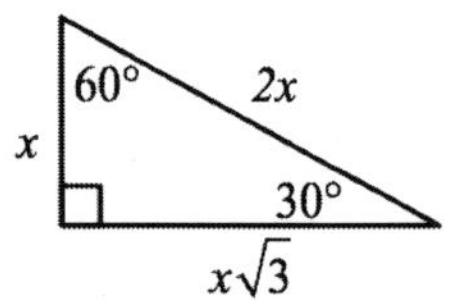

Special Right Triangle

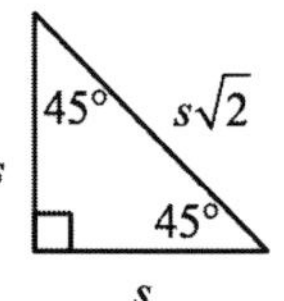

Special Right Triangle

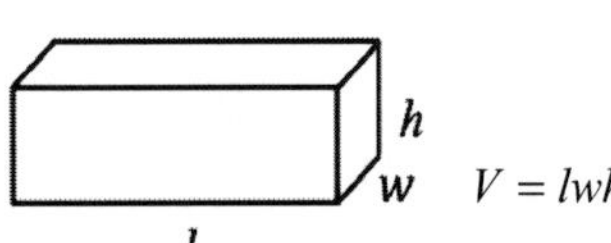

$V = lwh$

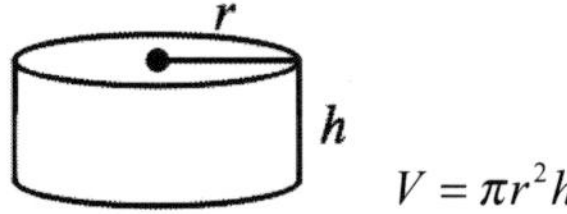

$V = \pi r^2 h$

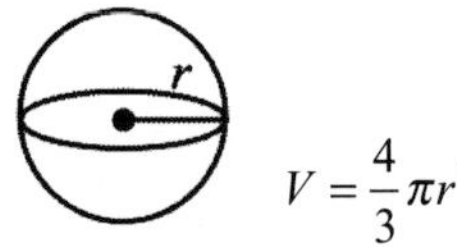

$V = \frac{4}{3}\pi r^3$

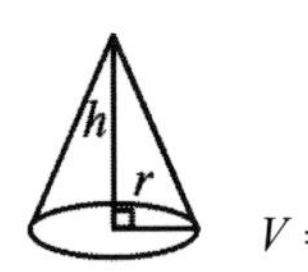

$V = \frac{1}{3}\pi r^2 h$

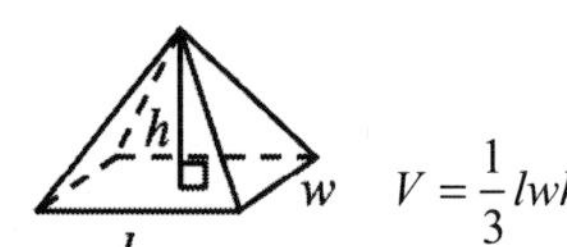

$V = \frac{1}{3}lwh$

There are $360°$ in a circle.
There are 2π radians in a circle.
There are $180°$ in a triangle.

CONTINUE

1

$$g(x) = x^2 - m$$

In the equation above, m is a constant. If $g(3) = 1$, what is the value of $g(5)$?

A) 1
B) 7
C) 8
D) 17

2

If $f(x) = 3 - 2x$, what is $f(x+3)$ equal to?

A) $-3-2x$
B) $-3+2x$
C) $9-2x$
D) $9-6x$

3

$$y = 4x + 2$$
$$x + y = 17$$

If (x, y) is a solution to the sytem of equations above, what is the value of x?

A) 3
B) 8
C) 11
D) 14

4

For which of the following expressions is there a value of x for which the expression has a negative value?

A) $1+x^2$

B) x^2-1

C) $|x-3|+4$

D) $|5-x|$

CONTINUE

5

Jessica works as a saleswoman for a computer wholesale company. Each month, Jessica is assigned a certain allotment of computers to attempt to sell. In an ongoing effort to improve her sales, Jessica is attempting to reduce the number of unsold computers in her allotment each month. If at the end of the third month Jessica had 22 computers remaining, at the end of the sixth month she had 13 computers remaining, and the number of remaining computers each month decreases linearly, which of the following best describes the reduction of Jessica's remaining computer stock between the third and sixth months?

A) The remaining number of computers at the end of each month decreases by 2 per month.
B) The remaining number of computers at the end of each month decreases by 3 per month.
C) The remaining number of computers at the end of each month decreases by 9 per month.
D) The remaining number of computers decreases by 3 every 3 months.

6

If $\frac{m+1}{m}=\frac{5}{4}$, which of the following is equivalent to m?

A) $\frac{1}{4}$

B) $\frac{4}{9}$

C) 2

D) 4

7

Which of the following is equivalent to the expression $(2x+y)(2y-x)$?

A) $3xy-2x^2+2y^2$
B) $5xy-2x^2+2y^2$
C) $4x^2-y^2$
D) $3xy$

8

Line l is perpendicular to the line $4x+2y=10$. What is the slope of Line l?

A) -2

B) -1

C) $\frac{1}{2}$

D) 2

9

$$15x + 45y = 210$$

The equation above represents a 210-mile trip that a cyclist recently took. If the cyclist averaged 15 mph on her bicycle and 45 mph for the portions that she drove her car, which of the following best depicts the variable y?

A) The number of miles that the cyclist rode her bicycle
B) The number of miles that the cyclist drove her car
C) The amount of time that the cyclist rode her bicycle
D) The amount of time that the cyclist drove her car

10

$$5x + y = 11$$
$$ax + 2y = 24$$

If the value of a is equivalent to 10, how many ordered pairs (x, y) satisfy the system of equations above?

A) 0
B) 1
C) 2
D) Infinitely many

11

Which of the following is the solution set to the equation $\sqrt{x^2 + 3} = \sqrt{-4x}$?

A) $\{-3\}$

B) $\{-1\}$

C) $\{-3, -1\}$

D) $\{1, 3\}$

12

$$\frac{10}{8 - 4i}$$

If the expression above is converted to the form $a + bi$, what is the value of b? (Note: $i = \sqrt{-1}$)

A) -1

B) $\frac{1}{2}$

C) 1

D) 2

13

Allison and her husband decided to buy bicycles for their two children. One of the bikes was $50 more expensive than the other bike. If Allison paid for both bikes on her own and paid a 7% sales tax, which of the following expressions, using x as the price in dollars of the cheaper bicycle, represents the amount of money that Allison paid in total?

A) $2x+50$
B) $2x+53.50$
C) $2.14x+53.50$
D) $1.07(x+50)$

14

$$10x = x^2 - 20$$

Which of the following is a negative solution to the quadratic equation above?

A) -10
B) $10-6\sqrt{5}$
C) $5+3\sqrt{5}$
D) $5-3\sqrt{5}$

15

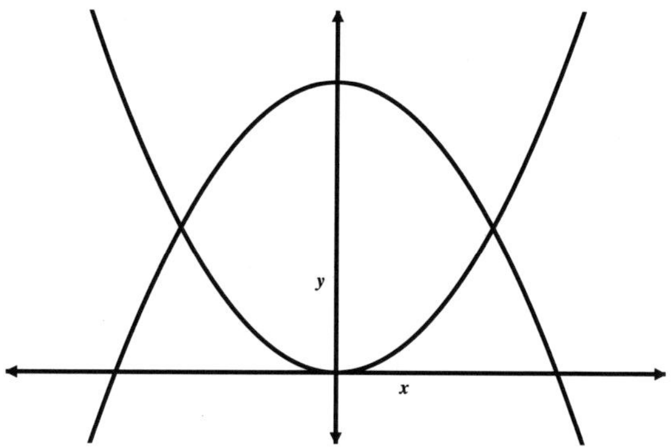

The functions $y = x^2$ and $y = h - x^2$, where h is a constant, are graphed in the xy-plane above. The ordered pairs (x, y) and $(-x, y)$ are the points or intersection for the two graphs, where x is a positive integer. Which of the following could be the value of h?

A) 1
B) 4
C) 8
D) 12

CONTINUE

DIRECTIONS

For each question from 16-20, solve and enter your answer in the grid-in section of your answer sheet as described below.

A. Write out your answers in the boxes at the top of each column in order to help you fill in the circles accurately. Remember, you will only receive credit for the circles that are filled in correctly, not for the written answer at the top of the columns.

B. Mark only a single circle in each column.

C. There are no negative answers.

D. If the problem has more than one correct answer, grid only one of the correct answers.

E. When your answer is a **mixed number**, such as $1\frac{1}{2}$, it should be entered as 1.5 or $3/2$. You cannot enter a mixed number because there is no room to fill in a circle that represents a space.

F. If you enter a **decimal answer** with more digits then the grid can handle, the answer may be rounded or truncated, but it absolutely must fill the entire grid.

Answer: $\frac{8}{21}$

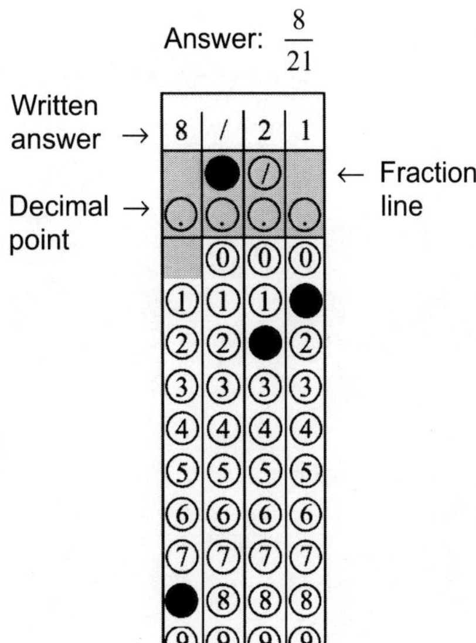

Answer: 6.4

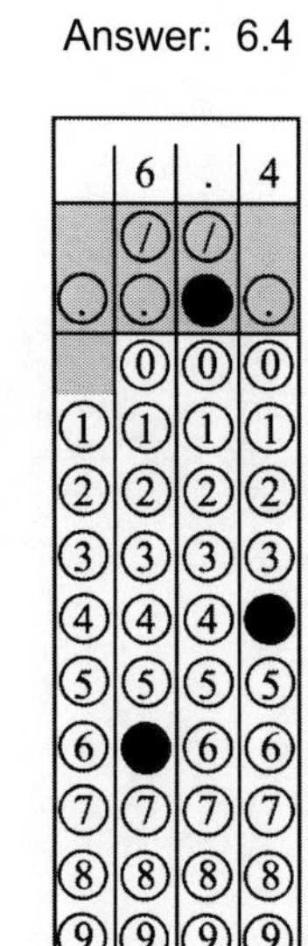

The ways to correctly grid $\frac{7}{9}$ are:

7 / 9

. 7 7 7

. 7 7 8

Answer: 102 - both positions are correct

REMEMBER: You can begin writing your answers in any column as long as there is enough space. Leave unused columns blank.

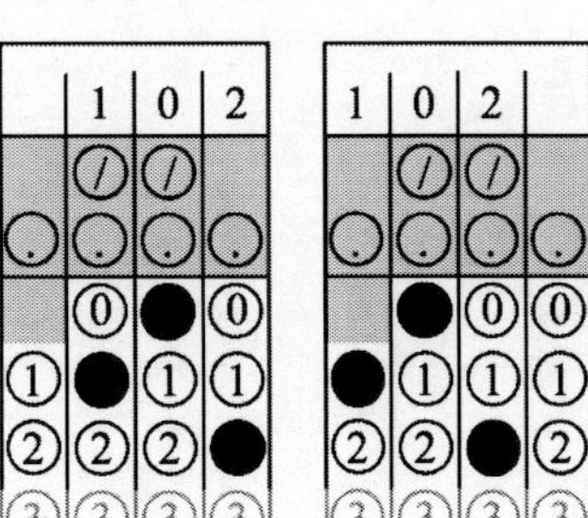

CONTINUE

16

In a right triangle, x is the measure, in degrees, of one of the acute angles. If $\sin x = 0.8$, what is the value of $\cos(90° - x)$?

17

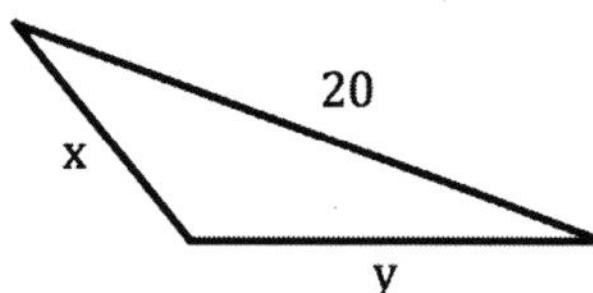

If $x = 11$ in the triangle above and y has an integer value, what is the difference between the maximum value of y and the minimum value of y?

18

$$x^3 - 2x^2 + x = 0$$

The equation above is true for how many values of x?

19

$$y^2 + 2x^2 = \frac{17}{16}$$
$$y = x^2 - 1$$

If (x, y) is a solution to the system of equations above and $x > 0$, what is the value of x?

CONTINUE

20

$$F_{Grav} = \frac{m_1 \bullet m_2}{D^2}$$

According to Newton's law of universal gravitation, the force of gravity between two objects is proportional to the product of the objects' masses divided by the square of the distance separating the objects. This relationship is shown in the equation above. If the masses of both objects stay the same and the distance between the objects doubles, by what percent does the force of gravity between the objects decrease?

STOP

Math Test - Calculator

28 MINUTES, 19 QUESTIONS

DIRECTIONS

For each question from 1-15, choose the best answer choice provided in the multiple choice bank and fill in the appropriate circle in the provided answer key. Alternatively, for questions **16-19**, answer the problem and enter your answer in the grid-in section of the answer key. Refer to the directions given before question 16 as to how to enter your answers for the grid-in questions. You may complete scratch work in any empty space in your test booklet.

NOTES

A. Calculator usage **is allowed**.
B. Variables, constants, and coefficients used represent real numbers unless indicated otherwise.
C. All figures are created to appropriate scale unless the question states otherwise.
D. All figures are two-dimensional unless the question states otherwise.
E. The domain of any given function is all real numbers x for which the function, $f(x)$, is a real number unless the question states otherwise.

REFERENCE

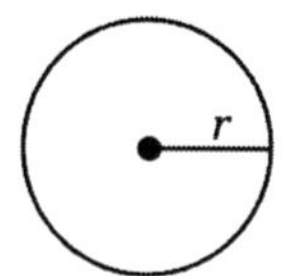

$A = \pi r^2$
$C = 2\pi r$

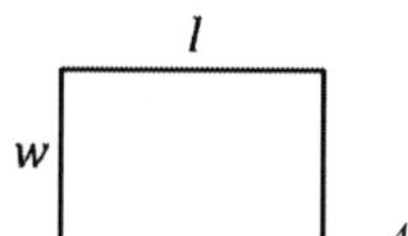

$A = lw$

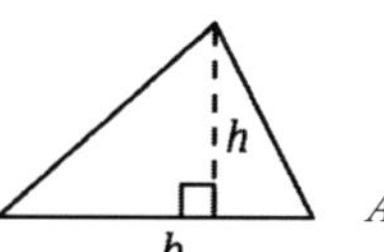

$A = \frac{1}{2}bh$

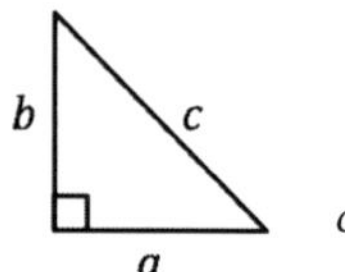

$c^2 = a^2 + b^2$

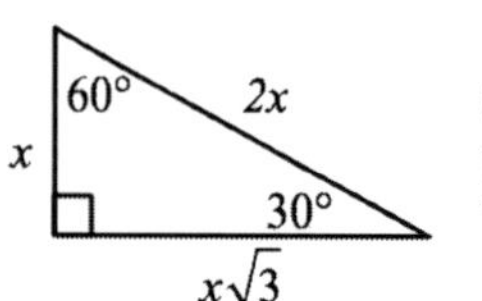

Special Right Triangle

45° $s\sqrt{2}$ s 45° s

Special Right Triangle

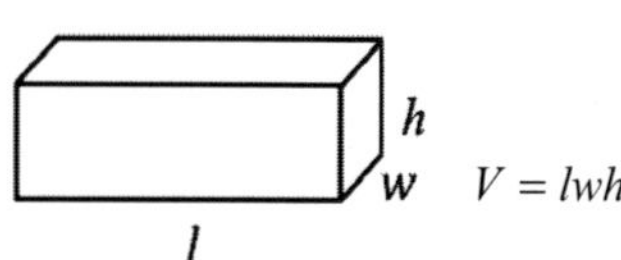

$V = lwh$

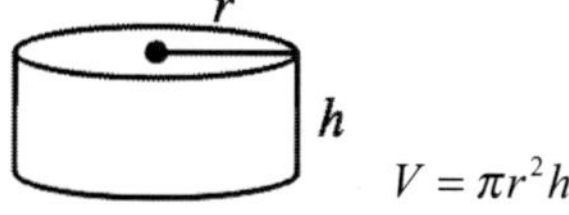

$V = \pi r^2 h$

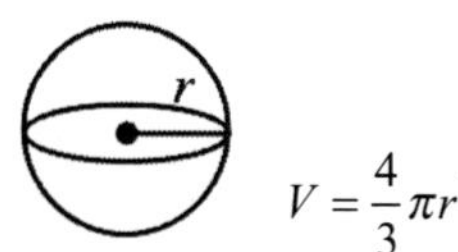

$V = \frac{4}{3}\pi r^3$

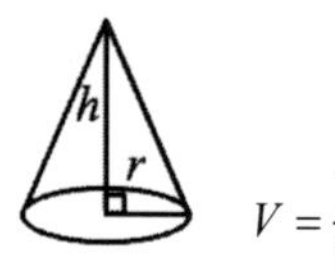

$V = \frac{1}{3}\pi r^2 h$

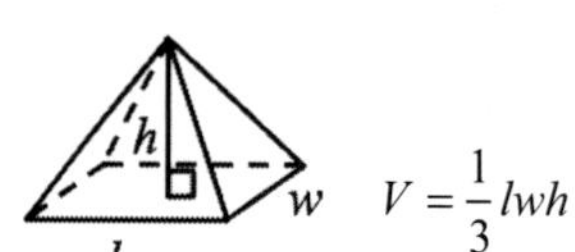

$V = \frac{1}{3}lwh$

There are $360°$ in a circle.
There are 2π radians in a circle.
There are $180°$ in a triangle.

CONTINUE

1

If $\frac{r}{2} = 18$, what is the value of $r+2$?

A) 11
B) 20
C) 36
D) 38

2

Customers are given price quotes for oil changes based on the equation $P = Rh + l$, where l represents the price of the oil chosen. In the equation, P represents the total price of the oil change, R is a constant that represents the hourly labor rate, and h is the number of hours. If a customer elects to use premium oil instead of standard oil, which of the following will change?

A) P only
B) P and l
C) P and h
D) P, R, and l

3

To date, the number of U.S. presidents that have served one term or less is one greater than the number of presidents that have served more than one term. If p represents the number of presidents that have served more than one term and there have been a total of 43 U.S. presidents, which of the following equations is true?

A) $p - 1 = 43$

B) $2p + 1 = 43$

C) $1 = 43 + 2p$

D) $\frac{p+43}{p} = 3$

4

Given that $m^{\frac{3}{2}} = r$, which of the following is equivalent to $\sqrt{m}$?

A) $\sqrt{r}$

B) $\sqrt[3]{r}$

C) $\sqrt[3]{r^2}$

D) r^2

CONTINUE

5

A line in the xy-plane goes through the points (k, k^2) and $(1, k)$. Which of the following expressions is equivalent to the slope of the line?

A) k

B) $k-1$

C) $\frac{1}{k}$

D) $k(k-1)$

6

A parabola with the equation $y = x^2 - 9$ is graphed in the xy-plane. If A and B are two coordinate points that lie on the parabola and share common y-values, what is the x-coordinate of the midpoint of Segment AB?

A) 0

B) $\frac{3}{2}$

C) 3

D) $\frac{9}{2}$

Questions 7-8 refer to the following information.

Faculty	Math	English	Total
Full-time	2	3	5
Part-time	4	9	13
Total	6	12	18

The number of full-time and part-time faculty at a private tutoring center in 2019 are categorized by department in the table above. The school's overall staff has increased by 12.5% since the year 2010.

7

If a part-time employee is selected at random, what is the probability that they are a member of the math department?

A) $\frac{2}{9}$

B) $\frac{1}{3}$

C) $\frac{4}{13}$

D) $\frac{2}{3}$

8

The private tutoring center hired how many new employees since the year 2010?

A) 2

B) 4

C) 6

D) 16

CONTINUE

9

The variable y is inversely proportional to the square root of the variable x. When y is 12, x is 9. What is the value of y when x is 16?

A) $\frac{9}{4}$

B) 4

C) 9

D) 16

10

Dean wanted to know whether or not students in his school preferred to use the graphing calculators provided by the school or the calculators built into their smartphones. Dean went to 8 randomly selected math classes and in each of those classes he observed the students sitting in the front row to see which calculator they were using in class. Dean discovered that 78% of the students were using graphing calculators provided by the school. Which of the following is the strongest reason that Dean's sample produced biased results and his discovery was *not* usable?

A) The size of the sample
B) The size of the population
C) The fact that he observed students instead of surveying them
D) The seating location of the observed students

11

It takes Rachel 20 minutes to ride her bike to school. If Rachel rides her bike at an average of 15 mph and her sister Danielle rides her skateboard to school at an average of 10 mph, how many minutes earlier must Danielle leave in order for the sisters to arrive at the school at the same time?

A) 5
B) 10
C) 20
D) 30

12

$$2x+3y=1$$
$$-6x-9y=-3$$

The system of equations above has how many solutions?

A) 0
B) 1
C) 2
D) Infinitely many

CONTINUE

13

The graph of the equation $y=(x+1)(x-19)$ in the xy-plane is a parabola with vertex $(\sqrt{c-19},-c)$. Which of the following is equivalent to $\sqrt{c}$?

A) 10
B) 81
C) 100
D) $\sqrt{c}$ cannot be determined.

14

$$(x+d)(x+1)=x^2+fx+10$$

In the equation above, d and f are constants. If the equation is true for all values of x, what is the value of f?

A) 9
B) 10
C) 11
D) 12

15

$$F=\frac{9}{5}C+32$$

The equation above can be used to determine temperature F, measured in degrees Fahrenheit, based on the temperature C, measured in degrees Celsius. Which of the following statements is true?

A) The temperature measures 32 degrees Celsius when the temperature measures 0 degrees Fahrenheit.
B) A change of 1 degree Fahrenheit is equivalent to a change of nine-fifths of a degree Celsius.
C) A change of 5 degrees Fahrenheit is equivalent to a change of 9 degrees Celsius.
D) A change of 5 degrees Celsius is equivalent to a change of 9 degrees Fahrenheit.

CONTINUE

DIRECTIONS

For each question from 16-19, solve and enter your answer in the grid-in section of your answer sheet as described below.

A. Write out your answers in the boxes at the top of each column in order to help you fill in the circles accurately. Remember, you will only receive credit for the circles that are filled in correctly, not for the written answer at the top of the columns.

B. Mark only a single circle in each column.

C. There are no negative answers.

D. If the problem has more than one correct answer, grid only one of the correct answers.

E. When your answer is a **mixed number**, such as $1\frac{1}{2}$, it should be entered as 1.5 or $3/2$. You cannot enter a mixed number because there is no room to fill in a circle that represents a space.

F. If you enter a **decimal answer** with more digits then the grid can handle, the answer may be rounded or truncated, but it absolutely must fill the entire grid.

Answer: $\frac{8}{21}$

Written answer → 8 / 2 1 ← Fraction line

Decimal point →

Answer: 6.4

The ways to correctly grid $\frac{7}{9}$ are:

7 / 9 | . 7 7 7 | . 7 7 8

Answer: 102 - both positions are correct

REMEMBER:
You can begin writing your answers in any column as long as there is enough space. Leave unused columns blank.

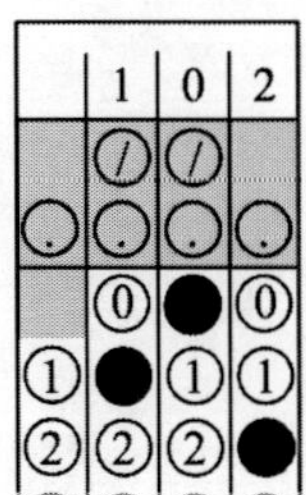

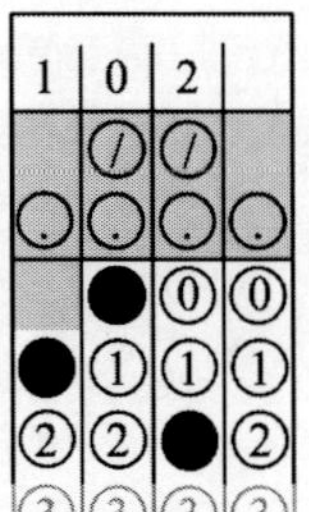

CONTINUE

16

In the equation $(x^2-5)(x^2+5)=-9$, what is the only positive value of x that satisfies the equation?

17

Triangle TUV is isosceles and has a right angle at U. A is the midpoint of TU and B is the midpoint of UV. In Triangle AUB, what is the tangent of $\angle UAB$?

Questions 18-19 refer to the following information.

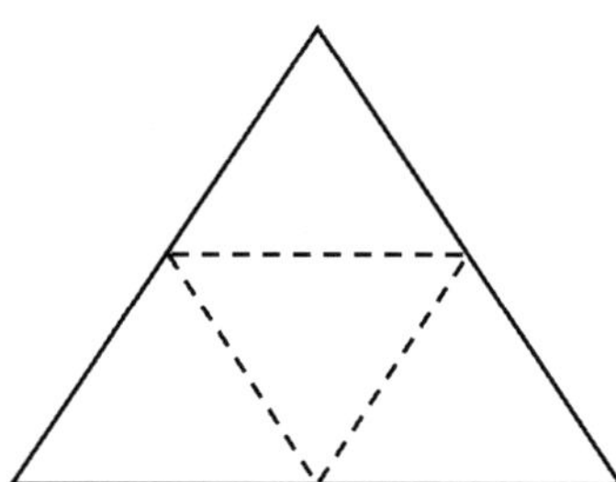

The equilateral triangle pictured above has been cut from a piece of square construction paper. One edge of the construction paper was used as one of the edges of the triangle. The other two edges were cut to create the triangle. The area of the original, uncut piece of construction paper was 144 square inches.

18

If the triangle were to be cut along the dotted lines to form four smaller equilateral triangles, a single smaller triangle's area, in its most simplified form, would be $x\sqrt{3}$. What is the value of x?

19

If the triangle with the dashed edge pictured above were to be divided into four smaller equilateral triangles, the area of the largest equilateral triangle above would be what percent larger than the area of one of these smaller equilateral triangles?

STOP

No Test Material On This Page

Math Test - No Calculator

25 MINUTES, 20 QUESTIONS

DIRECTIONS

For each question from 1-15, choose the best answer choice provided in the multiple choice bank and fill in the appropriate circle in the provided answer key. Alternatively, for questions **16-20**, answer the problem and enter your answer in the grid-in section of the answer key. Refer to the directions given before question 16 as to how to enter your answers for the grid-in questions. You may complete scratch work in any empty space in your test booklet.

NOTES

A. Calculator usage **is not allowed** in this section.
B. Variables, constants, and coefficients used represent real numbers unless indicated otherwise.
C. All figures are created to appropriate scale unless the question states otherwise.
D. All figures are two-dimensional unless the question states otherwise.
E. The domain of any given function is all real numbers *x* for which the function, $f(x)$, is a real number unless the question states otherwise.

REFERENCE

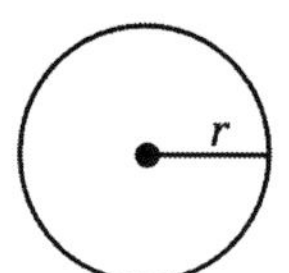

$A = \pi r^2$
$C = 2\pi r$

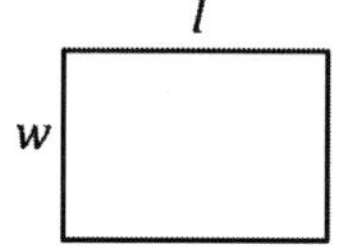

$A = lw$

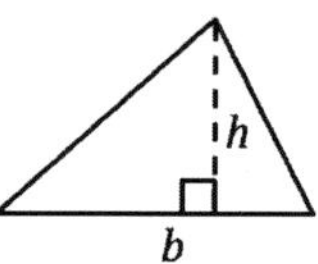

$A = \frac{1}{2}bh$

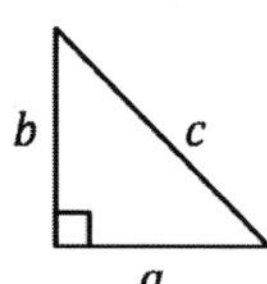

$c^2 = a^2 + b^2$

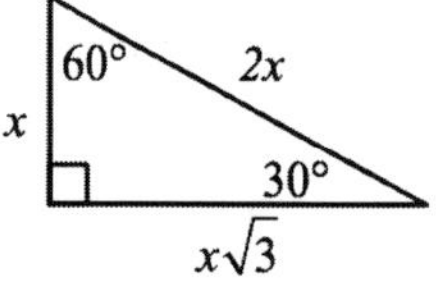

Special Right Triangle

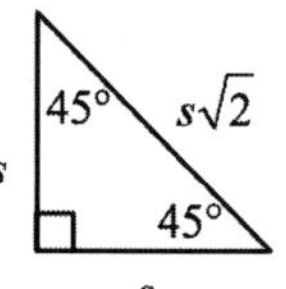

Special Right Triangle

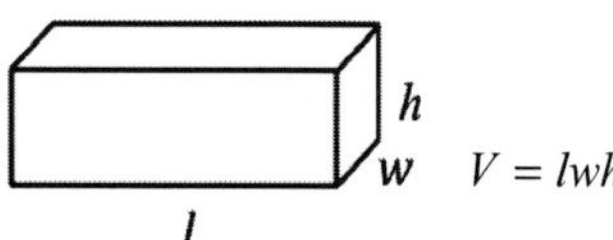

$V = lwh$

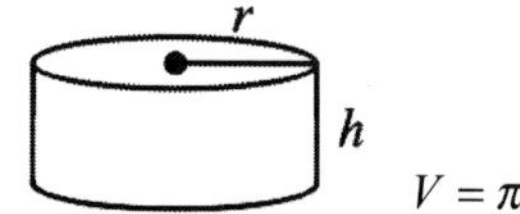

$V = \pi r^2 h$

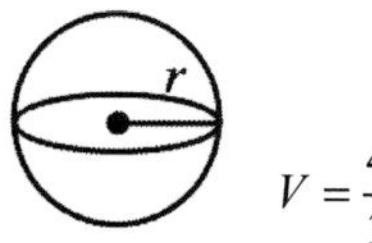

$V = \frac{4}{3}\pi r^3$

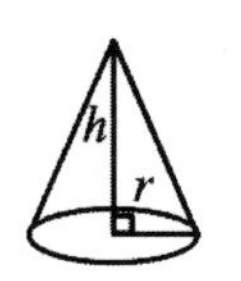

$V = \frac{1}{3}\pi r^2 h$

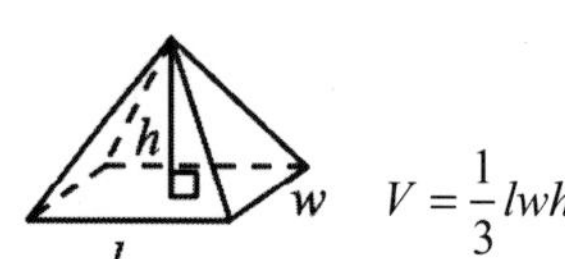

$V = \frac{1}{3}lwh$

There are 360° in a circle.
There are 2π radians in a circle.
There are 180° in a triangle.

CONTINUE

1

Which of the following systems of linear equations has no solutions?

A) $2x+y=16$
$4x+2y=16$

B) $2x-y=8$
$4x+2y=16$

C) $x-y=6$
$x+y=2$

D) $x-y=1$
$4x=12$

2

The average of two positive integers that differ by 10 is less than 10. What is the greatest integer value possible for the larger number?

A) 10
B) 11
C) 14
D) 15

3

Eliana is five years younger than four times her son's age. If Eliana is x years old, which of the following expressions represents the sum of Eliana's age and her son's age?

A) $4x-5$

B) $5x-5$

C) $\frac{x+5}{4}$

D) $\frac{5x+5}{4}$

4

$$P(y)=125{,}000(1.5)^{y}$$

The population growth model for a certain city is shown above, where y represents the number of years that have passed. Which of the following statements is true?

A) The population after one year has passed is 125,000 people.
B) The population will increase by 50% each year.
C) It will take more than two years for the population to double.
D) The population grows in a linear fashion.

CONTINUE

5

Line k is given by the equation $y = x + 12$. Another line, Line j, is parallel to Line k and passes through the origin. Which of the following points lies on Line j?

A) $(1,13)$
B) $(0,12)$
C) $(-1,-1)$
D) $(-1,1)$

6

$$\frac{4}{x} + \frac{8}{2x} = 16$$

Which of the following values of x is a solution to the equation given above?

A) $\frac{1}{2}$

B) 1

C) $\frac{3}{2}$

D) 2

7

Caroline is renting a table at a guitar show and selling vintage guitar picks that she found in a box in her grandfather's attic. Caroline must pay \$30 per hour to rent the table. In the first hour she sells 48 picks at \$0.50 each. If she decides to raise the price to \$1.00 for each pick and rents the table for only one more hour, how many picks must she sell in the second hour if she wants to make a profit of \$50?

A) 80
B) 86
C) 160
D) 172

8

In the equation $bx^2 + bx + 1 = 0$, b is a positive constant. If $2x + 1$ is the only factor of the equation, what is the value of b?

A) 1
B) 2
C) 4
D) 8

CONTINUE

9

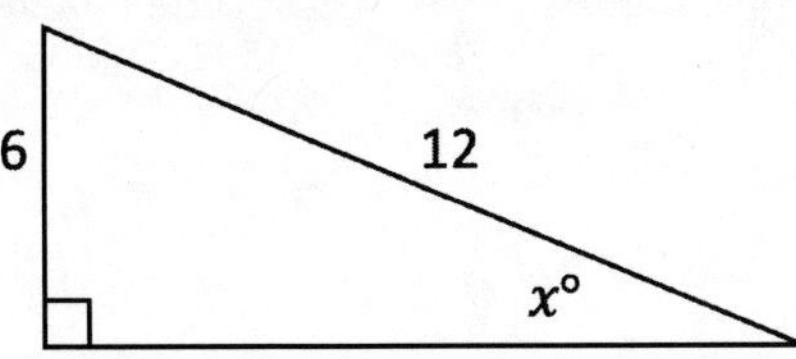

Given the figure above, which of the following is equivalent to $\tan x$?

A) $\frac{1}{2}$

B) $\frac{1}{\sqrt{3}}$

C) $\sqrt{3}$

D) 2

10

Angeline recently purchased 200 feet of fencing, 25 fence posts, and 10 bags of concrete for \$3,350. Her friend purchased 200 feet of fencing and 15 fence posts for \$2,750. What is the cost, in dollars, of buying one fence post and one bag of concrete?

A) 30

B) 45

C) 60

D) 75

11

Suppose that $f(x) = 2x + 3$ and $g(x) = x^2$. If $g(f(x)) = 1$, which of the following is a possible value of x?

A) –2

B) –3

C) –4

D) –5

12

$$10b = \frac{b+90}{b+\frac{1}{10}}$$

What positive value of b makes the equation above true?

A) 1

B) 3

C) 4

D) 9

13

$$x+3\overline{)x^3+6x^2+11x+6}$$

What is the product of the roots of the quotient given above?

A) -6
B) -2
C) 1
D) 2

14

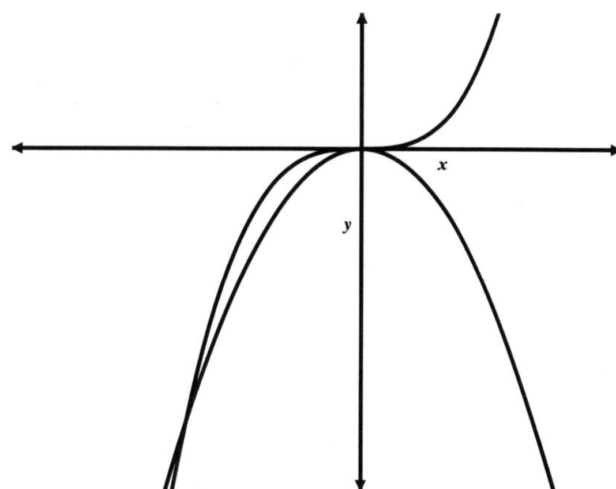

The functions $y=-x^2$ and $y=\frac{1}{2}x^3$ are graphed on the xy-plane above. If both functions were to be shifted vertically by 4 units, what would be the product of the y-values of the points of intersection?

A) 0
B) 2
C) 4
D) 8

15

What is the slope of a line that is perpendicular to the line that intercepts both the origin and the vertex of the parabola defined by the equation $V(x)=-3(x+2)^2+6$?

A) -3

B) $-\frac{1}{3}$

C) $\frac{1}{6}$

D) $\frac{1}{3}$

CONTINUE

DIRECTIONS

For each question from 16-20, solve and enter your answer in the grid-in section of your answer sheet as described below.

A. Write out your answers in the boxes at the top of each column in order to help you fill in the circles accurately. Remember, you will only receive credit for the circles that are filled in correctly, not for the written answer at the top of the columns.

B. Mark only a single circle in each column.

C. There are no negative answers.

D. If the problem has more than one correct answer, grid only one of the correct answers.

E. When your answer is a **mixed number**, such as $1\frac{1}{2}$, it should be entered as 1.5 or $3/2$. You cannot enter a mixed number because there is no room to fill in a circle that represents a space.

F. If you enter a **decimal answer** with more digits then the grid can handle, the answer may be rounded or truncated, but it absolutely must fill the entire grid.

Answer: $\frac{8}{21}$

Written answer → 8 / 2 1 ← Fraction line

Decimal point →

Answer: 6.4

6 . 4

The ways to correctly grid $\frac{7}{9}$ are:

7 / 9   . 7 7 7   . 7 7 8

Answer: 102 - both positions are correct

REMEMBER: You can begin writing your answers in any column as long as there is enough space. Leave unused columns blank.

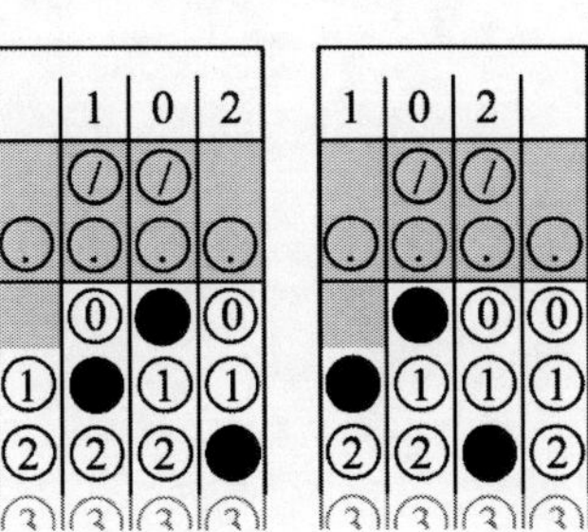

16

$$\frac{(a^2b^3)^{-2}(b^{-1})^{-6}}{(4a^2)^{-2}(ab^{-6})^0}$$

If the expression above simplifies to the form $16(ab)^n$, the exponent n is equivalent to what integer?

17

$$(x-1)(x-7) \leq -1(3-x^2)$$

What is the least value of x that satisfies the inequality given above?

18

Gretchen purchased a combined total of 38 boxes of binder clips and paper clips. If the binder clips cost \$2.50 per box, the paper clips cost \$1.75 per box, and Gretchen spend a combined total of \$86 on boxes of clips, how many more boxes of binder clips did she buy than boxes of paper clips?

19

$$(x+4)^2+(y-4)^2=16$$

The circle defined by the equation above intersects the set of coordinate axes at how many points?

CONTINUE

20

$$\frac{1}{3+2i}$$

If the complex number above were to be rewritten in the form $k+bi$, where k and b are both fractional constants, what would be the value of $k+b$?

STOP

Math Test - Calculator

28 MINUTES, 19 QUESTIONS

DIRECTIONS

For each question from 1-15, choose the best answer choice provided in the multiple choice bank and fill in the appropriate circle in the provided answer key. Alternatively, for questions **16-19**, answer the problem and enter your answer in the grid-in section of the answer key. Refer to the directions given before question 16 as to how to enter your answers for the grid-in questions. You may complete scratch work in any empty space in your test booklet.

NOTES

A. Calculator usage **is allowed**.
B. Variables, constants, and coefficients used represent real numbers unless indicated otherwise.
C. All figures are created to appropriate scale unless the question states otherwise.
D. All figures are two-dimensional unless the question states otherwise.
E. The domain of any given function is all real numbers *x* for which the function, $f(x)$, is a real number unless the question states otherwise.

REFERENCE

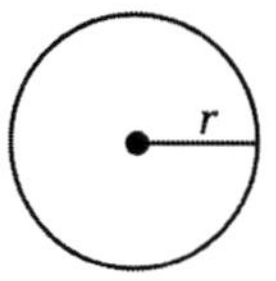

$A = \pi r^2$
$C = 2\pi r$

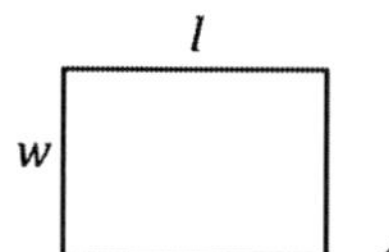

$A = lw$

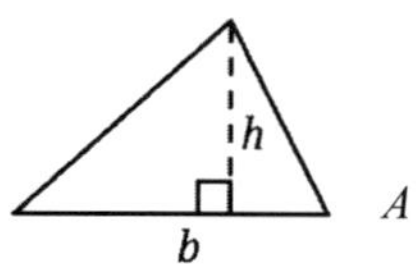

$A = \frac{1}{2}bh$

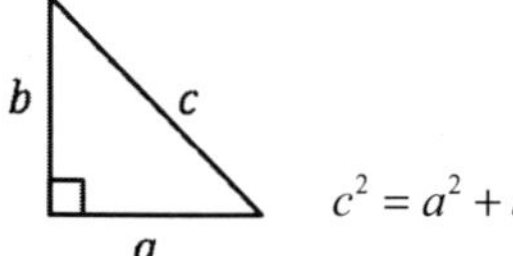

$c^2 = a^2 + b^2$

60° $2x$ x 30° $x\sqrt{3}$

Special Right Triangle

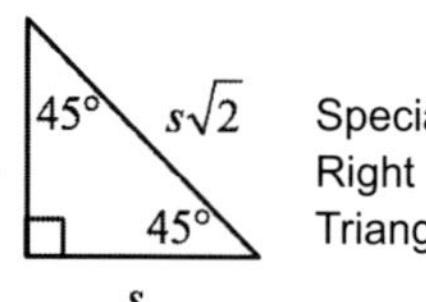

Special Right Triangle

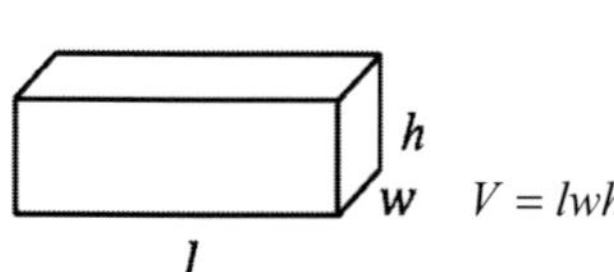

$V = lwh$

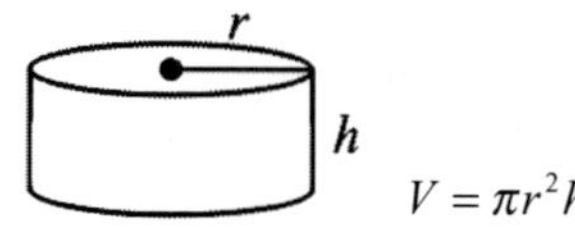

$V = \pi r^2 h$

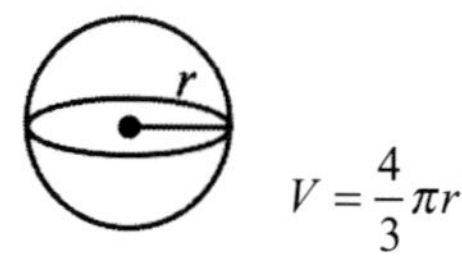

$V = \frac{4}{3}\pi r^3$

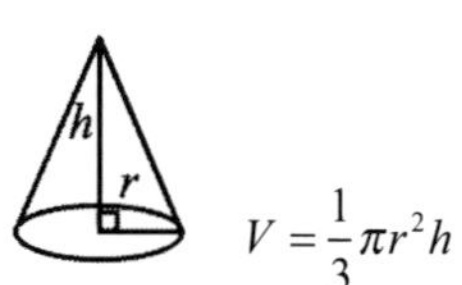

$V = \frac{1}{3}\pi r^2 h$

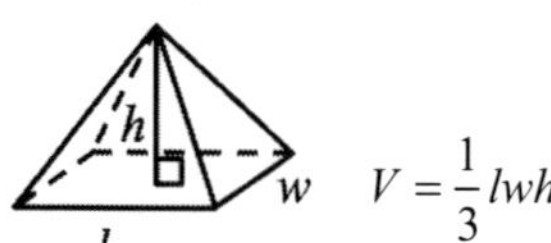

$V = \frac{1}{3}lwh$

There are $360°$ in a circle.
There are 2π radians in a circle.
There are $180°$ in a triangle.

CONTINUE

1

$$x-4y=13$$
$$x+3y=-1$$

Which of the following ordered pairs (x, y) satisfies the system of equations above?

A) $(5,-2)$
B) $(9,-1)$
C) $(1,-3)$
D) $(8,-3)$

2

A company that designs and installs home theaters estimates the cost of a job, in dollars, based on the equation $C=P+125h+250q$, where C is the total cost of the job, P is the price of the equipment, h is the number of hours worked by the installer, and q is the number of hours worked by the electrician. In the equation, what does the constant 250 represent?

A) The cost of installer labor per hour.
B) The cost of electrician labor per hour.
C) The total cost of installer labor.
D) The total number of electrician labor hours.

3

If it takes 8 men 3 full days to frame a house once the foundation has been set, how many men would it take to frame a house in 48 hours?

A) 6
B) 12
C) 18
D) 24

4

	6th Graders	7th Graders	8th Graders	**Total**
Nov.	42	50	62	154
Dec.	68	84	60	212
Apr.	40	22	72	134
Total	150	156	194	400

The two-way table above categorizes middle school students by grade level and the month in which they plan to take their family vacation during the school year. If a middle school student from the study is selected at random, what is the probability that the student is in the sixth grade?

A) $\frac{21}{200}$

B) $\frac{21}{75}$

C) $\frac{3}{8}$

D) $\frac{77}{200}$

5

$$\sqrt{2t^2 - 72}$$

Given that t is a negative integer, for how many values of t is the expression above equivalent to a real number?

A) 11
B) 12
C) 13
D) Infinitely many

6

If $28 = \dfrac{7}{h-2}$, what is the value of $h-2$?

A) $\dfrac{1}{4}$

B) $\dfrac{1}{2}$

C) 2

D) 4

7

$$\frac{x^a x^b}{x^2} = x^2$$

If x is a positive integer, what is the value of $2a+2b$?

A) 2
B) 4
C) 6
D) 8

8

Abigail purchases a new handbag that has a suggested retail price of $80. The store is having a storewide 20% off sale and Abigail has a coupon for 20% off as well. Which of the following equations represents the final price of the handbag, in dollars, after a 7% sales tax has been applied?

A) $p(x) = 80(.20)(.07)$
B) $p(x) = 80(.20)^2(.07)$
C) $p(x) = 80(.60)(1.07)$
D) $p(x) = 80(.80)^2(1.07)$

CONTINUE

Questions 9-12 refer to the following information.

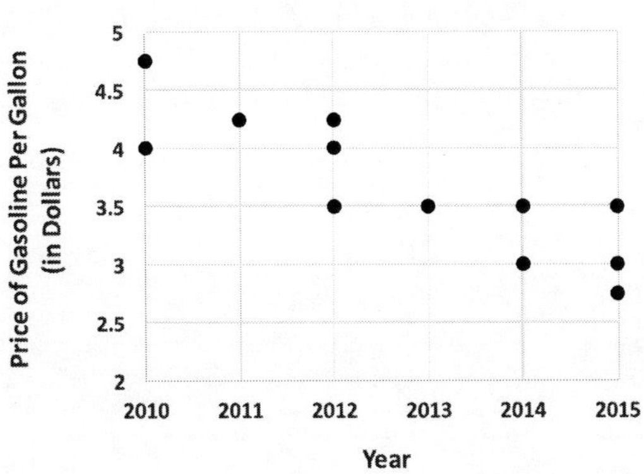

The scatterplot above shows the price per gallon of gasoline, in dollars, from the year 2010 to 2015. All twelve data points were collected randomly from the state of New Jersey over the course of the six years.

9

What was the range, in dollars, of the price of gasoline in the year(s) that had the greatest range?

A) 0
B) 0.50
C) 0.75
D) 1

10

Which of the following equations best models y, the price of gasoline in dollars, x years from the year 2000?

A) $y = -0.24x + 4.35$
B) $y = -0.24x + 6.75$
C) $y = -0.5x + 4.75$
D) $y = -0.5x + 9.75$

11

If the linear trend present in the scatterplot was proven to continue through the year 2017, which of the following would be the best estimate of the price of a gallon of gasoline in the year 2017?

A) \$2.40
B) \$2.65
C) \$2.90
D) \$3.15

12

In the year 2012, the three gas prices collected were randomly sampled and the average price was calculated to be \$3.92. A margin of error for the gas prices was calculated to be \$0.35. Given the average price and the margin of error, which of the following is the best inference that can be made about the price of gas per gallon in the year 2012?

A) The average price of a gallon of gasoline in the country falls between \$3.57 and \$4.27.
B) The average price of a gallon of gasoline from the sampled gas stations in the country falls between \$3.57 and \$4.27.
C) The average price of a gallon of gasoline in the state of New Jersey falls between \$3.57 and \$4.27.
D) The average price of a gallon of gasoline from the sampled gas stations in the state of New Jersey falls between \$3.57 and \$4.27.

CONTINUE

13

Martha went to the store to purchase paper plates and plastic utensils for a party she was hosting at her home. Packages of paper plates were priced at \$2.50 each and bags of plastic utensils were priced at \$1.75 each. If Martha spent a total of \$15.50 and purchased 8 items, how many bags of utensils did she purchase?

A) 2
B) 3
C) 5
D) 6

14

Which of the following equations can produce a negative value for y?

A) $-3+y=x^2$

B) $-3+y=|x+1|$

C) $y=|x+1|-1$

D) $y=0$

15

$$R=\frac{\pi(n-2)}{n}$$

The equation above is used to determine the measure, in radians, of a single angle in a regular polygon with n sides. Which of the following equations gives the number of sides, n, in terms of R, the radian measure of the angle?

A) $n=-\frac{2\pi}{R-\pi}$

B) $n=\frac{R-\pi}{2\pi}$

C) $n=-2\pi(R-\pi)$

D) $n=-2(R-\pi)$

CONTINUE

DIRECTIONS

For each question from 16-19, solve and enter your answer in the grid-in section of your answer sheet as described below.

A. Write out your answers in the boxes at the top of each column in order to help you fill in the circles accurately. Remember, you will only receive credit for the circles that are filled in correctly, not for the written answer at the top of the columns.

B. Mark only a single circle in each column.

C. There are no negative answers.

D. If the problem has more than one correct answer, grid only one of the correct answers.

E. When your answer is a **mixed number**, such as $1\frac{1}{2}$, it should be entered as 1.5 or $3/2$. You cannot enter a mixed number because there is no room to fill in a circle that represents a space.

F. If you enter a **decimal answer** with more digits then the grid can handle, the answer may be rounded or truncated, but it absolutely must fill the entire grid.

Answer: $\frac{8}{21}$ Answer: 6.4

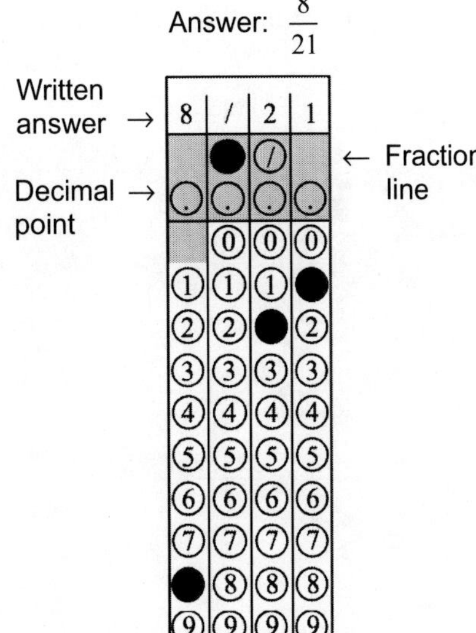

The ways to correctly grid $\frac{7}{9}$ are:

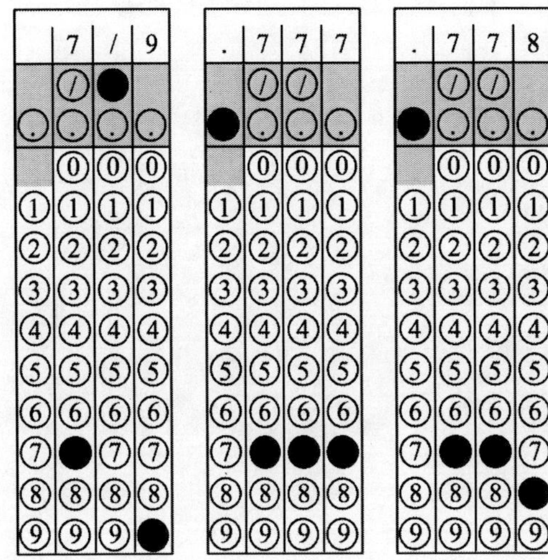

Answer: 102 - both positions are correct

REMEMBER: You can begin writing your answers in any column as long as there is enough space. Leave unused columns blank.

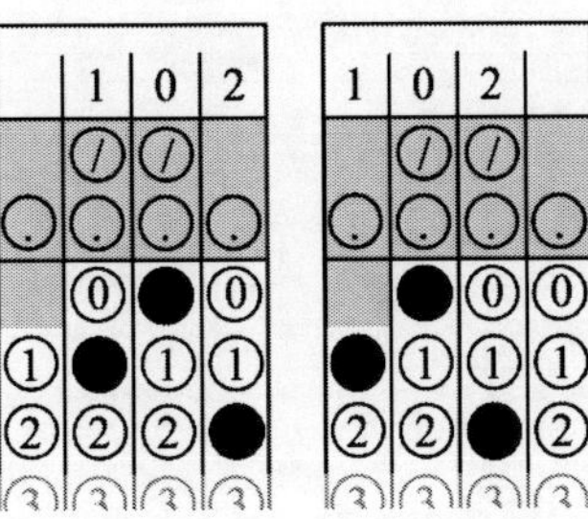

CONTINUE

16

A physics teacher gives prizes to her students in the form of power points. Power points can be used to purchase prizes that the teacher keeps on hand in the classroom. The teacher gives out tickets that are worth either 15 power points or 25 power points. If the teacher has given out at least two of each type of ticket and has given out a total of 230 power points so far this year, what is one possible number of 15-point tickets that the teacher has given away?

17

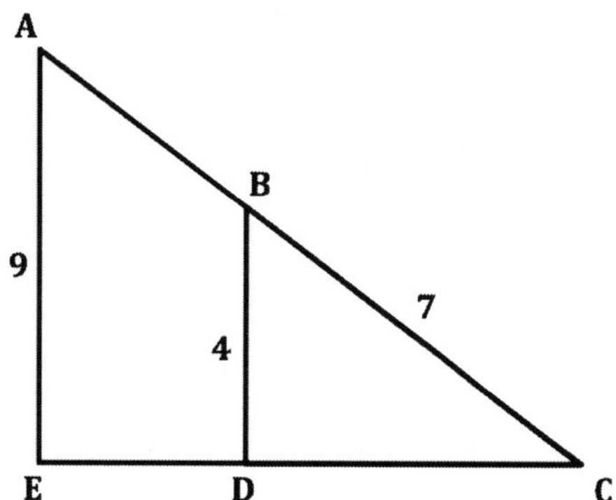

In the diagram above, $\angle AEC = \angle BDC = 90°$. If the length of Segment EC is written in the form $k\sqrt{33}$, where k is a positive constant, what is the value of k?

Questions 18-19 refer to the following information.

$$Account\ Balance = I(1+\frac{r}{100})^t$$

A college student uses the equation above to calculate her savings account balance based on her initial deposit to the account, I, the annual growth rate of her account, r, and the number of years, t, that the money remains in the account.

18

If the student's savings account accrues interest at a rate of 1.5% per year, what is the value of r?

19

42 months after the account was initially opened, the student's savings account balance was exactly $1,316.86. To the nearest dollar, what was the initial amount of money deposited in the account?

STOP

No Test Material On This Page

Math Test - No Calculator

25 MINUTES, 20 QUESTIONS

DIRECTIONS

For each question from 1-15, choose the best answer choice provided in the multiple choice bank and fill in the appropriate circle in the provided answer key. Alternatively, for questions **16-20**, answer the problem and enter your answer in the grid-in section of the answer key. Refer to the directions given before question 16 as to how to enter your answers for the grid-in questions. You may complete scratch work in any empty space in your test booklet.

NOTES

A. Calculator usage **is not allowed** in this section.
B. Variables, constants, and coefficients used represent real numbers unless indicated otherwise.
C. All figures are created to appropriate scale unless the question states otherwise.
D. All figures are two-dimensional unless the question states otherwise.
E. The domain of any given function is all real numbers *x* for which the function, $f(x)$, is a real number unless the question states otherwise.

REFERENCE

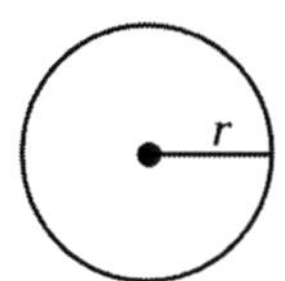

$A = \pi r^2$
$C = 2\pi r$

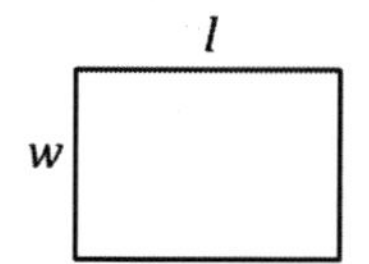

$A = lw$

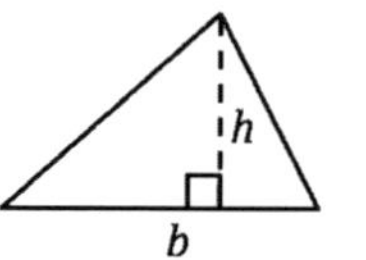

$A = \frac{1}{2}bh$

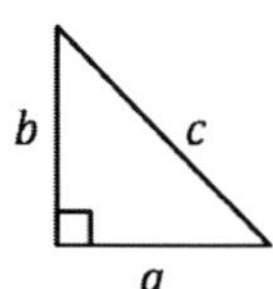

$c^2 = a^2 + b^2$

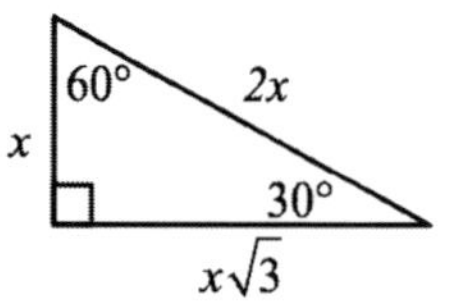

Special Right Triangle

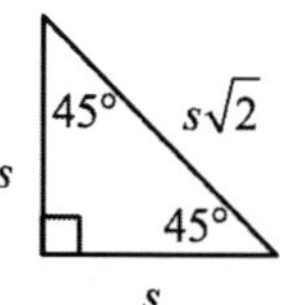

Special Right Triangle

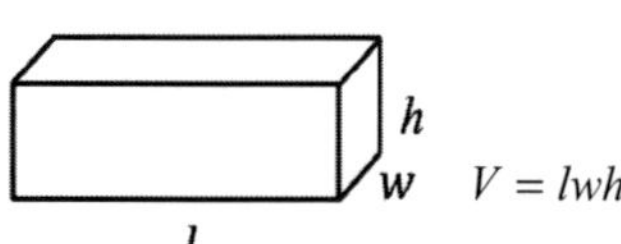

$V = lwh$

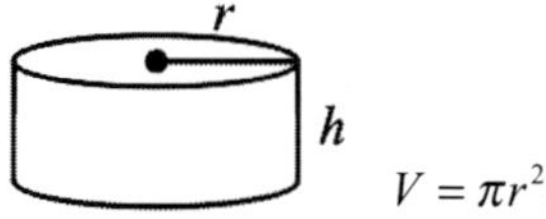

$V = \pi r^2 h$

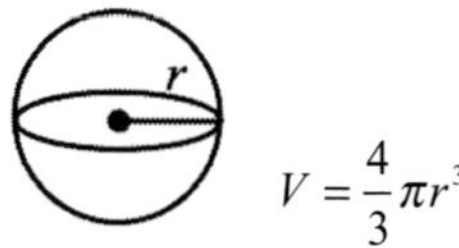

$V = \frac{4}{3}\pi r^3$

$V = \frac{1}{3}\pi r^2 h$

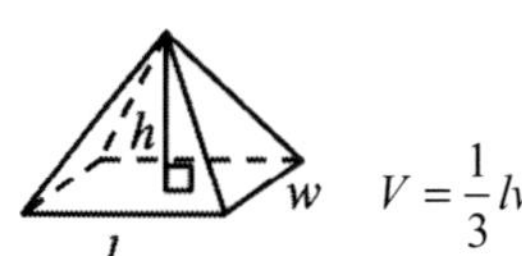

$V = \frac{1}{3}lwh$

There are $360°$ in a circle.
There are 2π radians in a circle.
There are $180°$ in a triangle.

CONTINUE

1

The enrollment in an art class at a local art museum follows a linear model represented by the equation $n = 56 - 2y$, where n represents the number of students enrolled in the art class y years after 2005. Which of the following statements is *not* true?

A) The initial student enrollment in the year 2005 was 56 students.
B) The enrollment has been steadily declining since 2005.
C) There were 36 students enrolled in the year 2015.
D) The average number of students enrolled in the art class from 2005 to 2015 was 48 students per class.

2

$$\frac{3(k+2)}{2} = \frac{3k+2}{4}$$

Which of the following is the value of k in the equation above?

A) $-\frac{10}{3}$

B) -3

C) $\frac{3}{10}$

D) 3

3

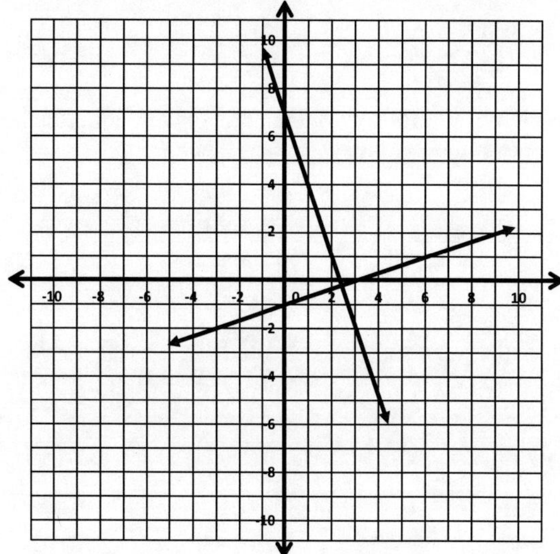

The lines $y = \frac{1}{3}x - 1$ and Line k are graphed on the xy-plane above. If the two lines are perpendicular to each other and Line k intersects the point $(3, -2)$, what is the y-intercept of Line k?

A) -1

B) 0

C) $\frac{5}{2}$

D) 7

4

If $\frac{x}{3} = \frac{3}{x}$ and x is a positive integer, which of the following is equivalent to $\frac{1}{x}$?

A) $-\frac{1}{3}$

B) $\frac{1}{9}$

C) $\frac{1}{3}$

D) 3

CONTINUE

5

$$\frac{16}{y^2} = \frac{4}{x}$$

Which of the following equations is *not* equivalent to the equation given above?

A) $y^2 = 4x$

B) $x = 4y^2$

C) $y = 2\sqrt{x}$

D) $y = -2\sqrt{x}$

6

Given the polynomial $f(x)$, if $f(5) = 0$, which of the following must be a factor of $f(x)$?

A) x
B) $x + 5$
C) $x - 5$
D) $x^2 - 25$

7

If we know that $y = x^3 + 2x^2 + 1$ and $z = x^2 - x$, which of the following is equivalent to $y - xz$?

A) $x^2 + 1$
B) $3x^2 + 1$
C) $x^3 + x^2 + x + 1$
D) $x^3 + 2x^2 - x + 1$

8

Which of the following expressions results from simplifying the expression $\frac{2-i}{2+i}$?
(Note: $i = \sqrt{-1}$)

A) $\frac{5-4i}{5}$

B) $\frac{3-4i}{5}$

C) $\frac{3-4i}{3}$

D) $\frac{5-4i}{3}$

CONTINUE

9

$$x + 4y = 9$$
$$5x + 2y = 27$$

If (x, y) is a solution to the system of equations above, what is the value of $6x + 6y$?

A) 5
B) 6
C) 30
D) 36

10

Nina currently has $842 saved. Nina works for a clothing retailer and last week she made $342 after working three 6-hour shifts. If Nina is paid hourly, which of the following equations can be used to calculate her total savings in the future, *S*, given *h*, the number of hours she works from this moment forward?

A) $S = 19h$
B) $S = 342h$
C) $S = 19h + 842$
D) $S = 19h + 1{,}184$

11

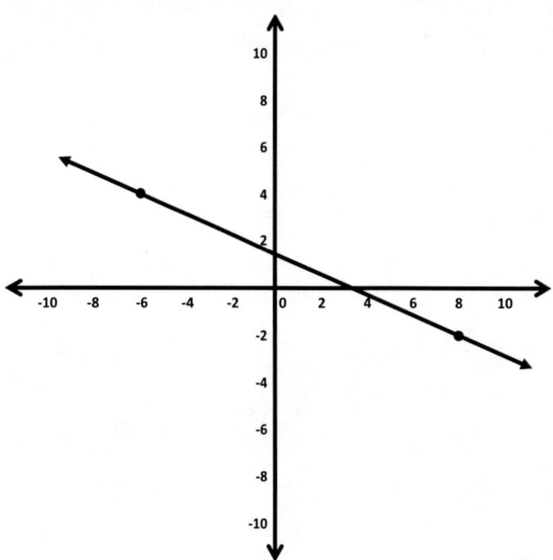

Given that the slope of the linear function graphed above is $-\frac{3}{7}$ and that the line goes through the point $(8, -2)$, what is the *x*-coordinate of the *x*-intercept of the line?

A) $-\frac{10}{3}$

B) $-\frac{3}{10}$

C) 3

D) $\frac{10}{3}$

12

What are the solutions to $7x^2 - 42x + 63 = 0$?

A) $x = \pm 3$
B) $x = -3$
C) $x = 3$
D) $x = \pm 9$

CONTINUE

13

Given $g(x) = 3(x-3)^2 + 35$, how many integer values of x exist that make $g(x) < 0$?

A) 0
B) 2
C) 5
D) Infinitely many

14

The graph of $y = (2x-6)(x-7)$ is a parabola in the xy-plane. If Point A is the vertex of the parabola, what are the coordinates of Point A?

A) $(5,-8)$
B) $(5,8)$
C) $(-5,8)$
D) $(-5,-8)$

15

$$4x + y = 4(x + y) - 3$$
$$x - 8y = 1$$

If (a,b) is the solution to the system of equations above, what is the value of the quotient $\frac{b}{a}$?

A) $\frac{1}{9}$

B) $\frac{1}{3}$

C) 3

D) 9

CONTINUE

DIRECTIONS

For each question from 16-20, solve and enter your answer in the grid-in section of your answer sheet as described below.

A. Write out your answers in the boxes at the top of each column in order to help you fill in the circles accurately. Remember, you will only receive credit for the circles that are filled in correctly, not for the written answer at the top of the columns.

B. Mark only a single circle in each column.

C. There are no negative answers.

D. If the problem has more than one correct answer, grid only one of the correct answers.

E. When your answer is a **mixed number**, such as $1\frac{1}{2}$, it should be entered as 1.5 or $3/2$. You cannot enter a mixed number because there is no room to fill in a circle that represents a space.

F. If you enter a **decimal answer** with more digits then the grid can handle, the answer may be rounded or truncated, but it absolutely must fill the entire grid.

Answer: $\frac{8}{21}$

Written answer → 8 / 2 1 ← Fraction line

Decimal point →

Answer: 6.4

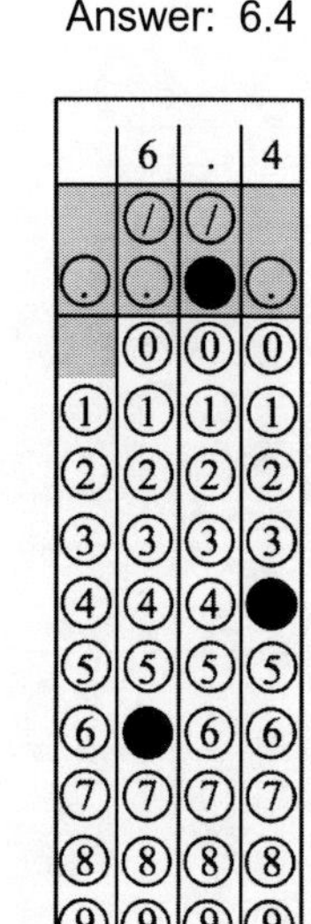

The ways to correctly grid $\frac{7}{9}$ are:

7 / 9   . 7 7 7   . 7 7 8

Answer: 102 - both positions are correct

REMEMBER: You can begin writing your answers in any column as long as there is enough space. Leave unused columns blank.

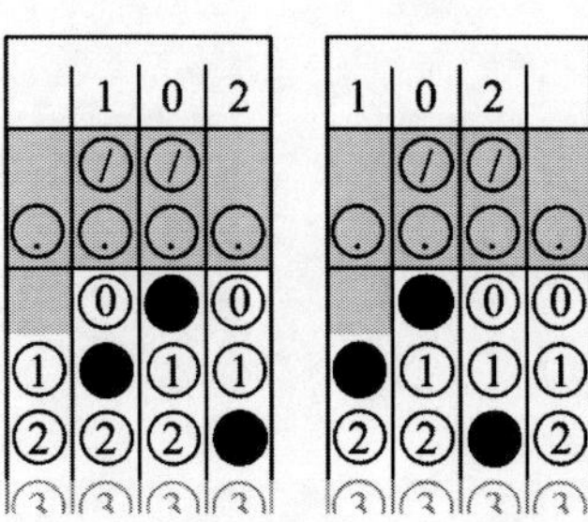

16

If $x+\frac{81}{x}=18$, what value of x makes the equation true?

17

$$\cos\left(\frac{\pi}{2}-\frac{\pi}{6}\right)$$

If $\frac{\pi}{2}-\frac{\pi}{6}$ is the radian measure of an angle, the expression above is equivalent to what value?

18

$$\frac{x^4+8x^3+3x^2-29x-7}{x+7}$$

Given that $x \neq -7$ and that the remainder of the quotient above is given in the form $\frac{b}{x+7}$, what is the value of b?

19

Suppose that the function $f(x)=-2(x+2)^3+1$ and that $g(x)=f(x+2)$. What is the value of $g(-5)$?

20

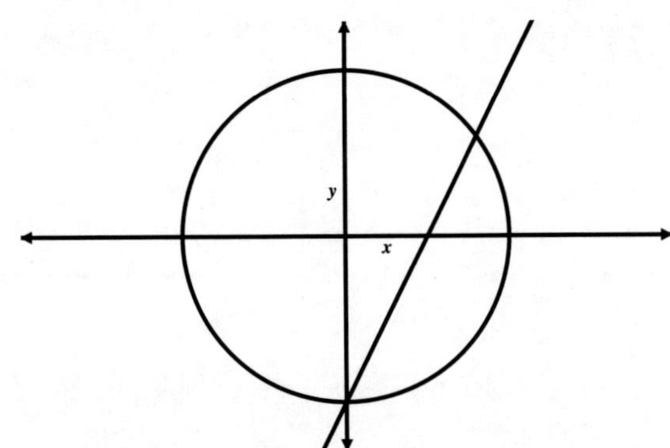

The circle above has the equation $x^2 + y^2 = 1$ and the line has the equation $y = 2x - 1$. If (c, d) is one of the points of intersection of the circle and the line and both c and d are positive, what is the value of c?

STOP

Math Test - Calculator

28 MINUTES, 19 QUESTIONS

DIRECTIONS

For each question from 1-15, choose the best answer choice provided in the multiple choice bank and fill in the appropriate circle in the provided answer key. Alternatively, for questions **16-19**, answer the problem and enter your answer in the grid-in section of the answer key. Refer to the directions given before question 16 as to how to enter your answers for the grid-in questions. You may complete scratch work in any empty space in your test booklet.

NOTES

A. Calculator usage **is allowed**.
B. Variables, constants, and coefficients used represent real numbers unless indicated otherwise.
C. All figures are created to appropriate scale unless the question states otherwise.
D. All figures are two-dimensional unless the question states otherwise.
E. The domain of any given function is all real numbers *x* for which the function, $f(x)$, is a real number unless the question states otherwise.

REFERENCE

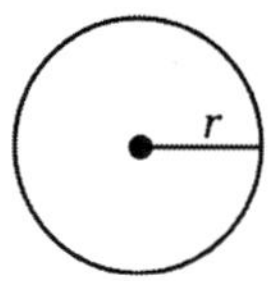

$A = \pi r^2$
$C = 2\pi r$

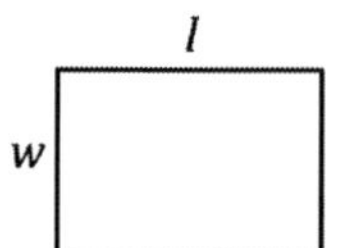

$A = lw$

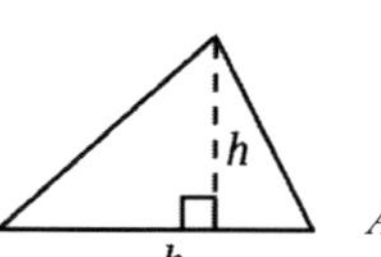

$A = \frac{1}{2}bh$

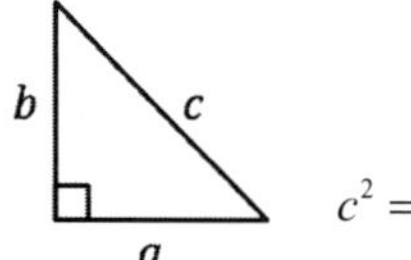

$c^2 = a^2 + b^2$

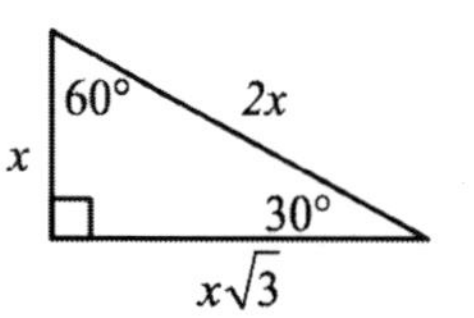

Special Right Triangle

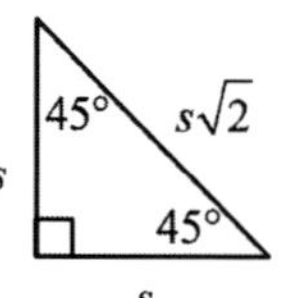

Special Right Triangle

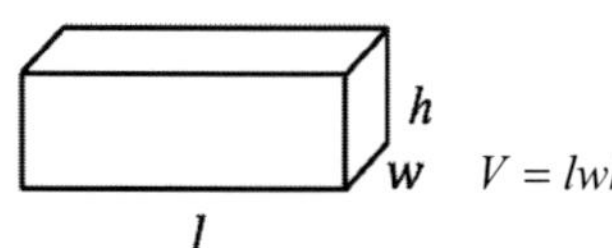

$V = lwh$

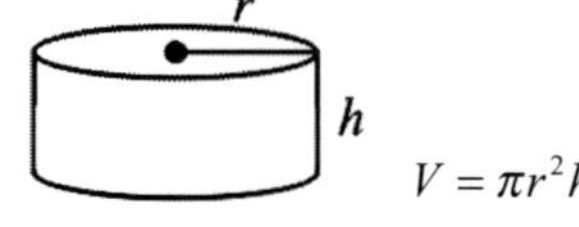

$V = \pi r^2 h$

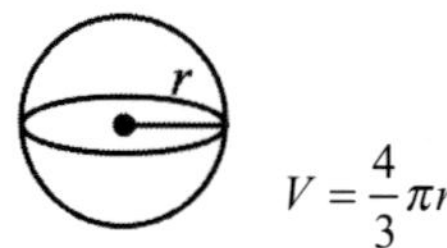

$V = \frac{4}{3}\pi r^3$

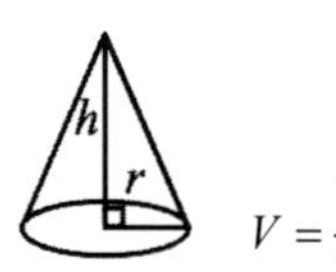

$V = \frac{1}{3}\pi r^2 h$

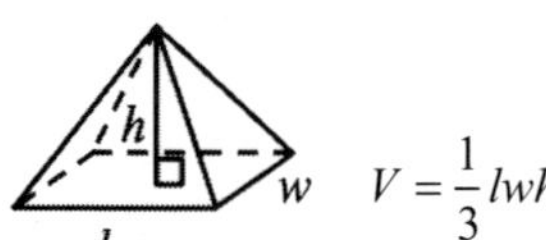

$V = \frac{1}{3}lwh$

There are $360°$ in a circle.
There are 2π radians in a circle.
There are $180°$ in a triangle.

CONTINUE

1

The chief financial officer of an alternative bio-fuel company progressively raises the price of a single gallon of the company's fuel based on the equation $P = 3.75(1.02)^m$, where P is the price per gallon and m is the number of months that have passed. What is the meaning of the constant 3.75 in this equation?

A) The initial price of the fuel is $3.75 per gallon.
B) The price of the fuel after one month has passed is $3.75 per gallon.
C) The price of the fuel will increase by 3.75% each month.
D) The price of the fuel will increase by 375% each month.

2

The director of an SAT school estimates the number of summer classes, c, in terms of s, the total student enrollment for the summer program, using the model $c = \frac{s}{18} + 3$. Based on the model, what is the number of students that the director expects to have in each class?

A) 3
B) 6
C) 18
D) 21

3

The ratio of the number of Juniors to the number of Seniors in a study hall is 5:7. If there are a total of 84 students in the study hall, how many more of the students are Seniors than Juniors?

A) 49
B) 35
C) 14
D) 7

4

	Colors			
	Red	**Blue**	**Grey**	**Black**
Top	12	8	16	24
Bottom	24	32	4	28
Total	**36**	**40**	**20**	**52**

A group of students at Union High School were categorized by the color of the top or the bottom of their gym class outfits in the table above. If a student is selected at random, what is the probability that they are wearing a red top?

A) $\frac{1}{2}$
B) $\frac{1}{3}$
C) $\frac{1}{5}$
D) $\frac{3}{37}$

CONTINUE

Questions 5-7 refer to the following scatterplot.

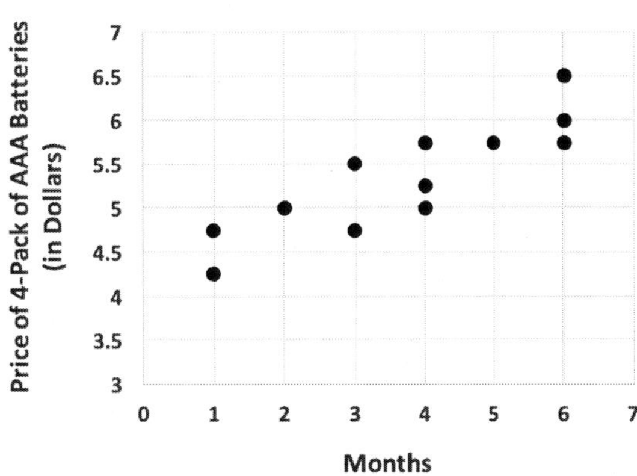

From February through July of 2018, the prices in dollars of randomly selected 4-packs of AAA batteries throughout the country were plotted against the number of months since January 1st, 2018. This data is displayed in the scatterplot above.

5

Which of the following is closest to the average price of the 4-packs of AAA batteries collected in May?

A) \$5.13
B) \$5.33
C) \$5.50
D) \$5.75

6

Which of the following is the range in prices of all of the 4-packs collected prior to May?

A) \$0.75
B) \$1.25
C) \$1.50
D) \$2.25

7

If a line of best fit were to be calculated for the data in the scatterplot, which of the would most likely be the equation of that line?

A) $y = 0.17x + 4.25$
B) $y = 0.17x + 4.50$
C) $y = 0.33x + 4.20$
D) $y = 0.33x + 4.50$

8

$$8x - y = 19$$
$$x + 2y = -38$$

Which of the following ordered pairs (x, y) is the solution to the system of equations above?

A) $(-1, -27)$
B) $(0, -19)$
C) $(1, -11)$
D) $(2, -3)$

CONTINUE

9

$$(xy^3 - 2xy + x^2) - (-xy^3 - 2xy)$$

Which of the following expressions is equivalent to the expression above?

A) x^2
B) $2xy^3 + x^2$
C) $-4xy + x^2$
D) $2xy^3 - 4xy + x^2$

10

Line m is perpendicular to the line $y = -\frac{1}{2}x - 2$ and passes through the point $(2,4)$. Which of the following points also lies on line m?

A) $(-4,-2)$
B) $(-2,0)$
C) $(0,8)$
D) $(8,16)$

11

$$m(x+b) + rx = 12x + 32$$

If m, b, and r are positive integers, which of the following is *not* a value of r that satisfies the equation above?

A) 2
B) 4
C) 8
D) 11

12

$$\frac{1}{x+5} + \frac{1}{x+2} = \frac{1}{x^2 + 7x + 10}$$

Given $x \neq -5$ and $x \neq -2$, which of the following is a value of x that satisfies the equation above?

A) -3
B) -1
C) 0
D) 1

CONTINUE

13

If $h(x) = 2x - 3b$ and b is a constant such that $h(3) = 0$, what is the value of $h(6)$?

A) -2
B) 0
C) 3
D) 6

14

$$t = \frac{(4g-1)^n(4g-1)^{k-n}}{4g-1}(m-f)$$

Which of the following equations gives m in terms of g, n, k, f, and t?

A) $m = t(4g-1)^{1-k} - f$

B) $m = f(4g-1)^{k-1}$

C) $m = \dfrac{t(4g-1)^n(4g-1)^{k-n}}{4g-1}(f)$

D) $m = \dfrac{t(4g-1)}{(4g-1)^n(4g-1)^{k-n}} + f$

15

If $7^{2x} = 49a^2$ and $7^x = 8ab$, what is the value of b?

A) $\dfrac{7}{8}$

B) 1

C) 7

D) 15

CONTINUE

DIRECTIONS

For each question from 16-19, solve and enter your answer in the grid-in section of your answer sheet as described below.

A. Write out your answers in the boxes at the top of each column in order to help you fill in the circles accurately. Remember, you will only receive credit for the circles that are filled in correctly, not for the written answer at the top of the columns.

B. Mark only a single circle in each column.

C. There are no negative answers.

D. If the problem has more than one correct answer, grid only one of the correct answers.

E. When your answer is a **mixed number**, such as $1\frac{1}{2}$, it should be entered as 1.5 or $3/2$. You cannot enter a mixed number because there is no room to fill in a circle that represents a space.

F. If you enter a **decimal answer** with more digits then the grid can handle, the answer may be rounded or truncated, but it absolutely must fill the entire grid.

Answer: $\frac{8}{21}$

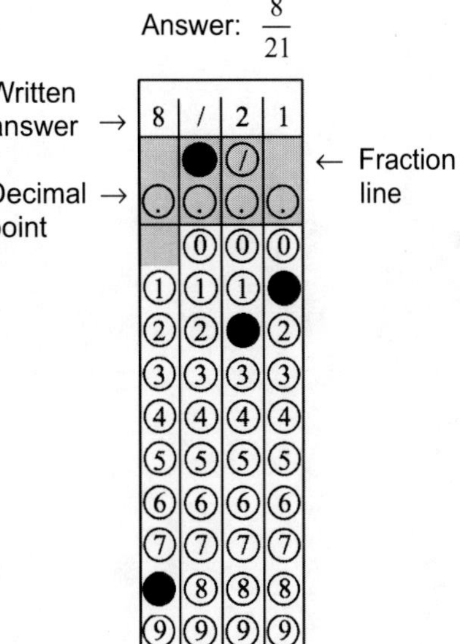

Answer: 6.4

6 . 4

The ways to correctly grid $\frac{7}{9}$ are:

7 / 9

. 7 7 7

. 7 7 8

Answer: 102 - both positions are correct

REMEMBER: You can begin writing your answers in any column as long as there is enough space. Leave unused columns blank.

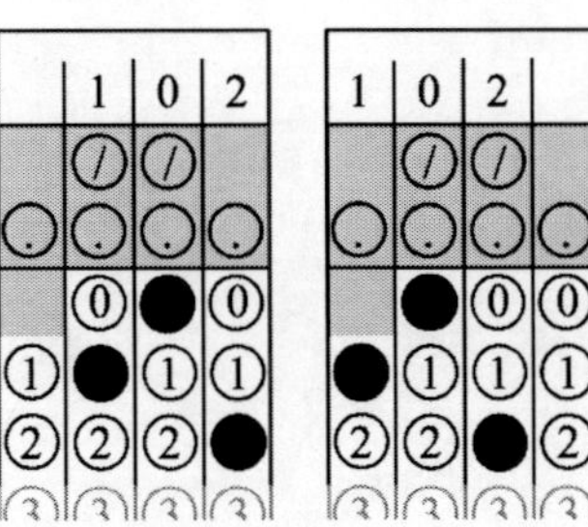

CONTINUE

16

$$y = 2^x + 1$$

If the y-intercept in the graph of the equation above is $(0, c)$, what is the value of c^2?

17

A triangle has one angle that measures $x°$ and another angle that measures $90°$. If $\sin x° = \frac{1}{2}$ and $\cos x°$ can be written in the form $n\sqrt{3}$, what is the value of n?

18

If $b^2 = \sqrt{6}$ and $x = \sqrt{\frac{32}{3} \bullet \frac{b^9}{b^3}}$, what is the value of x?

19

12 ounces of a 5% hydrofluoric acid solution are mixed with a 14% hydrofluoric acid solution to create a mixture that is 11% hydrofluoric acid. If there are 128 ounces in a gallon, how many gallons of 14% hydrofluoric acid are in the mixture?

STOP

No Test Material On This Page

Math Test - No Calculator

25 MINUTES, 20 QUESTIONS

DIRECTIONS

For each question from 1-15, choose the best answer choice provided in the multiple choice bank and fill in the appropriate circle in the provided answer key. Alternatively, for questions **16-20**, answer the problem and enter your answer in the grid-in section of the answer key. Refer to the directions given before question 16 as to how to enter your answers for the grid-in questions. You may complete scratch work in any empty space in your test booklet.

NOTES

A. Calculator usage **is not allowed** in this section.
B. Variables, constants, and coefficients used represent real numbers unless indicated otherwise.
C. All figures are created to appropriate scale unless the question states otherwise.
D. All figures are two-dimensional unless the question states otherwise.
E. The domain of any given function is all real numbers *x* for which the function, $f(x)$, is a real number unless the question states otherwise.

REFERENCE

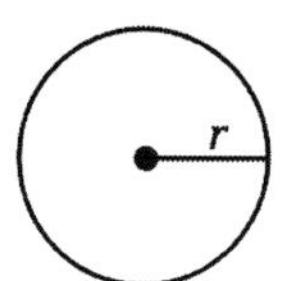

$A=\pi r^2$

$C=2\pi r$

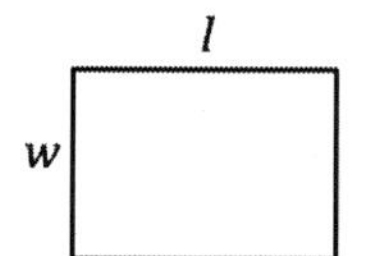

$A=lw$

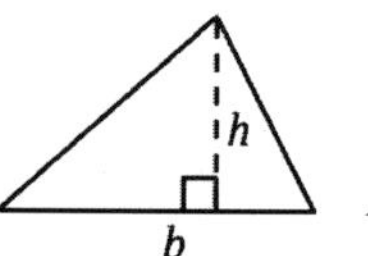

$A=\frac{1}{2}bh$

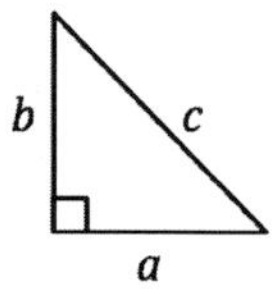

$c^2=a^2+b^2$

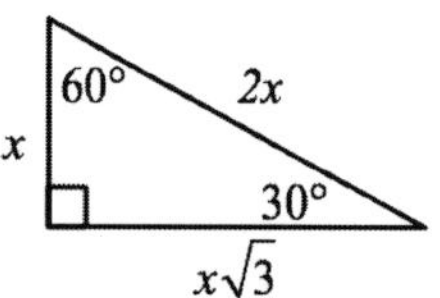

Special Right Triangle

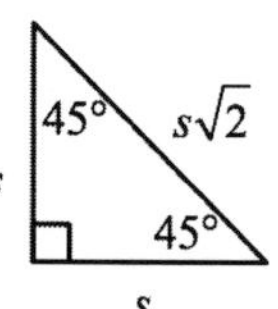

Special Right Triangle

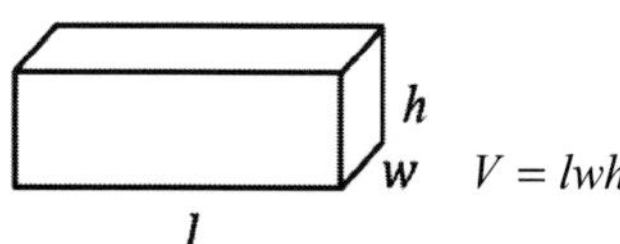

$V=lwh$

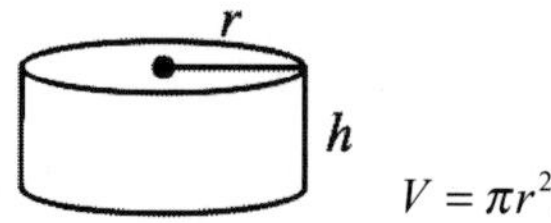

$V=\pi r^2 h$

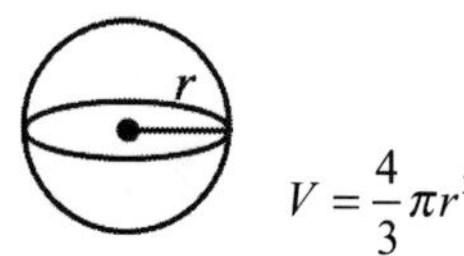

$V=\frac{4}{3}\pi r^3$

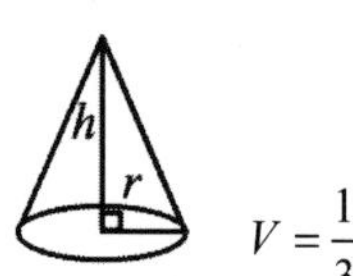

$V=\frac{1}{3}\pi r^2 h$

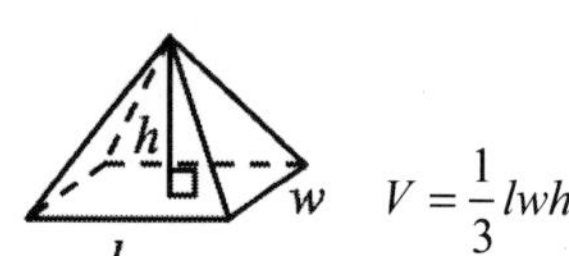

$V=\frac{1}{3}lwh$

There are $360°$ in a circle.
There are 2π radians in a circle.
There are $180°$ in a triangle.

CONTINUE

1

If $f(x) = 3x - 4$, what is the value of $f(2) + 3$?

A) 2
B) 5
C) 11
D) 13

2

$$\frac{x+y}{2} = 18$$
$$\frac{x-y}{3} = 12$$

If the ordered pair (x, y) is a solution to the system of equations above, what is the value of y?

A) 0
B) 12
C) 18
D) 36

3

In the equation $y = b(x+1)$, b is a constant. If $(4,4)$ and $(14, h)$ are solutions to the equation, what is the value of h?

A) $\frac{56}{5}$

B) 5

C) 12

D) $\frac{75}{4}$

4

Which of the following equations has no real solutions?

A) $x^2 - 1 = 0$

B) $5 - x^2 = -2$

C) $|x - (-3)| = 5$

D) $|8 - x| + 1 = 0$

CONTINUE

5

A man decided that he wanted to decrease the number of calories that he consumed daily in an effort to determine the daily calorie consumption that would allow him to maintain his current body weight. In the second week of this project he consumed 2600 calories per day and in the fifth week he consumed 2000 calories per day. If the man consciously reduced his calories at a constant rate, which of the following is true?

A) The number of calories consumed decreased by 100 calories per week.
B) The number of calories consumed decreased by 600 calories per week.
C) The initial number of calories consumed per day before the diet was 2800 calories.
D) The initial number of calories consumed per day before the diet was 3000 calories.

6

$$cd = 3 + d$$

If the equation above is true, which of the following equations must also be true?

A) $c = 3$

B) $c + 1 = 3$

C) $c - 1 = \frac{3}{d}$

D) $d = \frac{c-1}{3}$

7

The polynomial $20x^2 - 20x + 5$ is equivalent to which of the following expressions?

A) $5(2x-1)^2$
B) $2(5x-1)^2$
C) $5(2x-1)(2x+3)$
D) $2(5x-1)(2x-1)$

8

$$x = 2y$$
$$y = \frac{1}{4}x^2 - 6$$

The system of equations above has how many solutions where $x \leq 0$?

A) 0
B) 1
C) 2
D) Infinitely many

CONTINUE

9

If $\frac{1}{x}+2=\frac{4}{x}$, what is the value of x?

A) $\frac{2}{3}$

B) 1

C) $\frac{3}{2}$

D) 2

10

$$-16x=(x-3)^2$$

Which of the following is the minimum value of x that makes the equation above true?

A) -10

B) -9

C) -1

D) 1

11

Which of the following pairs of linear equations represents two lines that are perpendicular with respect to each other?

A) $2x+4y=5$
$2y-4x=5$

B) $3x+y=8$
$3y+9x=12$

C) $x+y=14$
$-x-y=7$

D) $3x+2y=11$
$4x-12y=13$

12

$$\frac{17}{4-i}=a+\frac{b}{2}i$$

For $i=\sqrt{-1}$, if the expression above is true for positive constants a and b, what is the value of b?

A) 1

B) 2

C) 8

D) 34

CONTINUE

13

Janice and Ariell were selling trinkets at a flea market and made a $3 profit on each sale. Janice sold three more than twice the number of trinkets that Ariell sold. If a represents the number of trinkets that Ariell sold and Janice and Ariell split the profits evenly, which of the following expressions represents the amount of money, in dollars, that each woman received?

A) $\frac{3a}{2}$

B) $\frac{9a}{2}$

C) $\frac{6a+9}{2}$

D) $\frac{9a+9}{2}$

14

$$x^2 + fx + gx + fg = 0$$

Which of the following expressions is equivalent to the sum of all of the roots of the equation given above?

A) $f+g$
B) $-(f+g)$
C) $1-f$
D) $-(1+g)$

15

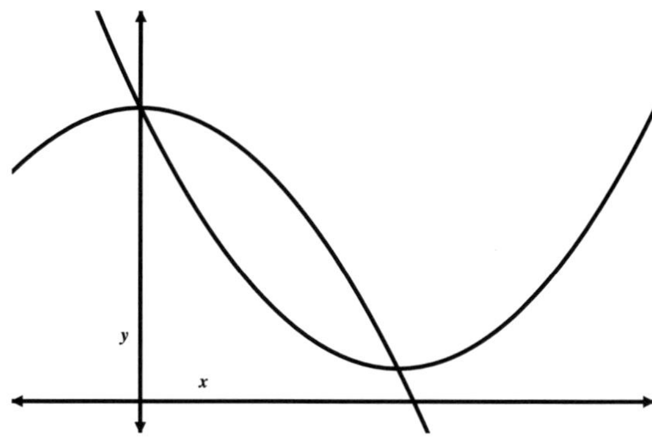

$$f(x) = 18 - x^2$$
$$g(x) = x^2 - 8x + 18$$

In the xy-plane above, the functions $f(x)$ and $g(x)$ intersect at the points A and B. If Line k passes through both A and B, what is the slope of Line k?

A) -4

B) -2

C) $-\frac{1}{2}$

D) $-\frac{1}{4}$

DIRECTIONS

For each question from 16-20, solve and enter your answer in the grid-in section of your answer sheet as described below.

A. Write out your answers in the boxes at the top of each column in order to help you fill in the circles accurately. Remember, you will only receive credit for the circles that are filled in correctly, not for the written answer at the top of the columns.

B. Mark only a single circle in each column.

C. There are no negative answers.

D. If the problem has more than one correct answer, grid only one of the correct answers.

E. When your answer is a **mixed number**, such as $1\frac{1}{2}$, it should be entered as 1.5 or $3/2$. You cannot enter a mixed number because there is no room to fill in a circle that represents a space.

F. If you enter a **decimal answer** with more digits then the grid can handle, the answer may be rounded or truncated, but it absolutely must fill the entire grid.

Answer: $\frac{8}{21}$

Written answer → 8 / 2 1

Decimal point →

← Fraction line

Answer: 6.4

6 . 4

The ways to correctly grid $\frac{7}{9}$ are:

7 / 9 | . 7 7 7 | . 7 7 8

Answer: 102 - both positions are correct

REMEMBER: You can begin writing your answers in any column as long as there is enough space. Leave unused columns blank.

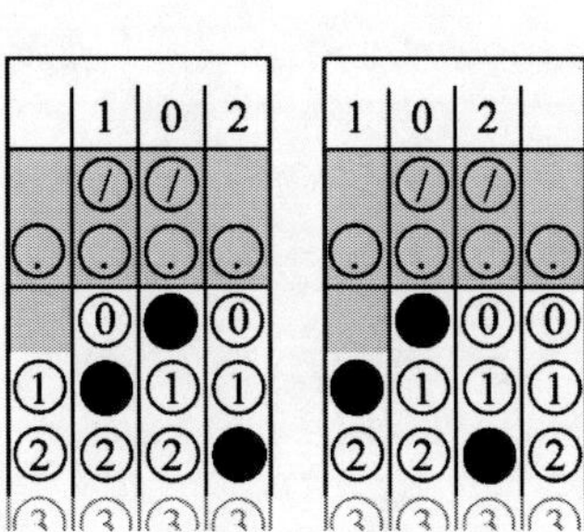

16

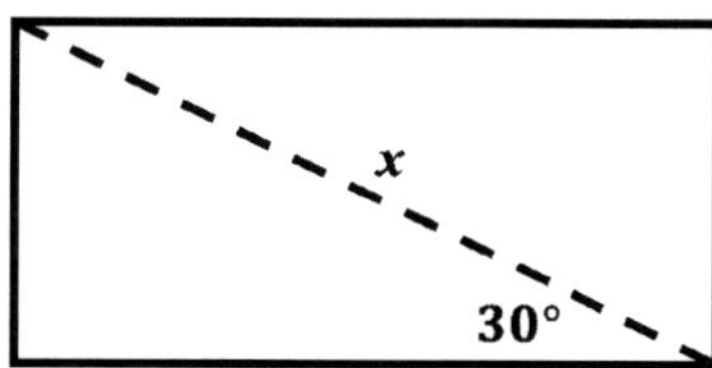

Mary is shipping a candle in a rectangular box. The candle, whose length is represented by x in the diagram above, has been placed diagonally on the bottom of the box and makes a $30°$ angle with the side of the box. If the area of the bottom of the box is $25\sqrt{3}$ inches and the candle fits perfectly on the bottom of the box from corner to corner, what is the length of the candle, in inches?

17

$$|x-5|-7<-6$$

If $x>5$, what is one possible value of x that makes the equation true?

18

$$y=-\frac{1}{2}x+3$$
$$y=-\frac{1}{4}x$$

The linear equations above intersect at the coordinate point (x,y). What is the value of x?

19

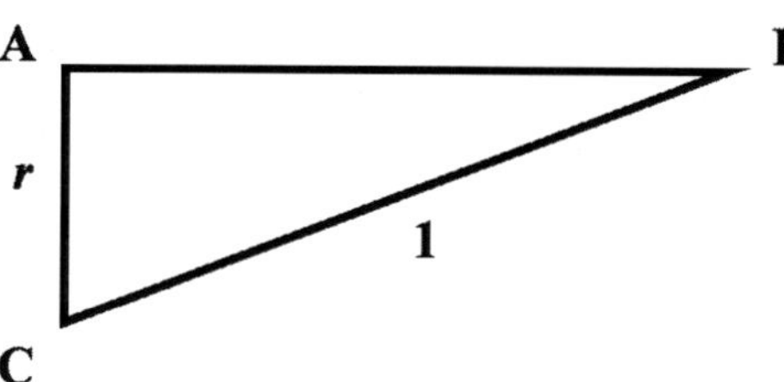

In the right triangle above, $\sin\angle ABC=r$. If $\cos\angle ABC=\sqrt{1+\frac{-k}{8}r^2}$, what is the value of k?

CONTINUE

20

At the surface of the ocean, hydrostatic pressure exerts 14.5 psi, pounds per square inch, of pressure on the human body. As you descend into the ocean, pressure increases in a linear fashion. At a depth of 165 feet below sea level, the force of hydrostatic pressure is 87 psi. At a depth of 231 feet, the force of hydrostatic pressure is 116 psi. At this rate, what is the increase in psi for a change of 33 feet in ocean depth?

STOP

Math Test - Calculator

28 MINUTES, 19 QUESTIONS

DIRECTIONS

For each question from 1-15, choose the best answer choice provided in the multiple choice bank and fill in the appropriate circle in the provided answer key. Alternatively, for questions **16-19**, answer the problem and enter your answer in the grid-in section of the answer key. Refer to the directions given before question 16 as to how to enter your answers for the grid-in questions. You may complete scratch work in any empty space in your test booklet.

NOTES

A. Calculator usage **is allowed**.
B. Variables, constants, and coefficients used represent real numbers unless indicated otherwise.
C. All figures are created to appropriate scale unless the question states otherwise.
D. All figures are two-dimensional unless the question states otherwise.
E. The domain of any given function is all real numbers *x* for which the function, $f(x)$, is a real number unless the question states otherwise.

REFERENCE

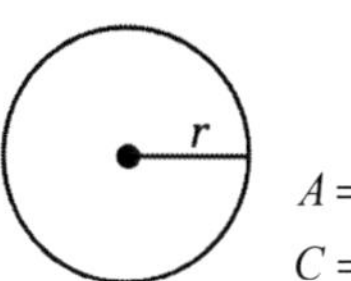

$A = \pi r^2$
$C = 2\pi r$

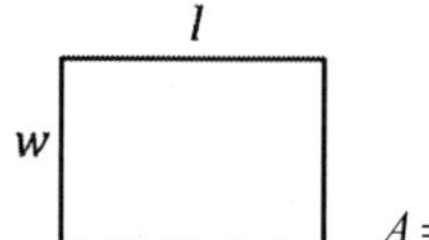

$A = lw$

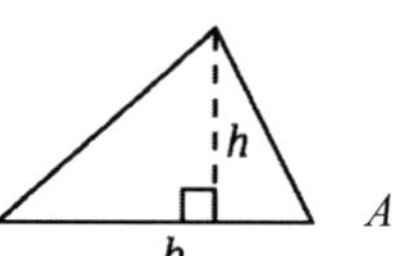

$A = \frac{1}{2}bh$

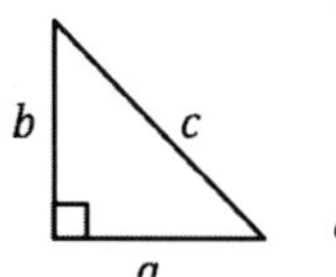

$c^2 = a^2 + b^2$

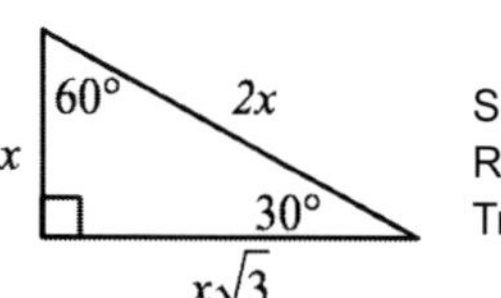

Special Right Triangle

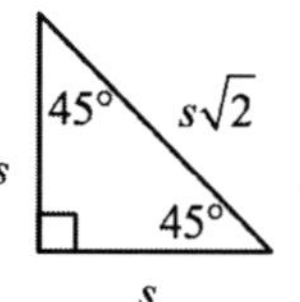

Special Right Triangle

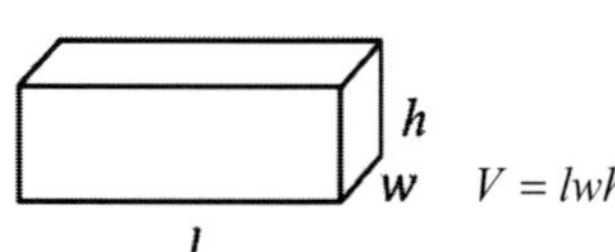

$V = lwh$

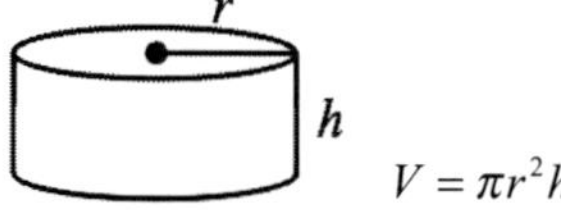

$V = \pi r^2 h$

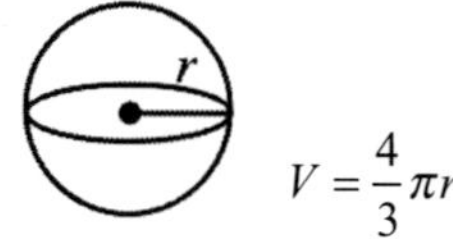

$V = \frac{4}{3}\pi r^3$

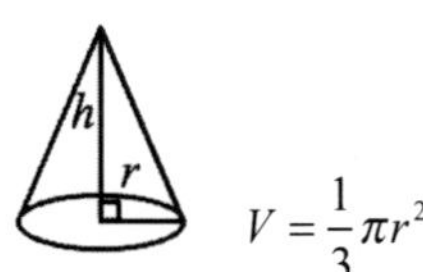

$V = \frac{1}{3}\pi r^2 h$

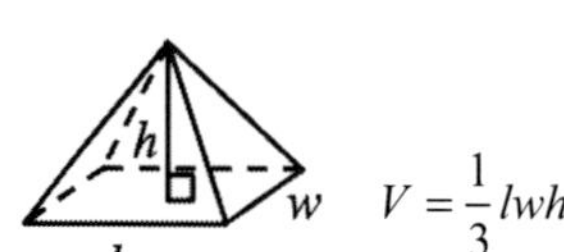

$V = \frac{1}{3}lwh$

There are $360°$ in a circle.
There are 2π radians in a circle.
There are $180°$ in a triangle.

CONTINUE

1

x	y
1	3
5	m
7	15
10	21

Given that the data collected above are solutions to a linear function, what is the value of m?

A) 5
B) 6
C) 9
D) 11

2

Lauren works part-time during her summer break in a local restaurant. The income she earns, I, can be calculated using the following model based on h, the number of hours she has worked: $I = 8h + 20$. Which of the following is true?

A) Lauren's income does not follow a linear model.
B) Lauren's hourly rate is $20.
C) Lauren makes $36 if she works for 2 hours.
D) Lauren only receives an hourly rate of pay.

3

One night, Nandita rolled a standard die 5 times in a row and rolled 5 fives in a row. If Nandita rolled the die a sixth time, what is the probability of her rolling another five on that particular roll?

A) $\frac{1}{46,656}$
B) $\frac{1}{36}$
C) $\frac{1}{6}$
D) $\frac{1}{2}$

4

Gerald's new motorcycle weighs exactly 242 kilograms. If he purchased a new seat which reduced the weight of the bike by 6 pounds, what is the overall weight of his modified bike in pounds?
(*1 kilogram = 2.2 pounds*)

A) 519.2
B) 526.4
C) 538.4
D) 545.6

CONTINUE

4

5

Suppose that $a^3 + 14a^2 = 51a$ and $a < 0$. What is the value of $a + 14$?

A) 17
B) 3
C) -3
D) -17

6

$$\frac{1}{a-1} \bullet y^3 = 7$$

Given the equation above, what is y in terms of a?

A) $\sqrt[3]{7a-1}$

B) $\sqrt[3]{7a-7}$

C) $7\sqrt[3]{a-1}$

D) $(7(a-1))^3$

7

Suppose that $4x - 3y = 24$. What is the value of $\frac{x}{3} - \frac{y}{4}$?

A) 2
B) 4
C) 6
D) 8

8

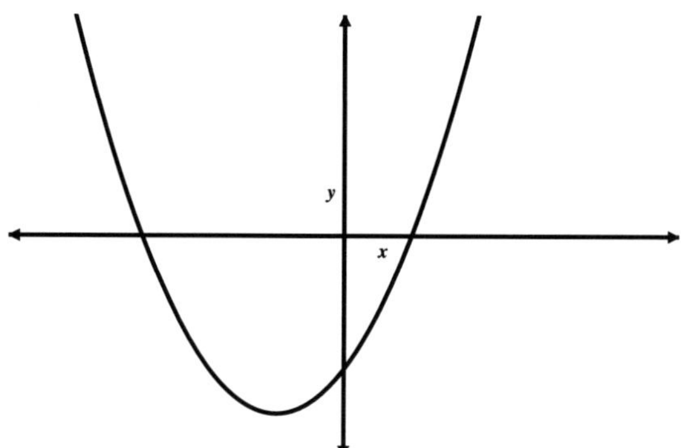

The graph of the parabolic function $y = 2(x-1)(x+3)$ is shown above. Which of the following is *not* true?

A) If $x = 1$, then $y = 0$.
B) The quadratic equation has both a negative and a positive root.
C) The axis of symmetry is $x = -1$.
D) The y-coordinate of the vertex is -4.

CONTINUE

Questions 9-11 refer to the following table.

	1	2	3	4	5	Total
Adults	13	35	103	82	17	**250**
Children	6	22	27	70	25	**150**
Total	**19**	**57**	**130**	**152**	**42**	**400**

At a large corporate-wide picnic, the 400 guests were asked to rank the activities at the picnic on a scale of 1 to 5, 5 being terrific and fun and 1 being insufficient and boring. The results are displayed in the two-way table above.

9

How many more adults gave an even number rank than children?

A) 25
B) 50
C) 75
D) 100

10

Which of the following is closest to the average rank given by the adults?

A) 2.5
B) 3.2
C) 3.6
D) 50

11

How much higher was the median rank of the children as opposed to the median rank of the adults?

A) 1
B) 10
C) 76
D) 100

12

If $y = x^2 + 1$ and $z = (x+1)(x-1)$, what is the value of yz in terms of x?

A) $x^4 - 1$
B) $x^4 + 1$
C) $x^4 + 2x^2 + 1$
D) $x^4 - 2x^2 + 1$

CONTINUE

13

$$\frac{2-3i}{1+i}$$

The expression above is equivalent to which of the following expressions?

A) $5-5i$

B) $\frac{1-5i}{2}$

C) $-1-5i$

D) $\frac{-1-5i}{2}$

14

What is the solution to the equation $x-\sqrt{x}=6$?

A) 4
B) 9
C) 27
D) 36

15

Given that $\cos x=\frac{4}{5}$ and that x is the measure of an angle in degrees, which of the following equations *cannot* be true?

A) $\sin x=\frac{3}{5}$

B) $\cos(90-x)=\frac{3}{5}$

C) $\tan(90-x)=\frac{3}{4}$

D) $\tan x=\frac{3}{4}$

CONTINUE

DIRECTIONS

For each question from 16-19, solve and enter your answer in the grid-in section of your answer sheet as described below.

A. Write out your answers in the boxes at the top of each column in order to help you fill in the circles accurately. Remember, you will only receive credit for the circles that are filled in correctly, not for the written answer at the top of the columns.

B. Mark only a single circle in each column.

C. There are no negative answers.

D. If the problem has more than one correct answer, grid only one of the correct answers.

E. When your answer is a **mixed number**, such as $1\frac{1}{2}$, it should be entered as 1.5 or $3/2$. You cannot enter a mixed number because there is no room to fill in a circle that represents a space.

F. If you enter a **decimal answer** with more digits then the grid can handle, the answer may be rounded or truncated, but it absolutely must fill the entire grid.

Answer: 102 - both positions are correct

REMEMBER: You can begin writing your answers in any column as long as there is enough space. Leave unused columns blank.

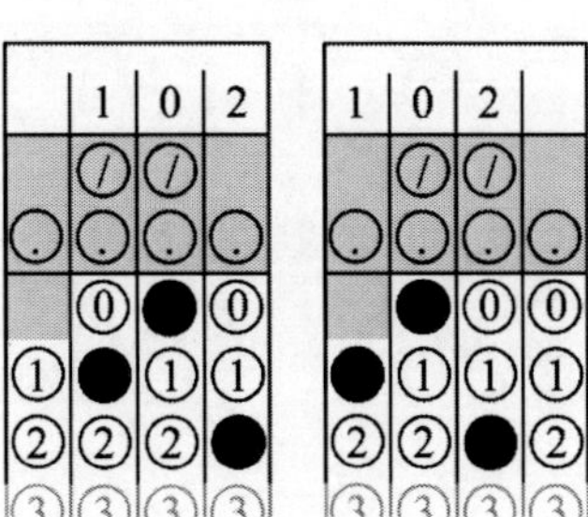

Answer: $\frac{8}{21}$

Written answer → 8 / 2 1

Decimal point →

← Fraction line

Answer: 6.4

6 . 4

The ways to correctly grid $\frac{7}{9}$ are:

7 / 9

. 7 7 7

. 7 7 8

CONTINUE

16

$$3x - 4y = 5$$
$$2x = y$$

Given the system of equations above, what is the value of the quotient of y and x?

17

The sum of a number k and 24 is 4 times the value of z. If k and z are both positive integers, what is the greatest possible value for k that is less than 20?

Questions 18-19 refer to the following scatterplot.

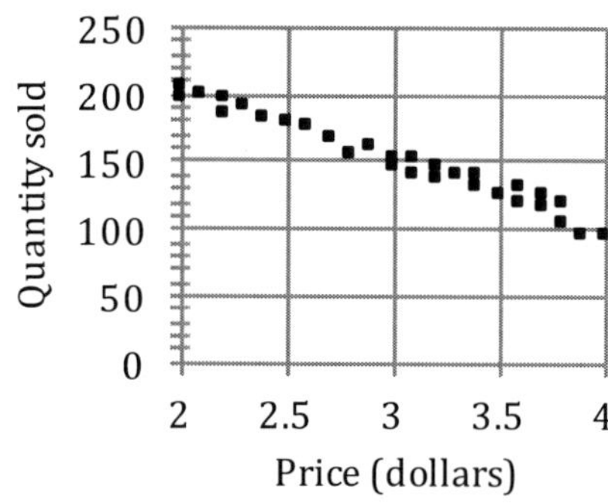

At a certain company, the more product they sell, the lower the price per unit will be. The quantity sold and price per unit of 30 randomly selected orders is displayed in the scatterplot above.

18

The equation for the scatterplot's best fit model was calculated to be $Q = -52.5p + 312.50$, where Q is the quantity of product sold given p, the price per unit. What would an employee of the company estimate for the price per unit, in dollars rounded to the nearest cent, for an order that had 97 products sold?

19

Of the randomly selected orders that had a price per unit greater than \$3.00, what fraction had quantities greater than 100?

STOP

No Test Material On This Page

Math Test - No Calculator

25 MINUTES, 20 QUESTIONS

DIRECTIONS

For each question from 1-15, choose the best answer choice provided in the multiple choice bank and fill in the appropriate circle in the provided answer key. Alternatively, for questions **16-20**, answer the problem and enter your answer in the grid-in section of the answer key. Refer to the directions given before question 16 as to how to enter your answers for the grid-in questions. You may complete scratch work in any empty space in your test booklet.

NOTES

A. Calculator usage **is not allowed** in this section.
B. Variables, constants, and coefficients used represent real numbers unless indicated otherwise.
C. All figures are created to appropriate scale unless the question states otherwise.
D. All figures are two-dimensional unless the question states otherwise.
E. The domain of any given function is all real numbers x for which the function, $f(x)$, is a real number unless the question states otherwise.

REFERENCE

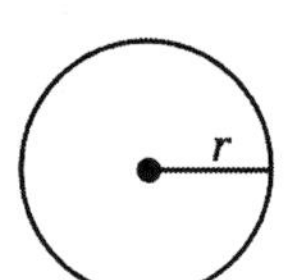

$A = \pi r^2$
$C = 2\pi r$

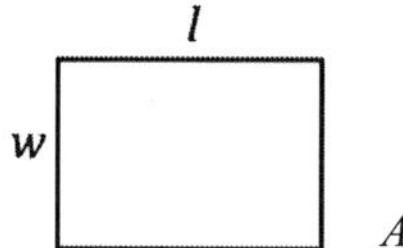

$A = lw$

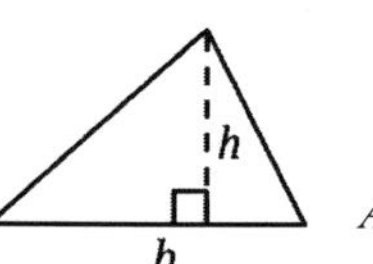

$A = \frac{1}{2}bh$

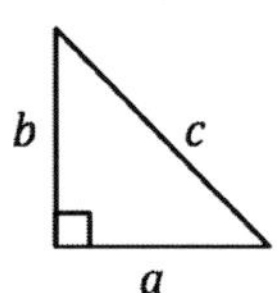

$c^2 = a^2 + b^2$

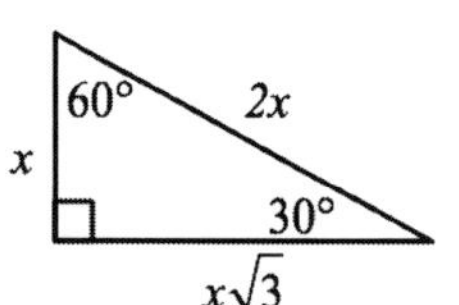

Special Right Triangle

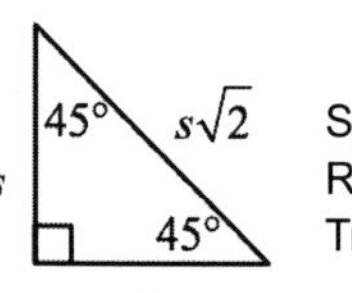

Special Right Triangle

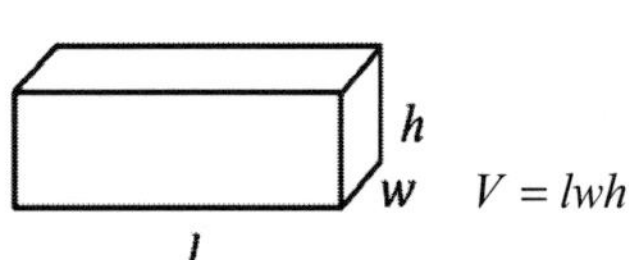

$V = lwh$

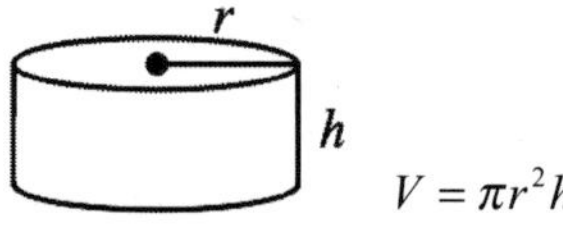

$V = \pi r^2 h$

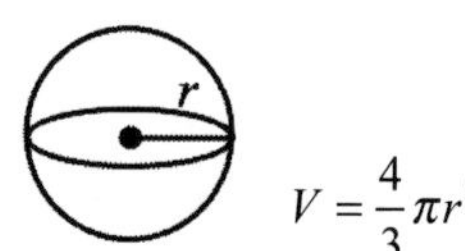

$V = \frac{4}{3}\pi r^3$

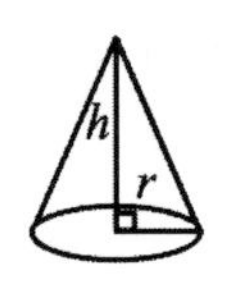

$V = \frac{1}{3}\pi r^2 h$

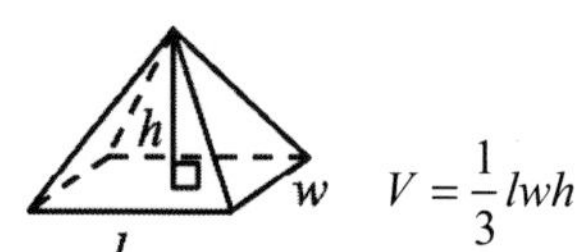

$V = \frac{1}{3}lwh$

There are $360°$ in a circle.
There are 2π radians in a circle.
There are $180°$ in a triangle.

CONTINUE

1

The height of a child in inches, H, with respect to time, t, in months, can be calculated using the equation $H = 36 + 0.4t$. Which of the following equations could be used to estimate the height of a child with respect to time for a child who is shorter but grows at a faster rate?

A) $H = 30 + 0.4t$
B) $H = 33 + 0.5t$
C) $H = 38 + 0.3t$
D) $H = 40 + 0.6t$

2

If $rt + 5 = 11$ and $r = 2$, what is the value of $4t$?

A) 6
B) 12
C) 16
D) 32

3

Given the equation $b^{\frac{3}{2}} = k - 1$, which of the following expressions is equivalent to $(k-1)^2$?

A) b^3
B) b^2
C) $\sqrt{b}$
D) $\sqrt[3]{b}$

4

32 students registered for an advanced art class. If the number of students registered for the standard art class is 10 less than three times the number of students registered for the advanced art class, how many students are enrolled in both classes combined?

A) 14
B) 86
C) 106
D) 118

CONTINUE

5

$$\frac{9}{4x} = \frac{x}{4}$$

If the equation above is true, what is the value of x^2?

A) 3
B) 9
C) 36
D) 81

6

$$x + 2y = 15$$
$$3x + 2y = 25$$

If (x, y) is a solution to the system of equations above, what is the value of $x + y$?

A) 1
B) 5
C) 10
D) 40

7

A linear function is graphed in the xy-plane and is represented by the equation $y = mx + b$, where m and b are constants. Which of the following coordinate points lies on the line?

A) $(0, y - mx)$

B) $(y - mx, 0)$

C) $(0, \frac{y}{mx})$

D) $(\frac{y}{mx}, 0)$

8

x	y
1	12
2	10
5	?
6	2

The table above represents a linear function. For the ordered pair $(5, y)$, what is the value of y?

A) 3
B) 4
C) 6
D) 8

CONTINUE

9

$$y = x^2 - 3x - 28$$

Two points, A and B, lie on the parabola above and share a common y-value. What is the x-value of their midpoint?

A) $\frac{1}{2}$

B) 1

C) $\frac{3}{2}$

D) 2

10

Which of the following systems of equations has no solutions?

A) $3x + 2y = 8$
$3x - 2y = 8$

B) $2x + y = 12$
$6x + 3y = 36$

C) $2x + 4y = 10$
$4x + 8y = 10$

D) $7x + y = 5$
$4x - y = 6$

11

Which of the following pairs of linear equations represents two lines that are neither parallel nor perpendicular with respect to each other?

A) $3x + 2y = 11$
$4x - 12y = 13$

B) $x + y = 14$
$-x - y = 7$

C) $3x + y = 8$
$3y + 9x = 12$

D) $2x + 4y = 5$
$2y - 4x = 5$

12

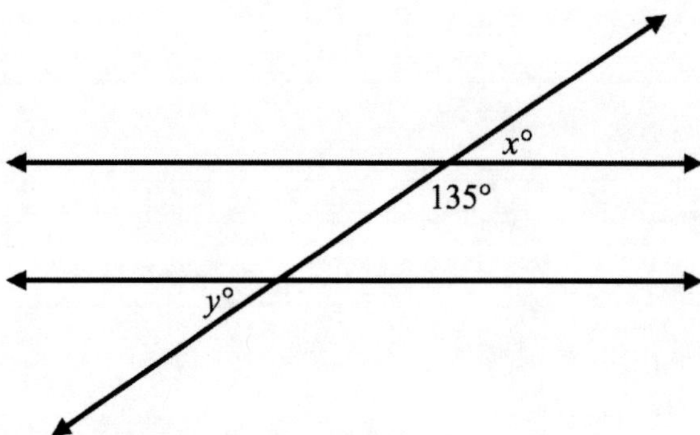

Given the diagram of two parallel lines and a transversal above, what is the value of $x - y$?

A) 0

B) 45

C) 90

D) 270

CONTINUE

13

$$\frac{2x^2+16x+32}{kx}=\frac{(x+4)^2}{x}$$

In the equation above, k is a positive constant and $x \neq 0$. What is the value of k?

A) $\frac{1}{2}$

B) 1

C) 2

D) 4

14

What are the solutions to $x^2-8x+4=0$?

A) $8\pm2\sqrt{2}$
B) $4\pm2\sqrt{2}$
C) $4\pm4\sqrt{3}$
D) $4\pm2\sqrt{3}$

15

$$M=4000(0.5)^{\frac{d}{30}}$$

A town has collected all of its old pumpkins in an effort to create natural fertilizer. The initial mass of the pumpkins is 4000 kilograms. The equation above is used to determine the mass of the pumpkins d days after the collection takes place. Which of the following statements is true?

A) The total mass decays by 5% each 30-day month.
B) The total mass decays by 50% every day.
C) The total mass decays to half of its original size every 15 days.
D) The total mass decays to one-sixteenth of its original size over the course of 4 months. (1 month = 30 days)

CONTINUE

DIRECTIONS

For each question from 16-20, solve and enter your answer in the grid-in section of your answer sheet as described below.

A. Write out your answers in the boxes at the top of each column in order to help you fill in the circles accurately. Remember, you will only receive credit for the circles that are filled in correctly, not for the written answer at the top of the columns.

B. Mark only a single circle in each column.

C. There are no negative answers.

D. If the problem has more than one correct answer, grid only one of the correct answers.

E. When your answer is a **mixed number**, such as $1\frac{1}{2}$, it should be entered as 1.5 or $3/2$. You cannot enter a mixed number because there is no room to fill in a circle that represents a space.

F. If you enter a **decimal answer** with more digits then the grid can handle, the answer may be rounded or truncated, but it absolutely must fill the entire grid.

Answer: $\frac{8}{21}$

Written answer → 8 / 2 1 ← Fraction line

Decimal point →

Answer: 6.4

6 . 4

The ways to correctly grid $\frac{7}{9}$ are:

7 / 9 | . 7 7 7 | . 7 7 8

Answer: 102 - both positions are correct

REMEMBER: You can begin writing your answers in any column as long as there is enough space. Leave unused columns blank.

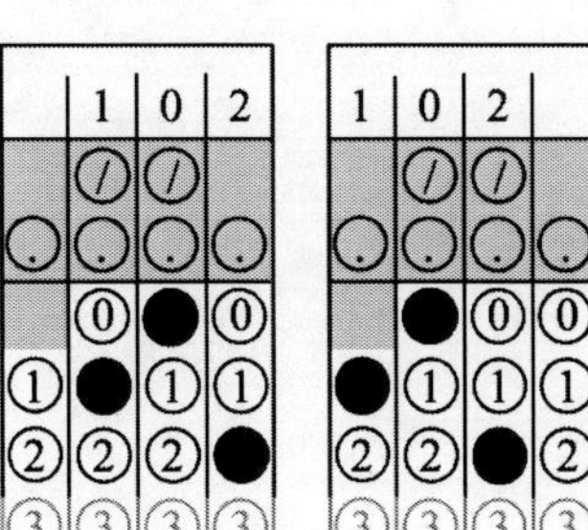

CONTINUE

16

$$5x^3 - 20x = 0$$

If $x > 0$, what is the only value of x that satisfies the equation above?

17

$$\frac{x}{2} + \frac{1}{5} = \frac{8}{5} - \frac{5}{4}$$

What is the value of x that makes the equation above true?

18

Two points A and B lie on Circle C and define an arc whose central angle measures $\frac{2\pi}{3}$ radians. If Triangle ABC were to be drawn, what would $\angle ABC$ measure in degrees?

19

At a restaurant, 6 patrons sat at a table and each patron ordered either the beef platter or the seafood platter. At the end of the meal, the final bill before tax and gratuity was \$190. If each beef platter was priced at \$25 dollars, each seafood platter was priced at \$35, and no other items were ordered, how many of the patrons ate seafood?

20

$$(x+2)^2+(y-2)^2+25=169$$

The equation above defines the base of a cylinder that stands 10 inches tall. What is the maximum distance, in inches, between any two points that lie on the surface of this cylinder?

STOP

Math Test - Calculator

28 MINUTES, 19 QUESTIONS

DIRECTIONS

For each question from 1-15, choose the best answer choice provided in the multiple choice bank and fill in the appropriate circle in the provided answer key. Alternatively, for questions **16-19**, answer the problem and enter your answer in the grid-in section of the answer key. Refer to the directions given before question 16 as to how to enter your answers for the grid-in questions. You may complete scratch work in any empty space in your test booklet.

NOTES

A. Calculator usage **is allowed**.
B. Variables, constants, and coefficients used represent real numbers unless indicated otherwise.
C. All figures are created to appropriate scale unless the question states otherwise.
D. All figures are two-dimensional unless the question states otherwise.
E. The domain of any given function is all real numbers x for which the function, $f(x)$, is a real number unless the question states otherwise.

REFERENCE

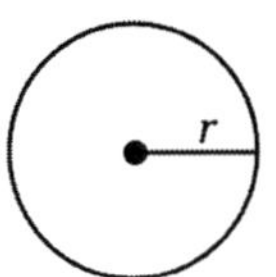

$A = \pi r^2$
$C = 2\pi r$

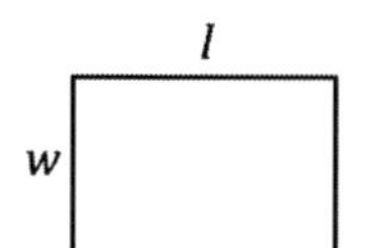

$A = lw$

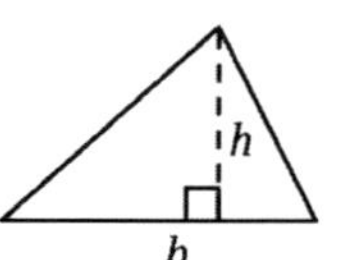

$A = \frac{1}{2}bh$

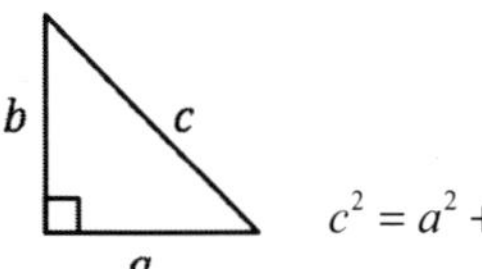

$c^2 = a^2 + b^2$

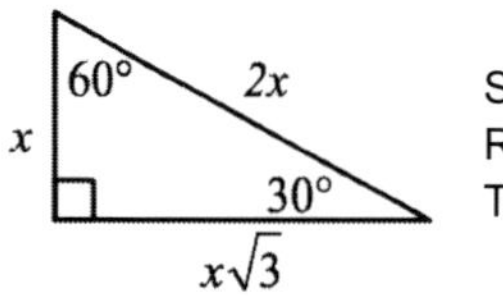

Special Right Triangle

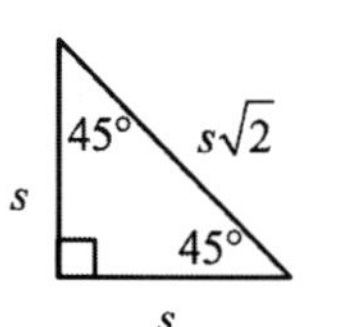

Special Right Triangle

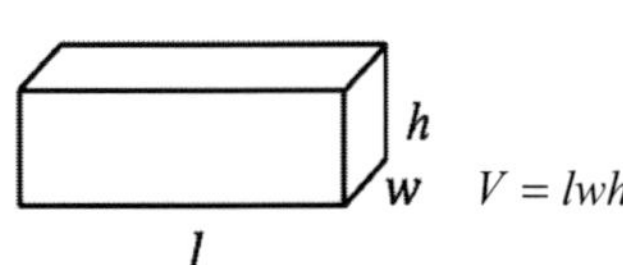

$V = lwh$

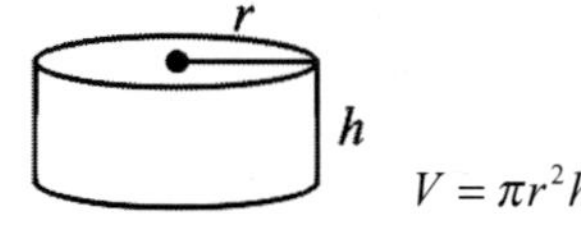

$V = \pi r^2 h$

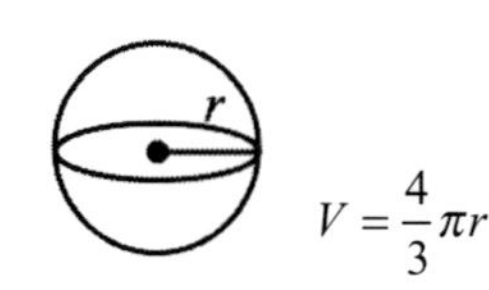

$V = \frac{4}{3}\pi r^3$

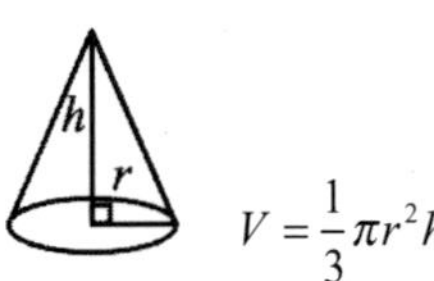

$V = \frac{1}{3}\pi r^2 h$

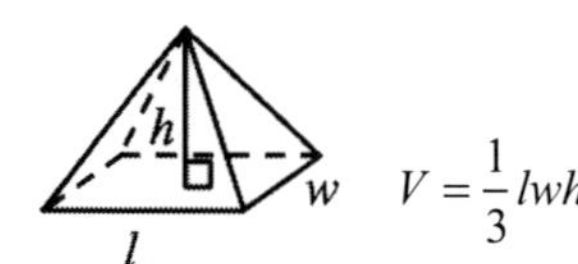

$V = \frac{1}{3}lwh$

There are $360°$ in a circle.
There are 2π radians in a circle.
There are $180°$ in a triangle.

CONTINUE

1

Lisa has been on a diet for the last 90 days. She measures her weight daily and finds that it decreases linearly. Her daily weight follows the model $w = 230 - 0.5d$, where w represents her weight in pounds and d represents the number of days since she started her diet. Which of the following statements is *not* correct?

A) The diet helps Lisa lose weight at the rate of a half of a pound per day.
B) It can be predicted that Lisa will weigh 187 pounds after 86 days on the diet.
C) Lisa weighed 230 pounds before she began her diet.
D) Lisa has lost a total of 46 pounds since she began the diet.

2

$$2(3x - 14) - 3 = 5(2x + 1)$$

The equation above is true for which of the following values of x?

A) -6
B) -7
C) -8
D) -9

3

Suppose that the expression $3x^3 + 18x^2 - 48x$ is equivalent to $3x(x + a)(x + b)$. What is the value of $a + b$?

A) 10
B) 8
C) 6
D) 2

4

Janette bought a jacket for \$45 at a discount clothing store. When she looked at the tag, she saw that the original price of the jacket was \$72. By what percent was the jacket discounted from the original price?

A) 37.5%
B) 50.0%
C) 62.5%
D) 75.0%

CONTINUE

5

Which of the following is the equation of a circle that has a circumference that measures 12π ?

A) $x^2+y^2=6$
B) $x^2+y^2=12$
C) $x^2+y^2=36$
D) $x^2+y^2=144$

6

245,000 divided by 500 is equivalent to which of the following expressions?

A) 4.9×10^1

B) 4.9×10^3

C) $\dfrac{2.45\times10^6}{500}$

D) $\dfrac{2.45\times10^5}{5\times10^2}$

7

The average SAT score for a group of students in Pennsylvania was 1050, with a standard deviation of 150 points. If the scores were approximately converted to PSAT scores by dividing each score by 10 and then subtracting 8, what are the mean, μ, and the standard deviation, σ, of the converted set of scores?

A) $\mu=97$ $\sigma=7$
B) $\mu=97$ $\sigma=15$
C) $\mu=105$ $\sigma=7$
D) $\mu=105$ $\sigma=15$

8

$$3y-2x=6$$
$$ky+3x=-7$$

Given the system of linear equations above, for what value of *k* would the two lines be perpendicular?

A) 6
B) 2
C) -2
D) -6

CONTINUE

9

An object is rising into the air and its height with respect to time is modeled by the parabolic equation $y = -2x^2 + 12x - 7$. At what coordinate point does the height of the object cease to increase?

A) $(6, -7)$
B) $(4, 9)$
C) $(3, 11)$
D) $(0, -7)$

10

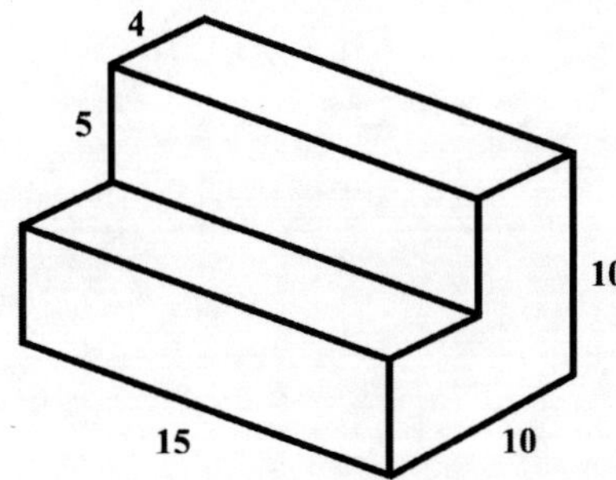

The measurements in the diagram above are given in centimeters. What is the volume of the modified prism above in cm^3?

A) 1050
B) 1200
C) 1250
D) 1500

11

A music store owner selling guitars and guitar supplies at a trade show charges $2 for the first two guitar stickers and $2 for each additional sticker after that. Which of the following equations represents the total cost for a customer who purchases *n* stickers?

A) $C(n) = 2n - 2$
B) $C(n) = 2n + 2$
C) $C(n) = 2n$
D) $C(n) = n$

12

Adele, Brutus, and Claire decided to survey students in their school to see if their school lunch menu should be modified to include more options. Adele randomly selected 200 students from the school to survey, Brutus randomly selected 400 students from the school to survey and Claire interviewed 500 students who volunteered to answer her survey. Data collected by which of the students *could* be used to make an inference about the entire student body?

A) Brutus
B) Claire
C) Adele and Brutus
D) Adele, Brutus, and Claire

CONTINUE

Questions 13-14 refer to the following information.

Aman purchased 15 bags of rock salt that had an average weight of 33 pounds. His business partner Li purchased an additional 13 bags which had a total weight of 390 pounds.

13

Approximately how much more is the average weight of all of the bags of rock salt combined compared to the average weight of Li's bags only?

A) 1.0 pounds
B) 1.2 pounds
C) 1.4 pounds
D) 1.6 pounds

14

After Aman used two bags of rock salt, the average weight of his remaining bags dropped to 31 pounds. After Li used three bags, the average weight of his bags increased to 33 pounds. What is the average weight of all of the bags that Aman and Li have already used?

A) 30.0 pounds
B) 30.4 pounds
C) 32.6 pounds
D) 44.2 pounds

15

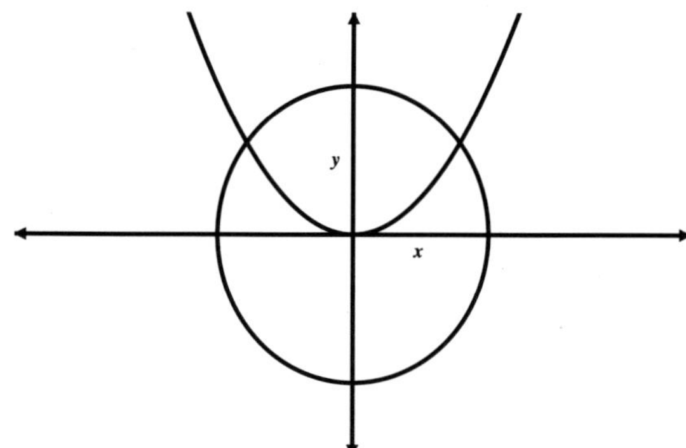

The parabolic equation $y = x^2$ intersects with the unit circle $x^2 + y^2 = 1$ in Quadrant 1 at Point A(x_a, y_a). What is the value of $\frac{(x_a)^2}{y_a}$?

A) 2

B) 1

C) $\frac{1}{2}$

D) $\frac{1}{4}$

CONTINUE

DIRECTIONS

For each question from 16-19, solve and enter your answer in the grid-in section of your answer sheet as described below.

A. Write out your answers in the boxes at the top of each column in order to help you fill in the circles accurately. Remember, you will only receive credit for the circles that are filled in correctly, not for the written answer at the top of the columns.

B. Mark only a single circle in each column.

C. There are no negative answers.

D. If the problem has more than one correct answer, grid only one of the correct answers.

E. When your answer is a **mixed number**, such as $1\frac{1}{2}$, it should be entered as 1.5 or $3/2$. You cannot enter a mixed number because there is no room to fill in a circle that represents a space.

F. If you enter a **decimal answer** with more digits then the grid can handle, the answer may be rounded or truncated, but it absolutely must fill the entire grid.

Answer: $\frac{8}{21}$

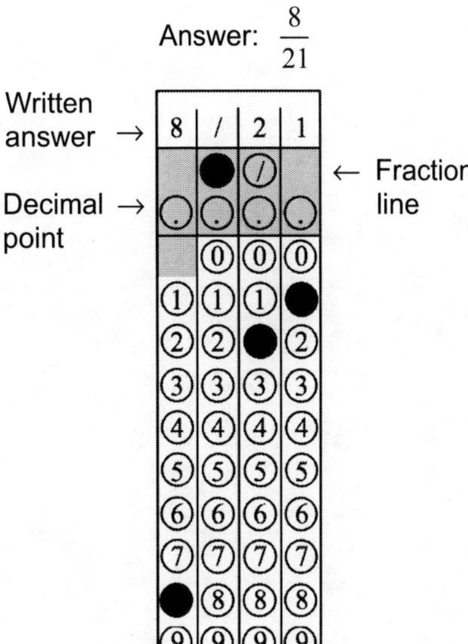

Answer: 6.4

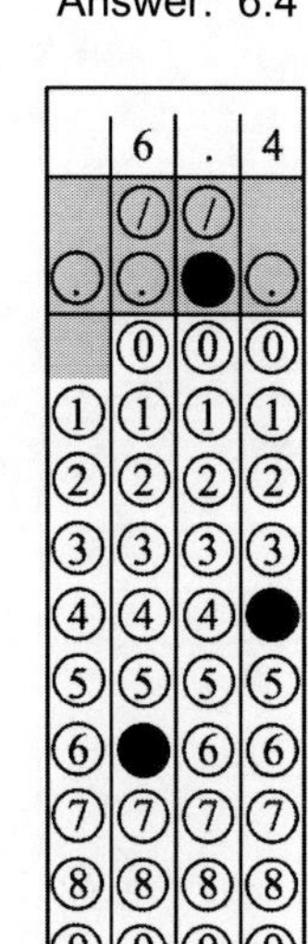

The ways to correctly grid $\frac{7}{9}$ are:

Answer: 102 - both positions are correct

REMEMBER: You can begin writing your answers in any column as long as there is enough space. Leave unused columns blank.

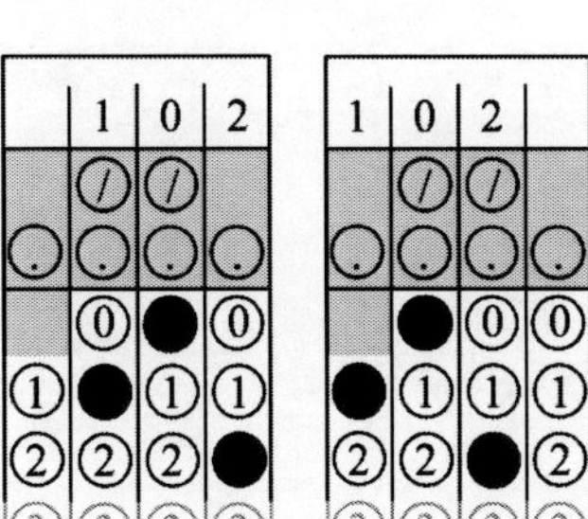

16

$$\frac{(x^2)^3(y^4y^5)}{(y^2)^4(x^7+x^7)}=1$$

Given the exponential equation above, $\frac{x}{y}$ is equivalent to what value?

17

$$-\frac{2(x-1)}{3}+\frac{3(x+1)}{4}=\frac{-x+3}{2}$$

For what value of x is the equation above true?

CONTINUE

Questions 18-19 refer to the following information.

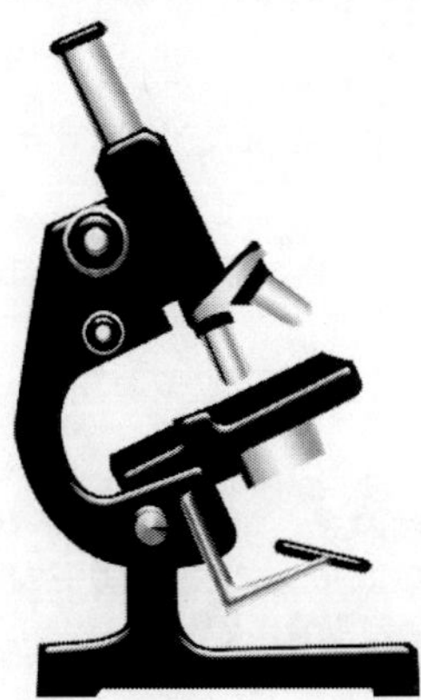

Nick is using a compound light microscope in his biology lab to conduct research on plant cells. The unit of linear measurement used to measure cells and their organelles is the micrometer (*um*). Nick finds that cells typically have diameters of between 10 and 50 micrometers; in his research, he uses both low- and high-power lenses. Most microscopes have a low-power field diameter of between 1,200 and 1,600 micrometers. The diameter of a high-power field can be determined mathematically using a simple proportion as follows:

L = Low-Power Magnification
H = High-Power Magnification
l = Low-Power Field Diameter
h = High-Power Field Diameter

$$\frac{L}{H} = \frac{h}{l}$$

18

If Nick uses a microscope with a 100-times low-power magnification lens and a 400-times high-power magnification lens, and direct measurement shows that the low-power field diameter is 1200 *um*, what is the diameter of the high-power field, in *um*?

19

Suppose that during his research, using the 100-times low-power magnification microscope with a low-power field diameter of 1200 *um*, Nick analyzes an extremely large cell whose diameter is in a ratio of 1 to 15 with the low-power field diameter. What is the diameter of the cell, in micrometers?

STOP

Math Test - No Calculator

25 MINUTES, 20 QUESTIONS

DIRECTIONS

For each question from 1-15, choose the best answer choice provided in the multiple choice bank and fill in the appropriate circle in the provided answer key. Alternatively, for questions **16-20**, answer the problem and enter your answer in the grid-in section of the answer key. Refer to the directions given before question 16 as to how to enter your answers for the grid-in questions. You may complete scratch work in any empty space in your test booklet.

NOTES

A. Calculator usage **is not allowed** in this section.
B. Variables, constants, and coefficients used represent real numbers unless indicated otherwise.
C. All figures are created to appropriate scale unless the question states otherwise.
D. All figures are two-dimensional unless the question states otherwise.
E. The domain of any given function is all real numbers x for which the function, $f(x)$, is a real number unless the question states otherwise.

REFERENCE

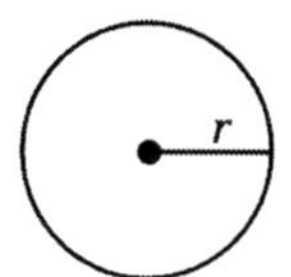

$A = \pi r^2$
$C = 2\pi r$

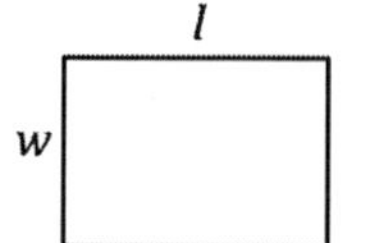

$A = lw$

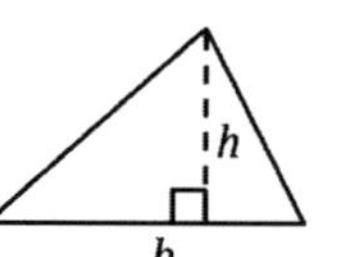

$A = \frac{1}{2}bh$

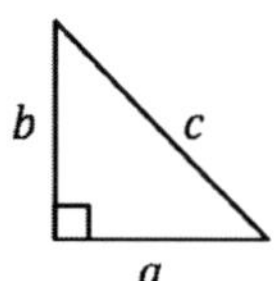

$c^2 = a^2 + b^2$

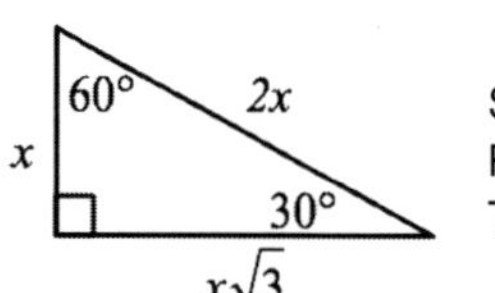

Special Right Triangle

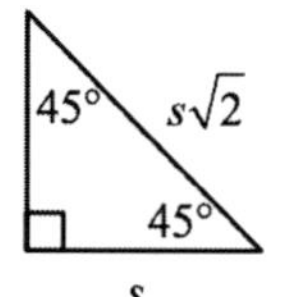

Special Right Triangle

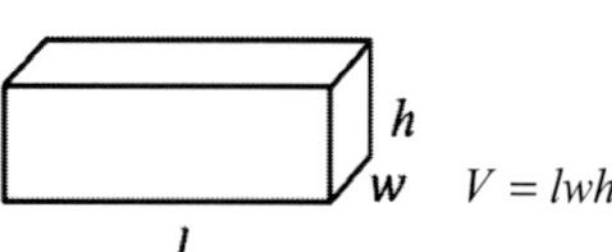

$V = lwh$

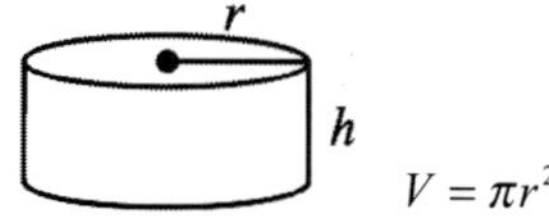

$V = \pi r^2 h$

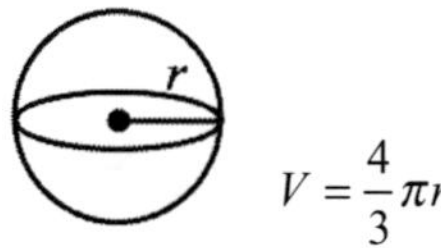

$V = \frac{4}{3}\pi r^3$

$V = \frac{1}{3}\pi r^2 h$

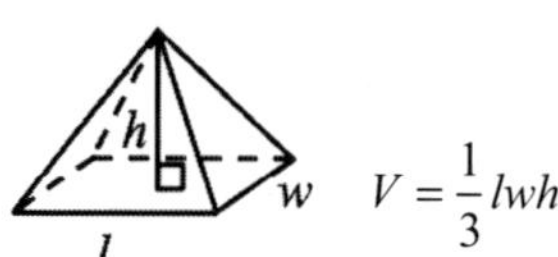

$V = \frac{1}{3}lwh$

There are $360°$ in a circle.
There are 2π radians in a circle.
There are $180°$ in a triangle.

CONTINUE

1

If $8x = 3 - 2x$, what is the value of $10x + 5$?

A) 3
B) 5
C) 8
D) 11

2

$$3x - 6y = 18$$
$$-x + 2y = -6$$

The system of equations above has how many real solutions?

A) 0
B) 1
C) 2
D) Infinitely many

3

$$(x-3)(x+1)^2$$

The expression above displays all of the factors of which of the following polynomial expressions?

A) $x^3 + 2x^2 - 5x - 3$
B) $x^3 + 2x^2 + x - 3$
C) $x^3 - x^2 - 5x - 3$
D) $x^3 - 5x^2 + 7x + 3$

4

$$200 - 5ma$$

The expression above is used to calculate the remaining amount of suspension cable, in yards, available to men at an excavation site, where m is the number of men at the site and a is the number of attempts to scale the front wall of the site made by each man. Which of the following is the best interpretation of the value 200 in this expression?

A) The amount of remaining cable at any point in time
B) The amount of cable distributed to each man
C) The amount of cable distributed to each man for each attempt to scale the wall
D) The initial amount of cable to be distributed among the men at the excavation site

CONTINUE

5

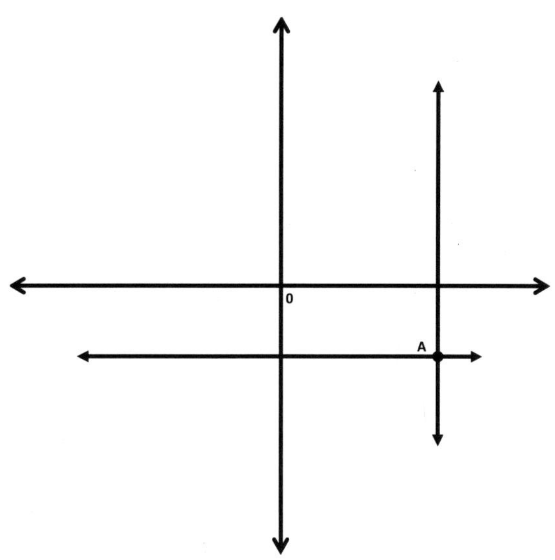

The lines $y = -5$ and $x = 12$ are graphed in the *xy*-plane above. What is the distance between Point A and the origin?

A) 12
B) 13
C) 15
D) 17

6

$$\sqrt{x^2 - 11} = 5$$

What is the least value of x that satisfies the equation above?

A) –6
B) –4
C) 4
D) 6

7

$$A = 180 - 2c$$

The equation above is used to calculate A, the degree measure of the third angle in an isosceles triangle with two congruent angles with degree measures of c. What is the least possible value of A, given that the value of c is at most 65?

A) 30
B) 50
C) 60
D) 130

8

If $4^{k+2} = 1$, what is the value of 4^{k+1}?

A) $\frac{1}{4}$

B) $\frac{1}{2}$

C) 4

D) 16

CONTINUE

9

$$\sqrt{-2+x^2}=y$$

Which of the following ordered pairs is a complex solution to the equation above?

A) $(-1,i)$
B) $(0,2i)$
C) $(1,-i)$
D) $(2,\sqrt{2})$

10

Segment AB has endpoints $A(0,0)$ and $B(6,6)$. Which of the following is the equation of a line that perpendicularly bisects Segment AB?

A) $y=-x+3$
B) $y=-x+6$
C) $y=-2x+6$
D) $y=-2x+12$

11

$$S=I(1+r)^t$$

The equation above is used to calculate S, the balance of money in a savings account, given I, the amount of the initial investment in dollars, r, the growth rate of the account, and t, the amount of time that has passed since the initial investment. Which of the following formulas gives r in terms of S, I, and t?

A) $r=\sqrt[t]{\frac{S}{I}-1}$

B) $r=\sqrt[t]{\frac{S}{I}+1}$

C) $r=\sqrt[t]{\frac{S}{I}}-1$

D) $r=\sqrt[t]{SI}-1$

12

$$(8+2i)(2-3i)(8-2i)$$

Which of the following complex numbers is equivalent to the expression above? (Note: $i=\sqrt{-1}$)

A) $12-24i$
B) $24-36i$
C) $68-136i$
D) $136-204i$

13

What is the sum of all of the roots of the equation $12m = 40 - 4m^2$?

A) -3
B) -2
C) 3
D) 5

14

The equation $g(x) = 220(0.76)^x$ is used to determine $g(x)$, the amount of clean oil, in grams, that is present in an engine x months after the oil has been changed. Which of the following statements is true?

A) The amount of clean oil is reduced by 76 grams each month.
B) The amount of clean oil after one month has passed is 220 grams.
C) The amount of clean oil is reduced by 24% each month.
D) The amount of clean oil is reduced by 76% each month.

15

$$\frac{x^2 + 3x + 5}{x - 2}$$

The equation above is equivalent to which of the following expressions?

A) $x + 1 + \dfrac{3}{x - 2}$
B) $x + 1 + \dfrac{7}{x - 2}$
C) $x + 5 - \dfrac{5}{x - 2}$
D) $x + 5 + \dfrac{15}{x - 2}$

CONTINUE

DIRECTIONS

For each question from 16-20, solve and enter your answer in the grid-in section of your answer sheet as described below.

A. Write out your answers in the boxes at the top of each column in order to help you fill in the circles accurately. Remember, you will only receive credit for the circles that are filled in correctly, not for the written answer at the top of the columns.

B. Mark only a single circle in each column.

C. There are no negative answers.

D. If the problem has more than one correct answer, grid only one of the correct answers.

E. When your answer is a **mixed number**, such as $1\frac{1}{2}$, it should be entered as 1.5 or $3/2$. You cannot enter a mixed number because there is no room to fill in a circle that represents a space.

F. If you enter a **decimal answer** with more digits then the grid can handle, the answer may be rounded or truncated, but it absolutely must fill the entire grid.

Answer: $\frac{8}{21}$

Written answer → 8 / 2 1

← Fraction line

Decimal point →

Answer: 6.4

6 . 4

The ways to correctly grid $\frac{7}{9}$ are:

7 / 9

. 7 7 7

. 7 7 8

Answer: 102 - both positions are correct

REMEMBER:
You can begin writing your answers in any column as long as there is enough space. Leave unused columns blank.

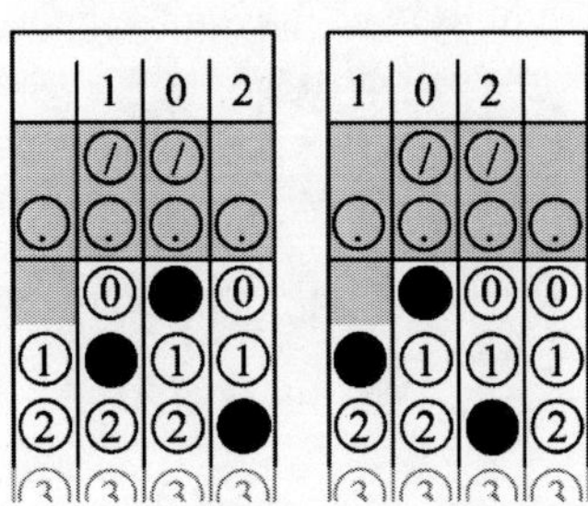

CONTINUE

16

$$bx + c = (5 - 2x) + 11(x - 1)$$

If b and c are constants and the equation is true for all values of x, what is the value of b?

17

Jack purchased an $85 mountain climbing activity pack and paid for the full transaction in cash. Jack had twenty-dollar bills, ten-dollar bills, five-dollar bills, and one-dollar bills at the time of the purchase. If Jack used at least three twenty-dollar bills and at least one of each other bill, what is the maximum number of five-dollar bills that he could have used?

18

$$Ax + y = 12$$
$$x + By = 23$$

If the coordinate point $(1,2)$ is the only solution to the system of equations above, what is the value of $A + B$?

19

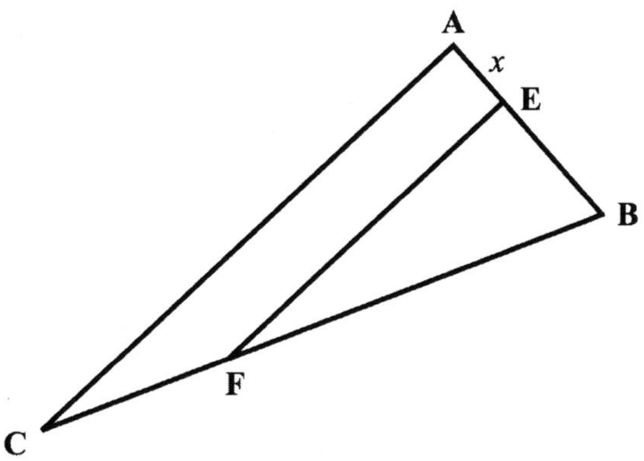

In the diagram above, AC is parallel to EF. $\triangle ABC$ is a right triangle in which the measure of AB is 5 and the measure of AC is 12. If the measure of CF is 3.9, what is the value of x?

20

A circle has a circumference that measures 12π inches. If the circle is divided into π equivalent arcs, what is the measure, in radians, of the central angle that defines each arc?

STOP

Math Test - Calculator

28 MINUTES, 19 QUESTIONS

DIRECTIONS

For each question from 1-15, choose the best answer choice provided in the multiple choice bank and fill in the appropriate circle in the provided answer key. Alternatively, for questions **16-19**, answer the problem and enter your answer in the grid-in section of the answer key. Refer to the directions given before question 16 as to how to enter your answers for the grid-in questions. You may complete scratch work in any empty space in your test booklet.

NOTES

A. Calculator usage **is allowed**.
B. Variables, constants, and coefficients used represent real numbers unless indicated otherwise.
C. All figures are created to appropriate scale unless the question states otherwise.
D. All figures are two-dimensional unless the question states otherwise.
E. The domain of any given function is all real numbers *x* for which the function, $f(x)$, is a real number unless the question states otherwise.

REFERENCE

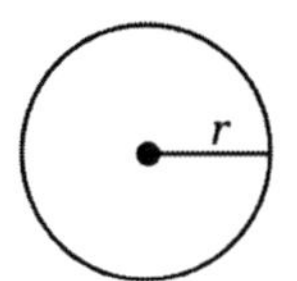

$A = \pi r^2$
$C = 2\pi r$

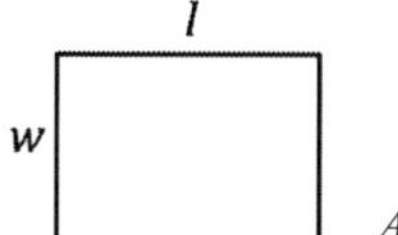

$A = lw$

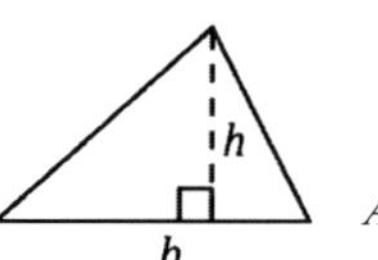

$A = \frac{1}{2}bh$

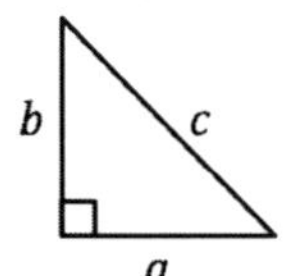

$c^2 = a^2 + b^2$

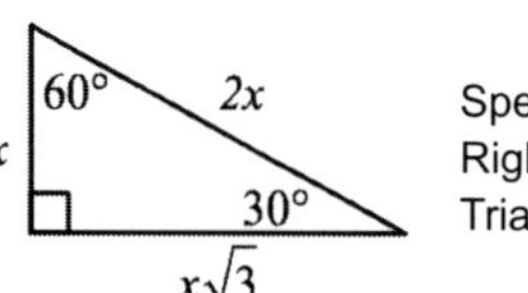

Special Right Triangle

45° $s\sqrt{2}$ s 45° s

Special Right Triangle

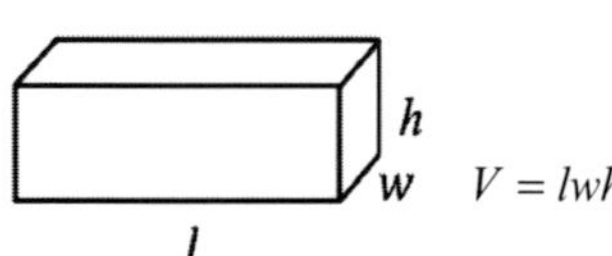

$V = lwh$

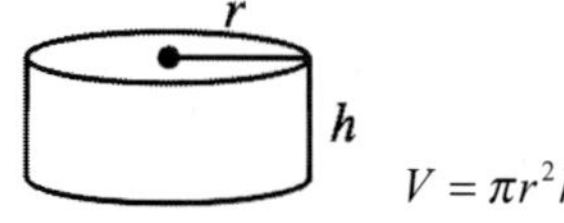

$V = \pi r^2 h$

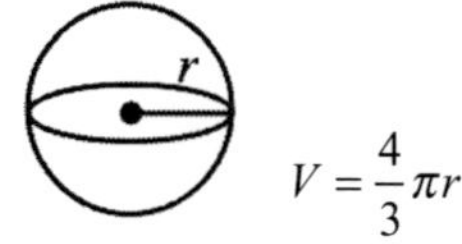

$V = \frac{4}{3}\pi r^3$

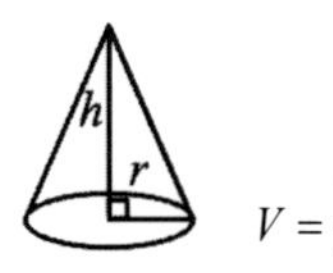

$V = \frac{1}{3}\pi r^2 h$

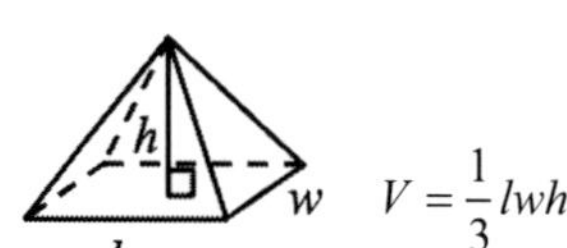

$V = \frac{1}{3}lwh$

There are $360°$ in a circle.
There are 2π radians in a circle.
There are $180°$ in a triangle.

CONTINUE

1

In the equation $xy = k$, k is a constant. If x is 4 when y is 9, what is x when y is 6?

A) $\frac{8}{3}$

B) 6

C) 18

D) 36

2

$$(3+i)-(2-2i)$$

Which of the following is equivalent to the expression above? (Note: $i=\sqrt{-1}$)

A) $1+3i$
B) $1-i$
C) $1-3i$
D) $5-i$

3

Drake ran 5 cell phone apps for m minutes. Each app uses d kilobytes of data each minute. Which of the following expressions is equivalent to the total amount of data, in kilobytes, that Drake used while running the five apps?

A) $5m+5d$
B) $5m+md$
C) $5+m+d$
D) $5md$

4

At her current job, Bernice receives bi-weekly paychecks and monthly commission checks. Bernice has set up a plan to save money for a car that she would like to purchase. The amount of money that Bernice has left to save can be calculated using the equation $R = 8{,}000 - 40w - 200m$, where R is the amount of money that remains to be saved, w is the number of weeks that have passed, and m is the number of months that have passed. Which of the following statements *cannot* be inferred from the equation?

A) It will take Bernice less than 2 years to reach her savings goal for the car.
B) Bernice plans to save $8,000 for the car.
C) Bernice puts $40 worth of each bi-weekly paycheck toward saving for the car.
D) Bernice puts $200 worth of each monthly commission check toward saving for the car.

CONTINUE

5

$$(2x^2 - xy) + (y^2 - xy) - (-y^2 - 2xy)$$

Which of the following is equivalent to the expression above?

A) $2x^2 - 4xy + 2y^2$
B) $2x^2 - 4xy$
C) $2x^2 + 2y^2$
D) $2x^2$

6

$$A = P(1+r)^t$$

The formula above gives the dollar amount accumulated, A, given an initial investment of P dollars at an interest rate of $100r$ % for t compounded interest periods. Which of the following gives r in terms of A, P, and t?

A) $r = \dfrac{A^t}{P^t} - 1$

B) $r = \sqrt[t]{\dfrac{A}{P}} - 1$

C) $r = \sqrt[t]{\dfrac{A}{P}} + (-1)^t$

D) $r = (AP)^t - 1$

7

If $\dfrac{4x}{y} = 3$, what is the value of $\dfrac{6y}{8x}$?

A) $\dfrac{1}{2}$

B) 1

C) 3

D) 4

8

Which of the following is equivalent to the original selling price, in dollars, of a jewelry box that was purchased for \$54 after two 20%-off coupons and 5% sales tax had been applied?

A) $54(.2)(.2)(.05)$

B) $54(.8)(.8)(1.05)$

C) $\dfrac{54}{(.2)(.2)(.05)}$

D) $\dfrac{54}{(.8)(.8)(1.05)}$

CONTINUE

9

$$f(x)=(k-x)^2+1$$

In the function f above, k is a constant greater than 1. If $f(3)=5$, what is the value of $f(4)$?

A) 2
B) 10
C) 11
D) 17

10

A line in the xy-plane passes through the point $(2,-3)$ and has solutions in Quadrant II. Which of the following could be the equation of the line?

A) $y=-3$

B) $x=2$

C) $y=\frac{3}{2}x-6$

D) $y=-\frac{1}{4}x-\frac{5}{2}$

Questions 11-12 refer to the following information.

A large sack of crumbled stone and dust was found to have an average density of 28 kilograms per cubic meter.

11

If the sack was placed on a large industrial scale and the weight was calculated to be 91 kilograms, how many cubic meters of crumbled stone and dust are in the sack?

A) 2.50
B) 2.75
C) 3.25
D) 3.75

12

If the unit of density used to measure the sack was converted to pounds per cubic foot, which of the following is closest to the density of the content in the sack using the new unit of measuement?

(1 kilogram = 2.2 pounds)

(1 cubic meter = 35.3 cubic feet)

A) 1.75
B) 2.77
C) 449.27
D) 2,174.48

CONTINUE

13

$$\frac{x^2-4y^2}{\frac{(x+2y)(x-2y)}{2}}$$

Which of the following is equivalent to the expression above?

A) $2(x^2-4y^2)^2$

B) $\frac{(x^2-4y^2)^2}{2}$

C) $\frac{1}{2}$

D) 2

14

If $2k+1=y$ and $4^k=B(2)^y$, what is the value of B?

A) $\frac{1}{2}$

B) 2

C) 4

D) The value cannot be determined from the information given.

15

The parabolic equations $y=3x^2-m$ and $y=-5x^2+m$ intersect at the point (x,y), where m and x are both positive integers. Which of the following could be the value of m?

A) 8

B) 24

C) 36

D) 48

4

DIRECTIONS

For each question from 16-19, solve and enter your answer in the grid-in section of your answer sheet as described below.

A. Write out your answers in the boxes at the top of each column in order to help you fill in the circles accurately. Remember, you will only receive credit for the circles that are filled in correctly, not for the written answer at the top of the columns.

B. Mark only a single circle in each column.

C. There are no negative answers.

D. If the problem has more than one correct answer, grid only one of the correct answers.

E. When your answer is a **mixed number**, such as $1\frac{1}{2}$, it should be entered as 1.5 or $3/2$. You cannot enter a mixed number because there is no room to fill in a circle that represents a space.

F. If you enter a **decimal answer** with more digits then the grid can handle, the answer may be rounded or truncated, but it absolutely must fill the entire grid.

Answer: $\frac{8}{21}$

Written answer → 8 / 2 1

Decimal point →

← Fraction line

Answer: 6.4

6 . 4

The ways to correctly grid $\frac{7}{9}$ are:

7 / 9 | . 7 7 7 | . 7 7 8

Answer: 102 - both positions are correct

REMEMBER:
You can begin writing your answers in any column as long as there is enough space. Leave unused columns blank.

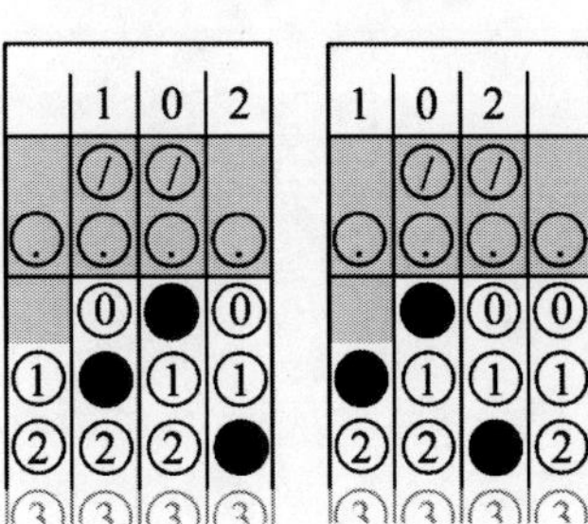

CONTINUE

16

$$4x + 2y = 12$$
$$5x - 3y = 4$$

What value of y satisfies the system of equations above?

17

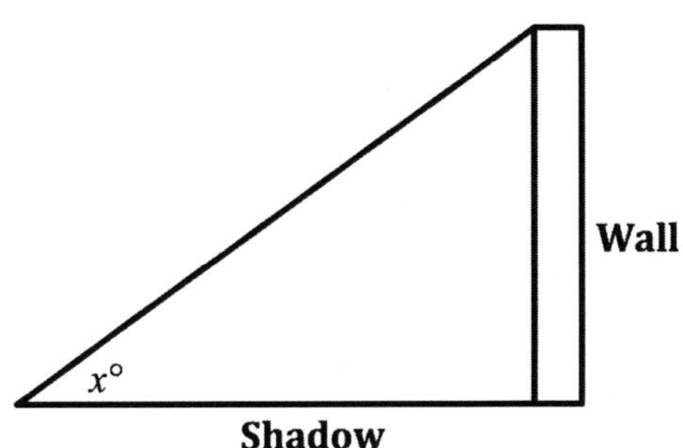

In the diagram above, the sun is shining from behind a wall and creates a shadow on the ground. The length of the shadow is exactly 24 feet and $\sin x° = \frac{3}{5}$. What is the height of the wall in feet?

Questions 18-19 refer to the following information.

A group of students at school A had an average SAT score of 1320 with a standard deviation of 80 points. A group of students at school B had an average SAT score of 1240 with a standard deviation of 90 points.

18

If the SAT scores of the group of students in school A were increased by 80 points each and then divided by 4, what is the standard deviation of the modified set of scores for the group of students in school A.?

19

If the combined average SAT score of the group of students in school A and the group of students in school B was 1260 and there were a total of 240 students in both groups, how many students were in the group from school B?

STOP

No Test Material On This Page

Math Test - No Calculator

25 MINUTES, 20 QUESTIONS

DIRECTIONS

For each question from 1-15, choose the best answer choice provided in the multiple choice bank and fill in the appropriate circle in the provided answer key. Alternatively, for questions **16-20**, answer the problem and enter your answer in the grid-in section of the answer key. Refer to the directions given before question 16 as to how to enter your answers for the grid-in questions. You may complete scratch work in any empty space in your test booklet.

NOTES

A. Calculator usage **is not allowed** in this section.
B. Variables, constants, and coefficients used represent real numbers unless indicated otherwise.
C. All figures are created to appropriate scale unless the question states otherwise.
D. All figures are two-dimensional unless the question states otherwise.
E. The domain of any given function is all real numbers x for which the function, $f(x)$, is a real number unless the question states otherwise.

REFERENCE

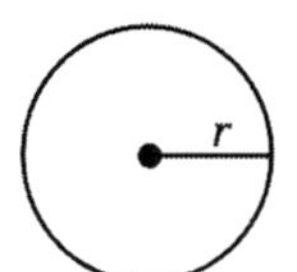

$A = \pi r^2$
$C = 2\pi r$

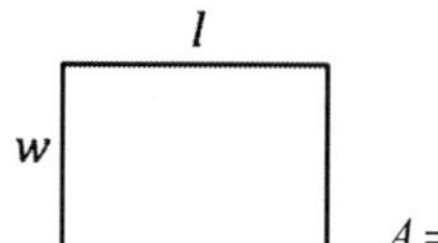

$A = lw$

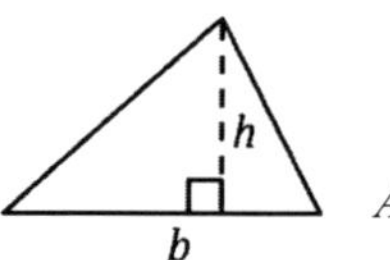

$A = \frac{1}{2}bh$

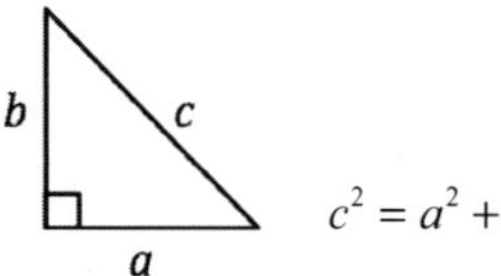

$c^2 = a^2 + b^2$

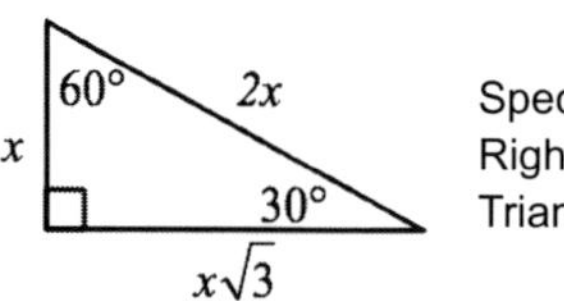

Special Right Triangle

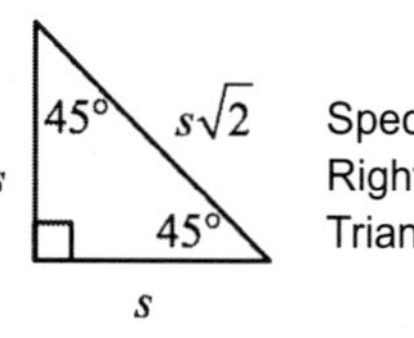

Special Right Triangle

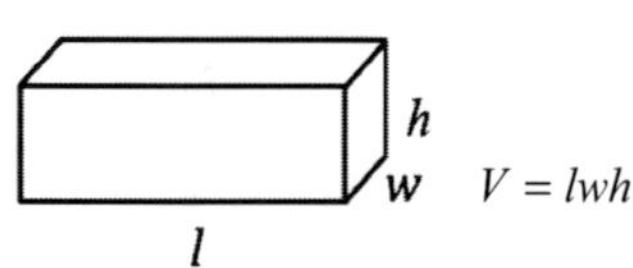

$V = lwh$

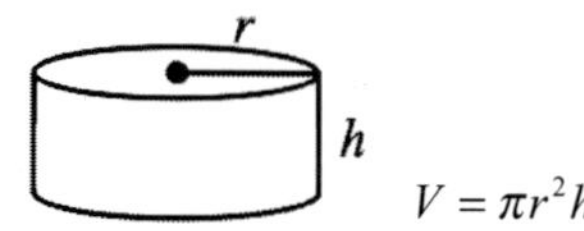

$V = \pi r^2 h$

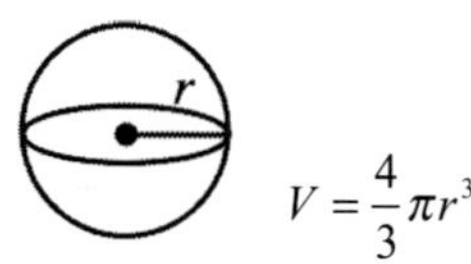

$V = \frac{4}{3}\pi r^3$

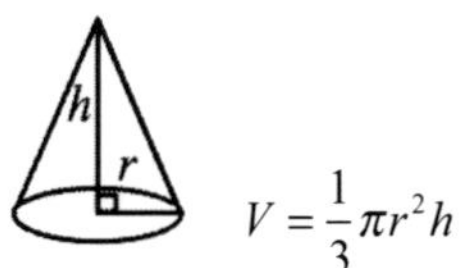

$V = \frac{1}{3}\pi r^2 h$

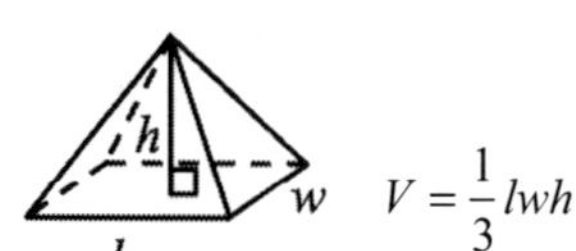

$V = \frac{1}{3}lwh$

There are $360°$ in a circle.
There are 2π radians in a circle.
There are $180°$ in a triangle.

CONTINUE

1

Alex goes Christmas shopping for his family with a total budget of \$200. Each pair of shoes in the store costs \$35, each pair of pants costs \$45, and each jacket costs \$55. If x, y, and z represent shoes, pants, and jackets, respectively, which of the following inequalities can be used to determine how many of each type of present Alex can buy and still stay within his budget?

A) $35x - 45y - 55z > 200$
B) $35x + 45y + 55z > 200$
C) $35x + 55z \leq 200 + 45y$
D) $35x + 45y \leq 200 - 55z$

2

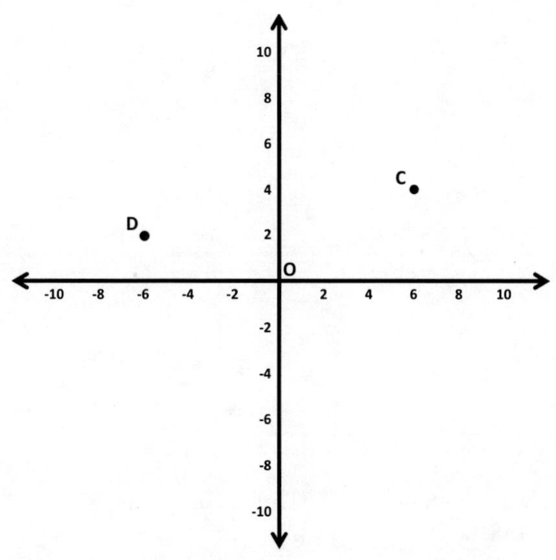

Point $C(6,4)$ and Point $D(-6,2)$ are in Quadrant I and Quadrant II of the xy-plane, respectively. If Line M passes through Point D and is parallel to Line OC, what is the y-intercept of Line M?

A) 3
B) 4
C) 5
D) 6

3

$$-1 < 3t - 2 < 1$$

Given the inequality above, which of the following is true of t?

A) $\frac{1}{3} < t < 1$

B) $1 < t < 3$

C) $-\frac{1}{3} < t < 1$

D) $-\frac{1}{3} < t - 2 < \frac{1}{3}$

4

Suppose that the initial number of bacterial colonies on a tissue sample is given by n_0. After a new anti-bacterial agent is applied to the tissue, the total number of bacterial colonies, n, reduces by half every 30 minutes. If t represents the time that has passed in minutes since the application of the anti-bacterial agent, which of the following equations can be used to predict the total number of remaining bacterial colonies?

A) $n = n_0(2t - 30)$

B) $n = \frac{n_0(\frac{1}{2})^t}{30}$

C) $n = n_0(\frac{1}{2})^{\frac{t}{30}}$

D) $n = n_0(2)^{\frac{t}{30}}$

CONTINUE

5

$$x^2+y^2=149$$
$$7x=10y$$

If (x, y) is a solution to the system of equations above, what is the value of y^2?

A) 100
B) 49
C) 25
D) 16

6

If the equation of Line l is $y=x+3$, which of the following equations would represent the new line if Line l were to be rotated 45 degrees clockwise about its y-intercept?

A) $y=3$
B) $x=0$
C) $y=x+6$
D) $y=-x+3$

7

$$\frac{4}{m-1}=\frac{6}{7y}$$

In the equation above, $m \neq 1$ and $y \neq 0$. What is the value of m in terms of y?

A) $m=\frac{14y}{3}-1$
B) $m=\frac{14}{3}y+1$
C) $m=\frac{7y}{3}+1$
D) $m=7y-1$

8

$$h(x)=x^3+2x^2-2x-4$$
$$f(x)=x^2-2$$
$$g(x)=x+2$$

Given the functions defined above, which of the following is true?

A) $h(x)=f(x)\bullet(x-4)$
B) $h(x)=g(x)\bullet(2-x^2)$
C) $h(x)=f(x)\bullet g(x)$
D) $h(x)=\frac{f(x)}{g(x)}$

CONTINUE

9

$$7x + y = 14$$
$$2x + 2y = 16$$

If the coordinate point (x, y) is a solution to the system of equations shown above, what is the value of xy?

A) 7
B) 8
C) 14
D) 28

10

Kristin bought a car in 2014 for \$24,500. If the car loses value at a rate of 7% per year, which of the following equations gives the value of the car in dollars, y, with respect to the number of years that have passed, x, since 2014?

A) $y = 24{,}500 - 0.93x$

B) $y = 24{,}500(0.93)^x$

C) $y = 24{,}500 - (1.07)^x$

D) $y = \dfrac{24{,}500}{(1.07)^x}$

11

$$\frac{10x^2 - 15xy}{4x^2 - 9y^2}$$

Which of the following expressions is equivalent to the expression above when it has been simplified fully?

A) $\dfrac{10x^2 - 15xy}{4x^2 - 9y^2}$

B) $\dfrac{5x(2x - 3y)}{4x^2 - 9y^2}$

C) $\dfrac{5x}{2x + 3y}$

D) $\dfrac{5x}{2x - 3y}$

12

$$f(x) = x^3 + x^2 + 7x$$

If m is the number of real roots of the equation written above, what is the value of m?

A) 0
B) 1
C) 2
D) 3

CONTINUE

13

Given that $i=\sqrt{-1}$ and that $m=4i^4+3i^3+2i^2+i$, which of the following expressions is equivalent to m?

A) $6+4i$
B) $2+4i$
C) $6-2i$
D) $2-2i$

14

A unique flying device was tossed into the air and its height followed a perfectly semicircular flight path with respect to time in seconds. If the object was thrown upward from a height of 3 feet above the ground again reached a height of 3 feet 10 seconds later, which of the following equations best depicts y, the height of the flying object, in terms of x, the time that has passed in seconds?

A) $x^2+y^2=100$
B) $x^2+y^2=25$
C) $(x+5)^2+(y+3)^2=25$
D) $(x-5)^2+(y-3)^2=25$

15

$$\frac{m}{20}+\frac{m}{30}=1$$

Two laboratory interns at a medical research facility are tasked with sterilizing multiple large scale centrifuges. The job requires a complete mechanical disassembly of the machines, inspection of all moving parts, and complete sterilization of all parts of the machine that come in contact with human blood. After working on separate machines at different rates, the interns decide that they would perform their tasks more efficiently by working together. The equation above represents this scenario; when the equation is solved, m represents the amount of time in minutes it takes the two interns working together to complete the sterilization of one centrifuge. Which of the following best describes the term $\frac{m}{30}$?

A) The amount of time it takes the intern with the slower rate to sterilize one centrifuge.
B) The amount of time it takes the intern with the faster rate to sterilize one centrifuge.
C) The portion of each centrifuge that is sterilized by the intern with the slower rate.
D) The portion of each centrifuge that is sterilized by the intern with the faster rate.

CONTINUE

DIRECTIONS

For each question from 16-20, solve and enter your answer in the grid-in section of your answer sheet as described below.

A. Write out your answers in the boxes at the top of each column in order to help you fill in the circles accurately. Remember, you will only receive credit for the circles that are filled in correctly, not for the written answer at the top of the columns.

B. Mark only a single circle in each column.

C. There are no negative answers.

D. If the problem has more than one correct answer, grid only one of the correct answers.

E. When your answer is a **mixed number**, such as $1\frac{1}{2}$, it should be entered as 1.5 or $3/2$. You cannot enter a mixed number because there is no room to fill in a circle that represents a space.

F. If you enter a **decimal answer** with more digits then the grid can handle, the answer may be rounded or truncated, but it absolutely must fill the entire grid.

Answer: $\frac{8}{21}$

Written answer → | 8 | / | 2 | 1 | ← Fraction line

Decimal point →

Answer: 6.4

| | 6 | . | 4 |

Answer: 102 - both positions are correct

REMEMBER: You can begin writing your answers in any column as long as there is enough space. Leave unused columns blank.

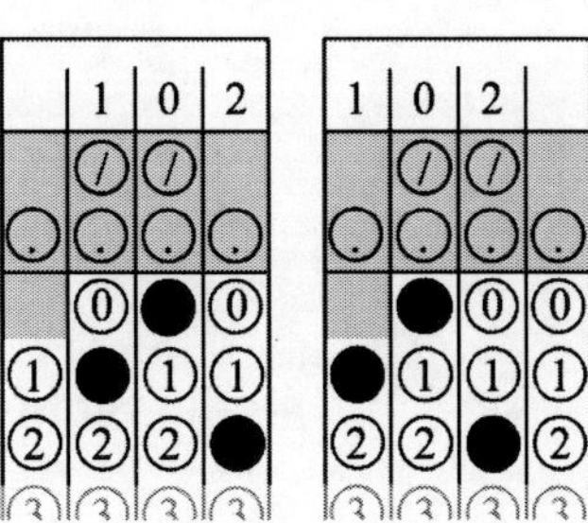

The ways to correctly grid $\frac{7}{9}$ are:

| | 7 | / | 9 |

| . | 7 | 7 | 7 |

| . | 7 | 7 | 8 |

16

If $x = \frac{1}{4}$ and $y = 2$, what is the value of $\frac{1}{2}x^3y^4$?

17

Given $\cos x = \dfrac{1}{2}$, where x is the radian measure of an angle and $0 < x < \dfrac{\pi}{2}$, what is the value of $\sin(x + \dfrac{\pi}{6})$?

18

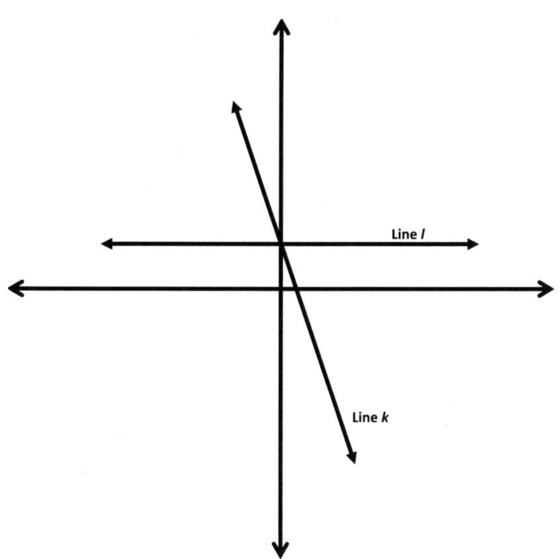

Line l is parallel to the x-axis and has the equation $y = b$. Line k has a slope of -2.2 and has the equation $y = -\frac{b}{2}x + b$. If the coordinate point $(4, q)$ lies on Line l, what is the value of q?

CONTINUE

19

A mechanical engineering student is testing the strength of a propulsion device that he has created. The student currently has the device rigged to propel tennis balls. The device is so powerful that measuring the height of a tennis ball launch or even the speed of the ball while traveling through free air would not appropriately gauge the strength of the device since wind velocity, pressure changes, and atmospheric elements would greatly affect the results. The student decided to position the propulsion device at the surface of a peaceful lake and fire the tennis ball down into the water, using the ball's ultimate depth and bouyant resistance to calculate the machine's potential power. The student believes that the results will be better controlled in this experimental setup. The propelled tennis ball's depth below the surface could be estimated using the equation $d=-5t^2+70t$, where d is the depth in feet of the tennis ball t seconds after the device is fired. What was the estimated maximum depth, in feet, that the tennis ball could reach?

20

$$y=(x+2)^2$$
$$y=Kx-5$$

If the system of equations above has only one solution and both x and y have positive values, what is the value of K?

STOP

Math Test - Calculator

28 MINUTES, 19 QUESTIONS

DIRECTIONS

For each question from 1-15, choose the best answer choice provided in the multiple choice bank and fill in the appropriate circle in the provided answer key. Alternatively, for questions **16-19**, answer the problem and enter your answer in the grid-in section of the answer key. Refer to the directions given before question 16 as to how to enter your answers for the grid-in questions. You may complete scratch work in any empty space in your test booklet.

NOTES

A. Calculator usage **is allowed**.
B. Variables, constants, and coefficients used represent real numbers unless indicated otherwise.
C. All figures are created to appropriate scale unless the question states otherwise.
D. All figures are two-dimensional unless the question states otherwise.
E. The domain of any given function is all real numbers x for which the function, $f(x)$, is a real number unless the question states otherwise.

REFERENCE

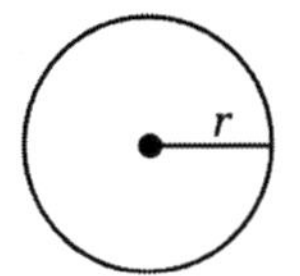

$A = \pi r^2$
$C = 2\pi r$

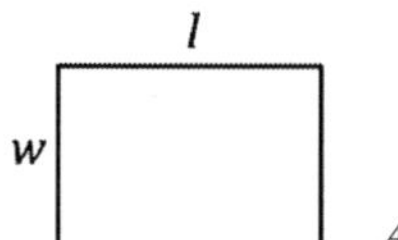

$A = lw$

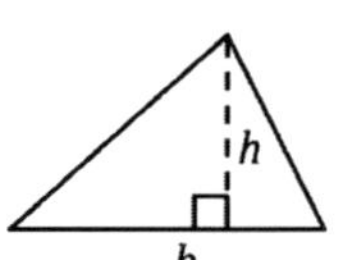

$A = \frac{1}{2}bh$

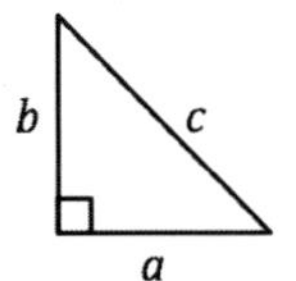

$c^2 = a^2 + b^2$

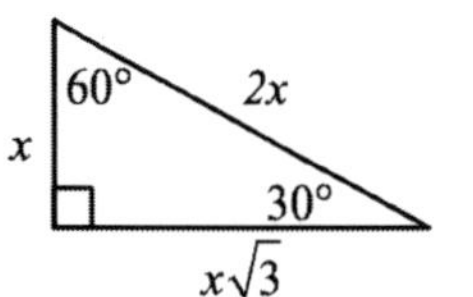

Special Right Triangle

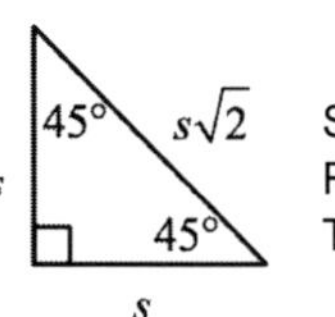

Special Right Triangle

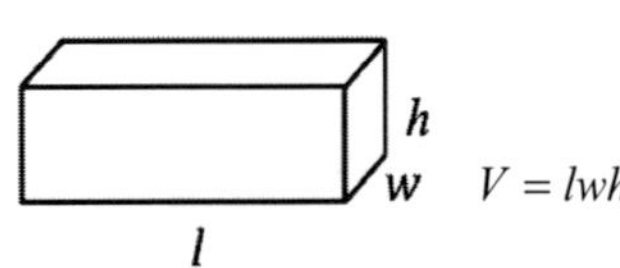

$V = lwh$

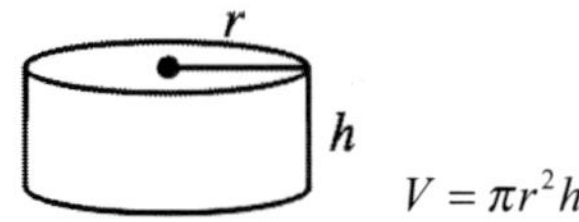

$V = \pi r^2 h$

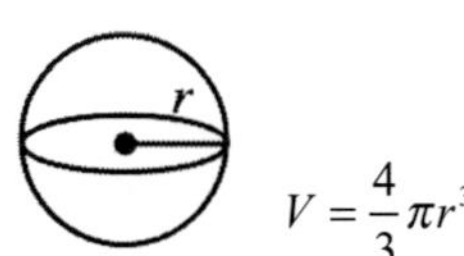

$V = \frac{4}{3}\pi r^3$

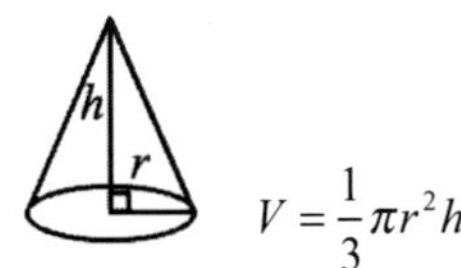

$V = \frac{1}{3}\pi r^2 h$

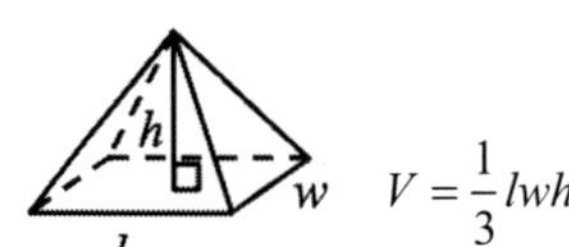

$V = \frac{1}{3}lwh$

There are $360°$ in a circle.
There are 2π radians in a circle.
There are $180°$ in a triangle.

CONTINUE

1

$$y = \frac{1}{2}x + b$$

If the line defined above intercepts the point $(8, 2)$ and the point $(12, a)$, what is the value of a?

A) 4
B) 3
C) 2
D) 1

2

Alda asked a randomly selected group of 50 people for their most recent systolic blood pressure reading. After collecting the data she calculated that the mean systolic blood pressure reading for the group was 128 mmHg with a margin of error of 5 mmHg. If Alda wants to reduce this margin of error as much as possible, she should do which of the following?

A) Resample with only 25 people
B) Sample the same group again and take the mean of all 100 readings
C) Randomly sample 50 more people
D) Randomly sample 100 more people

3

The median long jump distance for 12 field athletes was 20' 10". Which of the following *would not* change the median long jump distance?

A) If a new competitor jumped further than the rest of the competitors

B) If a new competitor jumped less than the rest of the competitors

C) If a new competitor jumped the average distance of the middle two distances when they are placed in order

D) If a new competitor jumped a distance that equaled the sum the middle two distances when they are placed in order

4

If $G(x) = 12 - x^2$, which of the following expressions is equivalent to $G(2x)$?

A) $12 - 2x^2$
B) $12 - 4x^2$
C) $24 - 2x^2$
D) $24 - 4x^2$

CONTINUE

5

$$x = 3y$$
$$\frac{y}{2} = \frac{x+3}{3}$$

If (x, y) is a solution to the system of equations above, what is the value of x?

A) -6
B) -2
C) 2
D) 3

6

$$m\left(\frac{1+p}{m}\right) = \frac{4}{5}$$

Given the equation above, which of the following is also true?

A) $m = \frac{9}{5}$
B) $p = -\frac{1}{5}$
C) $mp = \frac{9}{5}$
D) $mp = -\frac{1}{5}$

7

Bernardo was traveling by car on a cross-country trip. Six hours into his trip he passed his grandparents' town and his car's odometer read 28,200 miles. 4 hours later, when he passed his uncle's town, his car's odometer read 28,440 miles. If Bernardo's speed remained constant throughout the trip, which of the following statements is true?

A) Bernardo's average speed between his grandparents' town and his uncle's town was 40 mph.
B) Bernardo's average speed between his grandparents' town and his uncle's town was 64 mph.
C) Bernardo's odometer read 27,840 miles at the start of the trip.
D) Bernardo's odometer read 27,960 miles at the start of the trip.

8

$$\sqrt{x+3} = x+1$$

Which of the following lists all of the values of x that are real solutions to the equation above?

A) -2, 1, and 0
B) -2 and 1
C) -2
D) 1

CONTINUE

Questions 9-12 refer to the following information.

Quantity ($)	Models (x=number of customers for the day)
Sales, $S(x)$	$S(x) = 9.50x$
Cost, $C(x)$	$C(x) = 450 + 5.75x$
Profit, $P(x)$	$P(x) = S(x) - C(x)$

The table above defines the sales model, cost model, and profit model for a small company that sells replacement drive chains for bicycles and unicycles.

9

On average, each customer that makes a purchase from the company spends how many dollars?

A) 3.75
B) 4.50
C) 5.75
D) 9.50

10

If the company were to put a dollar value on what it costs them on average for each additional paying customer, what would this value be?

A) 3.75
B) 5.75
C) 450
D) 455.75

11

What is the minimum number of customers that the company would estimate they need to make a purchase in order to turn a positive profit?

A) 47
B) 48
C) 120
D) 121

12

If the company were able to reduce their initial cost by 50% and reduce their cost per paying customer by $0.75, how many fewer paying customers would they need to see in order to still turn a positive profit?

A) 50
B) 51
C) 70
D) 71

CONTINUE

13

Daryl and his older brother went to a local theme park. Daryl's ticket cost x dollars as a regularly priced admission, but his older brother had a coupon for 30% off the regular admission price. If Daryl and his older brother decided to split the cost of admission evenly, which of the following expressions represents the price they each paid in terms of x?

A) $\frac{1.7x}{2}$

B) $\frac{0.7x}{2}$

C) $\frac{x+0.7}{2}$

D) $\frac{1+0.7x}{2}$

14

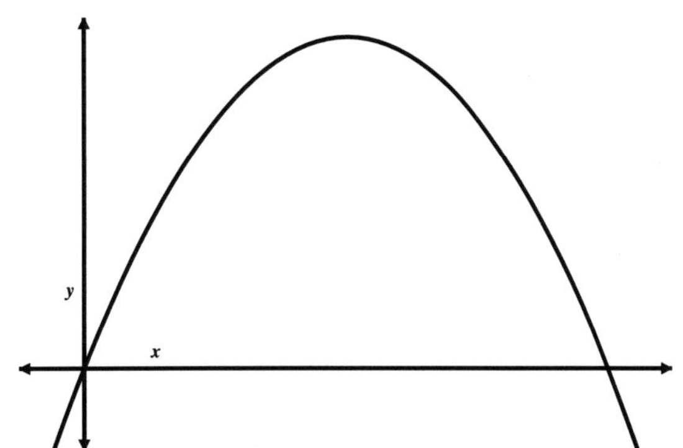

Line l intercepts the origin and the vertex of the parabola above. If the parabola has the equation $f(x) = -x^2 + 8x$, what is the slope of Line l?

A) $\frac{1}{4}$

B) 1

C) 4

D) 16

15

$$\frac{-j \pm \sqrt{j^2 + 4d}}{2}$$

The expression above represents all of the solutions for which of the following equations?

A) $x^2 + jx - d = 0$

B) $x^2 - jx + d = 0$

C) $x^2 + \frac{j}{2}x - d = 0$

D) $\frac{1}{2}x^2 + \frac{j}{2}x - d = 0$

CONTINUE

DIRECTIONS

For each question from 16-19, solve and enter your answer in the grid-in section of your answer sheet as described below.

A. Write out your answers in the boxes at the top of each column in order to help you fill in the circles accurately. Remember, you will only receive credit for the circles that are filled in correctly, not for the written answer at the top of the columns.

B. Mark only a single circle in each column.

C. There are no negative answers.

D. If the problem has more than one correct answer, grid only one of the correct answers.

E. When your answer is a **mixed number**, such as $1\frac{1}{2}$, it should be entered as 1.5 or $3/2$. You cannot enter a mixed number because there is no room to fill in a circle that represents a space.

F. If you enter a **decimal answer** with more digits then the grid can handle, the answer may be rounded or truncated, but it absolutely must fill the entire grid.

Answer: $\frac{8}{21}$

Written answer → 8 / 2 1

← Fraction line

Decimal point →

Answer: 6.4

6 . 4

The ways to correctly grid $\frac{7}{9}$ are:

7 / 9

. 7 7 7

. 7 7 8

Answer: 102 - both positions are correct

REMEMBER:
You can begin writing your answers in any column as long as there is enough space. Leave unused columns blank.

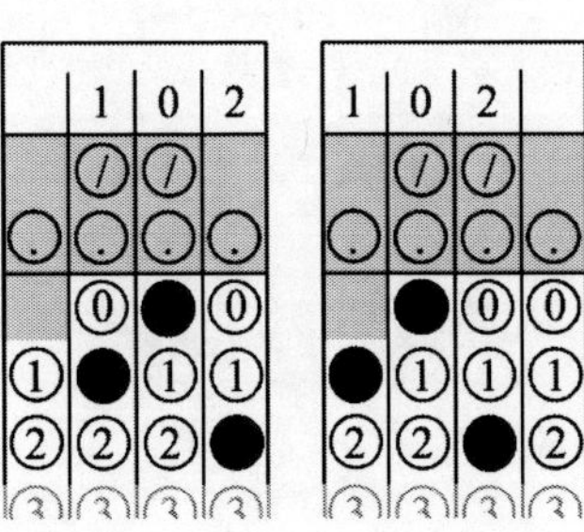

CONTINUE

16

$$4x = 8y + 16$$
$$2y = x + 4$$

How many ordered pairs (x, y) satisfy the system of equations above?

17

$$0 = x^3 + 3x^2 - 4x - 12$$

The equation above is true for what positive value of x?

18

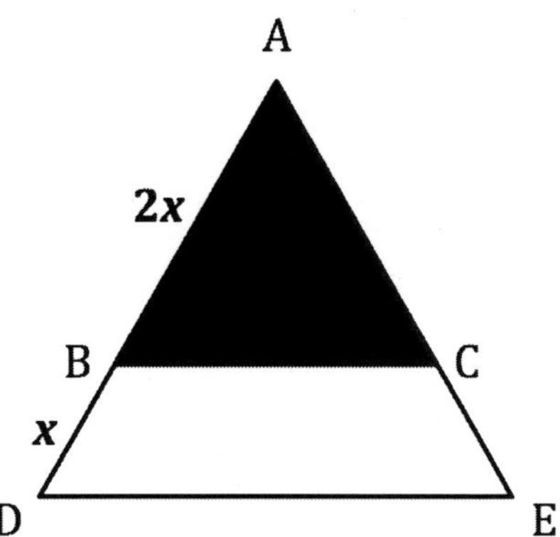

Triangle ABC and triangle ADE are equilateral triangles and the length of segment AB is twice the length of segment BD. If the area of the shaded region is a and the area of the unshaded region is b what is the value of $\frac{b}{a}$?

19

Xavier's weight, w, decreases linearly with respect to n, the number of miles that he runs on an elliptical machine. Xavier weighed 188 pounds after he had run a total of 35 miles and 183 pounds after he had run a total of 95 miles. If Xavier's current weight can be calculated with respect to the number of miles he has run using the equation $w = -Mn + P$, where M and P are positive constants, what is the value of M?

STOP

No Test Material On This Page

Made in United States
North Haven, CT
14 October 2022

25457025R00224